Christian
Engagements
WITH
Judaism

Christian Engagements

WITH

Judaism

W. D. Davies

TRINITY PRESS INTERNATIONAL
Harrisburg, Pennsylvania

Trinity Press International, P.O. Box 1321, Harrisburg, PA 17105
Trinity Press International is a division of the Morehouse Group.

Cover design by Jim Gerhard.

Library of Congress Cataloging-in-Publication Data
Davies, William David, 1911–
    Christian engagements with Judaism / W. D. Davies.
      p.   cm.
    Includes bibliographical references and index.
    ISBN 1-56338-268-7 (alk. paper)
    1. Judaism – Relations – Christianity. 2. Christianity and other religions – Judaism. I. Title.
BM535.D348 1999
261.2'6–dc21   99-29534

Printed in the United States of America

99   00   01   02   03   04   10 9 8 7 6 5 4 3 2 1

Dedicated to Rachel,
with our gratitude

Contents

Part IV
AN AMERICAN INTERPRETATION OF JUDAISM

Foreword

I met Professor Davies in 1977, when I was privileged to attend, in my first semester of graduate school at Duke University, his seminar on Matthew. That course determined the direction of much of my subsequent life, for out of it eventually grew our joint work on a commentary on Matthew.[1] The fifteen years that it took us to complete our project brought me much, including the opportunity to continue learning from Professor Davies, who at some point, although he never ceased to be mentor, also became my friend, W.D. My debts to him are many, and reach beyond the academic to the personal. But only of the former do I write here. In general, his approach to the New Testament through Jewish sources has been a worthy model for imitation, and it has inspired me as it has others. In particular, much of what I have myself written has been in response to his publications or (more often than he knows) to remarks made face-to-face. It accordingly gives me great satisfaction to contribute a foreword to this, his third volume of collected essays.[2]

If it is true that the unexamined life is not worth living, then it is equally true, as Professor Davies tells us in his opening chapter, that the unexamined book is unacceptable. Living his own maxim, he has examined the Book, the Bible, and along the way he has made more than his fair share of discoveries. Fortunately, in his numerous books and articles he has shared them.[3] In "An Odyssey in New Testament Interpretation," he seeks to review in short compass what he has learned and what it means. The article opens with characteristic caution: the distances of geography, language, time, and culture require that we make heroic efforts to understand the Jews and Christians of antiquity. But notwithstanding the immense obstacles, learning is possible.

---

1. *The Gospel according to Saint Matthew*, 3 vols., ICC (Edinburgh: T. & T. Clark, 1988, 1991, 1997).

2. The previous collections are: *Christian Origins and Judaism* (London: Longman & Todd, 1962; reprint, New York: Arno Press, New York Times, 1973), and *Jewish and Pauline Studies* (Philadelphia: Fortress Press, 1984).

3. For an overview of Professor Davies' contributions to biblical studies see Douglas R. A. Hare, in Donald K. McKim, ed., *Historical Handbook of Major Biblical Interpreters* (Downers Grove, Ill.: InterVarsity Press, 1998), s.v., "Davies, W(illliam) D(avid)." For a complete list of Davies' works through 1976 see Robert Hamerton-Kelly and Robin Scroggs, eds., *Jews, Greeks, and Christians: Religious Cultures in Late Antiquity: Essays in Honor of William David Davies*, SJLA 21 (Leiden: E. J. Brill, 1976), 1–10.

And so too is progress. For if the history of Christianity and the history of critical scholarship have strongly tended to see Christianity and Judaism as antithetical, we have more recently found good reasons to rethink this bit of conventional wisdom that has had such dire consequences. Professor Davies' own works are among those good reasons. Indeed, rethinking conventional wisdom regarding the relationship between Judaism and Christianity constitutes the central theme of his lifelong labors. In the introduction, he reviews his own work on Paul, on Matthew, and on The Land — all topics examined afresh in the present volume — which have helped to bring about the "silent revolution in our approach to the New Testament. To put it in a nutshell, the New Testament has been increasingly re-Judaized." The key sentences for me in this chapter are the following: "Christianity in the New Testament is not a new, distinct religion over against Judaism, but a new interpretation of Judaism in the light of Christ. It does not abandon Judaism but rather absorbs it, so that the substructure of Christianity remains Jewish. Judaism, in other words, is not 'before' Christianity, something that Christians have left behind, but rather somehow within it, something that Christians carry along with them." Even if his book on The Land reveals deep differences between Judaism and Christianity on this subject — something Davies in his honesty makes plain — most of his writings constitute a sort of cumulative case for the truth of these three sentences about the character of New Testament Christianity.

There is, as Professor Davies is anxious to emphasize, more here than just getting our historical facts straight. We understand ourselves by understanding our past, so if we indeed learn that there was, at the origin of Christianity, an "essential continuity" between it and Judaism, then the repercussions for today's world may be considerable. It is for this reason that, as he explores the past, Davies speaks with hope for the future, and of the possibility, made real in his own life, for "mutual respect and engagement" between synagogue and church.

In chapter 1, "In Search of 'The Center' of Judaism," Professor Davies shows us that he is not just interested in Judaism as a means to understanding Christianity. He also wants to understand Judaism in and of itself. So in this essay he explores the problem of how one might succinctly characterize what Judaism is and has been, and whether it can be defined by a particular historical pattern. In his typical wide-ranging fashion, he carefully considers what others have said. Along the way we are treated to quotations from all epochs of Jewish history, so that no one period is given predominance. Four subjects receive treatment in turn — Torah, The Land, the people of Israel, and the Messiah. From all this we get no simple answers. We rather go back and forth, pursuing objection after objection and qualification after qualification, until we finally come to the conclusion that talk of "essence" is inappropriate. This, however, is not the end of the matter. Professor Davies finally reverts to the metaphor of the heart to characterize that confluence of factors — Torah, Land, people, Messiah — that have characterized Judaism throughout most of its history.

One may ask, in response to chapter 1, whether the difficulty of defining "Judaism" should perhaps be related to the problem we have in defining other referential terms. The truth is that we usually have trouble gaining absolute clarity about any noun, if by that is meant listing characteristics that invariably belong to it or what it refers to. It is difficult to define "chair" in a way that fits all chairs, or "religion" in a way that fits all religions. All we can do, as Wittgenstein observed, is draw up a list of "family characteristics," things that tend to recur but may be absent from this or that instance of "chair" or "religion." This is just how common nouns work in the world. Do not Wittgenstein's words about "a complicated network of similarities overlapping and criss-crossing: sometimes overall similarities, sometimes similarities of detail"[4] apply well to the various sorts of Judaism, ancient and modern?

The reader of chapter 1 who knows Davies' other works will know well that, although this chapter treats Judaism on its own terms and does not bring Christianity into the discussion, the four specific themes examined — Torah, Land, the people of Israel, and the Messiah — have all been near the center of Professor Davies' various investigations of the New Testament. This means that he has throughout his career been seeking to relate Christianity to what is most characteristic of Judaism. His very influential book, *Paul and Rabbinic Judaism: Some Rabbinic Elements in Pauline Theology*, has a chapter on "The Old Torah and the New,"[5] and his second book is entitled, *Torah in the Messianic Age and/or the Age to Come.*[6] Another book, *The Gospel and the Land: Early Christianity and Jewish Territorial Doctrine,*[7] which opened a whole new avenue of investigation for New Testament scholars, sought to understand what Jesus and early Christians made of the Jewish doctrine of The Land. As for the people of Israel, Davies' interest in that subject is on display in *Paul and Rabbinic Judaism,* in the chapter on "The Old and the New Israel" (pp. 58–85), and again in his presidential address to the Studiorum Novi Testamenti Societas in 1976, "Paul and the People of Israel."[8] Davies has also been preoccupied with messianism throughout his career. One of the central

---

4. See *Philosophical Investigations: The English Text of the Third Edition,* trans. G. E. M. Anscombe, 2d ed. (New York: Macmillan, 1958), §66, 32.

5. Still in print in the fiftieth-anniversary edition of Sigler Press, 1998. See pp. 147–76.

6. Society of Biblical Literature Monographs 7 (Philadelphia: Society of Biblical Literature, 1952). See further chapters 4 and 7 herein and "Law in the New Testament," in *Jewish and Pauline Studies,* 227–42.

7. Berkeley: University of California Press, 1974.

8. *NTS* 24 (1977): 4–39; reprinted in *Jewish and Pauline Studies* (Philadelphia: Fortress Press, 1984), 123–52.

themes of *Paul and Rabbinic Judaism* is that much of the apostle's theology grew out of his conviction that the Messiah had come; the importance of Jewish messianism for understanding the early church in general is the subject of Davies' Albert Schweitzer Memorial Lecture delivered to the Society of Biblical Literature and the American Academy of Religion in 1975, entitled "From Schweitzer to Scholem: Reflections on Sabbatai Svi."[9] Here he takes us into the fantastic world of comparative messianism. In this area he has been a pioneer: others are only now beginning to follow.[10]

"Canon and Christology" is the subject of chapter 2. Here Professor Davies first looks into a neglected but rather interesting topic, namely, whether the Jewish and Christian canons have true parallels elsewhere. He suggests that Hinduism may supply such, but when he turns to the Greco-Roman world he does not find anything closely comparable to the authoritative collections reckoned sacred by Jews and Christians. One question that comes to mind while reading the argument is whether the Temple Scroll, whose author felt free at points to rewrite the Pentateuch, does not reveal an attitude to the Torah rather different from what we usually assume to have been the rule in Judaism. But the main point is well taken. Also convincing is the explanation: "The crises of the sixth century B.C.E. and of the first century C.E. demanded the reaffirmation of Jewish identity, and this was largely in part achieved through the development and ultimate fixation of the canon." For Jewish identity was tied up with formative and spectacular historical events — exodus, Sinai, exile — the memories of which were preserved in scripture. Next Davies goes on to remind us of the importance of the oral Torah, and then, at the end, he suggests that for early Christians Jesus functioned much like the oral Torah did for Jews. Here his argument that Christ functions as Torah, an argument for which he is otherwise known and which appears herein in other chapters,[11] is given a new twist. He seems to be saying not that Paul and others clearly conceived of Jesus Christ as the oral Torah, but that the traditions about him and his death and resurrection *functioned* for them like oral Torah: those traditions were the living tradition that interpreted the written text. This is a rather interesting correlation whose implications remain unclear to me. We may hope that someone else will attempt to unfold it further.

In chapter 3, on "Torah and Dogma," Professor Davies discusses whether

---

9. *JBL* 95 (1976): 529–58; reprinted in *Jewish and Pauline Studies*, 257–77.

10. My own attempt to bring millenarian studies into the subject of the historical Jesus was partly inspired by Davies' essay (which I still remember excitedly reading for the first time in 1976, before I knew I was to be his student at Duke); see *Jesus of Nazareth: Millenarian Prophet* (Minneapolis: Fortress Press, 1998). Note also Joel Marcus, "Modern and Ancient Jewish Apocalyptic," *JR* 76 (1996): 1–27 (Marcus refers to Davies on p. 1, n. 2).

11. See esp. chapter 6.

the relationship between Christianity and Judaism is best characterized as one of schism or unrelieved antithesis. He begins by considering, in a different way than in chapter 1 herein, how best to characterize Judaism. Is it a way of life or a set of beliefs? After all the necessary hesitancy and qualification, he leans toward the traditional view that Judaism is not primarily "opinion, doctrine, or dogma" but rather "practice, observance in trust, and joy." Christianity, on the other hand, despite its halakic elements, which are too often underestimated, is in the end more rooted in dogma. Why this should be so is unclear, although Davies offers the interesting speculation that "it is the awareness of sin that makes the theologian," so that whereas the introspective conscience of Christianity has encouraged a preoccupation with dogma, a different ethos has animated Judaism, with its greater optimism about the human condition. Whatever the explanation, it occurs to this reader that if Christianity indeed carries within itself the foundational pattern of the exodus, in which deliverance is followed by the giving of Torah, then Christianity has focused its reflection upon the opening act, the act of redemption, whereas Judaism has perhaps concentrated its attention upon the second act, the subsequent gift of the commandments.

Having established that there is a significant difference of emphasis here, Davies goes on to inquire about the situation in the New Testament. Here he suggests that one can find three different attitudes. There were Jewish Christians who were unaware of any essential break between Judaism and Christianity. There were others, including the author of John's Gospel, who perceived a sharp antithesis. And there were still others who thought firstly in terms of fulfillment. In this last category are Matthew and Hebrews as well as Paul (although many would instead link the apostle to the Gentiles with John). With all this in mind, Davies then goes on to consider whether the gulf between Christian dogma and Jewish halakah can ever be overcome. But after briefly looking into Bultmann's demythologizing program, which does away with the dogmatic and particularistic scandal of the creeds, and into the possibility of a contemporary (and admittedly nontraditional) halakic Christianity, it is recognized that Christianity is inescapably christological, so that there will always be a dogmatic difference between its adherents and Judaism. So the most we can hope for — and it is not little — is mutual tolerance, respect, learning, and perhaps even affection. Differences we will always have with us.

The postscript to chapter 3 refers us to recent studies which offer evidence that, in the first centuries of the Christian era, "Christians and Jews were not always in dogmatic conflict." Indeed, there appears to have been a number of people who did not think of themselves as either Christians or Jews but both. To the evidence gathered there, one wonders about one of the groups that J. Louis Martyn, Raymond E. Brown, and others have divined in the background of John's Gospel.[12] They seem to have been Jews who attended synagogue and believed in Jesus as Messiah but did not proselytize. John disapproved of them. But in their own eyes they may have been precisely the sort of people Davies is thinking of, that is, people who defy our neat categorization: they may have thought of themselves as neither Christian nor Jewish but both.[13]

Chapter 4, entitled "Law in Christianity," is the shortest in the book. It nicely illustrates the assertion in the introduction that Judaism somehow remains within Christianity. For here Professor Davies argues that the early church thought of itself as undergoing a new exodus and being given a new Torah, that new Torah being "the law of Christ" (Gal. 6:2). In other words, the structure of Christianity is largely the structure of Judaism. But it is not just the structure that is the same. Davies also instructs us, as have so many Jewish scholars in this century, that the content of early Christian moral teaching was largely taken over from Jewish sources. So here again we see the continuity that the centuries have all too often forgotten.

In this chapter the relationship of church and synagogue is not the only practical concern. Professor Davies asks us whether a proper understanding of the moral teaching of the New Testament does not have something to say to modern theological debates over ethics. There has been a tendency to set a prescriptive morality over against an *agape* morality. But if the New Testament can hold them together in tension, perhaps we should ask ourselves whether this is not the better course of wisdom, so that we should reconsider our habit of seeing the two things as antithetical.[14]

The first three sections of chapter 5, which is on "David Roberts and the Promised Land in Jewish and Christian Tradition," conveniently summarize the complex subject of the Jewish doctrine of The Land, a subject touched upon in several of the chapters herein and which Davies has treated at length in two books.[15] The next section recapitulates the Christian response to that doctrine, which has been to personalize holy space: it "personalizes 'holy space' in Christ, who, as a figure of history, is rooted in The Land; He cleansed the Temple and died in Jerusalem and lends His glory to these and to the places where He was, but, as living Lord, He is free to move wher-

---

12. J. Louis Martyn, in *History and Theology in the Fourth Gospel*, rev. ed. (Nashville: Abingdon Press, 1978); Raymond E. Brown, *The Community of the Beloved Disciple* (New York: Paulist Press, 1979), 71–73.

13. One may also refer to the recent interpretation of the Matthean community offered by Anthony J. Saldarini, *Matthew's Christian-Jewish Community* (Chicago and London: University of Chicago Press, 1994).

14. See further Davies' essays on "The Moral Teaching of the Early Church" and "The Relevance of the Moral Teaching of the Early Church," in *Jewish and Pauline Studies*, 278–88 and 289–302, respectively.

15. *The Gospel and the Land* and *The Territorial Dimension of Judaism* (Berkeley: University of California Press, 1982; reprint, Minneapolis: Fortress Press, 1991).

ever He wills." Once again, then, it is Christocentrism that transforms Jewish doctrine and makes Christianity something different from Judaism: "[W]here Christianity has reacted seriously to the realia of Judaism, whether negatively or positively, it has done so in terms of Christ, to whom all space and all places, like all things else, are subordinated."

With all this in mind Davies turns to the art of David Roberts (1796–1864), the Scottish Presbyterian who is so famous for his paintings of the Holy Land. Several questions are asked: How is it that it was a Gentile Christian, not a Jew, who did most justice to The Land in art? How accurate is the old wisdom that Jewish thinking discouraged the development of representational art? To what extent did theology inform Roberts's work? Was he influenced by Jewish teaching about The Land? What does Roberts's focus on holy places tell us about him and his admirers? In supplying us with tentative answers to these and other questions, we again learn something about the character of Judaism, the character of Christianity, and the differences between the two.

Chapter 6, on "Paul and the Exodus," may be viewed as an enlargement of chapter 4. It first establishes in detail that Paul considers the Christian dispensation to be a new exodus. It then vigorously argues that, for the apostle, it is not just that the saving event of Jesus has its typological correlate in the deliverance from Egypt, but what Galatians 6:2 calls "the law of Christ" is somehow analogous to the Law given on Sinai, to the Law of Moses. Davies underlines the importance Paul's moral teaching and observes, no doubt rightly, that "the standard of teaching to which you were committed" (Rom. 6:17) functions much as the Law does in Judaism, so that "[a]t no point is Paul without law (*anomos*); he is always with law (*ennomos*). To this extent Paul is at one with Matthew who also places the law of Christ in a context of the grace of Christ." Others might resist these words, which characteristically attempt to bring Paul and Matthew together.[16]

Even more controversial is the claim, first made in *Paul and Rabbinic Judaism*, that Jesus is and has brought the new or messianic Torah. Paul nowhere explicitly says this, so Davies can only argue that this was his "implicit intention." Critics have been quick to note this. This admission, however, is hardly fatal to the thesis, and one cannot but think that resistance to his proposal may stem partly from the still widespread feeling that Law and grace are antithetical. Davies may not, in his book *Torah in the Messianic Age and/or the Age to Come*, have found much evidence from early Judaism for a messianic Torah, but the tradition that an eschatological figure will bring instruction is attested in many texts from diverse times and places, beginning with Isa-

---

16. See further *The Setting of the Sermon on the Mount* (Cambridge: Cambridge University Press, 1964), 313–66.

iah 42:1–4, where "the servant" brings "torah."[17] Surely then Davies' thesis merits more sympathetic attention than it has received. There remain many issues that beg further exploring in this connection. Does the tradition that Moses embodied Torah have anything to say to Davies' proposed equation of Torah with Christ in Paul? Since it is plausible enough that some of Paul's Judaizing opponents interpreted Jesus as a new Moses, does the apostle's failure to be explicit about certain features of the new Christian exodus have its explanation in his desire to distance himself from antagonists? Is Paul's use of "the law of Christ" illumined by the "new commandment" of John 13:34 or the "new law" of *Barnabas* 2:6, and can these three expressions really be independent formulations, or is there not here an early tradition to be traced? And, finally, given all the attention being paid today to the importance of allusions to scripture in Paul, would a thorough history of the interpretation of Jeremiah 31 — a text which prophesies the interiorization of the Torah and which is referred to in 2 Corinthians 3 and 6 — shed any light on the proposed equation of Torah with Jesus, who is, so to speak, internalized in Paul (e.g., Rom. 8:10 ["Christ is in you"] and Gal. 2:20 ["it is Christ who lives in me"])?

"Paul and the Law" is the subject of chapter 7. Its brevity does not correspond to its importance.[18] Four main points are made. The first two, that "Law" (*nomos*) cannot be always be equated simply with "commandment" and that Paul's attitude toward the Law cannot be isolated from his messianic, that is, eschatological situation, are lessons learned from a better understanding of Judaism. The second two, that Paul's letters show change and development in his thinking about "Law" — a fact more and more admitted — and that they feature explicit moral imperatives that constitute a rigorous "way of Christ," follow from a closer reading of Paul's letters. Contemporary Pauline scholarship is in the process of coming to terms with at least three of these propositions. One is still unsure, however, that it has really begun to tackle in convincing fashion the ways in which Paul's eschatological convictions influenced his thinking about Torah.

Chapter 8 shows us again Davies' conviction that investigation of the critical exegesis of the New Testament is not just an academic exercise but has implications for present thought and practice: we must go there and back again. He begins by examining how Paul, through the symbols of the cultivated olive and wild olive in Romans 9–11, expressed the conviction that there is still a place for the Jewish people in the Christian dispensation.[19]

---

17. See further my book, *The New Moses: A Matthean Typology* (Minneapolis: Fortress Press, 1993), 185–87.

18. For a fuller treatment of the subject see Davies, *Jewish and Pauline Studies*, 91–122.

19. See further Davies, "Paul and the Gentiles: A Suggestion concerning Romans 11:13–24," in *Jewish and Pauline Studies*, 153–62.

Davies then shows us at length how Jacques Maritain effectively used Paul, and Romans 9–11 in particular, in his opposition to anti-Semitism, whereas Voltaire, who did not have such a high regard for Paul, fell into the prejudice of anti-Judaism. Davies even asks whether "Voltaire was a link in Western intellectual history between the anti-Judaism of classical paganism and the anti-Semitism of our age." However that may be, this is the sort of careful work that should give pause to those who, like Rosemary Radford Ruether, have accused Paul of being an anti-Semite. The truth rather seems to be, to revert to Davies' opening chapter, that, in its origins, Christianity, including the Pauline mission, was not an intrinsically anti-Judaic phenomenon.

With chapter 9 we turn from Paul to the Gospels. "A Different Approach to Jamnia: The Jewish Origins of Matthew's Gospel and Messianism" is an attempt to understand better Matthew's thought about Jesus. The focus is on the Gospel's prologue, chapters 1–2. Davies first looks at the theme of the new creation, which he discussed earlier in *The Setting of the Sermon on the Mount* (pp. 67–73). All of his points are well taken, even though the commentators for the most part continue to ignore them. Here he enlarges his earlier case by observing that in Philo we have proof that the first book of the Bible was already known as "Genesis" by the first century of the common era, a fact that increases the likelihood that Matthew's opening words, *biblos geneseos,* would have sent ancient readers back to the creation narratives. Davies could also have added that a recently released Dead Sea Scroll fragment, 4Q521, adds more confirmation, for it all but proves that Genesis 1:2 ("The Spirit of God was hovering over the face of the waters") lies behind the imagery of the dove at the baptism.[20]

The next three sections cover, respectively, Jesus as Davidic Messiah, as the Son of Abraham, and as one "greater than Moses." The treatment of the last subject is particularly noteworthy, for it seems to mark a change from Davies' earlier position. *The Setting of the Sermon on the Mount* urges that although Matthew knew of the interpretation of Jesus as one like Moses, "the restraint with which the New Exodus and New Moses motifs are used is noticeable" (p. 92). In the present chapter, however, Davies does not so express himself. He rather now sees additional parallels between Jesus and Moses and indeed tells us that while he had "long resisted" the direct parallel between the mountain of Matthew 5:1–2 and Sinai, his doubt has now been overcome. Being the author of the study that changed his mind about this, I am happy to record this reversal of opinion. On one point, however, one might wish to quibble. Davies' title for his third section is "The Greater Moses." But in actually reviewing the various passages, nothing is said or intimated

---

20. See Matthew 3:16 and my article, "The Baptism of Jesus and a New Dead Sea Scroll," *Biblical Archaeology Review* 18 (1992): 58–60.

about Jesus being greater than Moses, so one wonders about the formulation. Does it not perhaps misplace the emphasis? Perhaps this expression focuses on a presupposition — without question Jesus is for Matthew greater than Moses — and so misses the main point of the parallels. Matthew and his Christian readers had no anxiety about Jesus being greater than Moses, and they had no interest in denigrating the lawgiver. So what justification do we have for construing the parallels as something other than parallels? Why turn them rather into statements of inequality?[21]

"Aspects of the Jewish Background of the Gospel of John" is the subject of chapter 10. The reader familiar with Davies' work on Matthew will experience a strong sense of *déjà vu*. For here he tries to do for John what he did for Matthew in *The Setting of the Sermon on the Mount*, namely, to show that the Gospel can be understood in part as a reaction to Jamnia, if that be defined as the post-70 attempt of certain rabbis, descendants of the Pharisees, to consolidate a shattered Judaism and to establish their own authority.[22] He makes the obvious point that it is precisely the Pharisees who are Jesus' opponents in John and moreover appeals to the work of J. Louis Martyn, who persuasively argued that John's Gospel reflects the Jamnian reformulation of the *Birkath ha-Minim* near the end of the first century.[23] Davies then goes on to make his own novel contributions. The first is the observation that John's sophisticated reinterpretation of Jesus' miracles as signs may owe something to the early rabbinic playing-down of the miraculous, which was partly a response to Christian claims for Jesus. In short, "While retaining his 'miracles' as 'signs,' did he partly at least lend them a new, more sophisticated signification in order to undercut the rabbis' objection to 'miracles'?" Interestingly enough, although Davies does not mention the fact, the critical rabbinic spirit toward miracles may also appear in Matthew (see, e.g., 7:21–23 and 24:23–28), which is also, as he has shown us, plausibly given a Jamnian setting. Davies' final point is that John's statements on holy space may partly represent a reaction to the post-70 glorification of The Land. John can be read as opposing the view that the Spirit is confined to The Land, a view found in the *Mekilta*.[24] In the Fourth Gospel, The Land, like the Torah, is displaced, or rather replaced by a person, Christ. Here we see how, as discussed in chapter 3, it is christological conviction that alters the basic elements of Judaism and seemingly moves us toward a new religion.

---

21. For a further description and evaluation of Davies' work on Moses in Matthew, the interested reader may consult my book, *The New Moses*, 298–306.

22. His case is convincing, and I have myself defended it in "The Structure of the Sermon on the Mount," *JBL* 103 (1989): 423–45. It is also upheld throughout our commentary on Matthew.

23. *History and Theology in the Fourth Gospel*.

24. See Davies, "Reflections on the Spirit in the *Mekilta*: A Suggestion," in *Jewish and Pauline Studies*, 72–83.

Chapter 11, on "Israel, the Mormons, and the Land," takes us to an unexpected area, Mormonism. But it is not long before we see the connection with what has come before: Mormonism shows us one Christian group's very positive engagement with Judaism. Much of this engagement, such as the claim of being physically descended from Abraham, rests upon historically problematic premises. But the Jewish self-conception, if that is the right term, and the thoroughgoing adoption of Jewish concepts may, Professor Davies offers, stand in continuity with early Jewish Christianity and so recover in a way a neglected part of the Christian heritage. Perhaps the most absorbing part of this essay is the exposition of Mormonism as an illustration of the old eschatological teaching that the end will be like the beginning. Here we learn that Mormonism appears to have held the apocalyptic and priestly together as well as eschatology and Law. We further discover that Mormonism can be understood as a millenarian movement, and that there are intriguing parallels between it and the Sabbatian messianic movement. This is the sort of cross-cultural comparison that, although fraught with hazard, so often brings illumination. One suspects that a comparison between early Mormonism and the Essenes (presuming them to have been the sect behind the Dead Sea Scrolls) might prove fruitful.

Chapter 12, "The Mormon 'Canon,' " continues the discussion of Mormonism in chapter 11 as well as the treatment of canon in chapter 2. Following a lengthy discussion of the formation of the Mormon canon, Professor Davies turns to "the question of how the emergence and development of the Mormon canon compares and contrasts with the process of canonization in early Christianity." The focus is on the differences — the larger size of the Mormon canon, for example, and the speed with which it established itself — and their explanation. Here the importance of the fact that Jesus, as opposed to Joseph Smith, did not write anything that we know of gains its full force. So too the fact that books were not so plentiful and cheap in the first century as in Smith's day. Again this is the sort of imaginative comparing — or in this case contrasting — across time, space, and culture that enlarges the understanding.

There are additional interesting parallels, unremarked upon by Davies, that invite exploration. The comment of Wilford Woodruff, that "I would rather have the living oracles than all the writings in the books," reminds one of the attitude of Papias, an attitude that surely other early Christians shared: "I do not think that I derived so much benefit from books as from the living voice of those that are still surviving."[25] In addition, Professor Davies says at the beginning that "the attitude of the Church of Jesus Christ of Latter-day Saints, or the Mormons, to scripture is unusual — undeniably radical if not

---

25. Eusebius, *H.E.* 3.39.

unique." He qualifies this later on by referring to those Jewish Christians who
believed that the Hebrew Bible had suffered corruption. He could, however,
have added that Marcion had a similarly radical conviction about Luke and
the Pauline Epistles: they had to be edited in order to be freed of the ecclesiastical corruption they had allegedly suffered. There is also a parallel with
those Islamic theologians (such as Bīrūī) who have said that Jews and Christians corrupted the texts of their scriptures. Perhaps we are here looking at a
phenomenon not uncommon to the history of religions.

The epilogue, " 'Mystical Anti-Semitism' Reconsidered," is a response to
a book by Joel Carmichael, the editor of *Midstream.* In his book Carmichael
contends that anti-Judaism has been *sui generis,* and that the reason lies in
Christian theology. Specifically Christian beliefs about Jesus as the Son of
God who was killed by "the Jews" have led to the paradoxical conviction
that, although the Jews lived in abject poverty, without social or political
power, they were nonetheless extraordinarily powerful, the cosmic opponents
of the Incarnate God, and so demonic. That paradoxical conviction in turn
has been the engine behind the long, devastating history of anti-Judaism in
the West.

The rejoinder of Davies, whose expertise in the history of both Judaism
and Christianity gives his critique authority, is manifold. He reminds us,
among other things, that the status of the Jews was not much affected by
Christian doctrine during the early centuries (when, one might add, the likes
of Origen and Gregory of Nyssa were learning much from Philo the Jewish
philosopher); that there was, because of political and economic, not theological factors, a marked deterioration in the treatment of Jews in the eleventh
century; that some of the hatred of Jews occurred against the will of certain
church leaders and theologians; that we cannot utterly separate Christian
anti-Judaism from pre-Christian hostility to Jews; that the main impetus toward the initial Christian confrontation with Judaism was not this or that
Christian idea but the undeniable success of the Gentile mission; and — this
point is powerful — that anti-Judaism actually became more virulent as the
hold of Christian theology upon the West diminished.

Professor Davies has the better of the argument, if only because he fully
grasps the great lesson of Marx and of so many subsequent historians and
sociologists: ideas often have less power to move history than we imagine,
and the fixation by a group upon one idea as opposed to some other is often
due less to that idea's intrinsic power or appeal but rather to a host of contingent environmental factors, political, social, and economic. One recalls
that the theological arguments for the Crusades, put forward in so many ser-
mons, cannot be taken at face value: they scarcely end the historian's need
to seek for further explanations. The truth is that the Christian theological tradition, including the New Testament, is full of many different and

often contradictory statements about much, including the Jews. So, just as the New Testament has been, depending upon people's communal and social contexts, quoted both to advance the cause of women and to keep them in their traditional places, so too the New Testament has been quoted both to further anti-Semitism and (as Professor Davies shows in chapter 8 and indeed throughout these collected essays) to oppose it. Thus the truly instructive inquiry, in accord with Davies' procedure, must be into the circumstances that have caused too many Christians, at various times and places, to speak and act against the Jews, to take up and develop those parts of the tradition that demonize the Jews rather than those that glorify them. We must look into why the universal mechanism of scapegoating, so usefully uncovered in the writings of René Girard, has manifested itself exactly where and when it has, with the Jews as the scapegoats.

In our time certainly Jewish-Christian relations have been mightily affected by nontheological factors. The increased number of Christians involved in Jewish-Christian dialogue is largely due to two extratextual, extratheological factors, one being that large and hideous event known as the Holocaust, the other being the modern spirit of tolerance, which was born, after the wars of religion, in the Act of Toleration and the Enlightenment and has continued to enlarge itself since. That spirit, so increasingly needful (if sometimes also perverted into an excessive relativism) in our increasingly pluralistic world, discourages us from thinking of one religion as better than another. It is no wonder, then, that more and more Christians have buried the term "supersessionism" and all that it entails and have instead, with Professor Davies, sought common ground between Jews and Christians.

·

In the postscript to chapter 3 Davies follows his teacher and friend, David Daube, in speaking of "New Testament Judaism." It is a provocative phrase. But justification for it appears scattered throughout this collection of essays, as well as throughout the whole corpus of Davies' writings. For he has shown us again and again that in many of the earliest Christian sources we behold not a new religion but a religious movement within Judaism. Unlike Buddhism, which seems in its origins to have been an attempt to replace the religion of its day, Hinduism, Christianity began as a reform movement. Important Christian figures, including some New Testament writers, did not forsake Judaism: they rather, just like Jesus of Nazareth, worked within it. They reconceived their native faith in the light of their eschatological and christological convictions as well as their own religious experience — reconceived it but did not abandon it;[26] and their influence has endured, so that

---

26. See further Davies' essay, "Paul and Jewish Christianity according to Cardinal Daniélou: A Suggestion," in *Jewish and Pauline Studies,* 164-71.

Christian convictions and practices have always carried within themselves Jewish convictions and practices: our salvation is indeed of the Jews. The full realization of this fact in our time, a realization reflected and furthered in the writings of W. D. Davies, has meant great gain, both for understanding the first century and for understanding ourselves.

DALE C. ALLISON, JR.

Preface

The fourteen papers in this volume, written in the last twenty years or so, are reprinted almost exactly in their original forms. I have not attempted to bring them up to date, except in chapters 1, 3, and the epilogue, where I have added brief notes to indicate where the discussion has moved on. A shortened form of the epilogue has appeared in the *Festschrift* for my friend and former colleague Professor Dan Via.[1]

First of all, I thank Professor Dale C. Allison (now of the Pittsburgh Theological Seminary), with whom I have been privileged to work ever since he came to Duke as a graduate student. In addition to making helpful comments on each of the essays, he accepted the invitation of the publisher to isolate the common concerns which unite them despite their variety, and connect them with others of my writings. His contribution has greatly enriched the volume.

My former pupil, Dr. Arthur Bellinzoni, Professor of Religion at Wells College, Aurora, New York, readily took responsibility for seeing this work through the press; Dr. Huw Walters of the National Library of the University of Wales, Aberystwyth, Dyfed, helped me with the bibliography, as did Professor Roger Loyd and Mrs. Roberta Schaafsma, Director and Associate/ Reference Librarian, respectively, of the Divinity School Library at Duke. My thanks also go to the cooperative and invigorating Dean of the Duke Divinity School, Dr. L. Gregory Jones. Ms. Sarah Freedman, faculty secretary at the Divinity School, with her extraordinary skill and equally extraordinary generosity, made it possible for the essays to appear at this time. Dr. James Fodor, Visiting Lecturer at Duke, very thoroughly aided with the proofs, compiled the indices, checked the passages cited in French, and made highly helpful comments on the substance of the essays. I extend my acknowledgment to all the publishers listed below who gave their gracious permission to reprint these essays. Dr. Harold W. Rast, Director of Trinity Press International, and his staff have been very considerate and efficient.

All the teachers, colleagues, and other scholars — mostly Christian — who have helped me across the years are too numerous to mention: to them all

---

1. In *Perspectives in Religious Studies: Essays in Honor of Dan O. Via*, ed. Perry V. Kea and A. K. M. Adam (Macon, Ga.: Mercer University Press, 1996), 129–45.

my gratitude remains. Certain Jewish scholars who made possible the engagements enclosed in this volume I must name. First my gratitude goes to the president and General Assembly of the World Union of Jewish Studies, Jerusalem, for making me an Honorary Life Member of their Council, and also to the American Society of Jewish Research for electing me a fellow. My colleagues at the Jewish Theological Seminary of America were always supportive, especially Abraham Heschel, my former neighbor in New York, whose religious sensitivity, imaginative scholarship, generosity in sharing his learning, and magnanimity of spirit and enthusiasm were infectious. His one-time pupil Jacob Neusner, who holds him in deepest reverence, has had an immense influence on Jewish and Christian studies. The late Judah Goldin, University of Pennsylvania, the very incarnation of the Midrashic spirit, and Arthur Hertzberg, historian and theologian, have constantly been a source of kindness, stimulus, and insight, as also have been L. H. Feldman of Yeshiva University and Raphael Loewe of London University. More recently, I have been challenged in discussions with and by the writings of Daniel Boyarin of the University of California at Berkeley. Since the inauguration of the Program in Judaic Studies at Duke in 1972, its members — Kalman Bland, Carol and Eric Meyers — have been colleagues to whom I could always turn for illumination. It was Dr. Eric Meyers who suggested the illustration for the jacket of this book: a medallion enclosing both Jewish and Christian symbols from a marble chancel screen with relief decoration found in the West Church in Pella in Jordan, where Jewish Christianity arrived in the first century.

This collection of essays is a swan song in an almost lifelong endeavor for a deeper understanding of Judaism among Christians and of Christianity among Jews. I am persuaded that such a task may prove to be increasingly fruitful in unpredictable and unimaginable ways. Among many reasons for my persistence in this endeavor is that sharing in it were the two great teachers to whom I owe most, one a Jew and one a Christian. David Daube was rooted in an Orthodoxy which, however etiolated through German and later British and American academic and other influences, informed his whole life. He was my tutor and for over sixty years my closest friend. He died as I have been bringing this work to a close. Adequately to express what I owe to David, and to describe the "magic" of his presence, is impossible. It was he who taught me to think of "New Testament Judaism" — a phrase which when I first heard it from his lips I found very startling, but no longer. My other teacher was the intensely Christian C. H. Dodd. He taught me two thoughts which I have long known by heart, though I cannot now find them in his written works: first, that "the whole course of history...remains plastic to the will of God" and secondly, that "our destiny lies in the eternal order where 'Eye hath not seen, nor ear heard, neither have entered into the heart of man, the things which God hath prepared for them that love him.'" Dodd here cites Paul in

1 Corinthians 2:9, where the Apostle himself draws upon the Scriptures of his own people in Isaiah 64:4. These words apply not only to the texts in which Dodd used them but to those of the present work dealing with Jews and Christians: they provide the ground for our endeavor and our hope.

At the end of this list of acknowledgments comes the most deserved of all. This volume could not have appeared without the constant and selfless help of the distaff side of this household. The plural pronoun in the dedication to our daughter indicates that it is from both Eurwen and myself.

W. D. DAVIES

18 July 1999

Acknowledgments

Introduction, "An Odyssey in New Testament Interpretation," first published as "My Odyssey in New Testament Interpretation," *Bible Review* 5, no. 3 (June 1989): 10–18. Awarded the Fullner Prize for best essay of the year by *Bible Review* (published by Biblical Archaeology Society, 4710 41st St., NW, Washington DC 20016).

Chapter 1, "In Search of 'The Center' of Judaism," first published as "The Nature of Judaism," *Revue d'Histoire et Philosophie Religeuses* (Paris: Presses Universitaires de France) 75, no. 1 (January–March 1995): 85–113. This constitutes the second of my Kearns Lectures communicated to the Graduate School of Religion, Duke University. The first was published as "Reflections in Retrospect 1959–1980," *Duke Divinity School Review* (Fall 1981): 27–49.

Chapter 2, "Canon and Christology," first published in *The Glory of Christ in the New Testament: Studies in Christology in Memory of G. B. Caird,* ed. L. D. Hurst and N. T. Wright, 19–36. Oxford: Clarendon Press, 1987.

Chapter 3, "Torah and Dogma: A Comment," first published in *Harvard Theological Review* 61, no. 2 (April 1968): 87–105. Reprinted in *Papers from the Colloquium on Judaism and Christianity Held at Harvard Divinity School, Oct. 17–20, 1966,* with paper by D. Flusser and introduction by K. Stendahl. Cambridge: Harvard University Press, 1968.

Chapter 4, "Law in Christianity," first published as "What Is the Significance of the Law in Christianity?" in *Concilium: International Review of Theology* 98 (October 1974): 24–32. The theme of the issue was "Christians and Jews," and the issue was edited by Hans Küng and Walter Kasper.

Chapter 5, "David Roberts and the Promised Land in Jewish and Christian Tradition," first published in *Jerusalem and the Holy Land Rediscovered: The Prints of David Roberts (1796–1864),* 3–27. Durham, N.C.: Duke Museum of Art/Duke University Press, 1996.

Chapter 6, "Paul and the Exodus," first published in *The Quest for Meaning and Context: Studies in Biblical Intertextuality in Honor of James A. Sanders,* ed. Craig A. Evans and Shemaryabu Talmon, 443–63. Leiden: E. J. Brill, 1997.

Chapter 7, "Paul and the Law: Pitfalls in Interpretation," first published as "Paul and the Law: Reflections on Pitfalls in Interpretation," in *Paul and Paulinism: Essays in Honour of C. K. Barrett,* ed. M. D. Hooker and S. G. Wilson, 4–16. London: SPCK, 1982.

Chapter 8, "A Pauline Allegory in a French Context," first published as "Reflections on a Pauline Allegory in a French Context," in *The New Testament Age: Essays in Honor of Bo Reicke,* 1:107–26. Macon, Ga.: Mercer University Press, 1984.

Chapter 9, "A Different Approach to Jamnia: The Jewish Origins of Matthew's Gospel and Messianism," first published in *The Conversation Continues: Studies in Paul and John in Honor of J. Louis Martyn,* ed. R. T. Fortna and Beverly Gaventa, 378–94. Nashville: Abingdon Press, 1990.

Chapter 10, "Aspects of the Jewish Background of the Gospel of John," first published as "Reflections on Aspects of the Jewish Background of the Gospel of John," in *Exploring the Gospel of John: In Honor of D. Moody Smith,* ed. R. Alan Culpepper and C. Clifton Black, 43–64. Louisville: Westminster/John Knox Press, 1996.

Chapter 11, "Israel, the Mormons, and the Land," first published in *Reflections on Mormonism: Judaeo-Christian Parallels,* papers delivered at the Religious Studies Center Symposium, Brigham Young University, 10–11 March 1978, edited with an introductory essay by Truman G. Madsen, 79–97. Published by the Religious Studies Center, Brigham Young University, Provo, Utah, 1978.

Chapter 12, "The Mormon 'Canon,'" first published as "Reflections on the Mormon 'Canon,'" *Harvard Theological Review,* 79, nos. 1–3 (1986): 44–66. Reprinted in *Christians among Jews and Gentiles: Essays in Honor of Krister Stendahl on His Sixty-fifth Birthday,* ed. G. W. E. Nickelsburg and George W. MacRae, 44–67. Philadelphia: Fortress Press, 1986.

Epilogue, "'Mystical Anti-Semitism' Reconsidered," first published in shortened form as "Reflections on 'Mystical Anti-Semitism,'" in *Perspectives in Religious Studies: Essays in Honor of Dan O. Via,* ed. Perry V. Kea and A. K. M. Adam, 129–45. Macon, Ga.: Mercer University Press, 1996. Appendix first appeared as a contribution to the symposium on the Vatican-Israel Fundamental Agreement, *Midstream,* January 1995, 22–25.

Abbreviations

ABD	D. N. Freedman, ed., *Anchor Bible Dictionary*
ANRW	*Aufstieg und Niedergang der römischen Welt*
BDB	F. Brown, S. R. Driver, and C. A. Briggs, *Hebrew and English Lexicon of the Old Testament*
BETL	Bibliotheca ephemeridum theologicarum lovaniensium
Bib	*Biblica*
CBQ	*Catholic Biblical Quarterly*
ExpTim	*Expository Times*
HNT	Handbuch zum Neuen Testament
HUCA	*Hebrew Union College Annual*
ICC	International Critical Commentary
IDB	G. A. Buttrick, ed., *Interpreter's Dictionary of the Bible*
JAAR	*Journal of the American Academy of Religion*
JBL	*Journal of Biblical Literature*
JJS	*Journal of Jewish Studies*
JMES	*Journal of Middle Eastern Studies*
JQR	*Jewish Quarterly Review*
JR	*Journal of Religion*
JSNTSup	Journal for the Study of the New Testament — Supplement Series
JTS	*Journal of Theological Studies*
NovT	*Novum Testamentum*
NovTSup	Novum Testamentum Supplements
NTS	*New Testament Studies*

NTTS	New Testament Tools and Studies
RB	*Revue biblique*
SBLMS	Society of Biblical Literature Monograph Series
SBT	Studies in Biblical Theology
SJT	*Scottish Journal of Theology*
SNTS	Society for New Testament Studies
SNTSMS	Society for New Testament Studies Monograph Series
ST	*Studia theologica*
TU	Texte und Untersuchungen
TWNT	G. Kittel and G. Friedrich, eds., *Theologisches Wörterbuch zum Neuen Testament*
TZ	*Theologische Zeitschrift*
VC	*Vigiliae christianae*
WUNT	Wissenschaftliche Untersuchungen zum Neuen Testament
ZNW	*Zeitschrift für die neutestamentliche Wissenschaft*
ZRGG	*Zeitschrift für Religions- und Geistesgeschichte*

An Odyssey in
New Testament Interpretation

Karl Marx, when he was living in Highgate, London, was once asked to address a group of theologians. On his arrival, the meeting place was full of tobacco smoke, and Marx remarked, "Theologians always cloud the issues." When I remind theologians of this, they invariably reply, "Yes, and you in biblical studies always simplify them." If this be the case, the object we study, the Bible, is certainly not simple.

The first Bibles I ever saw were bound in black covers — Bible black as a poet called it. They stood out, unattractive and somehow odd and strange. They evoked the cromlechs — the large black stones, or megaliths — that dot so many hills in Great Britain. These black stones originally had a religious purpose. They conveyed the sense of awe and mystery and even terror that early Britons felt surrounded them.

For thousands of Jews and Christians, the Bible has been, and remains, a sacred, numinous, awesome book. Religious Jews believe that in the Bible the eternal has entered into time, the unseen has taken visible form, the unknown has become apparent, the intangible has become tangible in written documents that we can handle. The Law of God has become incarnate in print. For religious Jews, to read the scriptures, and even to quote from them, is to be put in touch with the divine order of being. That is why in Judaism the study of the Hebrew scriptures is worship. It is more important to study them than to obey them, it is said, because without study you will obey them in the wrong way.

But there is another aspect of the Bible that it is even more important to recognize. There are many *sacred* books, but not so many *canonical* books; that is, books that have been elevated by a religious community to be the rule of its life and faith, the authoritative source of its thinking and the ground of its identity — its foundation documents, as it were. Jewish identity and continuity are bound up with the scriptures. Jews are the people of the Book; the Bible, the book of a people.

The same is true, *mutatis mutandis,* of Christians. And because the Bible is the canonical authority for Jews and, through them, for Christians, it has

exerted an immense influence on the life of Western Europe. European culture has its ancient roots in Egypt, Greece, and Rome, but one of its chief
sources is a book — the Bible. By today, the influence of that book has
become worldwide.

Because of its sacred and canonical status, then, the Bible deserves attention: it is *there,* a black block, a megalith we cannot ignore. Millions are
content simply to feel its strange presence, to recognize its sanctity, and to
treat it with awe. But they reject any intellectual engagement with it. For
them, biblical criticism is impious. But this is to confuse reverence with
obscurantism and piety with ignorance. We prefer to follow Plato: The unexamined life is not worth living, and to accept the unexamined book is
unacceptable.

But *how* are we to examine it? There are four gulfs that separate us from
the Bible.

First, there is the gulf of geography. I remember a book beginning with the
words: "Hell is hot. Did you ever wonder why?" The reason given was that
hell is a biblical concept, and since the Bible was written in the Near East,
where the sun can burn one up and cause pain, hell was pictured as hot. In
the Norse sagas, by contrast, hell is icily cold, because the Scandinavians find
their enemy in snow and ice and cold. Dubious as all this may be, it points to
a truth. Geographic factors do enter into our engagement with the Bible —
the Bible belongs geographically to an alien Near Eastern world that we are
required to enter if we wish to understand the Book. This geographic gulf
is not now as serious as it once was. Modern photography and archaeology
and travel literature have made us more familiar with the Middle East. The
geographic strangeness of the Bible has been diminished, but it is still real.

The second gulf is the gulf of language. Languages are media of communication, but also of division. Do you recall your first visit to France, or
Germany, or any country where English was not spoken? Even within one
language there are problems in understanding: The United States and England, George Bernard Shaw once said, are separated by the same language.
The Hebrew scriptures were written — apart from a few Aramaic passages —
in Hebrew, a language which at that time was especially fitted for visions and
prophecy, and especially for poetry. It was much less suited for abstract philosophical and scientific thought. The New Testament is written in common,
or *koine,* Greek, the Greek largely of the marketplace and the street. Simpler to understand than Classical Greek, one would expect, but, because it is
influenced by Semitisms and Latinisms, presenting its own problems.

Can we ever fully understand another language? There are excellent translations of the Hebrew Bible and the New Testament, but translation is always
a betrayal to some extent. Before I came to the United States, I served on
the executive committee for the Bible translation called the New English

Bible (NEB). The late Professor C. H. Dodd was the director. After thirteen years, the translation was completed. Dodd had to prepare the preface to the translation. He had closed a rough draft of it by saying that "translation is an impossible art." Members of the committee objected to the adjective "impossible." Dodd did me the honor of asking me whether he should change it. We were both bilingual and knew that the adjective was justified. The adjective "impossible" remains in the preface. Every translation is only an approximation. Can we transcend the gulf of language? To some degree, yes. But how far?

Third, there is perhaps an even greater gulf — the gulf of time. Even in one generation we become strangers. How many fathers understand their sons; how many mothers their daughters? How much more difficult to understand people whom we know only through documents written thousands of years ago, in a strange land and in strange languages. There is not only a generation gap, but a generations gap. And the acceleration of the pace of change in our time has made cultural change ever more inescapable. London in 1800 was more like London in 100 than London today. Can we enter into the minds of people living thousands of years ago?

The combined result of all these gulfs leads to the fourth gulf, which we can put as a question. To what extent is it possible for a people of one culture to enter into the minds of people of another culture?

Despite the difficulties, one can, nevertheless, to some degree enter the world of the Bible.[1] The task of the Bible student is to enter that world and bring back from it what he finds: He must go there and back again.

At this point the question of how to go there, how to enter the biblical world, becomes crucial. The approach one takes to any phenomenon determines to a large extent what one sees. I remember, on entering New York from the sea on board the now-scrapped S.S. *Britannica,* seeing a city of skyscrapers glittering and shimmering in the sun. Manhattan seemed a fairyland. Later, I came to New York overland by car from the New Jersey side, past miles of dreary houses and black, belching factories. I saw the seamier, darker side of the city; it seemed a wasteland. I got two very different views.

How can we best approach the Bible? Here I shall indicate the way I have tried to follow, confining myself to the New Testament.

Modern critical scholarship of the New Testament began about the end of the eighteenth century in Europe during the Enlightenment, the movement that aimed at replacing faith with reason. The approach scholars took was predictable. First, since the New Testament was a Greek document, the view was natural that the main instrument for examining it would be Clas-

---

1. See on this question my article "Reflections on Thirty Years of Biblical Study," *SJT* (*Festschrift* for Hugh Anderson) 39 (1986): 43–64.

sical Greek. This was also very convenient because most biblical/theological scholars were then trained in the Latin and Greek classics; it was naturally tempting for them to use their classical skills in the biblical studies. In short, most biblical scholars looked at the New Testament through Greek-colored spectacles and, of course, what they tended to see was very Greek. Many found parallels to the teaching of Jesus in the Greek philosophers; they regarded Paul as a devotee of the Hellenistic Mystery religions and viewed the Fourth Gospel (John) and the Epistle to the Hebrews as imbued with something like the Hellenistic philosophy of Philo of Alexandria. I am drawing all this in broad black-and-white strokes, but not false ones.

New Testament scholarship in Britain, until as late as the 1930s, was dominated by the Greek, or Hellenistic, approach. For example, the great Cambridge Three — J. B. Lightfoot, B. F. Westcott, and F. J. A. Hort — were first and foremost, although not exclusively, scholars of Greek. Although they tried admirably to be objective and fair to their sources, they, nevertheless, wore both English- and Greek-colored spectacles. The strange elements they found in the New Testament that would not submit to the more-or-less rational and congenial Greek categories were relegated to unimportance and treated largely as a primitive vestige from secondary elements in early Christianity. These vestiges were primarily an embarrassment. For example, the kingdom of God — a standard Jewish phase — was interpreted to mean simply society organized by love. Its revolutionary, eschatological dimension was sidestepped: The gospel, according to some scholars, was the proclamation, centering on Jesus, of the love of God and the brotherhood of man. This was the essence of Jesus' teaching. And just as Jesus was turned into a refined Socrates or Plato, with touches of Francis of Assisi, or a sensitive English gentlemen (except that he had no bowler hat and umbrella), so Paul — the fiery *enfant terrible* of early Christianity — was draped in Hellenistic mysticism, tinged and somewhat emasculated with Stoic philosophy. For Greek-trained New Testament scholars, almost everything in the New Testament was suffused with a Greek light.

It was not only these scholars' Greek training that led to this. For nineteen centuries, with very rare exceptions, it had become customary to set Christianity over against Judaism as its antithesis. The Hebrew scriptures — which are never called the Old Testament in the New Testament — came to be called that. Implicitly the Old Testament was superseded by the new scriptures. The Old Testament stood for the law of God the judge over against the gospel of grace, of Christ the Son. Medieval Christendom relegated the People of the Book to the ghetto, and when the Reformation came, alas, the antithetical attitude toward Judaism, largely under Luther's influence, became even more marked: The religion of law had to be superseded by the religion of grace, as if Law and grace could not coexist.

Later, when historical criticism was applied to the Old Testament in the nineteenth century, this antithetical approach, which set the Old Testament against the New Testament, invaded the results of the new scholarship. The later history of the Jews was seen as one of decline to the aridity and banality of the law after the heights reached during the time of the prophets.

It is easy to caricature all this, and I do not wish to exaggerate, but it is fair to say that modern historical criticism until very recently did little to reveal any essential affinity between the New Testament and the Old Testament. Instead it concentrated on their differences. In this way, early historical criticism indirectly reinforced those scholars who thought of the New Testament in rather exclusively Greek terms.

Another reason for the preference for the Greek approach is seldom noticed. Paradoxically, it was the very movement called the Enlightenment, which elevated Reason with a capital *R* to supremacy and sought uniformity in all spheres, that reinforced an older approach in biblical studies. In countless directions the Enlightenment had immensely beneficial results; I would be the last to deny this. But in the biblical sphere, the Enlightenment helped to reinforce prejudice. For the Enlightenment, truth was universal: Truth is truth everywhere and for all peoples. What is not true for one is not true for another. What is truth for one is truth for all. There can be no *particular* truth given to any one *particular* people or person, no individual truth. The notion that there is one Chosen People — the Jews — to whom has been given *the* truth — and a special truth — was anathema. In the universalism and uniformity at which the Enlightenment aimed, the Jews as a Chosen People with a special revelation had no place. Some have found a connection between this Enlightenment view and the persecutions of the twentieth century. Some have suggested that Voltaire, the high priest of the Enlightenment, is in some ways the father of Hitler. But, in any case, the Enlightenment reinforced a pro-Greek stance among biblical scholars.

All these factors made it difficult for New Testament scholars — and Old Testament scholars — in the late nineteenth century to see the obvious. As a result, the Jesus of nineteenth-century scholarship is largely Platonized; and Paul, John, and the Letter to the Hebrews are Hellenized. This situation prevailed — although there were indications of a coming change, a few swallows before the summer — until the end of the nineteenth and the beginning of the twentieth centuries.

Then a German scholar and a Swiss scholar dropped a bombshell into the world of New Testament studies. The German scholar was Johannes Weiss and the Swiss scholar was Albert Schweitzer. They convincingly demonstrated that the most significant words and concepts in the New Testament must be understood in terms of Jewish apocalyptic sources and eschatological thinking. Terms like the resurrection, kingdom of God, the Son of Man, the Son of God, the judgment, justification, even Wisdom, were best to be understood in terms of Jewish literature and tradition, which had by New Testament times concentrated on the end of history in eschatology.

The evidence to which Weiss and Schweitzer appealed is so obvious to us now that one cannot imagine why it took so long to find it out. But it is the obvious that most easily eludes us.

Was the new thinking soon accepted? Not quite. Even though the evidence produced by Weiss and Schweitzer could not be denied, it could be sidestepped and reinterpreted. In Britain there was a polite unease and awkwardness: Could British classicist New Testament scholars believe that Jesus of Nazareth was an apocalyptic, wild-eyed fanatic convinced that the end of the world was at the door and that by dying he would bring it on? Could the Jesus of Albert Schweitzer — surely a deluded Jesus — be the object of New Testament faith? Scholars — not only in Britain — did their best to reject or qualify all this. My own revered teacher, Professor C. H. Dodd, for example, who was essentially a Platonist, hardly ever referred to Schweitzer and implicitly rejected his new evidence by re-Platonizing Jesus.

This was the situation even into the 1930s. But by then a serious question had been raised against what we may call the Christian-Classical alliance. At that time, several themes converged to convince me that this still predominant and almost exclusively Hellenistic approach to the New Testament had to be abandoned. First, I read the Greek New Testament itself. I came to it after years of immersion in Classical Greek and Semitic studies. Most of it I found easy to read. But to my amazement when I came to the Gospel of John, the so-called Fourth Gospel, I found it extremely difficult to translate, although I had been taught that it was the most Greek of all the Gospels. Its vocabulary is almost ridiculously simple. "I am the bread of life," "I am the light of the world," etc. Why, then, was it so difficult? It was because its prepositions and connecting terms and phrases, its relative pronouns particularly, were so awkward. But I discovered that, if these were translated into their Aramaic or Hebrew equivalents, they often made sense. I became convinced that what was in the scholarly mind the most Greek of the Gospels was in fact Semitic in its syntax and style. The Gospel of John was a Semitic document, it seemed to me, written in Greek. But, if so, what of the other New Testament documents? Could this be true of other parts of the New Testament as well?

About this same time, I was also reading in the literature of the Pharisees — the Mishnah (an authoritative collection of rabbinic legal discussions compiled around 200 c.e.) and other sources — and it became clearer and clearer that this literature was the product of the kind of world out of which much of the New Testament came. It was far nearer to the world reflected in the New Testament than were the Classical Greek and Hellenistic sources and illuminated it more.

Third, it was my good fortune at this time to come to know two extraordinary persons in England. One was a neighbor, an Anglican priest living in the small village of Barley in East Anglia, who had the finest private library of Judaica in the entire country and who did more to make his country aware of anti-Semitism than any person I know — James W. Parkes.[2] The other person was a Jewish refugee from Germany, Dr. (now Professor) David Daube, who at that time was Reader of Roman Law at Caius College, Cambridge. Daube became my tutor because, as an Orthodox Jew, he was intensely committed to Judaism and, at the same time, he was interested in Christian beginnings. Parkes and Daube compelled me to ask why Jews had suffered so much at the hands of Christendom; it was the time of Hitler. Contact with them, always immensely stimulating, gave me courage to pursue my hunch — now a conviction — about the essentially Jewish nature of many of the documents of the New Testament despite their Greek dress. (I must add that at the time I was unaware of all this and simply pursued my sources. One is not always aware of the *Zeitgeist* within which one works nor of the direct influences upon one.)[3]

Lastly, there was an archaeological discovery that, a little later, helped to redirect New Testament studies in the direction of a greater emphasis on its Jewish background — the discovery of the Dead Sea Scrolls. These were not as utterly revolutionary as was claimed at the time of their discovery. (Every new brush is thought to sweep clean.) But they did reveal certain aspects of Judaism that had hitherto been hidden or overlooked. The similarity of much in the scrolls, written in Hebrew, with much in the New Testament could not be denied. It became even clearer that the ark of the New Testament floated on Jewish waters.

The conviction that this was the right direction to follow led me to concentrate first on Paul. Paul had been pictured as the one who had taken the simple Palestinian gospel of Jesus and transformed it into an elaborate Hellenistic Mystery religion, and who had attacked the Law of Judaism. My method was to take the main elements in Paul's thought — the concepts of the flesh, of sin, the people of Israel, Wisdom, the Spirit, the death of Christ as sacrifice, the resurrection — and place all these, first, over against Hellenistic sources and, then, over against Semitic, Hebraic-rabbinic sources. In each case I was able to prove to my satisfaction that it was the latter that

---

2. His best-known work is *The Conflict of the Church and the Synagogue: A Study in the Origins of Anti-Semitism* (Philadelphia: Jewish Publication Society of America, 1934; reprint, New York: Atheneum, 1969).

3. Stephen Westerholm, "The British Connection: Dodd, Daube, and Davies," paper given at the "Torah/*Nomos* Seminar," annual meeting of the Canadian Society of Biblical Studies, 1983.

most illuminated Paul. I expressed my conclusions with far more reserve than I could have, simply stating that many aspects of Paulinism previously labeled Hellenistic were better understood as Pharisaic. Despite the difficulties presented by the rabbinic sources, I was able to bring light to much in Paul that had previously been obscure.

Then another very different character attracted me — the person who wrote the first Gospel, the Gospel of Matthew. Few documents have been more influential in Christian history than the Gospel of Matthew, partly because of its priority of place in the New Testament canon. But few documents have been more elusive. We do not know who the author was, and there is much debate still as to whether he was a Gentile or a Jewish Christian. I am convinced that he was a Jewish Christian who wrote good Greek — not a rare phenomenon in the first century. I ventured to examine the Sermon on the Mount from the Pharisaic point of view. I can easily illustrate the kind of thing that emerges from this study. Making the assumption that Matthew was written toward the end of the first century, I asked what contemporary movements were likely to have impinged on him. The time was after the failed revolt of the Jews against the Romans. In 70 C.E. Jerusalem was a city in ruins, the Jews were scattered, some sold into slavery. Palestine was desolate. The survival of Judaism seemed to be in jeopardy. So the sages — the leaders of the Pharisees — along with some other Jews, gathered, some say at a place called Jamnia (Yavneh), to rescue Judaism from extinction. They probably fixed the number of books that Jews were to regard as authoritative (canonical), the ordained persons authorized to teach the Law and expound it (the rabbis), and they established a calendar for all Jews everywhere. What we call Rabbinic Judaism came into being like a phoenix from the ashes of the revolt.

In the light of this background, I suggested that Matthew's Gospel, and particularly his Sermon on the Mount, was in part a reaction to Jamnia — a Christian response to it. The process that led to the codification of the Mishnah coincided with, and in a parallel way led to, the formation of the Gospel of Matthew.

I will illustrate this with only one point. The Sermon on the Mount has often been exaggeratedly praised as a piece of literature. It has many sparkling gems — individual sayings that are unforgettable — but their setting and arrangement has always been a problem. From a purely literary point of view, the Sermon on the Mount has always been very difficult to classify. But its arrangement is probably governed by Pharisaic tradition. In one of the tractates in the Mishnah we read: "On three things the world rests: Torah (the Law), Worship, and Deeds of social service [kindness]." This famous triad was in the air when the Pharisees were reorganizing at Jamnia, and Matthew, who was standing alongside that reorganization, used this triad, I believe, in ar-

ranging the Sermon on the Mount. He begins with Torah (5:17ff.), moves on
to true worship (6:1ff.), and, finally, to deeds of kindness (7:7ff.). The parallel
is not exact, but it is sufficiently close to be plausible. In other ways, it seems
to me, Matthew's Sermon on the Mount is a kind of Christian counterpart
to the Mishnah.[4]

When I had finished my study of the Sermon on the Mount, something
happened that led me to a more specifically theological aspect of the relations between Judaism and the New Testament. Just before the Six Day War
in 1967, I received a desperate letter from a distinguished professor of Talmud
at the Hebrew University of Jerusalem, Professor Ephraim E. Urbach. Dr. Urbach asked me to send a letter to the *New York Times,* in support of the Israeli
cause and to get others to do likewise, which in due course I did. However,
his letter was couched in religious language — Urbach is an Orthodox Jew.
He quoted the scriptures to prove that Jews had a divine right to the Land of
Israel. He assumed that as a Christian who had read the Hebrew scriptures,
I would agree with him and that a New Testament student would automatically lend his support to the Israeli cause. I realized with a pang that despite
my immersion in Judaism I had not paid attention at all to one of its peculiar emphases: The belief that there is an eternal connection among the God
of Israel, the People of Israel, and the Land of Israel. As one Jewish scholar
had put it: "Judaism is a fortunate blend of a land, a people and God." I was
driven to consider this important doctrine of Judaism which, partly at least,
is at the root of the conflict between the Arabs and the Israelis in the Middle
East. I assume that this doctrine of an eternal connection between people
and land rooted in a Divine Promise must have engaged early Christians who
wrote the New Testament. But what did they make of it? Did they dismiss
it, did they spiritualize it, did they transcendentalize it, or did they — at least
some of them — accept it? How do Christians in the New Testament view
the Land of Israel? Finding the answer to the question was very difficult. So
is the correlative question. If you accept this territorial doctrine of Judaism,
what of the claims of others besides Jews who live in the land and who have
lived there for centuries?[5]

I hope that I have said enough to show that during the last fifty years
there has emerged what is in effect a silent revolution in our approach to
the New Testament. To put it in a nutshell, the New Testament has been
increasingly re-Judaized.

But there has naturally been a reaction to all this. In abandoning the

---

4. See my *Setting of the Sermon on the Mount* (Cambridge: Cambridge University Press, 1964),
216–315.

5. On this question, see W. D. Davies, *The Territorial Dimension in Judaism* (Berkeley: University of California Press, 1982), and Davies, *The Gospel and the Land: Early Christianity and Jewish
Territorial Doctrine* (Berkeley: University of California Press, 1974).

predominantly Greek approach in favor of the Semitic, have we gone too far? Martin Luther once said that, as a group, human beings (and scholars belong to that category) are like a drunken peasant mounted on a donkey: If you push the person up when he falls on the left, he will fall down to the right; and if you push him up on the right, he will fall to the left. I was aware of this danger and, in fact, began my work on Paul by insisting that by the first century, Palestine, the home of the Jews, had already been for three centuries under direct Hellenistic influence, so that any neat division between what was Hellenistic and what was Semitic had to be rejected. The Pharisees have now turned out to be Hellenized and the rabbinic methods have turned out to be Aristotelian; Aristotle was the father of Rabbi Akiba. Out of the criticism of the old Hellenistic approach, there is emerging not simply a greater emphasis on the Jewish element, but also a recognition of the interpenetration, not the identity, of the Hellenistic and the Semitic. We have further begun to recognize that the Jews of the first century are not only Semitic, but also Mediterranean. The clear-cut dichotomies or divisions between the Hellenistic and the Hebraic or Semitic are not longer acceptable. We now recognize more and more that to some extent by the first century Hellenism itself had been Hebraized and Judaism itself Hellenized. There are now also other dichotomies that the scholarship of the last fifty years has questioned — those between Pharisaic and apocalyptic thought, and between Law and gospel.

There is one other aspect of Judaism that we have recently learned to appreciate more fully. Especially since the discovery of the Dead Sea Scrolls, it has become clear that before 70 C.E., in the time of Jesus, there was not one monolithic Judaism but many forms of Judaism. To understand such figures as Jesus and Paul, we have to ask not simply what was their relation to Judaism, but to which form of Judaism. In a sense, there were many Judaisms.

But you will be asking, what has all this to do with the significance of the New Testament? Is it important whether we think of it primarily as a Greek or Semitic document? I think it is, for many reasons. Let me remind you that the Bible has been the determinative canonical volume for the thinking of both the Jewish and Christian communities, and because these impinge in countless ways on the life of the world we live in, the way in which this canonical volume is interpreted becomes a matter of great importance. I shall mention three areas to illustrate this — three instances in which a Hellenistic interpretation of the New Testament may well have had an extraordinary influence on history.

The most obvious is that of the relationship between Jew and Gentile. History has been marred and stained by the absurdity and horror of anti-Semitism, partly — but only partly — because of our interpretation of the New Testament as a Greek document. This helped to create a climate within which anti-Judaism and later anti-Semitism became possible. Many of us have regarded Christianity as a *new* religion that superseded its mother religion, Judaism, and left it behind. Even Arnold Toynbee thought of Judaism as a *fossilized* form of religion. But the approach to the New Testament through Jewish eyes helps to correct this. Christianity in the New Testament is not a new, distinct religion over against Judaism, but a new interpretation of Judaism in the light of Christ. It does not abandon Judaism but rather absorbs it, so that the substructure of Christianity remains Jewish. Judaism, in other words, is not "before" Christianity, something that Christians have left behind, but rather somehow within it, something that Christians carry along with them. To recognize this essential continuity between the two faiths is a basis for mutual respect and engagement.

There is another area in which, some have suggested, the Hellenistic misinterpretation of the New Testament has had dire consequences — in the realm of politics and political theory. One of the major developments in twentieth-century political life has been the emergence and development of Marxism. This occurred *within* Christendom. How could this happen? Marxism began in Germany and flourished in Russia, where Christian communities had been most Hellenized. Marxism, it is often claimed, arose in protest against a Hellenized form of Christianity that had forsaken its Jewish roots. In this view Marx was the unwitting heir of the Hebrew prophets who had been submerged and forgotten in a Christianity that had substituted individual piety and mystic absorption for social justice. Christianity, in this view, transferred interest from the proper ordering of society in this world, with which Judaism is concerned, to preparation for another world that promised riches and revelation in the sky as compensation for poverty and pain on earth. The communal, social, and ethical concerns of Judaism, which Christianity had inherited, had been diluted and even abandoned by an increasingly Hellenized church. Thus Christianity had become the opium of the people and itself helped produce its own antithesis in a Marxism which developed into a kind of secular Jewish messianism — a religion that has its Messiahs in Marx and Lenin, its holy book in *Das Kapital,* its priesthood in the elite members of the Communist Party, and its kingdom of God in the hoped-for classless society of the future.

Third, the claim has been made — and not only by Jews — that much of the permissiveness, moral confusion, and legal nihilism of our time is a reaction to two factors:

1. To a Hellenized asceticism paradoxically nurtured in a Puritanism that has misinterpreted the Hebrew scriptures. (True, there are some ascetic strands in Jewish apocalyptic thought that contributed to this, but only to a minor extent.)

2. To the alleged opposition between gospel and Law, as if Law were a pariah, as it came to be viewed in much of the Protestant tradition of the West.

All this you will rightly claim is very speculative, and it is always dangerous to indulge in large, unprovable generalizations, although I do find much in them that is worthy of serious consideration. You will also rightly object that I have not pointed to the other side: the emphasis on newness in Christianity, its discontinuity with both Judaism and Hellenism. This question of newness, and the precise relation of the new to the old, I have deliberately ignored; it will have to await another occasion, although I am fully aware that for first-century Jews and Christians the gospel spelled "modernity"; it welcomed newness.

What, then, is the little harvest from what I have tried to say? It is simply this: that Judaism and Christianity need not be in opposition; that Christianity is not an anti-Judaic phenomenon, but itself, in its origin, a particular form of Messianic Judaism; that both Judaism and Christianity belong to the same family, so that the tension that inevitably exists between them need not develop into an antithesis.

I call it a little harvest because in twenty centuries since Jesus lived much has happened between Jews and Christians. So much, indeed, that merely to appeal to origins is not likely to allay mutual suspicions and distrust nor to counteract the horrors and distortions of history. Alas, history is in the saddle and rides us too much. But this little harvest may further help, however feebly, to initiate a new direction, a correction of misrepresentations and misinterpretations. To turn this small harvest into a full harvest will be the endless task facing the next generation. To encourage that generation as I myself have been encouraged, I quote the words of the rabbinic tractate *Pirke Aboth* (Sayings of the Fathers): "It is not given to you to complete the task, but also it is not given to you to desist from the task" of wrestling with the scriptures. The task of biblical interpretation is ongoing from generation to generation.

Part I

Judaism and Christianity

Chapter I

In Search of "The Center" of Judaism

Certain events and travails mutually reacting among Jews and Gentiles in the late nineteenth and first half of the twentieth century culminated in 1948 in the establishment of the state of Israel in the Land of Israel. Those events compelled the increasing recognition among Gentiles as well as Jews of the role of territory in the life of the Jewish people and their faith.

Still more recent events, in which Israelis and Palestinians have tragically confronted each other in the Intifada, have insured that that role be even more especially recognized and reexamined and more precisely assessed. A question which has occupied Jews across the centuries — the question of how important is "The Promised Land" in Judaism and (to use the customary but, as we shall see, inadequate terminology) what is the "center" or the "essence" of that faith — has now, because of the counterclaims of Palestinians and Israelis, Egyptians, and Lebanese, become agonizingly acute. What is it within Judaism as its "center" or "essence" without which it ceases to be itself?

However, there are many aspects to Judaism — much as in attempts to describe one "center" or "essence" in Christianity, there have been many answers, all open to criticism. So much is this the case that we might be tempted to think that we are engaged in a wild-goose chase. Is the question whether there is a center or essence to Judaism misplaced because it seems to imply that there is a single phenomenon, however complex, which we can designate "Judaism" — in the singular?[1]

---

1. When I began this essay, I asked the late Louis Finkelstein, then president of the Jewish Theological Seminary of America, for his judgment, and he replied as follows: "It is very difficult for me to formulate in a single sentence what might be called the essence of Judaism if that means that some things are more important than others. The Torah is what holds us together. We have to observe its laws and that can only be done by community. The Torah also commands that all of us, if we can do so, live in Israel and observe the commandments, which can only be fulfilled there. But I do not think that this means there is an essence of Judaism in the sense that some things are more important than others. The Divine Commandments are all equally important" (private communication, 12 June 1990). This response is similar to the comment made by D. C. Allison on this question when he suggested that the best definition of Judaism is in *Mishnah Aboth* 1:2. It reads: "Simeon the Just was of the remnants of the Greater Synagogue.

I

To begin with, it has been urged that there is no single phenomenon called "Judaism." Professor Jacob Neusner, for example, has insisted that there is a multiplicity of *Judaisms* — not a single comprehensive, overarching *Judaism.* He writes:

> A Judaism is a system made up of a world view, a way of life, and a social group that defines its life through that world view and lives in accord with the descriptions of that way of life. Through time there have been many Judaisms, that is, many Judaic systems that have defined for Jews the way they should live and understand their world.[2]

The term "system," as Neusner defines "a Judaism," clearly for him has much fluidity and flexibility. Indeed, his use of the term is so broad that it invites imprecision. For example, like Jacob Klatzkin[3] who sought to define "Judaism" in purely secular terms, Neusner regards even secular Zionism (despite its rejection of the received rabbinic system of "the dual Torah")[4] as "a Judaism" of the nineteenth and twentieth centuries, with all that this religiously implies. The net of Neusner's "Judaism" is so very widespread that it is a kind of Jewish catch-all. As is apparent in all his writings, Neusner himself can accept "a Judaism" without a revelation on Sinai or elsewhere. He finds a secular phenomenon such as Zionism, as he understands it — complex as it admittedly is and impregnated with traditional religious motifs — to be "a Judaism." In his eagerness to recognize many "Judaisms," he sidesteps the revelational origin of his own preferred "Judaism." This he can justify in terms of the definition of "a Judaism" offered by him which we indicated above. But if "Judaism" or "a Judaism" be so comprehensively defined, then, it seems to be implied presumably that *any* Jewish group holding *any* worldview and way of life can be designated "a Judaism."

We prefer, as does Raphael Loewe,[5] a more closely defined and restricted use of the term "Judaism" and deal only with those Jewish communities for

He used to say: 'By three things is the world sustained: by the Law, by the Temple-service, and by deeds of loving kindness'" (Danby's translation).

The difficulty of the responses by both Finkelstein and Allison is that they describe Pharisaic Judaism. The *Aboth* is a document of Pharisaism, and there are many aspects other than the Pharisaic to be considered. Our task here is not simply the Pharisaic interpretation of Judaism, but to go behind the unexpressed assumptions of the rabbis — behind Pharisaic Judaism — and to disclose these. For discussion of the *Pirke Aboth* as a Pharisaic document, see my essay in the John Knox *Festschrift,* reprinted in my *Jewish and Pauline Studies* (Philadelphia and London: Fortress Press, 1984), 27–48.

2. *Self-Fulfilling Prophecy: Exile and Return in the History of Judaism* (Boston: Beacon Press, 1987), 1.

3. Ibid., 207.

4. Ibid., 204.

5. Raphael Loewe, "Judaism's Eternal Triangle: Belief, Authority, and Peoplehood in Judaism," *Religious Studies* 23 (September 1987): 309–23.

whom their worldview or faith accepts and embraces an explicit revelational-theological dimension. The definition of "a Judaism" or "Judaism" in the terms used by Neusner simply of *any* Judaic group(s), even a secular one, invites the criticism that "Judaism" is ultimately simply an ethnic (not to say "tribal") phenomenon limited to persons of Judaic birth or adherence without reference to the religious tradition of the Jewish people. Is not this to lay all "Judaisms" (to use Neusner's terms) open to the charge that there is a "racial" element in their very essence, even while their very multiplicity makes a search for a center or for an essence such as we are engaged in even more a wild-goose chase? Raphael Loewe, we think, rightly restricts the term "Judaism" to a phenomenon "to which a theological dimension" is integral, a phenomenon of "revelational origin." He proposes the following definition.

> Judaism is a complex of faith and social ethics, of universal significance and possibly of universal relevance, resting upon the sanction of uncompromised and absolute monotheism expressing itself mainly through a pattern of religious symbolism, the cultural features of which are predominantly concrete and the transmission of which is predominantly by descent; and having as its object the general sublimating of the material concerns of humanity by pervading them with such spiritual considerations as will not compromise the monotheistic basis of the whole.[6]

This definition does not obviate the ethnic aspect of the Jewish faith, but it explicitly states that the ultimate sanction for that faith is not birth but "uncompromised and absolute monotheism."

Has our question been, then, answered? — that the center of Judaism is the One God? Neusner elsewhere seems to imply this when he defines Judaism otherwise than in the passage quoted above as a religion the first mark of which is "a world view which by reference to the *intersection of the supernatural and the natural worlds* accounts for how things are and puts them together into a cogent and harmonious picture."[7] In a private note he urged that there is the Persistent Presence — God — in and behind all Judaisms, self-contradictory as all this may seem to be.

We must agree that without the recognition that religious Jews have been aware of the presence of God in a way which brooks no denial, their history becomes inexplicable. It becomes the fruit either of a colossal illusion (a tragic and painful illusion, which they could have cast away conveniently had they so desired, as many of them do) or of the inescapable reality which

---

6. Ibid., 309.
7. Neusner, *Self-Fulfilling Prophecy*, 7.

has burned like a fire, however fitfully, among them. Speaking for myself, to a Gentile entering the religious tradition of Jews, one thing perhaps above all else shines clear: the religious certainty in Judaism about the reality of God seems to transcend or deny reason, and that often in the face of horrendous odds. The classic expression of this certainty is in Daniel 3:16–18 ("Shadrach, Meshach, and Abednego answered the king, 'O Nebuchadnezzar, we have no need to answer you in this matter. If it be so, our God whom we serve is able to deliver us from the burning fiery furnace; and he will deliver us out of your hand, O king. But if not, be it known to you, O king, that we will not serve your gods or worship the golden image which you have set up' "), but it is found ubiquitously in the sources.

But if we must agree that the One God as the Persistent Presence is in all "Judaisms," can we, then, assert that the essence or center of Judaism is simply monotheism? Certainly, as George Steiner has reminded us,[8] Judaism fully shares this with Islam and also, though more suspiciously, with Christianity. It is primarily Judaism that has most magnificently borne the weight of monotheism throughout the centuries. But monotheism has not been unique to Jews. There were monotheists among the ancient Greeks and elsewhere. Monotheism, then, is not the sole essential element which lends peculiarity to Judaism. This does provide a constant, indeed, its ultimate sanction. But monotheism does not by itself account for its other characteristics. At this point it is necessary to accept that the search for a single rational monotheistic center of the Jewish faith or essence is indeed misplaced. But recognizing that the center of Judaism is not a single phenomenon but a complex plurality of phenomena, at the same time we have equally to acknowledge that a few individual aspects of that faith have been given such prominence at various times or have so dominated Judaism in the perception of many that they seem to have been given primacy or a central position. Here two different kinds of phenomena are to be distinguished.

First, certain *isolated* or *single* phenomena have been accorded centrality or prominence. Four are inescapably noticeable: The Torah, The Land, The People, and (especially as Gentiles have looked upon Judaism) The Messiah. At different times and among different groups of Jews (and non-Jews), each of these has been accorded a centrality. But, second, we shall see that certain scholars have insisted that the essence or center of Judaism has been not so much a single phenomenon as a plurality of phenomena which constitute a well-defined "pattern" or conglomerate of phenomena, which have dominated it at all times and places. We begin with the single phenomenon.

---

8. In *Bluebeard's Castle: Some Notes towards the Redefinition of Culture* (New Haven: Yale University Press, 1971), 36–39; and see Davies, *Jewish and Pauline Studies,* 146.

The Torah

The first "isolated" aspect of Judaism that has presented itself as constituting the center or essence of Judaism to most Jews and certainly to most Christians, is the Torah, conceived of primarily as the first five books of the Tanak. Israel has often been called the People of the Book; Judaism, the religion of the Book (meaning the Torah). Years ago in Jerusalem I asked Professor Hiam Beinart, of Hebrew University, why Jews — despite their tragic history — have survived over the centuries. Apparently without any need for reflection, he immediately replied, "We have the Book." The implication was clear: for him, what has given life to the Jewish people is their possession of and by the Hebrew scriptures. These constitute the center of their faith. Josephus and others make it clear that this was so long before the first century; it became even more the case in the later rabbinic period. However, then as earlier, the scriptures, the written Torah, increasingly gathered round themselves an oral tradition which developed (though to a lesser extent than has often been claimed) by direct interpretation of the written Torah and probably even more by the accretion of independent materials. The Torah, conserved in the twofold form indicated — and that as interpreted by the rabbis, who after 70 C.E. emerged as the leaders of Jews — became the "canon" (if such a term can be used of Judaism) for religious Jews, the source of their self-understanding, and the guide for their conduct both individually and collectively.

On this view Judaism can be conceived of as "pan-halakic (to use a term popularized by Abraham Heschel); that is, every aspect of it is governed by the Torah. Without the Torah it cannot sustain itself, but with it, the Jewish people could persist wherever and whenever they choose to accept and embrace it. The touchstone of being religious for Jews became the attitude to the Torah. Neither time nor place can effectively and ultimately deny them the freedom to choose and live by the Torah. Tragically costly though their loyalty to the Torah has often been, Jews have been able to come to terms with life and to retain their identity even when and where all *outward* public observance of the Torah has been impossible. The classic example of this is the history of the Jewish Marranos of Spain and Portugal who persisted in their Judaism by necessarily recognizing solely the need of an inner consent to the Torah and a secret, private, and personal maintenance of its rites and customs. In this way in 1391 and later in the fifteenth century, thousands of Jews were able outwardly even to adopt Christianity in order to escape massacre and were not regarded as apostates by the rabbis.

In view of the role of the Torah in preserving Jewish existence over the centuries, it is natural that Judaism has been conceived as the religion of tough-minded rationalists, wryly ironic realists, and Jews as living within tightly drawn lines of legal restriction and self-imposed restraint — stern, pale, ascetic figures, the legalists of the Christian imagination.[9] Is it not altogether natural in the light of the ubiquity of the Torah in Judaism and Jewish history to make it the center of that faith?

Natural it is but not necessarily justified. Within and without Judaism, certain pressures have been at work to account for this apparent concentration and the centrality of the Torah in the faith.

From within there has been and still is the traditional emphasis upon the Torah among the Jewish sages from the beginning of the common era and before, to which we have already referred. The words of Josephus in *Contra Apion* 1, for example, are unambiguous and, though apologetic, surely significant. Then in the nineteenth and twentieth centuries, modern academic treatments of Judaism have reinforced the centrality of Torah from its very emergence. To reread the opening pages of G. F. Moore's *Judaism in the First Five Centuries of the Christian Era* is to realize again how this centrality of the Torah had come to be naturally accepted. Dealing with the pre-Christian centuries after the exile, Moore writes of "the creation of a normative type of Judaism" and "its establishment in undisputed supremacy throughout the wide Jewish world through the study of the scriptures and the discussions of generations of scholars...."[10] Until the 1940s the notion of a normative Judaism, as propounded by Moore, formed an academic consensus. By it was meant a Judaism governed by the centrality of Torah — a pan-halakic Judaism. A glance at the influential works of Solomon Schechter and Abraham Heschel, Jewish scholars; of Lagrange and Bonsirven, Roman Catholics; R. T. Herford, a Unitarian; and Strack-Billerbeck, Lutherans, confirms the academic pressure to concentrate on the central place of Torah for the understanding of Judaism.

What modern scholarship pointed to, the rabbinic leaders had long insisted upon: for them historical necessity had demanded and justified that concentration. Rabbinic Judaism came into being when certain symbols of the faith, the Temple, and the priestly sacrificial system in Jerusalem had been removed from control by Jews, and their land ravaged. The Torah alone remained as the focus of Jewish devotion and identity. Neusner has particularly emphasized how, deprived of geographic space by the destruction of their land and by deportation, and deprived of the luxury of time to wait for their rehabilitation by the destruction or eclipse of their messianism, the rabbis had to recognize a new kind of "space," a nonterritorial space, the Torah, which they could maintain and honor in obedience when The Land was

---

9. David Biale, *Power and Powerlessness in Jewish History* (New York: Schocken Books, 1986), 4. I have here borrowed some of Biale's terms.

10. *Judaism in the First Five Centuries of the Christian Era: The Age of the Tannaim* (Cambridge: Harvard University Press, 1927–30), 1:3.

not theirs to control, a nonterritorial space within which they could live in hope against hope. As long as Jews occupied their own land, they enjoyed in and through their geographic and historical remoteness a certain protection from the metaphysical "loneliness" which is endemic to the human condition. They were at home. To be in The Land ensured a certain tangible and psychological and spiritual security. Conversely, when they had been deprived of their land, they became exposed to social and civic homelessness — the political counterpart of the metaphysical "loneliness" of the human spirit. This "loneliness" could be experienced inside but especially outside The Land.

The sages who became the leaders of the Jewish people after the collapse of the state in 70 c.e. knew the threat of "homelessness" in their own land and in the Diaspora. The Diaspora spelled not only "scattering" but also "exile." After the abortive revolt of 135 c.e. under Bar Kokba, they faced an exile which, unlike the previous exile in Babylon (which lasted only half a century), seemed to stretch endlessly into the future until the Messiah came, "for ever." It lasted in fact until 1948. This meant that for the rabbis "history" seemed to have been swallowed up: the fulfillment of Jewish hopes would only come when historical time would come to an end or in the Age to Come when space and time would together disappear. Faced with such a situation in which they had no control over space or time, the rabbis developed a strategy to preserve their faith from disappearing in chaos. That strategy was to elevate the Torah as the chief, if not the sole, remaining emblem or symbol of their faith. Response to the Torah they could "control," since it was "a portable land," which, as we noted above, could be embraced outwardly or inwardly in all times and places.

And the instrument which they devised for this strategy was the Mishnah, the Jewish code of Law — to use crude shorthand — which, under Judah the Prince, the sages codified about the middle of the second century. The Mishnah sought to provide the way, the *halakah,* through the lonely wilderness that surrounded Jews and helped to enable them to come to terms with their defeat and the disorientation and destruction of their existence: it set forth "a map without territory" for the guidance of Jews in The Land and outside it, so that they could live according to God's will as revealed in the Torah. The sages could not reconquer The Land but they could and did discriminate between the pure and the polluted, the holy and the profane, "us" and "them," within and outside The Land.

The work of the sages preserved in the Mishnah was continued by later sages, eventually to produce the Palestinian Talmud and the Babylonian and still later the *Shulḥan Arukh.* Compiled by Joseph Karo and first published in 1565, this work succeeded in standardizing and creating a normative framework and guide for Jewish practice. The domain of the Torah was extended to every pocket of sacredness, every "small sanctuary" which Jews could

construct in their wanderings. The task of carving out "a way" moment by
moment, inch by inch, could not possibly succeed before the coming of the
Messiah: the rabbis could only pray that their task would not entirely fail
before He for whom they yearned came.[11] This Herculean rabbinic commitment and achievement to live according to the Torah, in their defeated and
dispersed condition, inevitably and naturally reinforced the tendency — already noted in Josephus, *Against Apion* — to find the heart of Judaism in the
Torah. The observance of the Torah was the insurance against the demise of
Judaism, the means of its survival. Among most religious Jews in the long
period following the collapse of the Jewish state in the late first century,
the centrality of the Torah, both written and oral, became an assumption.
Among Jewish scholars right up to the beginning of the twentieth century,
the same assumption seemed natural. The title of Solomon Schechter's work
Aspects of Rabbinic Theology[12] is significant: Schechter dealt only with aspects
of his theme. One might gather that he was not concerned with discover-
ing the center of rabbinic theology at all. However, in his treatment, it is
the Law that stands out as the dominant central aspect. His chapter on
"The Joy of the Law" especially, but also others, attests this unforgettably.
That G. F. Moore was in touch with Schechter and other scholars at the
Jewish Theological Seminary in New York, and under their influence, when
he formulated his understanding of "normative Judaism" is highly significant.
Moore breathed the same air as they did. Even later, when I taught at Union
Theological Seminary in New York City in the sixties, the leading scriptural
and Talmudic scholars there always left with me the unmistakable impres-
sion that Jewish scholarship not engaged with the Torah was secondary, if
not trivial. H. L. Ginsberg, Saul Lieberman, and Louis Finkelstein, and even
Heschel, come to mind.

But long before the time of Moore there were pressures *outside* Judaism
also to reinforce the centrality of the Torah. It is clear from Schechter's book
that he was acutely sensitive to criticism of the Torah by Christians of all per-
suasions. The medieval period had witnessed much discussion of the place of
the Law in Judaism; the medieval "disputations" or "trials" had brought the
question of the Law to the fore.[13] And especially after the Reformation, the
adversarial juxtaposition of Law and gospel — the one standing for Judaism
and the other for the Christian faith — became a marked feature of Protestant and other forms of Christianity. Law — standing for the quintessence
of Judaism — often became a pejorative term, as it still remains in some
quarters. It was only to be expected that Jewish scholars such as Schechter

---

11. I am deeply indebted to Jacob Neusner's works on all this and throughout this essay.

12. Published in London, 1909.

13. See Hyam Maccoby, *Judaism on Trial: Jewish-Christian Disputations in the Middle Ages*
(London: Fairleigh Dickinson Press, 1982).

reacted against what they regarded as unjustifiable and unfair criticism and denigration of the Torah. But this very reaction reinforced the centrality of Torah in both Jewish and Christian minds: scholarship does not develop in a vacuum. At the noted colloquium on Judaism and Christianity held at Harvard University after Vatican II in 1966, Torah was still taken as the quintessence of Judaism as over against dogma as the quintessence of Christianity. In writing a small volume recently, I assumed (unconsciously I now realize) that the heart or center of Judaism is Torah. I attempted no justification for this view: it did not occur to me that this was necessary. We have seen, however, that many forces had conspired to create this emphasis on Torah as center.

A complex, apparently contradictory approach to the centrality of Torah appears in the work of Jacob Neusner. At first he seems to have strengthened or confirmed the "bookish" or pan-halakic approach to Judaism. According to him, behind all "Judaisms" there is a single regulative governing and animating principle. For him the essential point of reference for understanding them all is clear: it is the pattern imposed upon Jewish history by the Jews who returned from the Babylonian Exile in 587–86 B.C.E. By about 450 B.C.E. these had completed the gathering together of the sources which make up the Torah and the prophetic books. From these sources — the Hebrew scriptures — in various unmistakable ways, a pattern of exile and return was stamped upon the minds of Jews. It is this pattern, according to Neusner, which is the center or essence of *all* Judaisms. We shall examine Neusner's "normative pattern" for all Judaism later. At this point we simply ask: is not the Torah, as the repository of his essential pattern, the center of Judaism? This would seem to be the logical outcome, at least by implication, of Neusner's position. However, he explicitly refuses to regard Judaism as the religion of the Book. "A Judaism," he writes, "is not a book, and no social group took shape because people read a book and agreed that God revealed what the book and they should do."[14] To us his divorce of the normative animating pattern of all Judaisms from the Book, the Torah, which contains it, seems questionable. Is he not straining at gnats? On the one hand he denies that Judaism in all its forms is a religion of the Book. But because the Book contains the normative pattern for all Judaisms, on the other hand does he not, by implication at least, affirm it as the religion of the Book? Our question later leads to further discussion of Neusner's views, because they point to another possible center for Judaism — a historical one, which again as we shall see by implication demands concentration, this time, on territory.

---

14. Neusner, *Self-Fulfilling Prophecy*, 14.

The Land

This reference to a territorial dimension points to another aspect of Judaism: the land of Israel, which for many Jews, especially in recent centuries, has been elevated to centrality or preeminence in their faith. The significance of The Land in the classical sources of Judaism — the Hebrew scriptures, the Mishnah, the Targumim, the Talmud Babli, and the Talmud Jerushalmi — and in the rich liturgical Jewish tradition, in popular custom and piety, we have indicated elsewhere:[15] it is unmistakable. And Jewish history confirms this abundantly. To anticipate what we write later, history bears witness to two kinds of engagement with The Land: first, with The Land regarded by religious Jews as divinely promised or sworn to the people of Israel, as the physical or geographic sphere for the expression of that people's life. And, second, there is engagement with The Land as significant not only geographically and politically but strictly spiritually, so that exile from it is not simply a scattering or dispersion but an expression and symbol of the metaphysical and spiritual homelessness of Jews, so that until the exile is ended they are doomed to an emaciated life, to the loneliness which the uprootedness of any people, but especially of Jews, always seems to involve, physical uprootedness being inseparable from spiritual uprootedness.[16] There is an umbilical geographic and spiritual relationship among The Land and the people and Yahweh which is inseverable and eternal: such has been the faith especially of religious Jews and, implicitly, even of many secular Jews.

In the nineteenth and twentieth centuries the political connotation of the Jews' exile has been to the fore, and the return to The Land in a physical sense has overshadowed its religious dimension. This was because of the rise of Zionism, which culminated in the creation of the state of Israel in 1948. The Zionist concern to return to The Land has often been interpreted as a new phenomenon unrelated to earlier efforts to return to The Land by Jews who were governed by religious or what we referred to as metaphysical or spiritual interests. But Zionism should not be isolated from those interests even when it ostensibly rejected them. Without the previous centuries-long religious engagement of Jews with The Land, it is doubtful whether Zionism could have developed as it did. That the movement chose for itself the name "Zionism," the religious evocativeness and appeal of which is unavoidable, is not accidental. The religious devotion to The Land across the

---

15. See W. D. Davies, *The Gospel and the Land: Early Christianity and Jewish Territorial Doctrine* (Berkeley: University of California Press, 1974; reprint, Sheffield, England: Sheffield University Press, 1994); and *The Territorial Dimension of Judaism* (Berkeley: University of California Press, 1982; reprinted with a symposium and further additions, Minneapolis: Fortress Press, 1991).

16. The political and metaphysical connotations of exile are most sensitively brought out by Arnold M. Eisen, *Galut: Modern Jewish Reflection on Homelessness and Homecoming* (Bloomington: Indiana University Press, 1987).

centuries we have traced elsewhere. Of its power, depth, tenacity, and animating power there can be no question: Zionism drew upon this devotion even when often despising it. The details of the ways in which this devotion expressed itself we cannot here pursue. We use one illustration only. Its power helps to explain the extraordinary influence of Sabbatai Zvi (1626–76) and his evocation of a very widespread, enthusiastic messianic fervor to return to The Land among Jews drawn from all classes all over Europe and the Middle East.[17] Much as it has been politically motivated, the Zionist movement is not without religious precedent. But the endemic Jewish devotion to the promised land being recognized, caution is in order. The reaction to the disillusion following upon the tragic outcome of Sabbatianism, with the apostasy of Sabbatai Zvi to Islam in 1666, took many complex forms. It produced increasing restraint and suspicion toward any messianic currents advocating a return to The Land, not only among the rabbinic leaders, who became increasingly cautious, nervous and suspicious in this matter, but among Jewish thinkers in general. Up until the late 1870s, there was, after Sabbatai Zvi, little concentration on The Land in messianic terms among them. The matter is complex.

Attitudes to The Land varied. Baruch Spinoza (1632–77), honored by more Jews for his integrity than for his theology, was a contemporary of Sabbatai Zvi: he could not but have encountered the Sabbatian movement. In his *Tractatus Theologico-Politicus* (1670), he treated The Land marginally and rejected the tradition about it. Along with God and the Chosen People, he assigned The Land to oblivion. The sentiment for The Land was a superstition which he demystified, just as he replaced Religion — "a tissue of lies and mysteries" — by Reason. He was profoundly influential.

In 1783, Moses Mendelssohn (1729–86) published a work, *Jerusalem*, in which he claimed that true religion is rational and universal. He retained the traditional laws of the Jewish faith, which for him are continuous, immutable, and always valid. However, there are no dogmas or "articles of faith." Reason alone is to govern the beliefs of Jews for whom there is freedom in doctrine even though conformity is demanded in action. Accordingly, "Jerusalem" meant for Mendelssohn "the Heavenly Jerusalem" in exile, where Jews would enjoy religious liberty and participate fully in the surrounding culture. The term "exile" was thus emptied of its customary connotation of homeless rootlessness and reinterpreted as simply "diaspora," scattering or dispersion. Legitimacy thereby was conferred on life outside The Land. For Mendelssohn "Jerusalem" had ceased to be a real tangible city and become simply a symbol of the true worship of God wherever people lived.

---

17. See Gershom Scholem, *Sabbatai Svi: The Mystical Messiah, 1626–1676*, trans. R. J. Zwi Werblowsky (Princeton: Princeton University Press, 1973).

Other Jewish thinkers also conferred legitimacy on the life outside The Land. Samson Raphael Hirsch (1808–88), the father of Modern Orthodoxy, in his *Nineteen Letters of Judaism* (1851), dealt only briefly with The Land; his main interest was in the exile. Similarly, Nochman Krochmal (1785–1840) and Abraham Geiger (1810–74), whose Reform prayer book, published in 1854, omitted all reference to the restoration of the Temple and the return to Zion, and even Heinrich Graetz (1817–91) placed their emphases, not on Jerusalem and The Land, but on making the exile a place where Jews could sustain their life. For Graetz (as well as for William Blake!), "Jerusalem" could be built anywhere. The mission of Israel to the world, and that not necessarily or at least not primarily in The Land, had replaced any concern or concentration on the need to return to it. Implicitly, if not explicitly, in the works of all these, The Land was deemphasized. Certain secular and religious thinkers in the period indicated above, as well as the rabbinic leaders, Orthodox and Reform, reveal this attitude. For such The Land was certainly not central and for some not even important: for them the strictly "religious" character of Judaism excluded direct political involvement on its behalf.

However, Jews in nineteenth-century Europe were not living in a vacuum, but in an atmosphere charged with emerging and growing nationalism and social change in France, Germany, and Italy. The result was predictable — the evocation and stimulation of the agelong devotion to The Land among many Jews and a consequent reengagement with it, even when the rabbinic leaders, the thinkers or intellectuals, and the historians were deemphasizing it.

Here the archetypal figure is Moses Hess (1812–75). Moved by the suffering of the masses, at first he became a Communist and in his first work, *A Holy History of Mankind by a Young Spinozist* (1837), he embraced a universalist commitment. The Chosen People had been made obsolete by Christianity: they had to disappear forever and a new universal "Jerusalem" built in Europe. But German nationalism had not left him untouched. Disappointed with the results of the emancipation of the Jews, he later, as he put it, "came back to my people," and in his work *Rome and Jerusalem* (1862) offered a new vision of the role of Jews in human redemption and emphasized their national character: for him Judaism had become *not* simply a religion. Just as other nationalistic movements in Europe had succeeded, so would that of the Jews: they would return to their own land, their national home, and at the same time be universally accepted. A socialist order in Israel would witness a renewed flowering of Judaism. This would coexist with large diaspora Jewish communities comfortably enjoying their civil rights. Even in the age of redemption there would be a partial exile, but it would be an acceptable one. However, the center of all Jewish existence would be in Palestine. The Land was to constitute a "central unity" for the whole of Jewry: modern means of communication would make this a possibility and a reality. For Hess a "sacred order" in Jerusalem would constitute for Jews "a spiritual nerve center." At home, on their own soil, "Jews would participate in the great historical movement [nationalism] of present-day humanity," and so they would contribute to the renewal of history and of the cosmos. In this way Hess combined the metaphysical or spiritual and political aspects of exile through his dynamic recognition of the centrality of The Land. That Hess became the father of later cultural and Socialist Zionism was natural: in him the prophetic hope of the Jewish past and the nationalist and socialist hopes of his contemporary Europe were wedded.

Less overwhelmed by the strictly nationalist dream, and more paradoxical, was Hess's contemporary Asher Levi Ginzberg (1856–1927). Aḥad Ha-am, as he was called, "the priest-prophet of the Jewish home-land," was not a believer (as Hess had not been). For him The Land as such was secondary to the goal of national regeneration. Before the soil of Israel could be transformed, the soul of Israel would have to be transformed. Soul not soil, "priests" not heroes, were the primary necessity for this. In an essay called "This Is Not the Way" (1889), he argued that the heart of the nation was the foundation on which The Land would be rebuilt — and as it was, alas, the nation was "fragmented and undisciplined." Efforts to settle on The Land were, therefore, premature: Israel was unprepared for this. Even though in *A Friendly Attack* (1891) he praised the efforts of the *Hovevei Zion* (Lovers of Zion), religious enthusiasts who had settled in The Land during the nineteenth century, later on in *Truth about the Land of Israel* (1893), Ginzberg warned that the nation was not ready to return to The Land: a Jewish state in Palestine could not emerge. Yet he urged that there should be a renewal of Jewish life with a "spiritual center" in Palestine: Israel was to be the inspiration not of the national "faith," i.e., Judaism, but of the national "spirit." And again as with Hess, the Palestinian "spiritual center" was to serve Jews who lived elsewhere. In Aḥad Ha-am, implicitly and even explicitly the focus on The Land was for the sake of life outside The Land. Since a Jewish state was unattainable, and under the existing "spiritual" condition of Jewry undesirable, The Land simply as "spiritual center" would have to suffice. Here is the paradoxical ambiguity of Aḥad Ha-am's thought. Although The Land was for him only a vehicle for the more important goal of national regeneration (on this score he has been called "the founder and principal theoretician" of "spiritual" Zionism), he did reassert the importance of The Land: what he kept out at the front door he let in at the back.

Ever since, The Land as "center" has haunted Jewry both religious and secular. This "center" has taken various forms. A. D. Gordon (1856–1922) reveals an understanding of The Land informed by the romanticism of the soil found in certain French and German nationalists and in Tolstoy. Engagement with the actual earth, the very soil of The Land, would demand and repay such labor: it would be in itself ennobling. But Gordon also drew upon the scriptures — Deuteronomy, Genesis, and Exodus. He used traditional biblical and rabbinic language, which lent great power to his message, although the thought he expressed through this scriptural and other Jewish traditional terminology was far removed from the actual meaning and intent of the religious leaders. The rabbis were certainly not romantics, whereas Gordon was a romantic who assumed the repudiation of the commandments in favor of the urges of nature, of eye and heart and feeling.

Gordon's thought lent itself to two emphases: on the one hand, to concentration on The Land itself, its very soil, as the necessary sphere for redemption. Direct, devoted engagement with the particular soil of the Holy Land alone could bring salvation and deliver his people from the horrible parasitism which, he thought, marked the Jewish life of the Diaspora. Both in the life of the individual and in that of the nation, since the individual was organically related to and dependent upon the people as a whole, only a return to the soil would bring renewal and a national awakening. On the other hand, the vanguard of spiritual elite which he called for in Eretz Israel, because of the organic unity of *all* Jews, would inspire all the people of Israel everywhere. The influence of those who had returned to its soil in The Land would so impinge on Jews everywhere that even those living outside The Land would no longer be in "exile." In this way, as with previously mentioned thinkers, the negation of the Diaspora is muted; it too can be redeemed through the spiritual center. Gordon, it is to be repeated, was not a believer. The leaders of Judaism would suspect his emphases on the direct ennobling influence of the soil, and certainly his dismissal of the necessity to keep the commandments.

However, a younger contemporary of Gordon's, who was to become more famous, Martin Buber, although less enamored of the romanticism of the soil as such, was to give a further twist to the discussion of The Land. Like Gordon, Buber had been influenced by European nationalism and romanticism, as well as by the traditional sources of Judaism. But he was also more aware of the need for a "political" expression for the life of Jews in The Land, that is, especially for a Jewish state. But, as were Aḥad Ha-am and Gordon, Buber was also concerned with the need for a spiritual revival of the people as a whole and of Israel as a "spiritual center," and as we indicated, less captured by the romanticism of the soil than was Gordon. For Buber, The Land was only a precondition for something beyond and greater than itself — the sanctity of the Jewish people. Buber's philosophy — his understanding of the I-Thou rather than the I-It relationship governing religious, and indeed human, life — universalizes "The Land." The spiritual center in Israel, although it needed political expression in a state, was to serve the periphery, the exile. Even Ben Gurion, political-nationalist as he was, thought of Israel as called to serve the whole of mankind — not to a splendid isolation, but to a mission for the world.

On the other hand, other thinkers had markedly different approaches. Buber's personalism had compelled him to wrestle both with and against The Land: there was always an ambiguity for him in this question. But in Franz Rosenzweig and E. Kaufmann, this ambiguity was overcome. They both forthrightly rejected the centrality of The Land as such. But Rosenzweig and Kaufmann had more extreme counterparts than Buber. There was Jacob Klatzkin for whom — believing as he did, like Nietzsche, that God was dead and without heir — only a return to The Land would deliver Jews from the "cemetery of the exile," which was worse than death, and lead to an authentic Jewish life. And later the chief theorist of religious Zionism, Rabbi Kuk, came to ascribe to The Land a messianic role.

The People

This incomplete glance at the way in which Jewish thinkers dealt with The Land evokes comment. First, the title of this essay is "In Search of 'The Center' of Judaism." But many of the Jewish thinkers to whom we have referred were secularists who rejected Judaism. Are their judgments, therefore, relevant? In reviewing the first volume of *The Cambridge History of Judaism: The Persian Period* (ed. L. Finkelstein and W. D. Davies, 1984), Fergus Millar, like other scholars, sharply criticized it for having failed to draw a distinction between Jews and Judaism. But how valid is such a distinction? Certainly it cannot be absolutized; in Judaism the connection between ethnicity and religion is inescapable. Even where it is deliberately rejected, as by the Jewish thinkers who abandon Judaism, this connection still remains; and even their very conscious rejection of it serves as testimony to the nature of Judaism. We have, therefore, not deemed it irrelevant to draw attention to such secular figures. They are "negative" witnesses to the significance of The Land.

But a second consideration is more important for the question we have raised as to whether The Land is to be conceived of as the center or essence of Judaism. Those religious and secular Jewish thinkers who were engaged with the question of The Land, apart perhaps from the romantic Gordon, were so engaged not because they regarded The Land as such as of emphatic and central significance, but because they were concerned with the condition of their own kinsmen, the Jews scattered throughout Europe. It was not a conceptual, theological, or devotional or pious tradition elevating The Land of promise that chiefly motivated movements of return to The Land. Even Samson Raphael Hirsch, the founder of modern Orthodoxy, no less than Abraham Geiger, the founder of Reform Judaism, did not emphasize

The Land nor the duty to return to it. The secular Jews who envisaged Pales-
tine as a spiritual center were governed by the needs of those outside The
Land; it was for their sakes, to a large extent, that they cherished a Spiritual
Center.

And then, third, note that it was only in the twentieth century that the
return to The Land was achieved. The question is inevitable: why then and
not before? The answers are equally inevitable — because of the growth of
European nationalism, which spurred strictly national sentiments among suppressed peoples, and concomitantly, because of the horrendous suffering of
Jews in Europe, born of particularly racist anti-Semitism. These were the
catalysts for radical Jewish involvement in the socialist, communist, and nationalist ferment of the nineteenth and twentieth centuries. To believe that
the Jews who created the Zionist movement were not, both consciously and
unconsciously, influenced by the tradition of the promised land among Jews
is unrealistic. The close texture of Jewish existence made this inevitable. But
that Zionism was primarily motivated by that tradition is not borne out by
the sources.

The bearing of all this on our theme is clear. Neither the book nor The
Land in isolation can be elevated to be the center of Judaism. The temptation so to elevate The Land was powerfully enhanced by the Zionist climate
of our time. The *Zeitgeist* has been favorable to this. But the temptation to
such an elevation must be resisted. What, then, or where is the heart of
Judaism?

The Jewish thinkers whom we have referred to, as we indicated, became
concerned with the land of Israel primarily because they were concerned
with the plight of the people of Israel. The Land for most if not all of
them subserved that concern: The Land was subordinate to the needs of
the People, the return to it inspired by that need. Are we not, then, to conclude that the heart of Judaism is strictly the people of Israel, the community
itself?

The claim is familiar that Israel is the People of the Book. Is it not even
more true that the Book is the book of a People? Is it not more accurate to
refer to the Bible — or rather, to the Tanak — as the Book of the People
of Israel, just as the whole of the Bible is the Book of the church? The
Book — not even "the Torah," in the strict, limited Pentateuchal sense —
has no chronological priority. It presupposes the existence of a community
or communities which gradually gave it birth and finally fixed its contents
and forms. From this point of view "people" — the actuality of the people
of Israel — is the heart of Judaism, its *sine qua non*. The claim that without
the Torah Israel could not exist is easily countered by the claim that without
"Israel" there would be no Torah. In the story of the exodus there already
exists people who are called to go to Sinai to receive the Torah, there to be-

come a uniquely covenanted people. That is why there can be no history of Judaism which is not the history of Jews. Kenneth Cragg has expressed the significance of the peoplehood of the Jews as follows:

> It seems clear that to believe in God is, in some sense, to believe also in ourselves. In what sense? will be the crucial question. From Moses, perhaps from Abraham, the Jewish people have had a sharply distinctive fusion, or amalgam, of faith in God and in themselves, a faith which wedded the divine reality to the necessity of them [themselves the people]. What obtained between God and this people was strictly covenantal in a relationship unique in the divine economy and — being unique in the divine economy — somewhat integral also to the divine nature.[18]

The result of this covenantal relationship between God and his People is that there is a "privacy" (a term I long ago learned from Bishop Cragg) in the religious experience of Jews which Judaism has preserved and cherished across the centuries and "which has resisted the Christian and other attempts to breach it." A mere glance at the section on the People of Israel, for example, in the *Rabbinic Anthology* of C. J. G. Montefiore and H. Loewe will abundantly indicate this.[19] In the work of Professor Arthur Hertzberg especially, the claim (in his often quoted words) is made unambiguously: "The essence of Judaism is the affirmation that the Jews are the chosen people, all else is commentary."[20]

However, much as it has to be recognized that emphasis on the continuity of the Torah, or of The Land as the case might be, was engendered and stimulated by circumstances and pressures from outside the Jewish community, so is it with the emphasis on the doctrine of "Chosenness." Hertzberg — we must believe — was led to insist upon its centrality by the character of the American society within which he lives and which demands a certain insidious conformity to its norms if Jews are to be "accepted." Just as in the sixth century B.C.E., the experience of Jews in the Babylonian exile led to a necessary emphasis on their "chosenness," if they were to survive the blandishments of Babylonian life, so in modern America Jewish survival depends upon its ability jealously to preserve its "chosenness."[21] The cost of

---

18. See Cragg's profound essay, "A Christian Judaica," in his *Faith and Life Negotiate: A Christian's Story-Study* (Norwich, England: Canterbury Press, 1994).

19. Selected and arranged with comments and introductions by C. J. G. Montefiore and R. Loewe (London: Macmillan, 1938).

20. *The Condition of Jewish Belief: A Symposium Compiled by the Editors of "Commentary" Magazine* (New York: Macmillan, 1966), 90. See further, A. Hertzberg and Aron Hirt-Manheimer, *Jews: The Essence and Character of a People* (San Francisco: Harper, 1998).

21. Of course, a society in which Jews are more and more accepted presents its own problems of assimilation, especially through intermarriage.

this preservation, which we cannot pursue here, has been brilliantly analyzed by John Murray Cuddihy in his essay "Jew: Rabbi Arthur Hertzberg and the Metaphoricality of Jewish Chosenness."[22] Limitations of space prevent further elaboration on the importance of the "People" for Judaism.[23]

The Messiah

In addition to the Torah, The Land, and The People, another aspect of Judaism has loomed large especially among Gentile and Jewish Christians; that is, the messianic. The elevation of the Messiah by Christians to particular significance is readily understandable, because the central focus of discussion and dispute between Jews and Christians has been the messianic claim made for Jesus of Nazareth. In their thought for the future some Jews did ascribe to a messianic figure a crucial role — he was to be a single figure often regarded as Davidic in origin. Among other Jews, such as those at Qumran, there were expected two messianic figures — a secular and a priestly one. But in the minds of most Jews, Christian concentration on the Messiah came to produce a cautious, even negative, reaction. Several recent Jewish scholars have expressed this. Rabbi Leibowitz[24] rejects the "Saviorism" of the Christian tradition. David Hartman[25] finds Messianic Christian claims "triumphalist": they are to be rejected because they abrogate the command and covenant of God with the People of Israel and crave for a certainty within history, through the Messiah, which it is not given to mortals to attain. So, too, for Arthur A. Cohen,[26] Judaism keeps the future "as empty of finality as possible": it has never had to explain (as Christians do) "a failed eschatology."

But apart from this natural Jewish reaction and rejection of the Christian emphasis, a glance at the frequency of the occurrence of the term "Messiah" in Jewish sources shows that it is not as dominating or crucial in them as Christian theology has presumed. There is little in the Tanak or in later Jewish sources to justify the elevation ascribed to the Messiah in Christian theology. E. P. Sanders has recently presented the evidence. His conclusion is fully justified that "the expectation of a messiah was not the rule. . . . The hope for [a Messiah] is missing from important sections of the prophetic corpus (such as in Isa. 40–66), but with such clear statements [as Jer. 23:5f.;

22. *Civil Religion and Protestant Task* (New York: Seabury Press, 1978), 101–55.

23. See my *Paul and Rabbinic Judaism*, 4th ed. (Philadelphia: Fortress Press, 1980), 58–85.

24. Yeshayahu Leibowitz, *Judaism, Human Values, and the Jewish State*, ed. Eliezer Goldman (Cambridge: Harvard University Press, 1992), 256–62.

25. *Conflicting Visions, Spiritual Possibilities of Modern Israel* (New York: Schocken Books, 1990), 4 and 264.

26. *The Myth of the Judeo-Christian Tradition* (New York: Harper & Row, 1970), 30, 33, 211.

Isa. 9:7] in the Bible it could not be completely surrendered by first-century Jews. Despite this, there are relatively few — strikingly few — references to a Davidic King in the literature of our period [63 B.C.E.–66 C.E.]."[27]

However, granting that a single, clearly established Messiah in Jewish hope for the future has been overemphasized, and cannot be regarded as "central" to Judaism, a hope for the future was and is *necessarily* endemic to that faith. We use the adverb "necessarily" here advisedly, because His activity in calling Israel into being and His promise to them committed the God of Israel to His people in the future as in the present and the past. To assure His people of their future was the expression of God's faithfulness in the classical sources of Judaism. E. P. Sanders offers a fourfold summary of the hope for the future in Judaism: it was (1) for the establishment of the Twelve Tribes of the Jews from all the world in Palestine and the rebuilding of its cities; (2) for the subjugation and conversion of the Gentiles; (3) for a renewed, purified, and glorious Temple; and (4) for purity and righteousness in both worship and morals.[28] These hopes were common, but not uniformly held, nor was the agent or agents destined to fulfill them only associated with the Davidic Messiah or other messianic figures. In the Qumran Scrolls the angels furthered those hopes, but it is God Himself who ushers in the final victory which assures their fulfillment. Those hopes centered, primarily, not on the individual, but on the people of Israel as a whole, on "freedom" for that people, and for a new age or order in which God's will would be done. Across the centuries those hopes have moved Jews, sometimes to quiet acceptance of dependence on foreign powers, to suffering and endurance, to a passive piety, tenaciously sustained by trust in the Divine, sometimes to violent political rebellion and assertion.

Moreover, it cannot be overlooked that under Persian and Greek influences especially many, if not most, Jews had hopes, albeit vaguely conceived, for a life after death. Though the Sadducees denied life after death, the Pharisees thought in terms of transmigration of souls, of rewards and punishments after death. The Essenes, like Josephus, recognized the soul as immortal and conceived of a future state for the dead comparable with the Greek "Isles of the Blessed." Such hopes were absorbed by Judaism and constitute part of the conglomerate that goes into its making. But they were not peculiar nor contributing to the marked differentiation of that Faith from others: only among Gentile and Jewish Christians has the messianic component been given centrality.

---

27. In *Judaism: Practice and Belief*, 63 B.C.E.–66 C.E. (Philadelphia: Trinity Press International, 1992), 295–96.

28. Ibid., 279–303, esp. 289ff.

II

So far, besides monotheism, we have pointed to four elements in Judaism — the halakic (or legal), the territorial, the ethnic, and the messianic — which each at various times in the course of Jewish history seem to have been elevated to centrality. But, on examination, each aspect points beyond itself to other elements in Judaism. Accordingly, it is not surprising that certain scholars have suggested not single, distinct elements, but "patterns" or "conglomerates" of elements as the clue to Judaism. And our treatment has made one thing clear. The term "center," in its precision, may suggest not only a certain detached "mathematical" coldness, but may also seem simply to evoke particular or isolated "geometric points," an austere reductionism, which make it seem inappropriate to apply to such a complex phenomenon as Judaism. The same is true of the term "essence," which, although often found in discussions of Christianity and other religions, again somehow seems more appropriately applicable to "substances" (whether in pharmacology or philosophy or theology) than to emotive religious phenomena. In recent discussions, therefore, the terms "center" and "essence" are often avoided.

For example, S. W. Sykes,[29] in an effort to find the essence of Christianity, after surveying the history of various efforts to define that essence came to the conclusion, with E. Troeltsch, that there was no reason to suppose that the essence of Christianity had to be a simple idea. It might contain tensions and oppositions within itself and not be amenable to any singular, direct formulation, or it might contain within itself the power to create new interpretations and to require repeated attempts at formulation. Likewise the "essence" of Judaism need not be (and as we have seen is not) simple, but multiple.

In this connection, words we used above of Jewish loyalty to the One God, that it "seems to transcend or deny reason," need emphasis, because they touch a point of sharp dispute among interpreters of Judaism in the last two centuries. When nineteenth-century Jewish theologians sought to commend their faith to the Western European mind, they presented it as rationalists, children of the Enlightenment, and as insecure emancipated members of a European society. They were anxious to fit into that society and tried to do so by emphasizing the rational in the faith of Jews to demonstrate the identity between Judaism and modern culture. Hermann Cohen (1842–1918) particularly interpreted Judaism as essentially a religion of reason.[30] He and others,

---

29. "Essence of Christianity," *Religious Studies* 7 (December 1971): 291–306.

30. In his posthumous work *Religion der Vernunft aus den Quellen des Judentums* (Frankfurt, 1929; English trans., 1972). See W. D. Davies, "The Territorial Dimension of Judaism," in *Intergerini Parietis Septym (Eph. 2:14): Essays Presented to Markus Barth on His Sixty-fifth Birthday*, ed. D. Y. Hadidian (Pittsburgh: Pickwick Press, 1980), 61–96, esp. 73.

like Leo Baeck, in imitation of or spurred on by Christians like Adolf Harnack, searched for the rational essence of Judaism. Later, Arthur A. Cohen, to be followed in different ways by Martin Buber and Gershom Scholem, revolted against this reduction of the complexity of Judaism to a single essence, Buber in the direction of existentialism, and Scholem in the direction of the history of Judaism in which he observed hitherto overlooked "subterranean" complexities in the Qabbalah. Abraham Heschel was also to go the way of mysticism. As Troeltsch had been led to reject the notion that the essence of Christianity had to be a single simple notion, so these Jewish scholars agreed that "Judaism, consisting of an anarchistic plurality of sources,"[31] is an open market of interpretations. Conflict of opinions is a necessity to unite its stream of traditions. It is understandable, therefore, that recent scholars have sought not for "a center" or for an "essence" of Judaism, but for "patterns" which represent it.

The triangular pattern that Raphael Loewe found (which we presented above on p. 17) holds in necessary tension three elements: peoplehood, authority (rabbinic), and belief. However, even though Loewe does ample justice to the monotheistic aspect, his definition barely does justice either to the ethnic or to the territorial dimension of Judaism. Is "universalism," though present, as marked in the classical Jewish sources as Loewe holds? Does he not underestimate the tenacity of Jewish "privacy"? His triangular pattern does not entirely satisfy, but his treatment is rich and impressive because it rightly recognizes that Judaism is held together as a body by a continual tension among the elements of Torah, Land, and People, the neglect of any of which leads to corrective reactions. This is the explanation probably of the recurrence of exile and return and of emphases reflected but corrected later in several spheres. The tensions within the conglomerate are mutually corrective.

We have previously noted Neusner's discovery of a historical pattern of exile and return as the mark of Judaism. He has given to the work of Max Weber a fresh dimension, insisting in a forceful manner that behind all "Judaisms," as he understands them, there is a single regulative or governing and animating principle, the pattern of exile and return imposed on Jews by their own history. We have already suggested that by implication at least, such a view paradoxically reinforces the centrality of the Torah, which records that history. But other considerations give us pause before we can endorse Neusner's approach.

The role played in Jewish history by exile from and return to the land of Israel has to be fully recognized. In the exile to and from Egypt leading to the

---

31. See David Biale, "Theology, Language, and History," in *Gershom Scholem: Modern Critical Views*, ed. with an introduction by Harold Bloom (New York, New Haven, and Philadelphia: Chelsea House, 1987), esp. 48, 56.

ultimate return under Moses, in the exile to and from Babylon leading to the return in the reign of Cyrus, in the exile after the fall of the state in 70 c.e. and the amazing return and creation of the state of Israel in the twentieth century — in all these events there is easily discernible, *mutatis mutandis,* a recurring "pattern." As Neusner once orally emphasized to the author, this "pattern" is not only literary or conceptual, not only imposed upon the data, but objectively verifiable and visible in actual historical events: it is not simply a matter of a subjective experience and interpretation, but of external, public happenings whose historicity or facticity needs no verification, so undeniable are they. Moreover, ever since biblical theologians have emphasized history as the revelatory sphere of the divine activity and the God of Judaism as "The God Who Acts," the appeal to history for the justification of Israel's faith, as later of that of the Christian community, has often been emphasized, sometimes even to the exclusion of other revelatory spheres, such as that of the created order, so that the pattern Neusner endorses fits well into much twentieth-century biblical theology.

Nevertheless, apart from the questionable divorce of the Hebrew scriptures from the pattern of exile and return (which the scriptures provide!), there are other difficulties about Neusner's position. *Is* this "pattern" the center or animating principle of all "Judaisms"? The wide-ranging historical presentation by Neusner, in his work *Self-Fulfilling Prophecy* of 1987,[32] in one direction evokes the work of Arnold Toynbee, though of course not in the understanding of Judaism as such. Like Toynbee, with his emphasis on a pattern of challenge and response as an instrument of or clue to historical interpretation, Neusner, too, has been enamored of his own pattern of exile and return, as we indicated. Toynbee and Neusner both have had a predilection for clarifying patterns, and they are not alone. However, not all scholars have found any patterns in history. In his *History of Europe,* H. A. L. Fisher could find no pattern in history.[33] But not so Neusner. In reviewing *The Cambridge History of Judaism* (vol. 1: *The Persian Period*), he criticized the work because its editors had offered no overriding theory to account for the history of that period, but presented only data, uncoordinated and unsystematized: they had presented no "pattern" to give coherence to the history of the period such as, presumably, the pattern of exile and return, endorsed by Neusner himself, could have provided through his detection of it behind all "Judaisms." But the unease which haunts many scholars about Toynbee's employment of a common pattern in so much of world history is also generated by Neusner's pattern in the history of Israel. Certain considerations engender this unease.

To begin with, the history of Israel is immensely long, varied, and complex.

---

32. Cited in n. 2.
33. See the preface to Fisher's *History of Europe* (London: Arnold, 1937).

That the pattern of exile and return does appear, often strikingly, cannot be denied. But how frequent is it? At best it is a very staggered pattern: between the occurrence of each instance of the pattern, there are long stretches of time, especially between the exile in the first century c.e. and the return in the nineteenth and twentieth centuries culminating in the creation of the state of Israel in 1948. Are not these examples of exile and return so widely separated in time that they can only with difficulty be directly related so as to illustrate or constitute a single historical "pattern"? Nor are the other phenomena interpreted as constituting a common pattern — the enslavement in Egypt and the exodus, the Babylonian Exile and the return — chronologically so closely related as both unmistakably to reveal a close pattern of exile and return. Is "a pattern" which did recur but only at such very long intervals, during which Jews successfully survived many horrendous assaults — is such a "pattern" likely to have been the animating principle of Judaism throughout its history? In addition, one overwhelming phenomenon in Jewish history — some have claimed in world history — must be regarded as unique, falling into no "pattern": the Holocaust.

Moreover, during one of the long intervals between exile and return, that between 70 c.e. and 1948, it became necessary for Judaism, in what came to prove to be its most dominant and enduring form, the rabbinic, to take a very cautious stance toward the expectation of a return to Palestine. Religious Jews never, or seldom, abandoned hope for an ultimate return, but at the same time, for most Jews, exile from The Land became an accepted condition. The return to it was not always found tempting, certainly not imperative. To document such a statement would not be difficult. Neusner himself has interpreted the country in which he now lives as the promised land from which there is no imperative need to return to the land of Israel. The single pattern of exile from and return to The Land, then, cannot be accepted as the heart of Judaism.

This prompts the further question of how far the nature of Judaism has not only been informed by those Jews who have lived in The Land but by those who have lived in the Diaspora outside it. David Vital refers to Judaism as "that great complex (not to say tangle) of history, high culture, belief, and social and ritual practice."[34] This tangle has evolved under inescapable and powerful influences from outside Palestine, not only through developments within Palestinian Jewry. The evidence, moreover, does not allow us to distinguish Palestinian and diaspora Judaism, as was once the academic custom. Whereas history attests to the manifold impact of exile, the pattern of exile and return, emphasized by Neusner, implies that the point of desire and

---

34. David Vital, *The Future of the Jews: A People at the Crossroads* (Cambridge: Harvard University Press, 1990), 1.

concentration for Judaism is The Land or the Torah that enshrines the promise of it. There is the cynosure, not elsewhere as we have already indicated.
While Neusner's emphasis on a pattern of exile and return points logically
by implication to the importance and centrality of the Torah, which presents
this pattern, a return also points by implication and again logically to another
dimension of Judaism as the central one: the territorial. And, finally, as Professor D. N. Freedman has pointed out, the emphasis on exile and return as
a pattern is more native to a cyclical view of history congenial to the Greeks
than to the purposive emphasis of the Hebrew scriptures.

For our immediate purpose we suggest, then, that implicitly the pattern
proposed by Neusner in fact elevates both the Book and The Land to centrality: the Book as the source of the pattern and the agent of its preservation
and perpetuation, and The Land as the desirable goal for Jews. This means
that the pattern of Neusner points away from itself as "the heart of Judaism" in two directions: in itself in isolation that pattern does not fulfill
the central role.

Another pattern or structure for Judaism has been proposed by E. P.
Sanders, a pattern which is endorsed by Neusner despite his criticism of it.
The structure is described by Sanders as follows:

> The "pattern" or "structure" of covenantal nomism is this: (1) God has
> chosen Israel and (2) given the law. The law implies both (3) God's
> promise to maintain the election and (4) the requirement to obey.
> (5) God rewards obedience and punishes transgression. (6) The law
> provides for means of atonement, and atonement results in (7) main-
> tenance or re-establishment of the covenantal relationship. (8) All
> those who are maintained in the covenant by obedience, atonement,
> and God's mercy belong to the group which will be saved. An im-
> portant interpretation of the first and last points is that election and
> ultimately salvation are considered to be by God's mercy rather than
> human achievement.[35]

"Covenantal nomism" covers those elements which we have isolated
above — the One God, the Law, the People. Only at two, not unrelated,
points does this schema fail to do justice to Judaism: The Land and the messianic future. It offers only a bare reference to "salvation." The territorial
dimension, although it is assumed, is not explicitly recognized. But these deficiencies being noted, it must be stated that the structure offered by E. P.
Sanders is the most satisfactory. Neusner himself accepted it as valid, despite
insisting on forceful criticisms.

---

35. *Paul and Palestinian Judaism* (London: SCM Press; Philadelphia: Fortress Press, 1977), 422.

The deficiencies to which we point are not to be isolated but should be understood in the full light of the treatment of Judaism by Sanders in his two works *Paul and Palestinian Judaism* (1977) and *Judaism: Practice and Belief, 63* B.C.E.–*66* C.E. (1992). In the latter he does recognize a territorial hope, but cannot claim to do full justice to the role of The Land in Judaism. Moreover, his treatment, it is essential to note, is confined to a specific period, 63 B.C.E. to 66 C.E. Does his pattern survive scrutiny in the long history of Judaism? For example, would his conclusions in the final chapter of *Judaism* (pp. 458–94), hold for the later rabbinic period? Certainly it is true of 63 B.C.E. to 66 C.E. that "different individuals and groups had different degrees of influence at various times and on various issues. Who ran what varied," but was it equally true of the rabbinic period? Loewe as we saw would think not.

The outcome of this all too brief study is that to seek for one center, one essence or even pattern of Judaism is misguided: it is best to look for the "heart" of Judaism. The term "heart" here is not simply a rhetorical device, but a deliberate substantial choice, because it evokes a *complexity* of relationships, not a simple organ. The heart, it will be recognized, has four chambers held in very delicate balance. The question we face is: what has and does enable Judaism to live and allows and inspires its various organs to function or, as the Puritan Philip Dodderidge would have put it: "What is its animating power?" To seek for "the heart" of Judaism in this sense is to inquire what has provided its continuity throughout and despite all its vicissitudes across the centuries, and what recurring norms or characteristics or patterns have marked and expressed its life. Given its immense complexity and variety, it is wise to recognize that the light of Judaism is less like that of a single torch (even that of monotheism) than that of a bundle or cluster of torches, each component differing in intensity at different times. The various aspects of Judaism, to which we have referred above — each now burning strongly and brightly, now flickering, now waning, and each enjoying its hour of prominence and even preeminence, and each suffering its hour of comparative eclipse and decline according to the need and demand of the times — occur together as a discernible complex conglomerate. And as Jean Juster warned us: "Il faut...ne pas d'essayer de diviser des choses indivisibles."[36]

Important also, however, is it that because of this, each aspect is always present and in living tension with each of the others; it is this very tension that holds them together as a conglomerate. To attempt to assign comparative importance to each of the torches of the light, which is the complex heart of Judaism, is beyond the purpose of this essay. We only note the recent

---

36. "One must not attempt to separate things that are indivisible." Quoted in G. F. Moore, *Judaism in the First Five Centuries of the Christian Era*, 3 vols. (Cambridge: Harvard University Press, 1927–40), 1:234.

statement of Yehuda Amitai as a suitable *point de départ* for such an assignment: "[T]here is a hierarchy of values in Judaism, and . . . those who fail to distinguish holiness from holiness will in the end fail to distinguish between the holy and the profane. We must consider the relative priority of three values. Israel, Torah, and the Land of Israel. . . . The interest of the people of Israel precedes that of the interest of the Land of Israel."[37] Is not such a position consonant with the underlying Divine Grace which would give priority to the personal, the human?

Because there is a final word. We rejected the terms "center" and "essence" as inappropriate. We even rejected the doctrine of monotheism, taken "neat," as the center or essence. Yet there *is* an ultimate, single animating power to which E. P. Sanders has rightly applied the term "center." It is not the abstract term "monotheism" to which he refers in using the term "center," but the underlying grace of the God who called the People of Israel into covenant and gave them the Torah and The Land and committed Himself to their future.[38] The centrality of an underlying "grace" in Judaism in this sense, we have to affirm. On this grace — differently expressed, as it has been and is, in each tradition — Judaism and Christianity both rest and in this grace lies the ground for their mutual respect. The Divine Grace is the blood of the heart of Judaism and the blood is the life, and it is *polupoikilos*, like the wisdom of God (Eph. 3:10).

---

37. Quoted in Ian S. Lustick, *For the Land and the Lord: Jewish Fundamentalism in Israel* (New York: Council on Foreign Relations, 1988), 128. But it is not irrelevant to add this comment on Amitai's words by Dr. Nahum Sarna (to whom I sent this chapter). In a letter dated 18 September 1995, Sarna wrote: "It seems to me that while such may have been true before 1939 [the outbreak of World War II], the matter is more complicated today in that the fate of the Land, and the fate of the people are inextricably intertwined. There is no doubt in my mind that should Arabs be victorious over Israel, another holocaust will certainly occur; the lives of five million Jews and the future of the Jewish people will be perilously insecure — without much concern or interest on the part of the rest of the world." These words remind us that the various emphases we have noted in this chapter did not arise in a vacuum, but under political and other pressures.

38. Sanders, *Judaism: Practice and Belief*, 277. See also Sanders's summation of "covenantal nomism," cited above, where the same grace is highlighted: "Election and ultimately salvation are considered to be by God's *mercy rather than human achievement*" (italics added). These words culminate Sanders's definition.

Chapter 2

Canon and Christology

Until recently, when costs increased and computers threatened their dominance, the abundance and cheapness of paper and writing materials led to their almost ubiquitous use in our culture. The temptation was easy to contrast this culture with previous more oral ones in which writing was not so pervasive. But, although the Greco-Roman and Jewish worlds of the first century, with which we are concerned, were less "a papyrus culture" than is ours of the twentieth, this should not be overemphasized. Those worlds were "if not literate, literary to a remarkable degree; in the Near East in the first century of our era writing was an essential accompaniment of life at almost all levels to an extent without parallel in living memory."[1] The reading of documents, written on papyrus or skin, was more widespread than is often acknowledged. Apparently, even in out-of-the-way Nazareth, Jesus could read, and assumed that his opponents in Galilee also could.[2]

At the same time there was a reserve about the written word among Greeks and Jews alike. This had long come to clear expression in Plato, who had urged that the invention of writing was a deceptive blessing.[3] For Plato's Socrates, so far from helping the memory, writing militates against it: it is no adequate substitute for living dialogue between teacher and taught. It is as if writing confines or even ossifies thought; at best what is written only serves as a reminder of what is already known. The profoundest truth cannot be encapsulated in writing; living thought needs the give-and-take of speech in dialogue. How widespread such an attitude was among the Greeks is disputed. However, though an emphasis in Plato, it was not a peculiarity of his. This attitude explains why in literary circles in Rome and Alexandria, and probably elsewhere in the Hellenistic age, "publication" did not signify the

---

1. C. S. Roberts in *The Cambridge History of the Bible,* ed. P. Ackroyd and C. F. Evans (Cambridge, 1970), 1:48.

2. Luke 4:15–30; Mark 2:25, 12:10, etc. See further Werner H. Kelber, *The Oral and Written Gospel* (Philadelphia, 1983), 78.

3. *Phaedrus* 274C–275A, in which Socrates is given the words "You have invented an elixir not of memory, but of reminding" (Loeb translation). Compare Xenophon's *Symposium* 3:5, and Diogenes Laertius 10.12 (Loeb translation 11.541).

41

appearance of a book or volume but was public recitation.[4] It was this same attitude, along with other probably more important factors, which led in Judaism to the prohibition of the writing of the oral law.[5] That, like John the Baptist, Jesus did not choose to write, even though he apparently could, may be indicative.[6] For Paul his letters were a necessary but, by implication, inferior substitute for his presence (Gal. 4:20; 2 Cor. 13:10; 1 Cor. 11:34). The documents of the early church were only tardily gathered together. Papias, bishop of Hierapolis (ca. 60–130 c.e.), makes clear this attitude in Christian circles. He explicitly preferred oral to written evidence: "I supposed that things out of books did not profit me so much as the utterance of a voice that lives and survives."[7]

This ambiguity toward written documents, in which writing was both widely practiced and yet often distrusted, raises the question whether in the Greco-Roman world the attitude of Jews toward their scriptures is to be regarded as peculiar to them. By the first century, religious Jews (it should not be overlooked that doubtless most, even among the Jews, were not such) regarded their sacred writings — the Pentateuch (which was given preeminence), the Prophets, the Writings (although not all finally fixed as an authoritative canon until the end of the first century, and possibly not even then) — as not simply "containing" but as "being" the very words of God himself, and therefore as binding, authoritative, perfect, unchangeable, and eternal. They were conceived to comprise all that Jews know and need to know, a gateway to another, and eternal, world; they represent the eternal breaking into time; the unknowable disclosed; the transcendent entering history and remaining here, available to mortals to handle and appropriate; the divine becoming apparent. To memorize them and even to quote from them is to enter into some sort of communication with ultimate reality.[8] And although recognized to be much in need of interpretation, so that the literal

---

4. On "publication," see S. Lieberman, *Hellenism in Jewish Palestine* (New York, 1962), 83–89; Roberts, *Cambridge History of the Bible.*

5. Jerusalem Talmud, *Megillah* 4.1, 74d (with which compare *Gittin* 66b; *Tem.* 14b): "That which has been expressed orally [must be transmitted orally] and that which has been expressed in writing [must be transmitted] in writing." See Lieberman, *Hellenism in Jewish Palestine*, 87. The Talmud contains no reference to a written Mishnah. The interdiction covered halakah and haggadah. R. Meyers, *TWNT* 9:34–35 regards this interdiction as legendary and refuses to press it for the rabbinic period. The interdiction has, moreover, been connected not with the kind of reserve toward writing found in the contemporary Greco-Roman world, but with the fear that two laws might emerge. The interpretations of the Qumran sectarians were not immediately written down, but some time after the death of the founder. For additional caution about overemphasizing the literary character of the Hellenistic world, see Kelber, *Oral and Written Gospel*, 17.

6. John 8:6.

7. Eusebius, *Ecclesiastical History* 3.39.1–7; 14–17. It is perhaps noteworthy that, much later, on the invention of printing, Islam allowed the printing of secular books, but forbade that of the Qur'an; so W. Cantwell Smith, *JAAR* 89 (1971): 137.

8. See my *Setting of the Sermon on the Mount* (Cambridge, 1964), 109–90, especially 156–90.

was not their only meaning, the scriptures were to be understood literally.[9] Immense care was taken to ensure that they were transmitted with strictest accuracy.[10] This Jewish attitude (though not universally held)[11] we shall examine later. At first encounter at least it is very far removed, indeed at the opposite pole, from Plato's attitude. Plato reveals little if any awareness of writings as containing divine truth, as treasures to be handed on to subsequent generations. Contrast the Library of Congress at Washington, which reminds us, each time we enter it, that books were for Milton the precious lifeblood of noble spirits and for Thoreau the treasures of the wisdom of the ages; they are not simply "reminders" but themselves of inestimable worth. Nothing of this is in Plato, nothing of the Jewish sense that in certain writings all truth is to be found, that what is needed is to excavate the inexhaustible mine of the divine revelation contained in the scriptures and bring to light treasures that lie hidden beneath the surface.[12]

I

Are there parallels in other religious traditions to the use made of scripture in Jewish and Christian circles? To answer this we must examine briefly a wide range of traditions and texts.[13] This much we can state: it is erroneous to regard all "sacred texts" as necessarily and automatically "canonical texts" such as are the Tanak and the Old and New Testaments in Judaism and Christianity respectively.

The Egyptian "sacred texts" probably owed their sacred character to their hieroglyphic script, not to their contents: they were treated with considerable liberty in transmission, and those who read them did not thereby acquire honor as did the readers of the Torah in the synagogue. They do not provide a parallel with the biblical canon.[14]

I here borrow phrases from W. Cantwell Smith, "The True Meaning of Scripture: An Empirical Historian's Non-reductionist Interpretation of the Qur'ān," *JMES* 1 (1980): 184.

9. Various senses of scripture were recognized, but the literal sense remained.

10. See B. Gerhardsson, *Memory and Manuscript*, pt. 1 (Uppsala-Lund, 1961), 1–191; H. L. Strack and G. Stemberger, *Einleitung in Talmud und Midrasch*, 7th ed. (Munich, 1982), 41–54.

11. The compiler of the Temple Scroll at Qumran (11QTemple) could insert his own halakah in the Pentateuch. See also *b. Yebamoth* 79a; *m. Berakoth* 9.5. See the chapter "Law in First-Century Judaism" in my *Jewish and Pauline Studies: Collected Essays* (Philadelphia, 1983).

12. Compare A. Cohen, *Everyman's Talmud* (London, 1932), 132. With this also goes an emphasis on oral learning and memorizing in Judaism; see Deuteronomy 31:19; *Lamentations Rabbah* 4:12.

13. In looking at the Egyptian, Near Eastern, and Semitic backgrounds, and at Hindu and Islamic sacred texts, I have no competence in the various original sources involved, and must rely on secondary works. I am particularly grateful to M. Meslin for allowing me to use his unpublished lecture, given at a colloquium at Strasbourg University in 1980 on the theme "La Bible est-elle une livre apart?"

14. See the mentions in Herodotus, *History* 11.36; Clement of Alexandria, *Stromateis* 6.4.37, 3; Diodorus Siculus (first century B.C.E.), *History* 11.4.

Somewhat closer parallels may be detected in Hinduism and Islam. The Sanskrit sacred texts were regarded as a unity, being of divine origin and possessing supreme authority, and underwent a process of something like canonization. Freedom to interpret these texts — resulting in a well-developed tradition (*Āgama*) which came itself to possess only slightly inferior status — did not imply freedom to modify them, which would entail exclusion from the community of Hinduism. Parallels here with Judaism and Christianity are not hard to find, even though the existence of different "sects" within Hinduism, each with its own claimed sacred texts, warns against such parallels being pressed too far. As for Islam, there are again parallels, this time between the Qur'an with its absolute authority and the Torah in Judaism, with, again, the development of a tradition (*Sunna*) facilitating its interpretation. Despite some difference, then, there are at least partial parallels in Hinduism and Islam to the phenomena of the interpretation of the Bible as a revelation from God, the literary forms which this assumed, the development of an explicatory and supplementary tradition alongside this and the "canonical" status afforded it, and to the influence which it has exerted on Western culture.[15]

What of the Hellenistic tradition? There is something to be said for applying the predicate "canonical" to the role of Homer in the Greek world of the first century.[16] Even when the content of poetry was questioned, the belief that poets were "the schoolmasters of grown men"[17] was unquestioned: and it was based on the conviction that good epic and lyric poets were inspired in a similar way to the Pythia at Delphi or such legendary figures as Bacchus and Sibyl.[18] Like those of these, the words of the poets were originally delivered orally, only subsequently being written down and collected. As early as the seventh century B.C.E. at the Delian festival, and elsewhere, Greeks assembled to hear their minstrels recite the Homeric poems. There was a public recitation of Homer every fourth year at the Panathenic festival. This, it has been claimed, is "analogous to the Jewish provision that once in every seven years the Law was to be read at the Feast of Tabernacles in the hearing of all Israel."[19]

A final possible parallel to the use of the Hebrew scriptures by Jews and early Christians comes from a later period when the dominance of the epic poets had long been under attack. In the first century or two of the Christian era there was much searching for ancient authority. The impulse to appeal to tradition which surfaced at the time in the Greco-Roman world emerged

---

15. W. Cantwell Smith has urged that the Bible has *not* influenced that culture as much as the Qur'an has influenced Islamic life: see *JAAR* 39 (1979): 133f.

16. See M. Hengel, *Judaism and Hellenism* (Philadelphia, 1974), 1:66.

17. Aristophanes, *Frogs* 1052ff.; compare 1032ff.

18. See Plato, *Phaedrus* 237c–d, 244–45; *Ion* 533–35.

19. B. S. Butcher, *Harvard Lectures*, 105, cited by James Adams, *The Religious Teachers of Greece* (Edinburgh, 1909), 9.

also in Judaism.[20] The appeal to the Hebrew scriptures in early Christianity is related to the same impulse.

II

But when all this has been recognized, is the place of the Tanak in Judaism and the early church adequately accounted for simply as the counterpart to the role played in Greece in an early time especially, but not exclusively, by Homer, and at a later date by the various philosophical traditions? The answer must finally be a qualified but unmistakable negative. There are significant differences between the approach to the Hebrew scriptures in Judaism and early Christianity and any understanding of their ancient poets, and literary and philosophical traditions by the Greeks before and after Plato. The differences can be summarized in one word, "canon," a word very often too loosely used in comparisons between Greek and Hebrew "sacred" texts.

A few preliminary considerations are pertinent. First, the Jews' attitude to their sacred writings induced the necessity to reproduce those texts without distortion. The Hebrew texts were transmitted with meticulous and scrupulous care. Although the evidence does not allow certainty, it is probable that such care was exercised before the first century. The texts discovered at Qumran seem to establish that the recension of the Masoretic text existed before the Christian era. Even an imperfect scroll such as 1QIsa deviates little from the Masoretic text. Contrast the care which this implies with the freer use and citation of scripture in the Targumim and Midrashim.

This is not the place to describe the process whereby Jewish copyists, long before it was fixed by post-Talmud Masoretes, ensured the preservation of the purity of the text of the Torah. There were probably pre-Christian specialists, scribes (*sopherim*), responsible for the official copying of texts.[21] These scribes were at first probably both "copyists," in the sense of being skilled in the mechanical art of writing, and persons who knew or were schooled in the scriptures.[22] The procedures for copying followed by the scribes probably have their parallel in the Hellenistic world, as do the rules of argumentation or of interpretation.[23] How much Jewish scribes owed to Alexandrian textual critics is hard to assess. As far as I am aware this question has not been seriously addressed. There *was* certainly an indigenous scribal tradition in Jewish Palestine. The Wisdom tradition implied a writing culture long established.

---

20. Ibid. A good example is the opening section of the *Pirke Aboth*, for which see my "Reflections on the *Aboth*," in *Jewish and Pauline Studies* (Philadelphia, 1983). Diodorus Siculus, *History* 1.9ff., is instructive at this point.

21. See Gerhardsson, *Memory and Manuscript*, 43.

22. For the situation after 70 C.E., see ibid., 51.

23. See D. Daube, *HUCA* 22:329ff., and his "Alexandrian Methods of Interpretation and the Rabbis," in *Festschrift Hans Lewald* (Basel, 1953), 22ff.

The translators of the LXX could send to the Temple authorities in Jerusalem for the best text of the Pentateuch. Most probably the translators of the scripture into Greek were influenced by the Alexandrian critical tradition.

Our specific concern is to discover whether the usage of Judaism in the treatment of texts of the Tanak points to a qualitatively different attitude toward those texts from that found in the Hellenistic world toward the sacred texts of Greece. The Hellenistic world, particularly at Alexandria and Pergamum, did seek to preserve its ancient texts, and the mechanical copying process followed by Jews came to be similar to those of the Greeks and Romans. But this insistence on the accurate textual transmission of the scriptures in Judaism seems to have become, probably by the first century and certainly later, more intense, anxious, and exacting than what we find in the Hellenistic milieu. Alexandrian critics labored to produce revised texts (*ekdoseis*) especially of the poets, and commentaries upon them. It was at Alexandria that Homer first became an object of critical study. But the attitude of editors to the texts of Homer (and, by inference, how much more to other texts) does not suggest the "religious anxiety" to observe the strictest possible exactitude that is clear in the transmission of the scriptures in Judaism. We can probably claim with some certainty that the work of Homeric critics such as Zenodotus (285–247 B.C.E.), Aristophanes (ca. 195 B.C.E.), and Aristarchus (180–145 B.C.E.) was simply governed by a textual and literary intent and lacked the intensity that a religious concern would be likely to have produced.

But what of the "canons" (κανόνες) of Alexandria as they are called? Do they not suggest that the ancient literature of Greece was elevated to a "canonical" status such as that achieved by the Tanak in Judaism and the Old and New Testaments in Christianity? To answer one must note what precisely were the concerns of the Alexandrian critics of the third and second centuries B.C.E. They aimed at discriminating authentic from spurious writings and at selecting the best writers in each kind from the enormous mass of literature which had come down to them — good, bad, indifferent. With this end in view they prepared lists (πίνακες) of poets: four heroic (headed by Homer), three iambic, four elegiac, etc. Crates prepared lists at Pergamum in which the leading writers of prose were given the prominence ascribed at Alexandria to the epic poets.[24] To be included in these lists an author had to achieve a certain excellence in the category concerned. For this reason the lists, so it has often been held, were called "canons" (κανόνες), and are to be understood as "canonical."[25]

First let it be noted that in fact the πίνακες of Alexandrian scholar-

---

24. L. Whibley, ed., *A Companion to Greek Studies* (New York, 1963), sec. 202, 175.
25. Ibid., 746.

ship were not called "canons." This term is very late as a translation for the πίνακες.[26] But, in addition to this devastating lexicographical point, was the critical intention at Alexandria comparable with that which led to the canonization of the scriptures of Judaism and Christianity? The fixing of the Alexandrian lists did reveal deep reverence, perhaps especially characteristic of the Hellenistic period, for the literary works of the ancients. But it seems that the criteria for excellence were exclusively literary: the chief responsibility for drawing up the lists was that of the two editors of Homer already mentioned, Aristarchus and Aristophanes. Their interests do not seem to have been the deeply religious ones which governed the Jews in fixing their canon. Primarily by literary discrimination, they were concerned to confirm the fame of the great authors of their people's past, not to provide a literature to govern their people in all the details of their lives in the present. The textual and so-called canonical intentions at Alexandria are perhaps not to be entirely distinguished from those of Judaism and Christianity, but they certainly do not share the same dimensions as in both the latter.

III

This brings us to the question as to the purpose of the fixation of the Jewish canon of scripture. To begin with, purely literary (as distinct from textual) criteria do not seem to have played a conscious part in the process. The concern of those who elevated the Torah, Nebiʾim, and Kethūbīm to canonicity was not to recognize, confirm, or confer any literary distinction upon them. Equally the lists of Alexandria and Pergamum do not seem to have been born of a deliberate concern to meet the urgent, immediate, and continuing needs of an ongoing self-conscious religious people or community. The "new" class of scholars engaged in editing Homer and other Greek writings in Alexandria and Pergamum were called διόρθωται, that is, "correctors." Jewish scribes would certainly have resented such a designation as impious: who would dare "correct" their sacred texts? This contrasts markedly with the concern that led to the fixation of the Jewish canon, as we shall see.

But before we deal further with their concern, the other phenomenon in the Greco-Roman world to which we referred previously again deserves

---

26. See R. Pfeiffer, *History of Classical Scholarship: From the Beginnings to the End of the Hellenistic Age* (Oxford, 1968), 207. Pfeiffer points out that the term "canon" was coined for the πίνακες (repertories or lists which we should call indexes) by David Ruhnken in 1768. The use of it for the πίνακες was not Greek, and it was not by the ancient Greek tradition that the use of "canon" for πίνακες was suggested to Ruhnken, but by the biblical. Eusebius *H.E.* 6, 25.3 "seems to be the earliest evidence for the canon of Scripture" according to Pfeiffer at p. 207, n. 4. See further J. Barr, *Holy Scripture: Canon, Authority, Criticism* (Philadelphia, 1983), 51, and my article "Reflections about the Use of the Old Testament in the New in Its Historical Context," *JQR* 74, no. 2 (October 1983): 105–36, to which the reader is referred for fuller treatment of much in the present chapter.

attention. Does this provide, at least, a partial parallel? As we saw, in the Hellenistic age the founders of schools of philosophy came to be highly revered and their words and works cherished. There were many such schools. What particularly interests us is the attitude each school reveals to the tradition — oral and written — originated by the founder. The tradition was not regarded as of intellectual or "philosophical" interest only. The tradition of the founder was to provide an inspiring, and normative, regulatory way of life: it provided a "rule" or "canon" by which the members of a particular school were to live. This scholastic "canonization" of a teaching founder's tradition, as we shall see, approaches in part the intent behind the canonization of the Jewish scriptures, which also were to provide a *halakah*, a way of life.[27] There is, however, an obvious difference. The canon of Judaism was to inform not simply the life of a particular school, although the interpretation of it could and did lead to the emergence of different "schools" within Israel, but that of a whole people.

This leads to the consideration of the underlying cause for the fixation of the Jewish canon. To grasp this would help to assess how far the Greco-Roman world offers more than formal parallels to that process.

To begin with, however much veneration for ancient texts and tradition the Greco-Roman world reveals, it provides only a pale and partial parallel with that implied in the constant, regular, daily reading of the Torah in the synagogue. The history of the synagogue is wrapped in obscurity, but there were synagogues in first-century Palestine and outside. Part of their activity was the reading and study of the scriptures which, although not altogether formally "fixed" as a "canon" until the end of the first century and possibly not even then, had achieved a prominent (for reasons we shall give later we deliberately avoid the adjective "normative") role in Jewish life. Certainly in this matter any dogmatism must be suspect, but the claim seems to be justified that by the first century the Torah had become a ubiquitous, ever present expression of Jewish religious life. Discussion has centered on whether the whole Torah was read annually or triennially in the first-century synagogues. In any case, the lectionary activity of the synagogue in that period points to an elevation of the sacred Hebrew texts for which there is no fully adequate parallel in the Greco-Roman world.[28]

Only recently has the nature of this elevation begun to be explored in depth. Previously the history of the canon was most often treated chrono-

---

27. On the role of philosophy in this connection, see A. D. Nock, *Conversion* (Oxford, 1933), 181; H. Wolfson, *Philo* (Cambridge, Mass., 1947), 1:8ff.; M. Smith in *Israel*, ed. M. Davis (New York, 1956), 80; E. J. Bickerman, *RB* 59 (1952): 49ff.

28. For the synagogue, see *The Cambridge History of Judaism*, vol. 3, forthcoming. Also see Jacob Mann, *The Bible as Read and Preached in the Old Synagogue* (Cincinnati, 1940). According to Mann (pp. 3ff.) the Palestinian Jewish lectionary was almost certainly triennial.

logically and factually without adequate attention either to the deep forces at work in its fixation or to the significance of the final form of the canon as such. Now it is increasingly urged that the emergence and formation of the canon in Judaism and Christianity was ultimately due to the necessity for the people of Israel, as later for the Christian churches, to define and pre-serve their identity. The primary impulse behind the elevation of the Torah and the Prophets, as later of the Writings, was the felt need in the disaster of the exile and later to reaffirm the "story" of Yahweh's dealing with his people. That disaster made the people of Israel — for the sake of their very survival — conceive of themselves increasingly, and more and more emphati-cally, as a "Chosen People," the record of whose origin and prescribed way of life and destiny they found in their ancient writings. These they revered and tried to preserve and elevate for the sake of their own continued existence. The sacred texts had become necessary to the continuing self-identity of the people of Israel; they became the book of a people and the people became a people of the book. The crises of the sixth century B.C.E. and of the first century C.E. demanded the reaffirmation of Jewish identity, and this was in part achieved through the development and ultimate fixation of the canon. The understanding of the canon thus crudely set forth here we owe especially to J. A. Sanders and Brevard Childs, who with varying emphases have called for a new canonical criticism.

And, despite the partial parallels to which we have pointed, we look in vain for a satisfactory parallel in the Greco-Roman world. Much as the epic poets, particularly Homer and Hesiod, were revered and regarded as "in-spired," they were never regarded as "gods," and certainly not as the voice of God, the creator of the universe. Contrast with this the Israelite view that Yahweh had spoken directly to Moses, and not only spoken to him but handed over the tablets on which he himself had written his commandments.

The same contrast applies to the esteem with which the traditions of the founders of the various philosophic schools were held. Some of the great philosophers were conceived of as having prophetic powers. But, as was the case with Homer and the poets, this did *not* connote their divinization: they were not "gods." But the tradition of Israel came to be directly traced to Yahweh himself, and, from the outset, its core in the Decalogue was in written form.[29] This placed the Torah outside the categories applied in the Greco-Roman world to its ancient literature, and the interpretation of it later in Israel still further removed it from anything in the Greco-Roman world.

This is reinforced by the way in which Homer was treated. Despite his

---

29. The accounts of the giving of the Law to Moses present problems which cannot be dealt with here.

attachment to Homer, Plato finally had to exclude him from the ideal state because he could corrupt morals.[30] The tragedians often found it necessary to correct Homeric notions of morality and of the gods. In the Hellenistic age, it is not Homer who is the teacher of the Greeks but philosophy. The kind of criticism of Homer and the epic poets which made necessary the rise of the allegorical method in the Greco-Roman world is not natural in their treatment of the Torah by Jews. Allegory does sometimes occur in Jewish sources but it is more native to the Hellenistic.[31] The approach of the Jews to their scriptures (which they regarded as of direct divine origin, though they were in some circles regarded as mediated by angels)[32] was qualitatively different from that of the Greeks to theirs.

Moreover, the kind of historical circumstances which provided the impetus for the formulation and later fixation of the Hebrew canon in Judaism were absent in Greece and in Greek history. The Jewish people came to understand themselves as having been called into being through an act of Yahweh in delivering them from slavery in Egypt. With this they later connected the giving of the Torah on Mount Sinai. The precise way in which the tradition of the exodus and the Sinaitic tradition of the giving of the Torah came to be conjoined does not directly concern us. Those two events came to dominate the memory of Israel. The emergence and continuance as a people were bound up with these; their ancient traditions and scriptures centered in them; the remembrance of these two events provided them with their identity as a people. Later another overwhelming event, the Babylonian Exile, engendered the necessity for the collecting of the traditions about those events and the setting in motion of the process which finally resulted in the Hebrew canon. The beginning of the formation of a canon was the means whereby Jewish identity survived the exile in the sixth century B.C.E. To understand the Hebrew canon, then, well-defined, extraordinary, historical memories — of the exodus, Sinai, and the exile — have to be recognized as formative.

When we turn to Greek history, there are no parallels of any comparable magnitude. The Greek identity seems not to have been determined by any outstanding, spectacular historical events. If we follow Herodotus,[33] that identity was forged out of the normal processes of human interaction and exchange arising from an agelong awareness of sharing in the same ethnic character, in the same religious tradition, and in the same language. Greek

---

30. *Republic* 607A. A Sophist could even call Homer a liar and hold him up to ridicule: so Dio of Prusa, *Discourse* 11.

31. See J. Bonsirven, *L'Exégèse Rabbinique et l'Exégèse Paulinienne* (Paris, 1939).

32. Gal. 3:19; Acts 7:38. See Davies, *Jewish and Pauline Studies*. See also Wolfson, *Philo*, 1:138ff.

33. See, e.g., *History* 8.144.

self-awareness was mainly a *cultural* awareness, not a strictly historical one in the sense that it was, as with Israel, the product of specific, overwhelmingly significant historical events. Greeks knew no exodus at their beginnings, nor, in the course of their history, an exile like that of the Jews to Babylon. Certain Greek city-states did experience exile and massive, cruel deportations, but the Greeks as a totality never faced such. When Persia threatened the existence of Greece, the threat was met and followed, not by exile, but by a period of efflorescence. It is probably significant that there is no one word for exile in classical Greek as there is in Hebrew (גלות, גולה) but rather several words emphasizing various aspects of the experience of exile. In Greek history there were famous "exiles," such as Odysseus, but no one overwhelming "Exile" in the Jewish sense.

Equally significant is it that, as Thucydides 1.3 points out, the term *Hellenes* for all Greeks occurs only late and then simply to distinguish them from the barbarians: whereas the Jewish people, despite the division between the kingdoms of Judah and Israel, came to think of themselves as constituted of one people from the beginning, through the exodus and Sinai. The Greeks never achieved such a "politically" unified conception of themselves. The independent city-states — not the land or country or people as a totality — were the foci of loyalty, but therefore *ipso facto* also of division and fratricide. Except under very great stress, such as the Persian invasion, the city-states hindered the development of a unified Greek world, despite the recognition of its cultural unity. The impulse to the formation of one authoritative "canon" to justify or preserve that unity was lacking: even reverence for Homer could not provide this. The geographical realities of Greece, as well as Greek history, then, militated against the emergence of anything comparable to the canon of Judaism in the classical period. In the Hellenistic period the diverse philosophical schools were also not conducive of a common Greek canon, but rather of individual "canons" for each school. The widespread cultural Hellenic identity does not seem to have required a concentrated literary identification through a "canon."

We have suggested that the notion of a "canon" of scripture in Judaism and Christianity has no adequate or satisfactory parallel in the Greco-Roman world. But our presentation has now to be seriously qualified. Two dangers have to be shunned: first, that of reading the role and authority of the Jewish and Christian canons, after they had been fixed, back to an earlier period; and, second, that of *underestimating* the variety of Judaism at the emergence of Christianity, and so of *overestimating the role of the Jewish scriptures in Jewish life at that time*. We have emphasized the importance of the scriptures in first-century Judaism. The probable fixation of the canon at the end of that century confirms this: it recognized what was already fact. But concentration on the written scriptures alone leads to distortion: this is why we previously rejected the word "normative" to describe the role of the Tanak in Judaism, and simply used the adjective "prominent."

At this point the development of the oral law in Judaism must be emphasized. After the Persian, and particularly in the Greek and Roman periods, Jews who were in Babylon and those who had returned to Palestine confronted new cultures. They faced the new demands and complex dilemmas of those new cultures: for these the ancient scriptures — important as they were in defining the origins and history, and safeguarding the identity, of the Jews — provided insufficient guidance. This, along with other factors, prompted a renewed development of the oral law alongside the written. Now for our purposes, contrary to what previous scholars have often asserted, it is strikingly noteworthy that the oral law of Judaism often bears little relation to the written Torah.[34] If the written Torah had enjoyed unswayed and normative authority, this is hard to understand. The strictly mishnaic collecting of oral laws, that is, without reference to scripture, *may* have preceded the midrashic method of relating the laws to the scriptural text, which was also practiced and culminated in the later Midrashim.[35] The two developments may have occurred side by side. Whether the mishnaic tendency was the prior we cannot ascertain. But the development of the oral law was *often* apart from the written law. According to some of the sages it came to take precedence over the written law. This indicates that the written law was not as all-dominating as our treatment may have implied. There was a very rich oral legal tradition alongside the written. This oral tradition, rooted in long-established custom, also came to be connected with the giving of the Torah to Moses on Mount Sinai. This meant that it too achieved the authority ascribed to scripture itself.[36] The relation of Jesus, Paul, and the early church to the Tanak must not be isolated from this phenomenon. In confronting Judaism at the first they faced primarily not only the written Torah, which so controls subsequent Christian thinking on this matter, but the oral tradition, which was perhaps the more dominant in the Jewish mind.

There is a concomitant factor. As we saw, the oral law was not always directly or indirectly connected with the Tanak. But it sometimes was. The development of the Midrashim points to this. This makes clear what is obvious otherwise, that between the Tanak and the New Testament lies a vast

---

34. *Mishnah Hagigah* 1.8 is particularly illuminating on the connection between the written and the oral tradition. The scribes, such as Ben Sirach, were not exegetes or midrashists, but expositors of Wisdom.

35. See J. Z. Lauterbach, *Rabbinic Essays* (Cincinnati, 1951).

36. This is the implication of *Mishnah Aboth* 1.1. See J. Neusner, "The Meaning of Oral Torah," in *Early Rabbinic Judaism* (Leiden, 1975), 1–33, and the forthcoming chapters by J. Goldin and D. Zlotnik in *The Cambridge History of Judaism*, vol. 4.

exegetical-interpretative activity within Judaism. This means that in confronting Judaism the early church, like Jesus and Paul, faced not only both a written and oral Torah but also ways of understanding these, that is, long-standing exegetical-interpretative traditions. They assumed these, and it was to these traditions of exegesis and interpretation rather than to the Tanak itself in its textual nudity that they related. Professor David Daube has long urged this. Recently he claimed:

> When dealing with the Old Testament in the New we ought to read it as it was read by Jews of that era. The references without exception come from their midst, are founded in their interpretation. If this often clashes with the pristine sense (or what we take to be such) it cannot be helped. We must still stick to it. Unless we do, we may miss parts of the New Testament message conveyed by means of the reference.[37]

Knowledge of varied and complex interpretations of the Tanak in first-century Judaism is a necessary prerequisite for understanding Jesus', and early Christian, engagement with it. To substantiate this claim is not possible here, but examples of the illumination afforded by the recognition of this approach are not hard to find. For the understanding of the use of the Old Testament in the New it matters little what *we* understand by an Old Testament text, but what it meant *to Jews* with whom Jesus and early Christians were in debate in the first century is of primary importance: this should be one of our exegetical axioms.

Apart, then, from certain general considerations pointing to certain parallels, but even greater dissimilarities, the Greco-Roman attitude to ancient texts helps little in our attempts to understand the early Christian engagement with the Hebrew scriptures. We are driven to consider anew the oral tradition and the exegetical-interpretative activity within Judaism. The recognition of the complexity of the attitude to the scriptures in the first-century Judaism suggested here — especially when the mishnaic, midrashic, and exegetical-interpretative developments are given due emphasis — helps to place their use by the writers of the New Testament in better perspective. Most of them wrote when there was much freedom, and many methods were employed in the approach to the scriptures even though they were so highly regarded. The canon was only in the process of being finally fixed for Judaism, just as the sages had not yet codified the oral law. From this point of view the New Testament is a document from a transition period in which Judaism had not come fully to terms with either its written or oral Torah. The use of the Old Testament in the New reveals reverence and a daring freedom

---

37. In a forthcoming lecture on "The Old Testament in the New." See especially *Mishnah Sanhedrin* 11.3, *Yadaim* 3.2.

of exegesis: but in this it was not unique, but probably typical: it was only its christological dimension and approach that was peculiar. Moreover, after the Hebrew canon had been fixed at twenty-two books with an unimpeachable ancestry, Christians continued to use and quote as scripture such books as Wisdom and Ecclesiasticus, which they had received as part of the Septuagint. Owing to our familiarity with a fixed, authoritative canon, confined by Protestantism to the Hebrew Bible, it is easy to conceive of the engagement of the early Christian movement, especially before 70 c.e., in too simplistic terms. They did use written Hebrew scriptures which they regarded as sacred: but these were still undefined in detail and had not yet achieved the express authority of "*The* Canon." Above all, they coexisted with a vast tradition of oral law and subtle and infinitely varied exegetical-interpretative traditions. It is in the light of this, not of any parallels with Hellenism, that the New Testament use of the Tanak is best approached.

Despite his possibly distorting enthusiasm, the words of Josephus, who claimed what we have here reiterated, are probably near the truth.

> ... how firmly we have given credit to these books of our own nation is evident by what we do; for during so many ages as have already passed, no one has been so bold as either to add any thing to them, to take any thing from them, or to make any change in them; but it is become natural to call Jews immediately, and from their very birth, to esteem these books to contain Divine doctrines, and to persist in them, and, if occasion be, willingly to die for them. For it is no new thing for our captives, many of them in number, and frequently in time, to be seen to endure racks and deaths of all kinds upon the theaters, that they may not be obliged to say one word against our laws and the records that contain them; whereas there are none at all among the Greeks who would undergo the least harm on that account, no, nor in case all the writings that are among them were to be destroyed; for they take them to be such discourses as are framed agreeably to the inclination of those that write them; and they have justly the same opinion of the ancient writers, since they see some of the present generation bold enough to write about such affairs, wherein they were not present, nor had concern enough to inform themselves about them from those that knew them.... [38]

Perhaps we have been able to suggest additional reasons why classical antiquity offers no adequate parallel to "The Canon" in Judaism and Christianity.

---

38. *Contra Apion*, bk. 1; pp. 861–62 in the Loeb translation.

IV

What light may these reflections on the nature of the Jewish canon throw on the topic of Christology?

We have seen that there is no significant parallel to the "canon" of Judaism in the first century. What has emerged is that the "canon" of Judaism is inextricably bound up with the search for the identity and for self-preservation and continuity of the Jewish community. But by itself the canon was not sufficient to serve this function adequately. It had to be interpreted and applied to the life of the community. This was achieved by the perpetuation and development of and obedience to the oral law. By this, among other things, the written Torah was minted down to guide the everyday living of faithful Jews. Both mishnaic and midrashic methods were applied to achieve this end. The significance of this development must be clearly recognized. Both Midrash and Mishnah involved what might be called the Judaization of the Tanak. That is, in Judaism the Tanak came to be interpreted in order to further and illuminate the self-understanding of Jews and to preserve their identity. The oral law and Midrash serve as a "fence" around the written law and *ipso facto* around the Jewish community. The Tanak was interpreted in the interests of elevating both the significance of the Torah and of the relationship of the people of Israel as such to Yahweh. This process of Judaization has made it necessary to distinguish Israelite religion and, indeed, the religion of the Tanak, from Judaism. That process was more checkered before 70 c.e. (for example, it is doubtful whether the Sadducees ever fully succumbed to it) than later. In Rabbinic Judaism, strictly so-called, the Judaization of the Tanak, and (some go so far as to claim) its subordination to the oral Torah, reached its apogee. The developed Rabbinic Judaism which emerged after the first century gave to the oral Torah, originally an accompaniment of the written Torah, an authority equal to the latter — if not a greater one. This helps to clarify the function of the oral Torah. Probably from the time of Ezra on it evolved to make sure that the Tanak was not treated as an isolated deposit, with overweening authority, but interpreted in the interests of the community. This was why in time the oral tradition became Torah, as much as the Tanak, and according to some even more than the latter.

We suggest that the due recognition of the oral tradition as the interpretative clue to the meaning of the Tanak in Judaism is relevant to our understanding of the Christology of the early church. We here use the term "Christology" not in its strict traditional sense to denote the doctrine of how God became man in Christ, but in the general sense of doctrine or teaching about Christ. And as in Judaism so in the history of Christian doctrine, the centuries after the first can best illumine the latter. Marcel Simon long ago pointed to the notion of Christ as a New Torah in the fathers. However, he made no attempt to connect it with the period of the New Testament or with its documents. Later, Daniélou was more receptive to such a connection and found anticipations of it in the New Testament. In *Paul and Rabbinic Judaism* we proposed that, for Paul, Christ had come to fulfill the role of a New Torah, although he never used that phrase. This suggestion has not been generally accepted. Apart from hesitancy especially on the part of Protestants to apply "legal" terms to the Lord of Grace, two reasons were advanced against it: first, the unacceptable appeal to Colossians and Ephesians, which many regard as non-Pauline or at best deutero-Pauline; second, the emphasis (which many regard as highly exaggerated and unwarranted) on the words of Jesus as constituting a new law. Moreover, it was often confidently asserted that Paul did not think of Christ in terms of the Law, as we had implied, but of the Law in terms of Christ, who is not a new Moses in Paul. Neither of these objections is insurmountable. There are pertinent anticipations of Colossians and Ephesians in earlier indubitably Pauline epistles, and the words of Jesus — the role of which we doubtless did underline too much — do play no mean part in Paul. The role of Moses in Paul's understanding is more difficult to deal with. Here, however, we are not concerned to reassert the interpretations of Christ as a New Torah in Paul without further refinement. Let it simply be noted that in speaking of Christ as Torah we were not thinking primarily of his words as constituting Torah but of the totality of his ministry and person, his cross and resurrection as having assumed for Paul the ultimate significance which Judaism applied to the Torah.

Such a position is simplistic and needs elaboration and refinement. The words in Torah remained authoritative for Paul: he is careful to insist that the life, death, and resurrection of Jesus are "according to the scriptures." The unchangeable "canon" remains "canon" for him. But just as, in Judaism, what was deemed to interpret the "canon" became itself "canon," so it came to pass for Paul that the life, teaching, death, and resurrection of Jesus became the exegesis of the canon (that is, of the Tanak) — a kind of equivalent of, and hence a substitute for, the oral tradition in Judaism as the clue to the scriptures. When he fought against obedience to the Law, he was not primarily opposed to the Tanak but to the oral tradition which was already being elevated to the status of the written Torah. In other words, for Paul the identity of the Christian community is preserved by the tradition about Christ: he now fulfills for Christians the role of the oral law in Judaism. But once this had been recognized the further elevation of Christ to be part of the "canon" was natural, as had been the elevation of the oral law to the same status in Judaism. Whether this stage was reached in Paul's mind we need not at this point determine. What we are concerned to suggest again is that, just as the oral Torah in Judaism implied the Judaization of the Tanak, so the elevation of the life, death, and resurrection of Jesus by Paul led to its

Christianization. Christ, we might claim, has become the "oral tradition" of Paul, the clue to his understanding of the Tanak.

From a different angle, Professor Daniel Patte has recently urged what amounts to the same thing, although he starts out not as we did from the canon and oral tradition of Judaism, but from the use of the scriptures in Paul. I can only refer the reader to his work. For example, of Paul's treatment of Abraham he writes:

> [T]he relation between the believers [the Christian community] and Christ is similar to that between the believers and Abraham. More generally, we may say that the relation of the believers to Christ is the same kind of relation which exists between scripture and its fulfillments in Christ and the believers. To put it another way, the Kerygma about Christ functions in Paul as an *"oral scripture."* This means that according to Paul's system of convictions, Christ, despite the fact that he is the Fulfillment of Scripture, *has the same status as Scripture.*[39]

A discussion of 1 Corinthians 15:3–11 leads Patte to the same conclusion: "Indeed, for Paul, Scripture is not merely the Old Testament Scripture, but also the Kerygma about Christ, and the story of the earlier believers' experience." It is not possible to pursue Patte's discussion, but it deserves careful consideration for its christological implications.

Outside the Pauline epistles, too, the New Testament points in other ways to a tradition, a way to be followed, which seems often to be equated with Christ Himself. This line of thought later breaks out more explicitly. In short, it is not unlikely that a consideration of Christ in the light of Torah both written and oral is still one fruitful way to approach the *mysterium tremendum* of his person.

---

39. *Paul's Truth and the Power of the Gospel* (Philadelphia, 1983), 213. Italics added.

Chapter 3

Torah and Dogma: A Comment

The suggestion has often been made recently that the relationship between Judaism and Christianity can be adequately described in terms of a "schism." This suggestion is worthy of serious consideration. It has much to commend it. It promises new possibilities (badly needed in view of past history), because "schism" can be healed. But its mere attractiveness and beneficial potential should not blind us to the problems involved. Because the term "schism" presupposes an underlying unity, its use to describe the relation between the two faiths preserves an emphasis which, in our given situation, where the dependence of the church on the synagogue is not sufficiently recognized, is too easily lost. And yet, without very careful definition, the term "schism" may be misleading. Who are to be schismatics? Is it Christians for leaving Judaism or Jews for rejecting the Christian Messiah and his people? As will become apparent in the following pages, there are two extreme positions to be avoided. On the one hand, that which regards the relationship between Judaism and Christianity at the present time as so close that that relationship is merely schismatic, and, on the other hand, that which regards that relationship as one of unrelieved antithesis.

I

The theme of our section of the colloquium is entitled "Torah and Dogma," and it is no doubt intended that the two terms in the title should stand for Judaism and Christianity respectively. Such a designation is understandable, but by no means unproblematic. It is important to recognize its implications

Editor's Note [from Krister Stendahl]: Professor W. D. Davies' reflections on Torah and dogma were presented as a comment on a paper which Professor Kornelius H. Miskotte, author of *Wenn die Götter schweigen*, presented to the colloquium. In his paper, entitled "The Great Schism," Miskotte surveyed the history of Jewish-Christian relations and opted for the term "schism" as theologically adequate and mutually beneficial in present and future dialogues between Jews and Christians. He did so with special reference to Rosenzweig and Barth (see below, n. 28). Here we present Professor Davies' comments as an independent contribution to the main theme of one of the seminars which made up the colloquium, namely, "Torah and Dogma." [The colloquium referred to is "The Colloquium on Judaism and Christianity," Harvard Divinity School, Cambridge, Massachusetts, 17–20 October 1966.]

and limitations. It implies that the characteristic mark of Judaism is *halakah* or *Torah* and that of Christianity *dogma*.[1] The one religion is primarily concerned with the "way to live" — *halak,* "to walk" — the other with the way to believe, with the proper creedal formulations.

This distinction between the two faiths cannot be pressed to the last degree. In a limited sense it can be claimed that Judaism demands certain beliefs. Scholars have pointed out a kerygmatic core in the Old Testament. Just as behind the New Testament there is a kerygma centered in an event — the life, death, and resurrection of Jesus of Nazareth — so in the Old Testament the exodus constitutes a kerygmatic core. This emerges clearly in passages where "creedal," confessional materials, older than the texts in which they occur, break through, as in Deuteronomy 26:5ff., which recapitulates the mighty deeds which gave birth to Israel (see also Deut. 6:20–24; Josh. 24:26–34; Deut. 4:32–34, etc.). The kerygmatic core in the Old Testament is a kind of confession of faith. Again the *Shema* expresses the quintessence of a Faith — if you like, a dogma of Judaism. Occasionally in the *Mishnah* an anathema is uttered against those who deny certain cardinal tenets of Judaism. A famous passage in *m. Sanhedrin* 10:1 reads as follows:

> All Israelites have a share in the world to come, for it is written, *Thy people also shall all be righteous, they shall inherit the land forever; the branch of my planting, the work of my hands that I may be glorified.* And these are they that have no share in the world to come: he that says that there is no resurrection of the dead prescribed in the Law, and [he that says] that the Law is not from Heaven, and an Epicurean. R. Akiba says: Also he that reads the heretical books, or that utters charms over a wound and says, *I will put none of the diseases upon thee which I have put upon the Egyptians: for I am the Lord that healeth thee.* Abba Saul says: Also he that pronounces the Name with its proper letters... (Danby translation)

Later on Maimonides was to issue his understanding of Judaism as a creed, and nineteenth-century movements in Judaism, both Conservative and Reform, sought to clarify the tenets of Judaism.[2] A British author, in a volume entitled *Judaism as Creed and Life,* summarizes Judaism as belief in God and human responsibility. The point is that there is a "dogma" or "creed" implicit, if not always explicit, in Judaism.[3]

---

1. By *dogma* I understand a truth necessary for salvation propounded by an authoritative council or organ of the church.

2. This emerges clearly in the lectures by Joseph L. Blau, *Modern Varieties of Judaism* (New York: Columbia University Press, 1966).

3. Morris Joseph, *Judaism as Creed and Life* (London: Macmillan, 1903).

But, when all this has been granted, the essential demand of Judaism is obedience to the Torah, the observance of the *Miṣwot*. The anathemas in *Mishnah Sanhedrin* 10 strike one as being haphazard: they are not the considered "dogmatic" pronouncement of an authorized body of leaders nor are they presented with the full-blasted force of a "dogma"; they do not stand out in any way from other materials in *Sanhedrin;* they are given no prominence, not to speak of preeminence.[4] Not dogmatic pronouncements, but legal directions are important. The musical *The Fiddler on the Roof* opens with a catching song on tradition. Precariously balanced as Judaism has been on the whims of the Gentile world, what has kept it alive is tradition — a way of doing things, a way of baking bread, sewing clothes, slaughtering animals, keeping the house clean. Judaism is a way. And the song asks: Whence is this tradition? Who gave it? Nobody quite knows; but it is *here,* and Jews live by it. True, the composer of *The Fiddler on the Roof* may be an *am haaretz.* But the song, nevertheless, illustrates the concern of Judaism. The primary concern is not the *understanding* of tradition, not the formulating of it in doctrine and dogma, although there is a search for the grounds of Torah, that is, the reasons for the commandments. The heart of the matter is rather *living* it, observing it, albeit with love, joy, and trust in God, the Father.[5]

It agrees with this that within Judaism "belief" can range at will. There are certain implicit, and sometimes explicit, basic principles to which we have already referred. But these apart, it is rightly (if humorously) asserted that where there are three Jews, there can be four opinions. For example, there is no one doctrine of the Messiah. It is easily possible for a Jew to claim to be the Messiah without incurring censure, provided he observes the *Miṣwot.* Herbert Danby is reported to have once said, playfully no doubt, that he once lectured in Jerusalem when there were six Messiahs in his audience. To observe the Law confers freedom for almost anything else and, to parody Augustine, a Jew might urge: "Observe the Law and believe what you like." There was some time ago, for example, the extreme but interesting case of an American rabbi who refused to believe in God and yet continued in the rabbinate.

Jewish scholars often affirm that what Judaism presents us with is a multiplicity of individual opinions, but no "theology." For example, a distinguished

---

4. In the discussion at Harvard, Professor Judah Goldin drew a conclusion exactly opposite to mine from this fact. That the "anathemas" are inserted without special introduction or emphasis means, in his view, that their outstanding importance was assumed. I hesitate to differ from such a rabbinist, but I fail in this instance to be convinced.

5. Abraham Heschel often reiterated this, as in his essay "No Time for Neutrality," in *Moral Grandeur and Spiritual Audacity: Essays,* edited by Susannah Heschel (New York: Farrar, Straus & Giroux, 1966), 137: "Our understanding comes by way of *mitzvah.* By living as Jews we attain our faith as Jews. We do not have faith in deeds; we attain faith through deeds." Heschel's criticism of Reinhold Niebuhr always makes this clear, as in Heschel's book *The Insecurity of Freedom* (New York: Farrar, Straus & Giroux, 1966), sec. 9, pp. 127–49, on "Confusion of Good and Evil."

Jewish scholar on reading the chapter in my work *The Setting of the Sermon on the Mount*, which deals with the concept of a New Torah, courteously commented that, while all the data in the chapter were correct, he wondered whether one could deal thematically, as I had done, with any idea in the rabbis. The rabbis were individuals holding diverse opinions. Certainly they held certain ideas which were theological, but they were not systematic theologians in any sense; they never constructed a theology for Judaism nor any dogmatic system.[6] It is significant that Samuel Schechter wrote a book not on rabbinic theology as such, but on *Some Aspects of Rabbinic Theology*, a title which suggests the fragmentary, unsystematic character of its theme; and it is often hinted that he had great difficulty in writing even on aspects of it.

Related to this, and perhaps determinative of it, is the fundamental fact that, however much exaggerated by Christian scholars, rabbinic piety is essentially nomistic in that it was the Torah given on Mount Sinai in a past age that was regulative for all life. "The Rabbis," writes Cohen, "would have denied that they were originators of Jewish thought. All they would have admitted was that they were excavators in the inexhaustible mine of the divine Revelation contained in the scriptures and brought to light treasures that lay hidden beneath the surface."[7]

In addition to all the above, another factor causes many modern rabbinic scholars to hesitate to formulate a theology of the rabbis, and that is the unexamined and unsifted character of the rabbinic texts on which such a formulation would have to be based. This can best be illustrated, for example, from the illuminating studies of Judah Goldin on various key texts. He shows how very fluid the rabbinic tradition was and how precarious any theological construction built upon them must be.[8]

The upshot of all this is that there is what might almost be called a consensus that Judaism is essentially halakic and not theological: it is not orthodoxy but orthopraxy that marks Judaism. Judaism — to use a term that has been used to express this point of view — is *pan-halakic*.[9]

There are Jewish scholars who hold a different view. Abraham Heschel

---

6. A biblical student cannot but ask whether, if the same standards were applied to the Old Testament as are applied to the rabbinic sources to deny the possibility of a rabbinic theology, biblical theology, as it has developed in our time, would ever have been possible. Does not it too often imply a system or connections between various documents and figures where none existed?

7. A. Cohen, *Everyman's Talmud* (London: J. M. Dent & Sons, 1932), 132. See R. T. Herford, *Pharisaism: Its Aim and Its Method* (London: Williams & Norgate; New York: G. P. Putnam's Sons, 1912), chaps. 1 and 2, and J. Bonsirven, *Le Judaïsme Palestinien au Temps de Jésus-Christ: Sa Théologie*, vol. 1: *La Théologie Dogmatique* (Paris: Gabriel Beauchesne,1934), 248f.

8. See, for example, J. Goldin, "The End of Ecclesiastes: Literal Exegesis and Its Transformation," in *Studies and Texts*, vol. 3: *Biblical Motifs*, ed. Alexander Altmann (Cambridge: Harvard University Press, 1966), 135–38.

9. I owe this phrase to A. Heschel's work *God in Search of Man: A Philosophy of Judaism* (London: Calder, 1955), 323, 328.

urged that *haggadah* can be made to reveal distinct theological currents of thought within Judaism. He distinguished a theological difference between the traditions emanating from the school of Rabbi Akiba and those from the school of Rabbi Ishmael, finding the one more mystical and the other more rational than the other.[10] Heschel's work has not been sufficiently assimilated and assessed,[11] and it would be presumptuous on my part to enter into this debate, but we may point out certain factors that are pertinent in its evaluation. The implication of Heschel's position is that in the Tannaitic period theological speculation of a sophisticated kind prevailed in rabbinic schools. One thing does suggest considerable speculation at least, even if it were not systematic, and that is the very extent of the haggadic material extant in rabbinic sources. It is far more extensive than strictly halakic material. Despite its formlessness, it is difficult to imagine that such extensive haggadah has merely a kind of fanciful, homiletical significance, devoid of all serious theological value. Would the haggadic materials have survived across the centuries, were merely this the case? Moreover, there are historical considerations which might have induced a diminution of theological interest in Judaism since Tannaitic times. Once Judaism came to occupy an inferior and despised position in a world where Christianity was dominant, particularly when it increasingly became confined to the ghetto, it was natural that it should be overawed by the intellectual, no less than by the material and political, dominance of Christianity. The very magnificence of the theological achievement of medieval Christendom had an inhibiting effect on any Jewish theological speculation that might have arisen. And, later, in the period when Jewry was emancipated from the ghetto, it was often understandably dazzled by the new world into which it entered. The lure and fascination of European culture often very naturally led to a neglect of Jewish theologizing. By and large, the intellectual energies of Jewry were consecrated to the newly opened, expansive, and insidious secular interests of nineteenth-century Europe, when assimilation became common. When Jewry did react "theologically" to Western culture, it was natural for it to do so either in a liberal fashion, which did not always foster theological profundity, or in a conservative fashion which led to renewed concentration on halakah. The neglect of theology by secularized and religious Jews in modern times is historically understandable.[12]

---

10. Three volumes of Heschel's work on this theme have already appeared (unfortunately only in Hebrew): *Torah min ha-shamayim be-aspaklaryah shel ha-dorot* (London and New York: Defus Shontsin, 1962–90). An English translation (*Torah from Heaven: The Theology of Classical Judaism* [New York: Continuum]) is forthcoming.

11. There is a review of the second volume by Jacob Neusner in *Conservative Judaism* 20, no. 3 (1966): 66–73.

12. At this point recent developments among Jewish thinkers must modify any present emphasis on the comparative absence of theological speculation in Judaism. Here only the briefest

However all this may be, it is probably true to claim that the *dominant* position still among Jewish scholars is that in Judaism not opinion, doctrine, or dogma matter primarily, but practice or observance in trust and joy.[13] The peculiar genius of Judaism is expressed not in creeds, like the Nicene or the Chalcedonian in Christianity, but in a law book, the Mishnah. While in certain Qabbalistic and mystical circles, which have persisted throughout Jewish history, a speculative, even esoteric, interest constantly emerges,

---

statement is possible. Since the tentative though influential work of Samuel Schechter, *Some Aspects of Rabbinic Theology* (London, 1909), and books of A. Marmorstein, *The Doctrine of Merits in the Old Rabbinical Literature*, Jews' College Publication, no. 7 (London, 1920), and *The Old Rabbinic Doctrine of God*, Jews' College Publications, nos. 10, 14 (London, 1927), there have been translations into English of *The Babylonian Talmud*, ed. I. Epstein (London: Soncino Press, 1935), and of *The Midrash Rabbah*, ed. H. Freedman and M. Simon, 9 vols. (London: Soncino Press, 1939), which have opened up those sources to the English-speaking world. Abraham Heschel, particularly, in many works revealed to the Jewish and Gentile worlds theological riches in his tradition, rabbinic and Hasidic, which have profoundly moved and influenced those worlds. For bibliography, see the collection of his works, *Moral Grandeur and Spiritual Audacity*, cited in n. 5 above. About the same time E. E. Urbach, Gershom Scholem, and Saul Lieberman enriched us by their studies. The works of Jacob Neusner have been immensely influential, both theologically and otherwise. Among his many studies I note as especially pertinent for this chapter the volume *The Incarnation of God: The Character of Divinity in Normative Judaism* (Philadelphia: Fortress Press, 1988).

More recently there are studies by David Novak, *The Election of Israel: The Idea of the Chosen People* (Cambridge: Cambridge University Press, 1995); Michael Wyschogrod, *The Body of Faith: Judaism as Corporal Election* (New York: Seabury Press, 1983); Frank E. Manuel, *The Broken Staff: Judaism through Christian Eyes* (Cambridge and London: Harvard University Press, 1992); Arthur Hertzberg, *Jews: The Essence and Character of a People* (San Francisco: Harper, 1998); David Weiss Halivni, *Revelation Restored: Divine Writ and Critical Responses*, Radical Traditions (Boulder, Colo., and Oxford: Westview Press, 1997).

The activity to which I here point indicates that there is a growing concern among Jews to examine the theology of their faith and to engage in theological discussions with Christians at a level which we must characterize as new. Stanley Hauerwas, who along with Peter Ochs is editing the series called Radical Traditions, has written an important foreword, "A Christian Perspective," to the book by Halivni in which he illuminatingly points to the impact of the Holocaust, and to what he regards as "the disestablishment of Christianity" in our time, as having compelled Jews to "do theology" and Christians to take that theology seriously (pp. xix–xxi). We cannot but hope that these new theological developments in Judaism will uncover connections — sinews — between the two faiths long tragically obscured by ignorance, misunderstanding, prejudice, and antagonism.

13. Perhaps Heschel himself would have agreed with this statement. He wrote eloquently of the "divinity of deeds" and the "wonder of doing" in Judaism. "A Jew is asked," he wrote, "to take a *leap of action* rather than a *leap of thought*" (*God in Search of Man*, 283). Heschel was concerned, of course, not to deny or even minimize the significance of halakah for Judaism, but to hold it in proper balance with haggadah. He traced the pan-halakic emphasis back to Spinoza down through Moses Mendelssohn: "With Spinoza, [Mendelssohn] maintains that Judaism asks for obedience to a law but not acceptance of doctrines. Judaism is not revealed religion in the usual sense of the term, but only *revealed legislation*, laws, commandments, and regulations, which were supernaturally given to the Jews through Moses. It demands no faith, no specific religious attitudes. The Spirit of Judaism is freedom in doctrine and conformity in action." [Heschel's text is here reproduced as it stands. Both quotations apparently are from Mendelssohn's *Jerusalem*, chap. 2. This is the only reference given by Heschel, who also referred to Hermann Cohen, *Die Religion der Vernunft*, 415ff. See Heschel, *God in Search of Man*, 321, 333.] How the question is exercising modern Jewry can be quickly gleaned from David Aronson, "Faith and Halakah," *Conservative Judaism* 21, no. 1 (1966): 34–48.

the mainstream of Judaism appears not to have taken kindly to this and has preferred to retain a kind of massive halakic simplicity, suspicious of speculation and uninterested in dogma. The actuality of obedience to the Torah, not theological interpretation of it, has been the hallmark of Judaism. The Torah is the peculiar property of Judaism: it is its heart. The clean challenge of the commandments (*Miṣwot*) cuts through all the sentimentality, mysticism, Gnosticism, and irrelevance of which, according to some Jews and many Christians, the Christian faith has been guilty. Leo Baeck especially has forcefully set forth the cleanliness of the commandment in Judaism over against the murky religiosity and the irrelevant piety of which Christianity is so often capable.[14]

And it is at this point that Christianity is usually claimed especially to differ from Judaism. "All the Christian objections to Judaism," wrote Schoeps, "and the corresponding Jewish replies pale into insignificance before the point of dispute . . . which was decisive in the life of Saul of Tarsus: whether the Law has not found its fulfillment and been abolished through belief in the Lord and Savior, Jesus of Nazareth."[15]

Now, the Christianity that emerges in the New Testament is not as opposed to Law as Baeck and other scholars, Christian no less than Jewish, have maintained. In Matthew, and even in Paul, there is room for Law, and for a new commandment in John. The early church often strikes one as a Bible class concerned with halakah. As Stendahl has suggested in his well-known book and in many publications, there is in the New Testament a halakic Christianity.[16] He has pointed out that whereas it has become customary for Christians to think of "Theology and Ethics" in that order, the opposite is true of Judaism, and in much of the New Testament including the Gospels.[17] The earliest Christians among other things were called those of "The Way" — of the Christian halakah. Probably this aspect of primitive Christianity has been neglected for a simple reason. The kerygma has so dominated recent scholarship that the didache, although recognized, has been unconsciously and consciously relegated to a secondary status. This is not the place to assess the role of the kerygma in the New Testament. Suffice that it has too often been rigidly and even wholly separated from the total life of the church

---

14. See Leo Baeck's chapters, "The Faith of Paul," "Mystery and Commandment," and "Romantic Religion," in *Judaism and Christianity: Essays*, translated with an introduction by Walter Kaufmann (Philadelphia: Jewish Publication Society of America, 1958), 139–292. On Leo Baeck, see now the excellent treatment of his work by J. Louis Martyn in *Jewish Perspectives on Christianity*, ed. Fritz A. Rothschild (New York: Crossroad, 1990), 21–41.

15. Hans Joachim Schoeps, *The Jewish-Christian Argument: A History of Theologies in Conflict*, trans. D. E. Green (New York: Holt, Rinehart & Winston, 1963), 40.

16. Krister Stendahl, *The School of St. Matthew and Its Use of the Old Testament* (Uppsala: C. W. K. Gleerup, 1954; 2d ed., 1968).

17. See Stendahl's article "Thy Kingdom Come on Earth," *The American Baptist Quarterly* 14, no. 1 (1995): 14–21, esp. p. 17.

and presented as a phenomenon in a vacuum. In fact, the kerygma was only one aspect of the life of primitive Christianity embedded in and accompanied by a rich communal life — a "way." This "way" has continued to inform the life of the church throughout the centuries. I am not competent to trace this fact historically in its various forms — in the imitation of Christ and otherwise. But one may hazard the statement that it is witness to the "way" among Christians, and not only a kerygma proclaimed, that has most furthered the Christian faith. In any case, it is well to recognize that a complete separation of Judaism as a religion of Torah from Christianity as a religion of dogma cannot be justified. Christianity too has a halakah.[18]

But once this be admitted, it has further to be stated at once that, in fact, Christianity in the course of time did develop dogmatic systems in a way which Judaism did not. I am not sufficiently versed in Jewish history to explain why this is so, that is, why Judaism did not succumb to refined dogmatic speculation as did Christianity (although Lurianic Qabbalah and other developments should not be overlooked). In addition to the historical considerations suggested above, one may hazard the suggestion that the Jewish halakah sufficiently safeguarded the uniqueness of Jewish faith. In the Torah, Judaism possessed a wall of fire which needed no dogmatic justification to surround and safeguard it, so effective was it. "What is the Jewish way to God? It is not a way of ascending the ladder of speculation? Our understanding of God is not the triumphal outcome of an assault upon the riddles of the universe or a donation we receive in return for intellectual surrender. Our understanding comes by the way of *mitzwah*." So wrote Heschel in "No Time for Neutrality."[19]

The most obvious reason why Christianity developed into dogmatic systems is that as the Palestinian faith spread throughout the Greco-Roman world, without the benefit of a full-blooded unmistakable fence such as the Jewish Torah, it had to define itself over against the various forces that threatened it. The evolution of the New Testament canon, the episcopate and, especially, in this connection, creed or dogma is the response of Christianity to Gnostic and other well-known pressures. Gradually the church became

---

18. For the justification for most of the above paragraph, see my *The Setting of the Sermon on the Mount* (Cambridge: Cambridge University Press, 1964), and Eero Repo, *Der Weg als Selbstbezeichnung des Urchristentums* (Helsinki: Suomalainen Tiedeakatemica, 1964). Reinhold Niebuhr, however, warned me of the dangers that lurk in the sentence (which I first used at Harvard and have here changed): "Christianity too is a halakah." He reminded me of the radical criticism of the Law implied and sometimes expressed in the ministry of Jesus and in the epistles of Paul. His point may be met, I think, by claiming that halakah in Christianity is not the means of salvation so much as its accompaniment. Christianity must always be antilegalistic even though it must never be antinomian. On the other hand, it should not be overlooked that for Judaism the Law is an expression of grace as well as a means to grace. The true emphasis in this matter is difficult of achievement.

19. In *Moral Grandeur and Spiritual Audacity*, 137.

Hellenized, and with Hellenization came orthodoxy, which culminated in the great dogmatic statements of the councils. *Belief,* not halakah, became important. The increasing separation of the church from its Hebraic root in the synagogue meant increasingly the predominance of dogma over Torah. I am tempted to think that, along with this separation, the threat of meaninglessness in the church increased. Judaism has always managed to retain a massive awareness of the purpose of God, an awareness that made refined theological speculation unnecessary. Christianity, more exposed to the winds of the world, perhaps, has had to battle more directly the meaninglessness of things, and this fight is one of the sources of its dogmatic evolution. It had to impose a meaning, creeds or dogmas, on meaninglessness in a way the more rooted synagogue could afford to neglect.

Has not the time now come for the church to recognize all this fully and by renewing its contact with the synagogue to restore the balance between kerygma and didache, dogma and Torah?[20]

II

Let us turn to the next point. Broadly speaking only, I have suggested that it is justifiable to think of Christianity in terms of dogma and of Judaism in terms of Torah. A concomitant of this is a factor which, more than any other, has always impressed me very forcibly. It is the absence in Judaism of a *crippling* sense of sin and guilt. One can hardly turn to any of the Christian classics, from the first century down through Augustine to Luther and thence to Barth and Niebuhr, without at times being overwhelmed by the profound sense of sin which everywhere apparently accompanies Christianity.

True, the sense of sin is not absent from the Old Testament, as in the familiar Psalm 139 and elsewhere. "Can the leopard change his spots?" is an Old Testament verse (Jer. 13:23). The Day of Atonement is a central festival of Judaism. True also that the power of the unconscious in Freud has been traced to roots in Jewish thought about the *Yeṣer ha-ra'*.[21] But by and large it

---

20. C. H. Dodd, in *Gospel and Law* (New York, 1951), and *"Ennomos Christou,"* in *Studia Paulina in honorem Johannis de Zwaan septuaginarii* (Haarlem: De Errem F. Bohn N.V., 1953), 96ff., reveals a striking sensitivity to this need to do greater justice to the halakic aspect of Christianity, as over against his clear separation of kerygma and didache in his *Apostolic Preaching and Its Developments: Three Lectures* (New York: Harper and Brothers, 1949). The fence of the Torah to surround Jews, it might be argued, is little different from the various customs which other ethnic groups (national and other) have observed in order to preserve their several identities. Doubtless there is an element of ethnicity in the Jewish concern to observe the fence of the Torah. But, as far as I am aware, the Jews have more unmistakably and peculiarly rooted their "fence" in a divine sanction — the giving of the Torah on Sinai — than have other groups, much as they too may have regarded their peculiar customs as ordained by their gods.

21. See N. P. Williams, *The Ideas of the Fall and of Original Sin* (London and New York: Longmans, Green, 1927).

is an invincible hope that wells up in Rabbinic Judaism. The commandment was given to be obeyed, and the implication is that man can obey it. Jewish history presents the most incredible record of justification for utter despair and yet of the persistence of hope. The evil *yeṣer* is recognized; the fall of Adam was momentous in its consequences; everything is determined. Yes: but free will is given (cf. *Aboth* 3:19). I do not recall any rabbinic passage where there is a pervading sense of the miasma of sin or anything like a doctrine of original sin. Sin is a sore to which the ointment of the Torah may be applied: significantly the evil *yeṣer* is an impulse, not a condition or state, as, for example, is sin in Paul. There are, it is true, passages in the Dead Sea Scrolls which approach the Christian sense of the miasma of sin, but even here sin is essentially transgression.[22] The air that Judaism breathes is that of the commandment — direct, fresh, simple. There is in Judaism, as compared with Christianity, little introspection, little preoccupation with conscience, for which it has no word, comparatively little torturing of the soul. Asceticism, for example, is largely alien to Judaism, although known to it, and is much more typical of what Jews now regard as the extremism of Christianity.[23]

How different is the history of Christianity where Sin, with a capital S, has been recognized as "exceeding sinful" from the beginning, where "the bondage of the will" is a familiar doctrine. I suggest that where "optimism" of the kind that pervades Judaism, despite the tragedies of its history, is dominant, dogma is likely to be secondary. It is the awareness of Sin that makes the theologian.[24] Dogma develops where there is torture, moral and intel-

---

22. See, e.g., the closing psalm of the Manual of Discipline. The pertinent passage reads as follows in Millar Burrows's translation (*The Dead Sea Scrolls* [New York: Viking Press, 1955], 388): "But I belong to wicked mankind, to the company of erring flesh, my iniquities, my transgression, my sin, with the iniquity of my heart belong to the company of worms and those who walk in darkness. For the way of a man is not his own ... (1QS xi 9f.). On all this section, see A. Heschel in *The Insecurity of Freedom*, cited above in n. 5.

23. See my article on "Conscience" in *IDB*; also Steven Fraade, "Ascetical Aspects of Ancient Judaism," in *Jewish Spirituality: From the Bible through the Middle Ages*, ed. Arthur Green (New York: Crossroad, 1986), 253–88.

24. In the colloquium I said, "It is Sin that makes the theologian" — using a shorthand for: "It is the awareness of Sin that makes the theologian." The phrase "Sin makes the theologian" (*Peccatum facit theologum*) is an unconscious corruption on my part of a Latin scholastic tag which I learned, long ago, at the feet of J. S. Whale; that is, *Pectus facit theologum*. I did not recall that he gave the source of the tag, so I wrote to him, and he replied: "I don't know how we've managed to get this a bit muddled, as though the old tag said *Peccatum* rather than *Pectus*. And I don't know who first used [or, should I say, *coined*] this enduring phrase. I shouldn't be surprised to find it in James Denney's Cunningham Lectures on Reconciliation — in the chapter on Augustine, where the great saint/sinner is described as having "an experiencing nature." You must drop the actual phrase, of course — "Sin makes the theologian"; but it is a false reading which is nevertheless saying something true. Christian theology presupposes and begins with sin, and man's immemorial predicament. Hence the opening words of Milton's P. L.... I can't plead guilty myself to having misquoted *pectus* as *peccatum* in any lecture I've ever given; but I remember how Wheeler Robinson used to remark with a chuckle about the inspired character

lectual. The introspective conscience of the West, which is alien to Judaism, is surely one of the sources of the dogmatic concentration of Christianity. The robust, halakic character of Judaism has not been conducive to theological subtlety, of any systematic kind, at least. The commandment to be done, not the creedal conundrum to be unraveled, has been the central concern of Judaism. I should be prepared to say that the chief differences in ethos between Jewish and Christian life, worship, and thought are all colored by the difference in intensity with which the two religions have wrestled with sin.

III

I move now to the third point. In this discussion it has been agreed that "Torah" and "dogma" are terms that can represent Judaism and Christianity. I assume also that the basic structure of Christianity in most of the New Testament documents is to a great extent parallel to that of Judaism. By and large the Christian dispensation or event was understood as a new exodus from the realm of slavery to sin, the old Egypt, to the life of a new Canaan. Christianity, it may be argued, emerges as a specific kind of Judaism with a new exodus and a new Moses and a new Sinai "in Christ." What, then, is the difference between the two faiths? This can be expressed somewhat as follows. Whereas in the complex often referred to as the exodus, at which Israel's redemption was wrought, Judaism came to place more and more emphasis on the Torah — that is, the demand uttered on Sinai, which was itself a gift, the figure of Moses being a colossus because he mediated the Torah — the church, as it looked back to the new exodus wrought in Christ, first remembered the person of Jesus Christ, through whom the new exodus was wrought, and who thus came to have for the church the significance of Torah. This is why ultimately the tradition in Judaism culminates in the Mishnah, a code of halakot, and in Christianity in the Gospels, in which all is subservient to Jesus as Lord.[25] What then is the essential dogma that has replaced the Torah of Judaism? As I argued in my work *Paul and Rabbinic Judaism*, it is the claim that the Torah now is Jesus of Nazareth, the Christ. There is a new ultimate in Jesus: the finality of Christ replaces the finality of Torah. To claim that

---

of certain false readings in scripture" (in a letter dated 3 February 1967). The horror expressed at the idea that "Sin makes the theologian" by some of the Jewish participants in the colloquium was typical, while the silent acceptance of it by the Christians was significant. In any case the idea is not alien to the history of Christian thought, however infelicitously I expressed it. As J. S. Whale also writes: "Luther's *pecca fortiter*, like Thomas's "O felix culpa!..." is a monstrously provocative statement of the truth that Christian Theology begins with peccatum!"

25. Much of this formulation I owe to Professor David Daube. As to how all this bears on the question of supersession, I draw attention to the penetrating and important study by Krister Stendahl, "Qumran and Supersessionism — and the Road Not Taken," where he argues for the need to disentangle Judaism and Christianity, in *Princeton Theological Seminary Bulletin* 19, no. 2 (July 1998): 134–42.

the gulf between Judaism and Christianity is merely a schism is to imply that this new finality can be expressed in terms consonant with Judaism. Can this be asserted?

The finality of Christ, to judge by the New Testament, can only be established even for Christians in terms of the Torah itself. It is a familiar fact that early Christians searched the scriptures in order to show that the Torah and the Prophets pointed to Jesus. Christianity from the first involved the interpretation of the scriptures, just as Judaism also involved an interpretation of them. The interpretation of the Old Testament variously given in the New Testament is governed by the assumption that Jesus is the Messiah. Throughout the New Testament, appeal is made to the Old. The life, death, and resurrection of Jesus of Nazareth and the emergence of the church are understood in terms of the Old Testament as its fulfillment. But although the New Testament writers draw upon the Old Testament to illumine what had happened in the gospel, they do not draw on all the Old Testament indiscriminately. There were some prophecies which they ignored and others which they modified. Not all Old Testament expectations were suitable for the events which they were interpreting. The New Testament is not dominated by the Old. It is the gospel itself that provides the pattern for the understanding of the Old: the New Testament interprets the Old in the light of Christ. It does not merely interpret Christ in the light of the Old Testament. To put the matter in another way, the New Testament does not paint a picture of its Lord out of all the colors found in the Old Testament. It uses the Old Testament selectively, in a creative way; it rejects some colors and uses others in the light of Jesus, the Christ.

And given the Christian presuppositions, this christological principle of interpretation is convincing — but only given the Christian presuppositions. Recall Scholem's view that Christian exegesis of the Old Testament interprets it against its very grain.[26] That is, it is forced and, therefore, unacceptable exegesis: it imputes to the Old Testament a meaning it never intended. Jewish interpretation, on the other hand, springs naturally from the text itself: it is native, indigenous. The kind of schematization that is found, for example, in Romans 9–11, which Christians have always found illuminating and inspiring in its vast historical and theological sweep, is a falsification of the intent of the Old Testament. The issue of the interpretation of scripture, both in its wider sweep and in matters of minute detail, has cropped up again and again

26. G. Scholem, "Religious Authority and Mysticism," *Commentary* 38 (November 1964): 31–39. Contrast with Scholem's view that of a Christian scholar, Gerhard von Rad: "The question should be put the other way around: how was it possible for the Old Testament traditions, and all the narratives, prayers, and predictions, to be taken over by the New Testament? This could not have happened if the Old Testament writings had not themselves contained pointers to Christ and been hermeneutically adapted to such a merger" (*Old Testament Theology*, vol. 2 [New York: Harper & Row, 1965], 333).

in Jewish-Christian dialogue and it still does and always will. It will necessarily remain with us because the christological principle of the interpretation of the Old Testament is implied in most forms of traditional and in all forms of authentic Christianity.

And, despite its rejection by Jewry, this implies that Christian thought, christological and other, can be expressed in categories derived from the root of Judaism, which is the Old Testament. And it is arguable that Jewish categories are, in themselves, sufficient to account for the essentials of later Christian dogma, even that of the Trinity. Daniélou, for example, has sought to show how, right down to the Council of Nicaea, Semitic categories were influential in the formulation of Christian dogma.[27] On this view, Christianity can be regarded as essentially a schismatic branch of Judaism. But is it only this?

IV

This brings me, finally, to the term "schism." Although such a model is attractive and has influenced the creative thinking of men like Rosenzweig and Barth,[28] I would merely ask the question, in conclusion, whether the New Testament itself supports the notion that the relation between Christianity and Judaism is that of a "schism." The New Testament has, almost traditionally, been understood to present that relationship in at least three ways.

First, there are documents in which there is little awareness of any essential break between Judaism and Christianity. Jesus has come as the Messiah, but the essential structure of Judaism has remained virtually unaltered. Acceptance of Jesus does not mean any radical break with Jewish practice or belief. All that has happened in Christianity is that Judaism is now in possession of its long-awaited Messiah, but his advent has not demanded perceptible change. The earliest Christians, Judaizers, and Jewish Christians who held this position have left few traces in the New Testament itself, although their presence can easily be discerned moving shadowily behind its pages, especially in the Pauline epistles. But they have left us noncanonical materials of fairly substantial extent. The Christianity which these reveal has been

---

27. Jean Daniélou, *Théologie du Judéo-Christianisme: Histoire des doctrines Chrétiennes avant Nicée*, vol. 1 (Tournai, Belgium: Desclée and Cie, 1957). On the first page he writes: "La théologie chrétienne utilisera à partir des Apologistes les instruments intellectuels de la philosophie grecque. Mais auparavant il y a eu une première théologie de structure sémitique." [Christian theology will find it useful to begin with the conceptual tools of the Greek philosophy of the Apologists. But before this there had been a first theology of Semitic structure.]

28. Professor Miskotte's paper did so interpret Barth with references to *Kirchliche Dogmatik* III:3, 247; IV:1, 749; IV:3b, 1005f.

examined anew and given great prominence by Schoeps.[29] He found Jewish Christianity to have been the chief bulwark in the primitive church against Marcion and the threat of Gnosticism. That Jewish Christianity disappeared almost without vestige is no indication of its real significance in history. From its point of view, the Christian faith is a reformation or revision of Judaism, involving little radical newness, that is, it is a schism. It is, indeed, merely Judaism with an addendum — Jesus the Messiah. We may agree with Schoeps that the disappearance of Jewish Christianity may be no criterion for what it connoted in its heyday, but many have regarded the disappearance as almost inevitable because it provided no ultimate *raison d'être* for Christianity alongside Judaism.

Second, at the opposite extreme, we find, in certain documents of the New Testament, the claim that the relation of Christianity to Judaism is one of sharp antithesis. This comes to clearest expression in the Fourth Gospel, where there is a sustained interpretation of the Christian faith which emphasizes that it challenges Judaism. On this view, Christianity is a revolution which so transforms Judaism that the latter can be regarded as radically reoriented. Yet it is true that the Fourth Gospel urges that salvation is from the Jews and uses categories that are derived from Judaism to expound Jesus' significance. But it does also look away from Judaism in its existing form. The newness of the Gospel is such that the old order of the waterpots has given place to the new wine of the Gospel. The quintessence of the Fourth Gospel's attitude may perhaps be understood in the story of Mary and the beloved disciple at the cross (John 19:25–27). Near the cross where Jesus hung stood his mother, with her sister, Mary, wife of Cleopas, and Mary of Magdala. Jesus saw his mother, with the disciple whom he loved standing beside her. He said to her, "Mother, there is your son"; and to the disciple, "There is your mother"; and from that moment the disciple took her into his home. Mary is the mother of Jesus. She is now handed over to the respectful care of his disciple. If Mary here stands for Judaism, the implication is clear. Judaism is the aged mother. She is honored and cherished, but a new order to which she has given birth has emerged. Mary — Judaism — is not rejected by, nor does she reject, the new order: they become mutually supportive. Such is the relation between Judaism and Christianity.[30]

---

29. *Theologie und Geschichte des Judenchristentums* (Tübingen: Mohr, 1949).

30. I used this symbolic interpretation in my work (intended for a popular audience) *Invitation to the New Testament* (1966), 492. The symbolism is suggested by A. Loisy, who is referred to, without specific annotation, by E. C. Hoskyns and F. N. Davey, *The Fourth Gospel* (1947), 530. See further, B. R. Gaventa, *Mary: Glimpses of the Mother of Jesus* (Columbia: University of South Carolina Press, 1995), 90–95. Instead of having Mary represent Judaism, Gaventa presents a more cautious view of what Mary signifies in this passage. See now the excellent discussion by Richard Hays on "Anti-Judaism and Ethnic Conflict," in *The Moral Vision of the New Testament: Community, Cross, New Creation* (San Francisco: Harper, 1996), 406–23, in which he discusses

To some, then, the gospel is a revision, if not a radical one, of Judaism; to others the gospel challenges Judaism antithetically. The third attitude is best represented perhaps in Matthew 5:17: "I came not to destroy but to complete." The immediate context in Matthew concerns the Law, but the attitude can be extended to cover the whole of Judaism. The Christian gospel has brought the intent of Judaism to full fruition. It has not only fulfilled the Jewish hope for a Messiah; it has brought with it a new Temple, a new Law, a new sacrifice, a new people. In all these cases the adjective "new" is meant to indicate not antithesis but fulfillment. What in Judaism was "shadowy," tentative, and preparatory is now fully realized in Christ. Readers of the Epistle to the Hebrews do not need to be reminded of the way in which the theology of that epistle is built upon the theology of Judaism as its "completion."

There is one figure, possibly the major figure of the New Testament, apart of course from Jesus, whom it is difficult to place in any of the categories indicated. Paul has been regarded, particularly by Jewish scholars, but also by Protestants dominated by Luther, as having broken with Judaism in a radical fashion. In particular, Jewish scholars have accused Paul of breaking down the fence of the Torah, and Christian scholars have set his doctrine of "justification by faith" over against the emphasis in Judaism on "salvation by work." But there can be little question that Paul remained throughout his life, in his own mind, within the pale of Judaism. Christ was for him the end of Judaism in the sense not of its annulment but of its fulfillment. By and large, we should classify Paul with Hebrews and Matthew rather than with the Fourth Gospel. To Paul, also, Christianity is not the antithesis of Judaism but its culmination.

The New Testament, then, presents us with three main alternatives, only one of which, the first mentioned above, justifies the use of the term "schism." I think it must be clearly recognized that there came a point when the two faiths — conceptually as well as historically — parted company, radically and not merely schismatically: that was where Christian dogmatic developments made the gulf between the two religions so deep that the term

---

the theme of Christian responses to Judaism more fully than we could do here. In particular, he deals with the Gospel of Luke far more adequately. In dealing with Romans 11, he urges that "Gentile Christians should not fall prey to the supersessionist illusion that we are the culmination of God's saving work." But in his treatment of the Fourth Gospel, while he rightly points out that in that Gospel "the Church's bitter polemic against the Synagogue is raised to the highest pitch in the New Testament" (424), Hays does not explicitly disavow supersessionist language. We may ask: do not his words about Romans 11 also apply to John? We cannot speak unqualifiedly of the supersession of Judaism by the gospel in the Fourth Gospel either: there is a commonality between Judaism and Christianity which there also is retained. The term "supersession" is extremely ambiguous. To abandon its use carries its own problems, as Bruce Marshall has forcibly set forth in *The Cambridge Companion to Christian Doctrine,* ed. Colin Gunton (Cambridge: Cambridge University Press, 1997), 81–101; see chap. 5, "Christ and the Cultures: The Jewish People and Christian Theology," with very helpful appended bibliography. However, the importance of the *Shema* in Christianity as in Judaism lends them both an unmistakable commonality.

"schism" becomes inapplicable. As long as Jesus was interpreted in strictly messianic categories and, indeed, in terms of Torah, a merely schismatic relationship between Judaism and Christianity is conceivable. But once Jesus is claimed to be God incarnate, and this is already the case in parts of the New Testament itself, then[31] the Rubicon has been crossed and Christianity stands outside the conceivable confines of Judaism, the quintessence of which is expressed in the *Shema*. If Christianity be interpreted kerygmatically in terms of the divinity of Jesus, the Christ, then we must speak of a new religion, not merely of a schismatic emergence. No Christian who has ever engaged in even the slightest discussion with Jews can doubt this. The doctrine of the incarnation is the Rubicon between the two faiths.

The question then emerges whether Christianity can ever be expressed in nonincarnational terms which would lessen the gulf between it and Judaism. There are two possibilities to be considered.

The first possibility is to recognize frankly that there is a viable interpretation of the gospel which does not require the affirmation of the historic creeds, couched as they are in mythological language which needs to be demythologized. It would seem that Bultmann, for example, if we are to follow one of his interpreters, did in fact give up the great dogmatic formulations of the Christian faith. Thus Ian Henderson writes:

> More important is perhaps to ask whether Bultmann's position in the controversy about myths leaves open the kind of Christology we find in the statements of Nicaea and Chalcedon. I do not think it does.... Now this issue is quite vital. For all signs are that Christianity is going to split on the Christologies of Nicaea and Chalcedon....[32]

Because it, apparently, removes the offense of Christology, could Bultmann's understanding of Christianity, then, be acceptable to Judaism, and could it be described as merely a schismatic phenomenon? Apparently so. The Jesus of Bultmann stands within Judaism. But here we are faced with a paradox. While for him Jesus stands within Judaism, Bultmann's understanding of the Christian faith is so divorced from the Old Testament and Judaism that the Jesus he presents is divested of any serious significance for Judaism and is thus, from the Jewish point of view, rendered innocuous. A Jesus who is merely a bearer of the Word and not the Word himself — and especially as the bearer of a Word not fundamentally rooted in Judaism, such as he is for Bultmann — offers no challenge to Judaism as such. In such a view of Jesus the Rubicon between Judaism and Christianity is not so much confronted as bypassed. The theological barrier to a Jewish-Christian *rapprochement* in the

---

31. On this, see R. E. Brown, "Does the New Testament Call Jesus God?" *Theological Studies* 26 (1965): 545–73.

32. *Rudolf Bultmann* (Richmond: John Knox Press, 1966).

dogmatic history of Christianity is thereby obviated; but it is also, from the Jewish point of view, trivialized. The possibility raised by Bultmann's view of Jesus not only raises in an acute form the question whether the dogmatic history of Christianity can or should be reversed, but also reveals the question whether, if such were the case, it would really interest Judaism.

The other possibility, which is hesitatingly raised here, is that which would interpret Christianity, not in kerygmatic, but in halakic terms. Let us again raise the question how far Christianity can cease to affirm the historic creeds and yet remain itself. That is, would it be possible to conceive of Christianity adequately, not primarily as a way of belief, a creed, but rather as a way of life, as *agape?* It is certain that if Christianity finds the essence of its life in creeds such as those of Nicaea and Chalcedon, there can be no ultimate *rapprochement* with Judaism. On the other hand, could not a halakically oriented Christianity be at home with Judaism or, at least, remain as a merely schismatic aspect of it? The answer to this question also, to judge from the history of the church, would seem to be that even a halakically centered Christianity has had christological implications that Judaism has not been able to accept. Even so conservatively halakic a figure as James, the brother of the Lord, was finally unacceptable to Judaism and died a martyr's death. How much less is any halakic Christianity conceivable in our time!

We seem to be driven to one conclusion. There is a christological factor, however expressed, in Christianity which — to use a phrase borrowed from Reinhold Niebuhr — is nonnegotiable even with its mother faith, just as there is a centrality of Torah in Judaism which is nonnegotiable. The dogmatic development of much of Christianity, in short, remains as the barrier to reducing the relation between the two faiths to a mere schism. But this, in itself, is not the tragedy of the history of the relations between the two faiths. Rather is it that the spirit of the halakah demanded by both has not been more truly pursued by both, so as to make possible, within their dogmatic difference, mutual tolerance, respect, learning, and even affection. At least the time is long overdue for Christians to recognize that the attempt to overcome Torah by dogma is long past: its almost total, ignominious failure is evident. This already points forward the emergence of a new era or at least new possibilities for Christian-Jewish relations.

Postscript

Since this last sentence was written in 1968, there have been significant developments. In certain aspects at least, this new era to which I here refer can be regarded as a return, *mutatis mutandis,* to a previous one — the pre-Constantinian era and even the immediately following centuries. Our understanding of the parting of the ways between Judaism and Christianity has been deepened.[33] From the beginning, the differing attitudes toward Judaism within the Christian movement were even more varied than previously recognized. In Section IV above we indicated three attitudes toward Judaism among Christians in the New Testament. For some their new faith was a revision of their mother faith; for others, an antithesis to it; and for others still, the completion of it. But these three attitudes did not exhaust the relationships between Christians and Jews: a far more complex situation is here oversimplified. As we have implied above, concentration on what was often regarded as a well-defined or itemized kerygma (brilliantly and very influentially set forth by C. H. Dodd especially)[34] may have led scholars to emphasize too exclusively the controversial and adversarial and even antagonistic and polemical approaches among early Christians to Jews.

In the early centuries Christians and Jews were not always in dogmatic conflict. James Parkes long ago urged that "there is every reason to believe that the common people [Christian and Jewish] were much more friendly with each other than the leaders approved of...."[35] This was noted also by Marcel Simon.[36] The Swedish scholar J. Jervell has emphasized the preoccupation of many Christians with the Jewish people and with the interplay between the rejection and acceptance of the gospel by Jews.[37] J. Louis Martyn has urged that there was not only opposition to Paul among Jewish Christians but also a law-observant mission to Gentiles.[38] The complexity of the situation is set forth in an article by R. E. Brown called "Not

---

33. See especially James D. G. Dunn, *The Parting of the Ways between Christianity and Judaism and Their Significance for the Character of Christianity* (Philadelphia: Trinity Press International, 1991).

34. *The Apostolic Preaching and Its Developments, with an Appendix on Eschatology and History* (London: Hodder and Stroughton, 1936). See also my "A Quest to Be Resumed in New Testament Studies," in *Christian Origins and Judaism* (London: Darton, Longman & Todd, 1962), 1–17; and H. J. Cadbury, "Acts and Eschatology," in *The Background of the New Testament and Its Eschatology*, ed. W. D. Davies and David Daube (Cambridge: Cambridge University Press, 1956), 300–322.

35. *The Conflict of the Church and the Synagogue* (Philadelphia: Jewish Publication Society of America, 1934), 94.

36. *Verus Israel: A Study of the Relations between Christians and Jews in the Roman Empire* (C.E. 135–435) (Oxford: Oxford University Press, 1986), 232.

37. See Jervell's many works, and most recently his *The Theology of the Acts of the Apostles* (Cambridge: Cambridge University Press, 1996).

38. See Martyn's Anchor Bible Commentary, *Galatians: A New Translation and Commentary* (New York: Doubleday, 1997), and "A Law-Observant Mission to Gentiles," in *Theological Issues in the Letter of Paul* (Nashville: Abingdon Press, 1997), 7–24. The brief introductory statement in part 1 of this volume, on "Paul and Christian Judaism" (305), is crucial, as is the whole of Martyn's work in this area, which is rich, subtle, and stimulating. He sets forth the agenda for much in the next stage of Pauline studies. Is David Daube correct in speaking of "New Testament Judaism," that is, that Paul too remains within Judaism, or is Martyn right in confining "Christian Judaism" to the opponents of Paul and to those who share their position? Is Martyn justified in his use of "Christian Judaism" only for Paul's opponents?

Jewish Christianity and Gentile Christianity, but Types of Jewish/Gentile Christianity."[39]

Recently several striking studies have further emphasized this complexity: first, a brilliant chapter by James D. G. Dunn called "Two Covenants in One: The Interdependence of Jewish and Christian Identity."[40] Supplying cogent supporting evidence, he writes as follows:

> In the early centuries of the common era, there is clear evidence of more diverse forms of both Judaism and Christianity. In particular, in the middle ground between them there were evidently many who did not think of themselves as *either* Christian *or* Jew. . . . there may have been an important dimension of both Judaism and Christianity which was marginalized and lost sight of in those early centuries by the emerging orthodoxies on each side, and which needs to be recovered now if we are to understand both Christianity and Judaism and their formative periods aright.[41]

In the period referred to, church and synagogue, Christianity and Judaism, were less separate and distinct than has traditionally been held.

Second, Stephen G. Wilson, a Canadian scholar, in an excellent, comprehensive study, while recognizing "elements of Christian anti-Semitism that were later to become standard fare," concludes as follows:

> Yet when we stand back from the detail, our survey of this crucial century [70–170 C.E.] suggests a considerable complexity. Even toward the end, we find an array of attitudes and motives that resist simple definition. Reducing the story to a single issue, trend or cause not only misleads but also hides the rich and subtle variations to which the evidence points. And this perhaps is the only overarching conclusion we can draw.[42]

Finally, in a forthcoming article, which he has kindly allowed me to consult, Dale C. Allison points out that the Epistle of James, which is usually dated toward the end of the first century, only once mentions the name of Jesus (in 1:1; the occurrence in 2:1 is probably not original) and is deliberately silent about the major elements of the Christian message or kerygma. Contrasting the situation in Matthew (which reflects tensions after 70 C.E. between certain Jewish Christians and the rabbinic authorities and synagogues under their influence) with that facing James, Allison writes:

---

39. CBQ 45, no. 1 (January 1983): 74–78.

40. In *Geschichte Tradition Reflexion: Festschrift für Martin Hengel zum 70 Geburtstag, 111, Fruhes Christentum, heraus gegeben von Hermann Lichtenberger* (Tübingen: J. C. B. Mohr/Paul Siebeck, 1996), 97–102.

41. Ibid., 106–7.

42. *Related Strangers: Jews and Christians, 70–170 C.E.* (Minneapolis: Fortress Press, 1995), 30.

[James] likely emerged from a group that, in its place and time, whether that time was before or after Matthew, was still seeking to keep relations irenic. It was yet within the synagogue (2:2) and so still trying to get along as best as possible with those who did not believe Jesus to be the Messiah. In such a context the Epistle of James makes good sense. The emphasis upon convictions rooted in the common religiosity of the wisdom literature, the omission of potentially divisive Christian affirmations, and the passages that can be read one way by a Christian and another way by a non-Christian would make for good will on the part of the latter and also provide edification for the former. James communicated, among other things, that *Jesus' followers are not apostates from Judaism, but rather faithful members of the synagogue who live according to the Jewish moral tradition, are faithful to the Torah, and oppose those who want — as no doubt was rumored of Paul and his disciples — to divide faith from works.* (Italics added)

That a document such as the Epistle of James, understood rightly, as we believe, in the way Allison proposes, was canonized in the fourth century, implies that for a long time there persisted a sensitive and respectful attitude toward Judaism among numbers of Christians. Allison's work especially reinforces the view that kerygmatic critical confrontation was not the only stance taken by Christians as they encountered Judaism.

All this raises the question whether the position (as we urged above in this essay) that the dogmatic development of Christianity remains the barrier to reducing the relation between Christianity and Judaism to a mere schism is valid. Have we too much overlooked that the New Testament canon itself contains elements which would question such a position? Overemphasis on the kerygmatic and dogmatic alone must not be said to have always separated Christians from Jews: they could live together, sometimes at least, in brotherly peace despite dogmatic differences.[43] The kind of sensitive approach to the mother faith witnessed to in the Epistle of James recalls the passage in John 19:25–27, where the relation to the mother faith on the part of Christians was thought of in terms of a family. The presence of Christian dogma alone, set against Torah, did not necessarily separate Jews from Christians and Christians from Jews. Nor should this altogether surprise us. James Parkes, among others, long ago made clear that factors other than dogma and Torah entered into Christian-Jewish relationships to vitiate them. Social, economic, polit-

---

43. The archaeological work of my colleague Eric Meyers has reinforced this position. With the only exception being that relating to Capernaum, the evidence points to much commonality of life and worship between Jews and Christians. They shared common places of worship and common endeavors. See Eric Meyers, "Early Judaism and Christianity in the Light of Archaeology," *Biblical Archaeologist* (1988): 69–79; "Jews and Christians in a Roman World," *Archaeology* (1989): 27–33 (with L. Michael White).

ical, and even intellectual factors have impinged upon those relationships from the first century onward. Christian dogmatic antagonism to Judaism has to be closely related to such factors. Before Constantine, and even for some time later, the gulf between Torah and dogma did not always spell hatred.[44]

The recognition of this fact and that Christian theology never has existed in a vacuum, but has always been exposed to the kind of factors we have pointed to, strengthens the hope that there can be a new era when that theology need not necessarily be opposed to Judaism, a new era when we can speak — as has my great teacher David Daube — of a "New Testament Judaism." That an immensely sensitive Jew such as David Daube, in a century in which his people have suffered more than in any other, was led to use such a phrase (which at first encounter must appear to many Jews and Christians as astounding) must cause pause, before we further congeal the opposition between Torah and dogma.[45] That this need not happen we can also hope, because of the new spirit of theological openness that has recently burgeoned in Judaism[46] and because of the new openness in contrition which many in the Christian world have in our time manifested.

---

44. See my early essay "Chosen People: The Approach to Anti-Semitism" for some bibliography, *The Congregational Quarterly* (London) 26, no. 4 (October 1948): 327–41.

45. C. H. Dodd, friend and colleague of David Daube, in reflecting on his own religious background wrote: "Its theoretical basis I can only describe as an etiolated Calvinism drained of the good red blood of dogmatic theology. It is strange to think on how small an allowance of positive dogma a religious system could maintain itself." See F. W. Dillistone, *C. H. Dodd: Interpreter of the New Testament* (Grand Rapids, Mich.: Eerdmans, 1977), 33–34. This, coming from an intensely Christian mind, demands pondering on the comparative importance of precise dogma and the life of the community — the church or synagogue — in maintaining religious life. See also the introduction to *The Collected Papers of David Daube on the New Testament*, ed. Calum Carmichael (forthcoming), where the attitude of Dodd and Daube to religions other than their own is set forth.

46. We refer elsewhere in this volume to a new spirit of theological openness in Judaism; see esp. n. 12 above.

Chapter 4

Law in Christianity

To a biblical student the study of Christian ethics in our time presents a confused spectacle. He cannot but be aware of a profound dichotomy within it. On the one hand, the Christian gospel is understood in many ethical writings as a gospel of liberation from Law, not only in its Jewish form, but, it would appear, in any form. Protestantism has witnessed a growing emphasis on an ethic without principles, an ethic governed by its context, often with little reference to the moral teachings of its own foundation text, the Bible. Catholicism has often become critical of its own tradition of moral theology and casuistry and disenchanted with Law, canonical and other.

On the other hand, in biblical studies there has been in many quarters a growing appreciation of the significance of Law not only in the Old Testament but in the New. One of the most illuminating developments in Old Testament studies has been the rehabilitation of the Law. Through the work of Alt, von Rad, Noth, Clements, Buber, Daube, and others, the influence of the covenant with its Law even on the prophets, whom we were formerly taught to regard as the opponents of the priests and their Law, has become clear. The prophets are emerging as teachers of the Law. Zimmerli has given a fascinating account of all this in *The Law and the Prophets* (1956). And just as the prophets have been connected with the Law that preceded them, Finkelstein has linked them with the sages and with the rabbinical Law that followed them.[1]

All this has had an effect on New Testament studies. But unfortunately Pauline polemic against the Law in Judaism and Jewish Christianity has so colored the minds of Protestants and even Catholics that it has been difficult for them both to give its due place to the Law in the corpus of revelation. What was argued by Paul against the Judaic and Judaizing interpretation of the Law was applied to the whole structure of the faith. But at long last we are being delivered from this inability to do justice to the value of Law in the biblical sources. We now see that the saving event of the exodus, which gave birth to Israel, is indissolubly bound up with the obligation to obey certain norms of conduct, that is, certain demands made by Yahweh. And in the

---

1. See L. Finkelstein, *New Light from the Prophets* (London, 1969).

New Testament also the early Christians born of a New Exodus, in Christ, were conscious of being bound to certain legal norms which they sought to live by and put into practice.

It is from this perspective that I write here. Such a perspective confronts serious difficulties especially in the Pauline corpus. If I largely ignore these, it is not because I am not aware of them but because to deal with them would require more space than is available.

By "the Law" I shall understand the moral demand made upon Christians and confine myself to the New Testament. This reveals varying emphases. Any neat presentation of early Christian teaching must immediately be suspect. But it is possible to indicate certain themes which convey the moral seriousness of the primitive church.

I begin with a central fact: through the life, death, and resurrection of Jesus of Nazareth, Christians believed that they were living "in the end of the days," in the time of fulfillment of the expectations of Judaism (Isa. 10:22; 34:4; 43:3; 45:17–22; 60:16; Gal. 4:4; Matt. 4:4, 6–7; 5:17–18; Mark 12:28–37). This fulfillment did not ignore the moral content of these expectations. The early church consciously accepted the moral concern of Israel as it was illumined and completed in the light of the life, death, and resurrection of Jesus. Thus in much of the New Testament the experience of the church was understood as parallel to that of the Jewish people. The emergence of the church was, not indeed that of a new Israel, but the entrance of Israel on a new stage of its history. In the creation of the church the exodus was, as it were, repeated. As a corollary to the experience of a New Exodus, the church understood itself as standing under the New Sinai of a New Moses. This complex of ideas largely governs Paul's references to the New Covenant (1 Cor. 11:23f.), Matthew's presentation of the Sermon on the Mount, Mark's new teaching (1:27ff.), and John's new commandment (13:34). What is clear is that "Law," that is, moral demand, is bound up with the Christian gospel, as it was bound up with the message of the Old Testament and Judaism. The structure of early Christianity is, in part at least, modeled upon or grows out of the structure of Judaism: that is, "Law" is integral to the gospel of the New Testament as it was to that of the Old. In both Testaments there is a "way" (*hodos*, halakah) which the People of God are to follow.

But what is this "way"? What "law" is integral to the gospel? This brings us to the motif that most governs the thought of early Christianity in morality. It reinterpreted the moral tradition of the Old Testament and Judaism in the light of Christ. It is the person of Christ that is normative for the understanding of morality in the New Testament. Just as early Christians reinterpreted the Temple, the Sabbath, Jerusalem, and all significant symbols of Jewish self-identity in terms of Christ, so they reinterpreted the Law. They found "in Christ" a new demand under which they stood, so that although the precise phrase does not occur — Christ became their "Law." I have urged elsewhere that Paul understood Jesus as taking the place of the Law. The demand of Christianity, that is, its Law, is concentrated in the Person of Christ.

This fact has three aspects which are exceedingly difficult to hold in proper balance. First, the moral life of Christians is molded by the actual life of Jesus of Nazareth, that is, his ministry of forgiveness, judgment, healing, teaching, which culminated in the cross. Second, it has its point of departure not only in the ministry of Jesus but in his resurrection. The resurrection was the ground for the emergence of the primitive community but it was also the immediate inspiration of its morality. The resurrection was not only a triumph of life over death but of forgiveness over sin. It was an expression, perhaps *the* expression, of God's grace in Christ, because the risen Christ came back to those who had forsaken him and fled, who had slept during his agony. He forgave their failure. The resurrection as forgiveness emerges clearly in 1 Corinthians 15:7ff.; John 20:1ff. It was of a piece with the whole ministry of Jesus, and the morality of the community which it created was to be a morality governed by grace, that is, it was the morality of forgiven men who had known the risen Lord as a forgiving Lord, and who in gratitude, the most ethical of all the emotions, gave themselves to the good life in his name. Third, the mode of the presence of the risen Lord in the community was that of "the Spirit." The coming of the Spirit — not merely a wonder-working power but of moral dynamism — should never be separated from the resurrection as grace. Like the resurrection itself, the coming of the Spirit is "an energy of forgiveness." Thus it became the source of morality because gratitude for forgiveness is the ground of Christian being. Love, joy, peace, righteousness, and every victory "in the moral sphere" are the fruit of the Spirit. The enthusiasm of the Spirit found its true expression in *agape.*

When, therefore, we say that "the Law" had been Christified, we mean that Christian morality had as its point of reference the life, death, resurrection, and living Spirit of Jesus Christ: inextricably bound together, these were the source of the demand under which the early church lived. And it is this that determines its manifold dimensions. These can be conveniently gathered together under two main heads.

Vertical Dimensions

We have seen that the ground on which the early church stood was the life, death, resurrection, and Spirit of Jesus Christ. To put the matter geometrically, it was their relation vertically to the risen Lord, the participation of the early Christians in the experience of being forgiven by the risen Lord and the Spirit, that lent them a common grace. They had been grasped by him and their response was primarily, through the prompting of the Spirit, to him.

All Christian fellowship was rooted in a particular event — the life, death, and resurrection of Jesus — and its morality is linked to the understanding of this event.

Now in much of the New Testament, though not in all, morality is understood in terms of the *appropriation* of this event, that is, the recapitulation of it in the life of the believer. The moral life is a life "in Christ"; it is the living out in daily conduct what it means to have died and risen with Christ. This is true of Paul and possibly of Matthew. For Paul the act by which a Christian acknowledged his faith and really began to live "in Christ" was baptism. This act symbolized a death to the old life under "the Law" and a rising to newness of life "in Christ" or "in the Spirit." By baptism the Christian through faith had died, had risen, had been justified: he was a new creation (Rom. 6:3; 1 Cor. 12:13; Gal. 3:27; 2 Cor. 8:9; 12:1; Phil. 2:5–8; Rom. 8:11). What was now necessary was for him to become what he was. His moral life is rooted in what he *is* — a new creation in Christ. Just as we call on each other "to play the man," so Christians are called upon "to play the Christian" — to *be* what they *are*. To use theological jargon, the imperative in Paul is rooted in the indicative. There is a vertical dimension to Christian living — an attachment to the Living Person of Christ, his life, death, and resurrection. So too in the Fourth Gospel the Christian is to reenact the self-giving of God in sending Christ into the world. The "love" which exists between the Father and the Son is to be reproduced in the relationships of the disciples to one another.

This vertical relationship has another aspect. Not only the imitation of God's act through dying and rising with Christ, but also the imitation of the "Jesus of history" played a part in the moral development of the early church. Early Christians looked to Jesus as their "identifying figure." Probably part of the reason for the preservation of stories about the life of Jesus, such as we have in the Gospels, was the desire to imitate Jesus in his acts. Christians were to take up the cross (Mark 8:34ff.). While persecution (taking up the cross literally) was always a possibility, more often Christians were called to imitate their Lord in the witness of the common way, less spectacular perhaps, but no less arduous than readiness to die — in love, forbearance, patience, mercy in messianic grace. (Compare Mark 8:34 and Luke 9:23.) Christ is an object of imitation to Paul as Paul himself expects to be such an object to his own followers (1 Cor. 11:1). He holds up qualities of the historic Jesus which are to be imitated (Rom. 15:3; 2 Cor. 10:1; 1 Cor. 8:8–9). The description of *agape* in 1 Corinthians 13 probably rests on the life of Jesus. For Paul every Christian is pledged to an attempted moral conformity to Christ. (Christ the Lord for him was not to be separated from the Jesus of history.) So too in the Fourth Gospel (John 13) and 1 Peter 2:2; 4:1ff., the life of Jesus is a paradigm of the Christian life.

There is a third aspect to the vertical dimension of Christian living. The Christian is also taken up into the purpose of God in Christ. To be a believer is to be directed to and by Jesus of Nazareth as the Messiah. That is, there is always an *eschatological reference* to Christian living: the Christian shares in the purpose of God in the salvation revealed in Jesus to be completed in the future. In the light of the redemptive purpose revealed in Christ, they made their decisions, they discerned the things that further and that hinder that purpose, and they became fellow workers with God. The life of Christians was sustained by the hope of the end, even as it was informed by the earthly Jesus. It was governed by a memory and an anticipation, "a lively hope."

Horizontal Dimensions

Early Christians were not exclusively oriented to the vertical realities indicated above. Early Christian morality contained a horizontal — a human, societal dimension. It is a morality born of the grace of the resurrection. The New Testament knows nothing of solitary religion and nothing of an individual morality — if, indeed, there be such. It points to a community with a life to live. This community was not to luxuriate in grace, absorbed in irrelevant, vertical privileges. As a community of grace, it took practical steps to give expression to grace in its life. How? We may summarize the answer under two main heads:

Christian Community

First, there was a constant concern among early Christians for the quality of their common life. This led to the experiment of the "communism" of the early chapters of Acts; it was the natural, spontaneous expression of life in the Spirit. This appears from the naivete of the experiment. It failed, not to be repeated in this form, but it witnessed to the societal or communal morality of the primitive community in its realism and its unpracticability. That experiment took place in the light of an absolute demand for *agape* informed by the intensity of the church's experience of forgiveness and, therefore, of grace.

This emphasis on the communal nature of the Christian way persists throughout the New Testament. It is rooted by a communal emphasis found in Jesus' choice of the Twelve, the nucleus of the new community. It is from this that here developed probably Paul's "Christ-mysticism" which issued not in "a flight of the alone to the Alone," but in building up the church. Along with rationality (1 Cor. 12:8; 14:13ff.; Rom. 12:2), Paul sets forth as the criterion of Christian action the building up of the church. In the Johannine literature the love of the brethren is a mark of the church.

Specific Moral Teaching

At first, in the awareness of its resources in grace, the church attempted to live in the light of certain moral absolutes. These absolutes constitute the peculiarity, though not the totality, of the teaching of Jesus. Under inevitable pressures it became necessary for the church to apply these absolutes to life. There began an attempt to transform the absolutes into practical rules of conduct, a Christian casuistry (see, e.g., Matt. 5:32ff.). This did not only occur in Jewish-Christian circles. The Pauline letters also appeal to the words of Jesus as authoritative. These words were at least one source of Paul's moral teaching. Two factors emerge clearly.

1. Paul interweaves words of Jesus almost unconsciously into his exhortations which means that these words were bone of his bone (compare Rom. 12:14; 12:17; 13:7; 14:13; 14:14; 1 Thess. 5:2; 5:13; 5:15 with Matt. 5:43; 5:39; 22:15–22; 18:7; 15:11; 24:43–44; Mark 9:50; Matt. 5:39–41, respectively).

2. There was a collection of sayings of the Lord to which Paul appealed (1 Cor. 7:10ff.; 9:14; 11:23ff.; 14:37; 1 Thess. 4:15–16). Not only in legislative matters did Paul find guidance in the words of Jesus, but in personal matters (Romans 7). In 1 Corinthians 7:25 a word of Jesus is a commandment *(entole)*: in two places we hear of the Law *(nomos)* of Christ (Gal. 6:2; 1 Cor. 9:20–22; see also Rom. 8:2). This is no declension to a primitive legalism but the recognition of the role of the words of Jesus (John 14:25–26). Sometimes the words of Jesus are summed up in one word — *agape* (Matt. 7:12; Rom. 13:8–10; 1 Cor. 8:1; 1 Corinthians 13; Col. 3:14; John 13:34–35; 1 John 3:1; 2:7–10; 4:7–16). The expression of love is multiple, but its essential nature is revealed in Christ's dying for men. It is this kind of act that is demanded of those who love.

The necessity which led to the application of the absolutes of Jesus to life led the church to take over for its own use codal material from Hellenism and Judaism. Most of Paul's letters and others reveal a twofold structure: a first part dealing with "doctrine" and a second dealing with "morality." Romans is typical. Chapters 1–11 are doctrinal: 12:1ff. deals with moral questions. The catechetical origin of much in the "moral sections" of the epistles is clear: they are largely drawn from instruction to converts at baptism. The presence of the imperative participle (e.g., in Rom. 12:9–10), a form found, but not common, in Hellenistic Greek but familiar in Hebrew legal documents, suggests that Paul and other Christian writers drew upon codal material, such as is found in the Dead Sea Scrolls (DSD 1.18ff.), the *Mishnah Demai*, and *Derek Eretz Rabba* and *Zuta*. There are parallels also in Hellenistic sources. The early church took over much pagan moral convention from the Jewish Diaspora: it borrowed from non-Christian sources: it not only domesticated the absolutes of Jesus but took over domestic virtues from the world.

This brings us to the last aspect of the New Testament moral teaching. That the church was able to draw upon moral teaching from Judaism and Hellenism means that there was a continuity between the moral awareness of Christians and of the non-Christian world. Wherein did this continuity lie? It lay probably in the doctrine of creation which the early church held. In the New Testament creation and redemption are congenial, as indeed in Judaism. The Messianic Age had cosmic dimensions for Judaism. So too in the New Testament the Creator and the Redeemer are one. Jesus can discover redemptive spiritual truths in the natural order (Matt. 5:43–48; and the parables), Paul finds in Christ the Wisdom, the creative agent of God, and John and Hebrews can find in him the Word by which all things were made. For the New Testament writers the good life is the truly natural life. Morality is rooted in creation.

The Law of Christ

In summing up, what, then, is the demand or Law of Christ as the New Testament understands it? There are specific commands of Christ, a body (though not to be utterly strictly defined) of moral teaching, a moral messianic Law which was regarded as bringing "the Law" of Judaism to its final form. Elements of this teaching, although simple in their forms, were stark in their demands, inescapable in their penetration, and, apparently, impossible of fulfillment. Other elements were more "ordinary," prescriptive, catechetical, and paraenetical. It is impossible to delete the prescriptive commandments from the New Testament. Christians brought with them to any situation which they faced a body of moral prescriptions and insights. They were not only, as were others, open to the demands of the context in which they moved, but they confronted that context with demands under which they stood. The New Testament also reveals moral casuistry. In addition, it borrowed concepts in the interpretation of "The Way," from the surrounding culture, pagan and Jewish.

But the prescriptive casuistry which was present was never very highly developed: it remained uncomplicated. It was never in danger of becoming the kind of casuistry against which Pascal wrote in the *Lettres Provinciales*, that in which practical ethics had become so befogged by fine distinctions and alternately meaningless definitions that it had ceased to be ethics of any kind, either practical or theoretical. This was because in the New Testament the moral teaching of Christ was not given autonomous centrality, but was always understood in the total context of the *agape* of the life, death, and resurrection of Christ and of the Spirit. The very commandments of Christ were subordinated to him. The self-giving exemplified in the cross was normative for all behavior even in obedience to his commandments. All the demands of God in Christ are placed under his rule, that is, are informed by *agape* which may be defined, in part at least, as openness to suffering and moral sensitivity. But — and this is important — *agape* itself needed to preserve, and even to protect itself in terms of prescriptions, which can both express *agape* and be a support for *agape*.

Now to isolate and emphasize the prescriptive elements in the New Testament is to risk a narrow, rigid, parochial legalism: to isolate the motif of the indicative-imperative is often so to individualize and "spiritualize" our interests as to endanger our moral concern. Only the sober realism of the prescriptions — themselves, however, kept captive to the obedience of Christ — can keep the indicative-imperative relationship healthy. We need what Leo Baeck called "the cleanliness of the commandment." So too the "imitation of Christ" can become banal, archaic, and "hippyish" if taken in isolation. Even the cross itself can become, in isolation, a distortion of "the Way," a warming of one's hands at the fires of martyrdom for one's own sake. The elements of the moral teaching of the New Testament are all to be interrelated; in this interrelationship is their strength and health, their mutual correction, and their safeguard against misleading distortion and enthusiasm.

Finally, it is not superfluous to point out the relevance of all the above to the current ethical debate. Those who favor a prescriptive ethic are impatient with the contextualists who emphasize the free response of *agape* in the *koinonia*. In between these extremes are those who favor "middle axioms." In the light of the New Testament the debate is unreal or misplaced. Each school can find support for its position in the New Testament. What is more important, they can all find themselves corrected there in the rich totality of the New Testament church, where the Law's "prescriptive morality," *agape* and *koinonia* morality, and middle axioms all coexist in mutual interaction. The relevance of the genius of the moral tradition of the New Testament is that it holds all these approaches in living and healthy tension. In short, I plead for the recognition of the place of Law in Christianity but that within the context of the *total* canon.

Chapter 5

David Roberts and the Promised Land in Jewish and Christian Tradition

A volume of lithographs of the Holy Land[1] by an artist brought up in the Scottish Presbyterian tradition provokes a question. Is the work of David Roberts another example of one of those ironies of history that Reinhold Niebuhr so often emphasized? The question arises because the Protestant tradition, to which Roberts belonged, was very austere and is usually deemed not to have been conducive to artistic expression in general and especially to that of religious themes. Moreover, his work may be ironic for another reason. Although Judaism seldom, if ever, calls it "the Holy Land" (an ap-pellation far more typical of Christianity),[2] its emphasis on the significance of the promised land of Israel can hardly be exaggerated. To express the pecu-liarity and importance of their land, the Jewish rabbis used the unadorned, but implicitly exclusive, term The Land (*Ha-aretz*), much as Homer never described Helen of Troy, "whose face launched a thousand ships," except in the briefest, stereotypical terms — "long-robed Helen, fair among women." We shall follow the rabbis in using The Land for what Christendom refers to as "the Holy Land." The reasons why, at the very beginning, we have evoked the notion of irony will become clear when we set Roberts's work over against the background of the role played by The Land in the Jewish soul through-out the centuries down to the present. At this point we simply ask whether it is not ironic that Judaism, which had so praised The Land, had to wait for a nineteenth-century Scottish Presbyterian artist, to attempt to do justice to its beauty in art.[3]

---

1. *Jerusalem and the Holy Land Rediscovered: The Prints of David Roberts (1796–1864)* (Durham, N.C.: Duke University Museum of Art/Duke University Press, 1996).

2. W. D. Davies, *The Gospel and the Land: Early Christianity and Jewish Territorial Doctrine* (Berkeley, Calif., 1974), 29f.; Moshe Weinfeld, *The Promise of the Land: The Inheritance of the Land of Canaan by the Israelites* (Berkeley, Calif., 1993), 203–8, 219–21.

3. I desire to acknowledge the help of Dr. Sarah Schroth, curator at the Duke Univer-sity Museum of Art; Professor Kalman Bland, the Department of Religion, Duke University;

The Marked Theological Tradition

Let us begin with the teaching about The Land in Judaism. Despite the vicissitudes of Jewish history, the sacred documents on which religious Jews have
rested — the Hebrew scriptures (the so-called Old Testament of Christians),
the Mishnah, the Midrashim, and the Talmud — the liturgies that they have
constantly celebrated, and the observances that they have kept across the
centuries all point to The Land as a very important aspect of Judaism. The
reader is referred to William D. Davies's *The Gospel and the Land: Early Christianity and Jewish Territorial Doctrine* for a fuller annotated treatment. Here we
merely summarize the main points of the evidence in defense of the position
indicated.

Two Hebrew terms have to be distinguished: *'adamah*, soil, land, earth;
and *'eretz*, which, while not always clearly distinguished from *'adamah*, bears
also the meaning of a politically defined territory. It is with *'eretz* in this latter
sense that we are concerned — that is, with the land of Israel as territory.
The boundaries of the promised land vary in different sources and are never
precisely defined.

The Evidence of the Classical Sources of Judaism

The doctrine of The Land finds its fundamental expression in the Pentateuch[4] but is also abundantly reflected in the other documents of the Tanak.
Two elements in the understanding of The Land are central. First, The Land
is regarded as promised, or, more accurately, as sworn by the deity (Yahweh), to the people of Israel. The earliest history of the tradition concerning
Yahweh's promise, on which there is no widespread critical agreement, is
complex. The most probable development seems to be in the recognition of
a promise of a territorial patrimony to the individual Abraham, to that of a
more extensive territory to the people of Israel, probably under the impact
of Davidic imperial ambitions. Alongside the belief in the promise, the conviction prevailed that this promised land belonged especially to Yahweh. Not
only did it necessarily belong to Him, as did all lands that He had called into
being, but it was His peculiar possession to give to His own people: the election of the people of Israel was bound up with His promise, His covenant,
to give His own land to them.[5] Out of the combination, or fusion,[6] of the
three elements involved in the promise — God, the People, and The Land —
there emerged the belief of religious Jews of the first century and later down

Dr. Hugh Walters, Llyfrgell Genedlaethol Cymru (The National Library of Wales); and Ms.
Nancy Sears, Dr. Leslie T. Henry, and Ms. Rebecca Gau.
    4. Gen. 15:1–6 (EJ); 12:1–3; 15:17ff. (JE); 17:1–14 (P).
    5. Davies, *Gospel and the Land.*
    6. Gershom Cohen, *Zion in Jewish Literature*, ed. G. S. Halkin (New York, 1961), 39.

to our own times in the indissolubility or eternity of the connection among these three realities.

This belief comes to clearest expression in the rabbinic sources: the Mishnah, the Midrashim, and the Talmud. That fact is remarkable and significant because across many centuries the sages (the rabbis), the authors and preservers of those sources, for good reasons, had increasingly suspected any disturbing concentration on hopes for a return to The Land in any messianic context as a snare and a delusion likely to distract their people from the essential task of living in obedience to the Torah. As we shall later indicate, the rabbis came to accept the need to acquiesce in the exiled life and to cooperate in foreign lands with foreign rulers. But paradoxically, they continued to shower their praises on The Land, emphatically expressing their concern for it and recognizing the ultimate indissolubility of Israel's connection with it: for them The Land is the covenanted land of a covenanted people, Israel.

The initial stimulus for this concern has been especially connected with the destruction of The Land by the Romans in the war from 66 to 70 C.E. Conditions in Palestine after 70 C.E. were economically difficult. As a result, there developed an increasing tendency for Jews to emigrate from Palestine to neighboring countries, especially Syria. The need to encourage Jews to remain in The Land, and not to depart from areas in it where they were permitted to live, was so urgent that the rabbis adopted a policy of extolling the virtues of The Land and encouraging settlement in it.[7]

But important as they were, economic factors were not the sole or even the main reason for the emergence of the doctrine with which we are concerned. As we have indicated, the roots of the emphasis on The Land are deep in the Tanak. The Tannaitic and other sources build on the Hebrew scriptures even though they respond also to economic and political realities. They point to the significance of The Land in the most unambiguous way. There is a kind of umbilical cord between Israel and The Land.[8] It is no accident that one-third of the Mishnah, the Pharisaic legal code, is connected with The Land. Nine-tenths of the first order of the Mishnah, *Zeraim* (Seeds), of the fifth order, *Kodashim* (Hallowed things), and of the sixth order, *Tohoroth* (Cleanness), deal with laws concerning The Land, and there is much of the same in the other parts of the Mishnah. This is no accident because the connection between Israel and The Land was not fortuitous, but part of the divine purpose or guidance, as was the Law itself. The choice of Israel and the Temple and of The Land was deliberate, the result of Yahweh's planning. The connection among Yahweh, Israel, The Land, Sinai, and the

---

7. W. D. Davies, *The Setting of the Sermon on the Mount* (Cambridge, 1964), 295f.; Cohen, *Zion in Jewish Literature*, 45f.

8. Cohen, *Zion in Jewish Literature*, 45f.

Temple is primordial: it is grounded in a necessity of the divine purpose and is, therefore, inseparable (*Lev. Rabbah* 13:2). And it is no wonder that the rabbis heaped upon The Land terms of honor and endearment. As previously noted, for them the land of Israel is called simply *Ha-aretz*, The Land; all countries outside it are *ḥutz la-aretz*, outside The Land. In *T.B.* (the Babylonian Talmud) *Berakoth* 5a we read: "It has been taught: R. Simeon b. Yoḥai says: The Holy One, blessed be He, gave Israel three precious gifts, and all of them were given only through sufferings. These are: the Torah, The Land of Israel, and the World to Come."

We have seen that behind the glorification of The Land stood passages in the scriptures. But in addition to this, two factors could not but increasingly stamp The Land upon the consciousness of Israel. The first is that the Law itself, by which Jews lived, was so tied to The Land that it could not but always recall The Land. As we have already stated, one-third of the Mishnah deals with The Land and all the agricultural laws in it, as those of the scripture itself deal with it. Consider Leviticus 19:23, 23:10, 23:22, 25:2, and Deuteronomy 26:1. These verses make it clear that the agricultural laws are to apply "in The Land." Further, only in Palestine could there be cities of refuge, which were so important in the civil law (Num. 35:9f.; Deut. 4:41f.; 9:1f.). True, there are laws not contingent upon The Land, and the distinction between these and their opposites was clearly recognized. But the reward for the observance of the laws was "life in The Land," as is implied in *Mishnah Kiddushin* 1:9–10. The Law itself, therefore, might be regarded as an effective symbol of The Land: it served as a perpetual call to The Land.

The second factor is that because it was The Land to which the Law most applies, The Land gained in sanctity. In *Mishnah Kiddushin* 1:9–10 — in the references to The Land, the walled cities of The Land, the wall of Jerusalem, the Temple Mount, the Rampart, the Court of Women, the Court of Israelites — it is the connection with an enactment of the Law that determines the degree of the holiness of each of these phenomena. And for our purposes especially, it is the applicability of the Law to The Land in *Mishnah Kiddushin* 1:6 that assures its special holiness. The implication is that Jewish sanctity is only fully possible in The Land; outside it only strictly personal laws can be fulfilled, that is, the moral law, sexual law, Sabbath law, circumcision, dietary laws, and so on. Of necessity, outside The Land territorial laws have to be neglected. The exiled life is, therefore, an emaciated life, even though, through suffering, it atones. A passage in *T.B. Sotah* 14a expresses this point of view in dealing with Moses' failure to enter The Land. Moses, outside The Land, is a suffering servant who atones.

In light of the above, it is not surprising that both the gift of prophecy — the gift of the Holy Spirit — and the gift of the resurrection of the dead were connected by some rabbis with The Land. For example, *Mekilta Pisḥa* 1 reveals the affirmation of Israel as the only land fit for prophecy and the dwelling of the Shekinah and mentions the efforts made to deal with the difficulties such a position confronted, for example, the fact that Yahweh had appeared outside The Land.

Again, in the view of some rabbis, the resurrection was to take place first in The Land, and the benefits of The Land in death are many (*Gen. Rabbah* 96:5). Some urged that those who died outside The Land would not rise: but even an alien (Canaanitish) slave girl who dwelt in The Land might expect to share in the resurrection (*T.B. Ketuboth* 3a). At the end of the second century Rabbi Meir, at his death, required that his remains should be cast into the sea off the Palestinian coast, lest he be buried in foreign soil. There is no space or necessity here to enlarge further. The desire to die in The Land, to possess its soil, to make pilgrimages to it — all these manifestations of attachment to The Land — history attests. Enough has been written to indicate that the primary documents of Judaism, the Tanak and Tannaitic Midrashim and the Talmud, are unequivocal in their recognition that The Land is essential to the true or complete fulfillment of the life to which Israel was called.[9]

The Evidence of the Observance

The liturgical practice of the synagogue offers the same witness. Throughout the centuries, beginning with the fall of Jerusalem in 70 c.e., the conscious cultivation of the memory of The Land, concentrated in Jerusalem and the Temple, has continued unbroken in Judaism. The rabbis at Jamnia, in demanding that the *Tefillah* (Prayer) or *Shemoneh Esreh* should be said three times a day, morning, afternoon, and evening (*Mishnah Berakoth* 4:1ff.), had in mind, among other things, the perpetual remembrance of Jerusalem and The Land. The prayers of *Shemoneh Esreh* for the morning and afternoon service corresponded to the morning and afternoon daily whole-offerings in the Temple. There was no time fixed for the evening *Shemoneh Esreh*, but on Sabbaths and festivals the *Shemoneh Esreh* was to be said four times (there being demanded an additional *Tefillah* corresponding to the "additional offering" presented on those days in the ancient Temple). Three times daily, then, the Jew was required to pray. Among other things, he was required to repeat the fourteenth benediction (dated by Dugmore [1944] to 168–65 b.c.e.), the sixteenth (possibly pre-Maccabean), and the eighteenth (40–70 c.e.) These read as follows:

> Be merciful, O Lord our God, in Thy great mercy, towards Israel Thy
> people, and towards Jerusalem thy city, and towards Zion the abiding

---

9. W. D. Davies, "Reflections on the Spirit in the *Mechilta*," in *Jewish and Pauline Studies* (Philadelphia, 1984), 72–83.

place of Thy glory, and towards Thy temple and Thy habitation, and towards the kingdom of the house of David, the righteous anointed one. Blessed art Thou, O Lord God of David, the builder of Jerusalem. (Benediction 14)

Accept [us], O Lord our God, and dwell in Zion; and may Thy servants serve thee in Jerusalem. Blessed are Thou, O Lord, whom in reverent fear we serve [or, worship]. (Benediction 16)

Bestow That peace upon Israel Thy people and upon Thy city and upon Thine inheritance, and bless us, all of us together. Blessed art Thou, O Lord, who makest peace. (Benediction 18)

That there was a deliberate concern with Jerusalem appears from the text in *Mishnah Berakoth* 4:1ff., where the rules concerning the *Shemoneh Esreh*, indicated above, are set forth and where *Mishnah Berakoth* 4:5 states that, according to R. Joshua (80–120 c.e.), "If [a man] was riding on an ass [when the time for the prayer is upon him] he should dismount [to say the *Tefillah:* Danby]. If he cannot dismount he should turn his face [toward Jerusalem]; and if he cannot turn his face, he should direct his heart toward the Holy of Holies." The centrality of The Land is clear. The same is also emphasized in *Numbers Rabbah* 23:7 on Numbers 34:2. The deliberate recalling of the Temple and thereby Jerusalem and The Land in the liturgy also appears from *Mishnah Rosh-ha-Shanah* 4:1–3 and *T.B. Baba Bathra* 60b.

Again other elements in the Jewish liturgy come to be *zeker lehoreban*, that is, in memory of the destruction of Jerusalem. For three weeks of sorrow, ending on the ninth day of the month of Ab, which is given over entirely for twenty-four hours to fasting, Jews annually recall the destruction of The Land. So much has that event become the quintessence of the suffering of Jewry that the ninth of Ab is recognized as a day on which disasters recurred again and again to the Jewish people. Connected with it significantly was the decree that the fathers should not enter the promised land. The passage in *T.B. Ta'anith* 29a that states this cannot easily be dated. But it is traced to an unknown rabbi whose works are explained by R. Ḥama b. Ḥananiah (279–320 c.e.). The pertinent passage is in *Mishnah Ta'anith* 4:6–7. As a matter of history, only the fall of Betar (the Beth Tor of the text), the last stronghold of Bar Kokba, captured by the Romans in 135 c.e., possibly occurred on the ninth of Ab. The First Temple was burnt on the seventh of Ab (2 Kings 25:8–9) or on the tenth of that month (Jer. 52:12); the Second Temple fell on the tenth (see the dictionaries). The essential feature of the liturgy for the ninth of Ab (which is the only twenty-four-hour fast apart from the Day of Atonement) was the reading of Lamentations and dirges. Later, on the fast of the ninth of Ab, an addition that concentrates on Jerusalem still further was made to the service. The prayer, as used today, begins with the words "O Lord God, comfort the mourners of Zion; Comfort those who grieve for Jerusalem." It ends with "Praised are You, who comforts Zion, Praised are You, who rebuilds Jerusalem."

So far, in showing how the sentiment for The Land remained powerfully active in Judaism after 70 C.E., we have mostly adduced materials from the haggadah (roughly the "homiletical" literature) and the liturgy of Rabbinic Judaism. There was also a more specifically halakic (or legal) approach to the question of The Land. The ramifications of this development we are unfortunately not competent to trace. We can only refer to two items. In the Jerusalem Talmud, in *Kilayyim* 7:5, ed. Krotoshin (or Venice) 31a, line 32 (Venice, line 25), *Orla* 1:2, ed. Krotoshin 61a, line 2 (Venice, line 9), there is a Jewish law that is quoted as giving to Israel a legal right to The Land. The law is translated by Saul Lieberman as, "Though soil cannot be stolen, a man can forfeit his right to this soil by giving up hope of ever regaining it." The argument is that "Israel" "never for a moment gave up hope of regaining the soil of Palestine. Never did they renounce their right to Palestine and never have they ceased claiming it in their prayers and in their teachings. It is on this foundation that [Jews] now claim that Eretz Israel belongs to them."[10] Not unrelated to this law is that of *ḥazakah* (prescription) in which the legal right of Israel to The Land was sought.[11] But how early such attempts were and how significant in the discussion of the relationship between Israel and Eretz Israel we cannot determine. The history of the halakic understanding of that relationship lies beyond the scope of this study, as does the relative place of haggadah and halakah in Judaism.[12]

Nevertheless, it is in the haggadah and the liturgy that the full force of the sentiment of The Land is to be felt. It cannot properly be seen except through Jewish eyes, nor felt except through Jewish words, such as those so powerfully uttered by Abraham Heschel in *Israel: An Echo of Eternity*, which is more lyrical outburst than a critical study, and in André Néher's moving essay, "Israel, terre mystique de l'Absolu," in *L'Existence Juive*.

So far we have referred to the evidence of the classical sources of Judaism.[13] The same theological conviction that there is an inseparable connection among Israel, The Land, and its God continued to be cherished throughout the medieval period and up to the modern. A rough division has been drawn between two periods. The first stretches up to the last revolt of

---

10. S. Lieberman, *Proceedings of the Rabbinical Assembly of America*, vol. 12 (New York, 1949).

11. See *Baba Bathra* 28a and notes in the Soncino translation for *ḥazakah*.

12. Jacob Neusner, "The Tasks of Theology in Judaism: A Humanistic Program," *JR* 59 (1979): 83–84, urges that "Halakah is Judaism's primary expression of Theology." Abraham Heschel would qualify this.

13. Cohen, *Zion in Jewish Literature*, 41.

Jews in the Roman Empire, in the hope of reestablishing a Jewish state, which
followed upon the imposition of harsh anti-Jewish statutes under Justinian
(483–565 C.E.), and later the brief three-year reign of Nehemiah, a messianic
figure, in Jerusalem from 614 to 617 C.E. It is legitimate to recognize up to
that time a living, if intermittent, hope and a violent activity directed toward
the actual return of The Land politically to Israel. From then on, especially
after the Arab conquest of The Land in 638 C.E. and the building of the
Mosque of Omar on the site of the Temple in 687–91 C.E., a mosque that
was to be a center for the Islamic faith, there was, it has been suggested, a
change. Jewish devotion to The Land came to express itself for a long period
not so much in political activity for the reestablishment of the state of Israel
as in voluntary individual pilgrimages and immigrations to The Land.[14] But
the division suggested between the two periods must not be made inflexible.
On the one hand, in the earlier period the rabbis were wary of political attempts to reestablish the kingdom of Israel in its own land. On the other
hand, in the Middle Ages there was much apocalyptic-messianic speculation
and probably much activity aimed at such a reestablishment: the history of
this has been largely lost, so that its full strength must remain conjectural
even if likely. The extent to which apocalyptic-messianism persisted, to break
out finally in Sabbatianism in the seventeenth century, is only now being recognized through the influence of the work of Gershom Scholem.[15] It fed into
the Zionist movement of our times. What we can be certain of is that Eretz
Israel, as an object of devotion and intense and religious concern, continued
to exercise the imagination of Jews after the fall of Jerusalem in 70 C.E. and
after the Arab conquest. It remained part of the communal consciousness of
Jews and has continued to do so up to the present time.

In this connection, two facts need to be borne in mind. First, the devotion
to The Land is not to be equated simply with the imaginative notions of other
peoples about an Ideal land — such as the Elysium of Homer, the Afallon of
Celtic mythology, the Innisfree of Yeats. Rather it was concentrated on an
actual land with a well-known history, a land known to be barren and rugged
and to offer no easy life though it was transfused, because it had been chosen
to be Yahweh's own and Israel's as an inheritance from him. Second, the influence of the familiar or customary division of history at the advent of Christ
into two periods, "before Christ" and "after Christ," has often tended to create the unconscious assumption among Gentiles that after the first century
Jews as a people ceased to have a common history.[16] No less a scholar than

---

14. F. W. Marquardt, *Die Juden und ihr Land* (Hamburg, 1975), 29 n. 1.

15. Gershom Scholem, *Sabbatai Sevi: The Mystic Messiah, 1626–1676,* trans. R. J. Zwi
Werblowsky (Princeton, N.J., 1973); W. D. Davies, "From Schweitzer to Scholem: Reflections
of Sabbatai Svi," *JBL* 95 (1976): 529–58.

16. Marquardt, *Juden und ihr Land,* 107ff.

Martin Noth saw Israel's history as having come to a ghastly end with the Bar Kokba revolt in 135 C.E.[17] But the Jews continued as a people, not simply as a conglomerate of individuals, after that tragic event. The Talmud, the primary document of Judaism in the Middle Ages and afterward to the present time, concerns itself with the way in which the Jews as a people should walk. The Talmud has a communal, national reference in its application of the Torah to the actualities of the Jews' existence. Its contents, formation, and preservation presuppose the continuance of the self-conscious unity of the people of Israel. It is this that explains the character of the Talmud: it adds Gemara to Mishnah, and Rashi (1040–1105 C.E.) to both, to make the tradition of the past relevant to the present. It is realistically involved with the life of the Jewish people over a thousand years of its history.[18]

And in the devotional life of the Jewish community, the relationship to The Land remained central.[19] To trace the various expressions of devotion to The Land among Jews across the centuries is beyond our competence. The most noteworthy is that of pilgrimage. The Law demanded that every male Israelite should make a pilgrimage to Jerusalem three times a year: at Passover, the Feast of Weeks, and the Feast of Tabernacles (Exod. 23:17; Deut. 16:16). During the Second Temple period even Jews of the Diaspora sought to observe this demand.[20] After the destruction of the Temple, pilgrimages, especially to the Wailing Wall, became occasions for mourning; there were pilgrimages throughout the Middle Ages to other holy places also. Individual Jews witness to this, a most famous example coming in the works of the "God-intoxicated" or "God-kissed" Jehudah Halevi, a Spanish physician born in Toledo in 1086. At the age of fifty he left his beloved Spain on a perilous pilgrimage to Zion. He died possibly before reaching Jerusalem, but not before expressing his love for The Land and Zion in unforgettable terms. "My heart is in the east, and I in the uttermost west — How can I find savour in food? How shall it be sweet to me? How shall I render my vows and my bonds, while yet Zion lieth beneath the fetter of Edom, and I in Arab chains? A light thing would it seem to me to leave all the good things of Spain — Seeing how precious in mine eyes it is to behold the dust of the desolate sanctuary."[21]

17. Martin Noth, *The History of Israel*, trans. Stanley Goodman (London, 1958), 448, 453f.; C. Klein, *Anti-Judaism in Christian Theology* (Philadelphia, 1975), 15–38.

18. Marquardt, *Juden und ihr Land*, 107f.; Jacob Neusner, "Why the Talmud Matters," *Midstream* 42 (January 1996): 17–21.

19. R. J. Zwi Werblowsky, "Israel et Eretz Israel," *Les Temps Modernes*, no. 253, B15 (1967): 374–75.

20. See, for example, *Mishnah Ta'anith* 1:3; *Aboth* 5:4; Josephus, *Wars* 6:9.

21. H. Brody, ed., *Selected Poems of Jehudah Halevi*, trans. Nina Salaman (Philadelphia, 1924), 2.

It was not only single, individual pilgrims who sought The Land, but groups of communities, as in the case of Rabbi Meir of Rothenburg (1220–93), who sought to lead a great number of Jews from the area of the Rhine to Israel. In 1523, David Reuveni led a messianic movement aimed at a return to The Land, which attracted the interest of communities in Egypt, Spain, and Germany. The living Jewish concern to establish an earthly kingdom in Jerusalem may have contributed to the formulation of the seventeenth article for the Confession of Augsburg of 1530.[22] The justification for such a concern was made luminously clear in the astounding response to the Sabbatian movement from the Yemen to western Europe.[23]

These data to which historians point cannot be ignored. However, we are not competent to assess the relative weight that should be given to the purely religious interest in The Land, which led individuals and groups to journey to Israel out of a desire to experience the mystical or spiritual power of The Land, rather than to a desire to escape and to right the wrongs of exile. Certainly, many pious Jews had no directly political concern. Their sole aim was to recognize that in The Land, as nowhere else, a relationship to the eternal was possible. A striking illustration of spiritual concentration on The Land is provided by Rabbi Naḥman of Bratzlov (1772–1810), who journeyed to Israel. He asserted that what he had known before that journey was insignificant. *Before*, there had been confusion; *after*, "he held the Law whole." Not that all he had desired was direct contact with The Land. This he achieved by simply stepping ashore at Haifa. He desired to return immediately. (Under pressure he stayed and visited Tiberias but never even went up to Jerusalem.) Again, the celebrated Maharal of Prague (Rabbi Yehuda Liwa of Loew — Ben Bezalel, 1515–1609) understood the nature and role of nations to be ordained by God as part of the natural order. Nations were intended to cohere rather than to be scattered. Nevertheless, he did not urge a political reestablishment of a state of Israel in The Land; he left that to God. Exile no less than restoration was in His will; the latter *would* come in His good time, but only then. (The promise of The Land would endure eternally. Return was ultimately assured [Lev. 26:44–45].)

Because of the kind of devotion we have indicated, despite geographical and political obstacles, at no time since the first century has the land of Israel been wholly without a Jewish presence, however diminished. The numbers of Jews living in The Land throughout the centuries have been variously estimated, but James Parkes rightly insisted that Jews in Palestine across the centuries were forgotten by historians. It is certain that in the nineteenth century, first under the influence of Rabbi Elijah, Ben Solomon Salman of

---

22. Marquardt, *Juden und ihr Land*, 131.
23. Scholem, *Sabbatai Sevi*.

Vilna, known as the Vilna Gaon (1720–97), a number of parties of Jews, soon to be joined by many others, went to Safed, in the Galilee, in 1808 and 1809, just a few years before David Roberts was born. These sought not simply contact with The Land of which they claimed that "even in its ruins none can compare with it," but permanent settlement.[24] Regarding themselves as representatives of all Jews, they assumed the right to appeal to other Jews for aid and reinforcement. Some, such as Rabbi Akiba Schlessinger of Preissburg (1832–1922), were driven to The Land by the realization of the increasing impossibility of living according to the Torah in Western society, which was becoming increasingly secular. For such people The Land became an escape and a refuge from modernism and secularism, a bulwark for the preservation of their religious tradition. After these early settlements to which we have referred, there were other efforts to reenter The Land by religious Jews whose history cannot be traced here. We must simply note that the Zionist movement, despite its strongly nationalistic, socialistic, and political character, is not to be divorced from this devotion to The Land. We shall deal with this later. Here we emphasize that during David Roberts's lifetime Jews were actively expressing profound devotion to The Land.

An Inescapable Historical Diversity

I have sought in the preceding pages to do justice to the theological role of territory in Judaism. Jewish theology as revealed in its sources seems to point to The Land as of the "essence" of Judaism.[25] In strictly theological terms, the Jewish faith could be defined as "a fortunate blend" of a people, a land, and their God. But this view has been criticized, because in any blend an item may be lost, and in the particular blend referred to, the essential and distinctive significance of The Land could be lost. As in discussions of the Trinity in Christianity, in which the personal identity of each member is carefully preserved and not simply blended, so in our understanding of Judaism the distinct or separable significance of The Land must be fully recognized. Judaism held to an election of a people and of its election to a particular land; Werblowsky rightly speaks of "une vocation, spirituelle à la géographie."[26]

But like Christian theology, Jewish theology has had to find ways of coming to terms with history. In this section we shall indicate certain actualities of Jewish history that must bear upon any answer to the question of the place of The Land in Judaism.

---

24. David Vital, *The Origins of Zionism* (Oxford, 1975), 7; Marquardt, *Juden und ihr Land,* 131ff.

25. See W. D. Davies, "Reflections on the Nature of Judaism," *Revue d'Histoire et de Philosophie Religieuses* (Strasbourg) 7 (1995): 85–111, on caution about the use of the term "essence."

26. Werblowsky, "Israel et Eretz Israel," 377.

In the first place, historically the term "Judaism" itself cannot be understood as representing a monolithic faith in which there has been a simplistic uniformity of doctrine either demanded or imposed or recognized about The Land, as about other elements of belief. Certainly this was so at all periods and in all sections of the Jewish community before 70 c.e. And despite the overwhelming dominance of the rabbinic form of Judaism, the history of the Jews since that date, though not to the same degree, reveals the same fissiparous, amorphous, and unsystematized doctrinal character. The concept of an adamant, uniform, orthodox Judaism, which was not stirred by dissident movements and ideas and by mystical, messianic yearnings that expressed themselves outside of or in opposition to the main, strictly rabbinic tradition, is no longer tenable. To define the place of Eretz Israel in Judaism requires the frank recognition that that place has changed or, more accurately, has received different emphases among various groups and at different times. However persistent some views of and attachment to The Land have been, and however uniform the testimony of the classical sources, there has not been one unchangeable, essential doctrine universally and uniformly recognized by the whole of Judaism. There is an illuminating controversy that circled around Maimonides (Rambam [1135–1204]) during the Middle Ages. In his *Dalalat al Harin,* translated into English as the *Guide to the Perplexed,* the Great Eagle never concerned himself directly with The Land. Although he was so concerned in his commentary on the Mishnah, his silence about The Land in the *Guide* caused dismay and dispute among the rabbis. Naḥmanides (1194–1270) was led to criticize the Great Eagle by insisting that there was a specific commandment (*mitzwah*) to settle in The Land, a *mitzwah* that Maimonides had ignored. Naḥmanides notes its absence in Maimonides' *Sepher-Ha-Mitzwah.* (For more information on Naḥmanides, see the *Encyclopedia of the Jewish Religion.*) In modern times, Reform Judaism in the United States, anxious to come to terms with Western culture, was careful to avoid any emphasis on any particularistic elements in Judaism that would set Jews apart from their Christian neighbors. Until recently, when external and internal pressures made themselves felt, the doctrine of The Land tended, in Reform Judaism in the United States, to be ignored or spiritualized. It was an embarrassment.

The demotion of The Land, along with the messianic idea and its disturbing potentialities, was no less evident in the Liberal Judaism of nineteenth-century Europe. Hermann Cohen (1842–1918) reveals how far the confused and confusing embarrassment with The Land went there, even among Jewish theologians. In 1880 he claimed that Judaism was already in the process of forming a "cultural, historical union with Protestantism."[27] It

27. Vital, *Origins of Zionism,* 207 n. 19.

is not surprising that Hermann Cohen could write such paradoxical words as the following: *"The loss of the national state is already conditioned by messianism. But this is the basis of the tragedy of Jewish peoplehood in all its historic depth. How can a people exist and fulfill its messianic task if it is deprived of the common human protection afforded by a state to its people? And yet, just this is the situation of the Jewish people, and thus it must needs be the meaning of the history of the Jews, if indeed this meaning lies in messianism."*[28] Cohen was concerned with the state and with Judaism, but by implication he not only questioned the messianic destiny of Israel in its own land, but, even if he still recognized it as a reality, he so domesticated that destiny in his western Europe that it bore little resemblance to the dynamism of the messianism expressed in previous Jewish history. Cohen's messianism eradicated the Davidic Messiah and the hope of a kingdom of God on earth — and with this any hope for The Land. Even though the Reform and Liberal Judaism factions in the United States and Europe have recently reintroduced an emphasis on The Land in response to contemporary events, which they could not ignore, that emphasis cannot obliterate their earlier nonterritorial or antiterritorial attitude. Not unrelated to this discussion in Reform and Liberal Judaism, though not directly connected with those movements, is the insistence by such figures as Aḥad Ha-Am (1856–1927) that Jews first needed to devote themselves to spiritual renewal, not to the occupation of territory. Aḥad Ha-Am founded a select and secret society in 1899 "dedicated to the notion that moral and cultural preparation had to precede the material salvation of the Jews."[29]

Second, in a historical examination it is necessary to recognize that the territorial theology with which we are concerned could not but gain increasing attention and therefore emphasis among recent students of Judaism because of the pervasive influence of the Zionist movement. The ascribing of a theological concern with The Land to Jews who entertain no definable Jewish theology, or who may even reject the tradition of their fathers, has become insidiously easy because of the Zionist climate within which so much of modern Jewry lives. The temptation to this ascription has been reinforced by an understandable sympathy toward the justification of the doctrine that the suffering of Jews in modern Europe so imperatively calls forth.

But sympathy by itself does not necessarily lead to historical truth. At this point it is important to emphasize the complexity and interpenetration of the many forces that combined to initiate the Zionist movement. It held together apparently irreconcilable points of view in a living tension. Any neat

---

28. Hermann Cohen, *Religion der Vernuft aus den Quellen des Judentums*, trans. Simon Kaplan (New York, 1972), 311–12; italics added.

29. Vital, *Origins of Zionism*, 156, 188–201.

dichotomies between religious and political factors in Zionism are falsifica-
tions of their rich and mutually accommodating diversity. To read Gershom
Scholem's autobiographical pages[30] is to be made aware of the impossibility of
presenting clean, clear lines in any picture of the Zionist movement. But this
much is certain: The territorial theology of Judaism should not be ascribed
directly (the qualifying adverb is important) to the many nonreligious Jews
who played a most significant part in Zionist history. The Zionist movement,
which has played so prominent a role in our time, was initiated by the Congress of Basel in 1897. It grew thereafter until in 1948, after an abeyance of
almost twenty centuries, there emerged the state of Israel. But the role of
Jewish territorial doctrine and sentiment in the movement has to be carefully assessed: it can easily be exaggerated. At first it was possible for some of
the leading Zionists to contemplate the establishment of a state outside The
Land altogether — in Uganda, in Argentina, in newly conquered Russian territories in Asia, in Asiatic Turkey, and in North America. The often silent
but almost ubiquitous presence of the religious tradition, with its concentration on Eretz Israel, however, caused those leaders to change their minds and
made the final choice of the Jewish homeland inevitable. Herzl, like other
Zionist secularists, was compelled to recognize this.

But Zionism remained an expression not only, and probably not even
chiefly, of the theological territorial attachment of Judaism, but even more an
expression of the nationalist and socialistic spirit of the nineteenth century.
In this sense it is a typical product of that century. An examination of the
history of Zionism makes its specifically religious motivation less significant
than an uncritical emphasis on territorial theology would suggest. Gershom
Scholem, in reply to an article by novelist Yeuda Bourla, wrote:

> I...am opposed, like thousands of other Zionists...to mixing up re-
> ligious and political concepts. I categorically deny that Zionism is a
> messianic movement and that it is entitled to use religious terminology
> to advance its political aims.
>
> The redemption of the Jewish people, which as a Zionist I desire, is
> in no way identical with the religious redemption I hope for the future.
> I am not prepared as a Zionist to satisfy political demands or yearnings
> that exist in a strictly nonpolitical, religious sphere, in the sphere of
> End-of-Days apocalyptic. The Zionist ideal is one thing and the mes-
> sianic ideal is another, and the two do not touch except in pompous
> phraseology of mass rallies, which often infuse into our youth a spirit
> of new Sabbatianism that must inevitably fail. The Zionist movement
> is congenitally alien to the Sabbatian movement, and the attempts to

---

30. Gershom Scholem, *On Jews and Judaism in Crisis: Selected Essays*, ed. Werner J.
Dannhauser (New York, 1976), 1–48.

infuse Sabbatian spirit into it have already caused it a great deal of harm.[31]

It seems that Scholem would here largely recognize Zionism as comparable with other nationalistic movements, such as those of Italy and many other countries in the nineteenth century. In a summary of forces that led to the triumph of Zionism, Scholem writes with greater fullness.

> If Zionism triumphed — at least on the level of historical decisions in the history of the Jews — it owes its victory preeminently to three factors that left their imprint on its character: it was, all in all, a movement of the young, in which strong romantic elements inevitably played a considerable role; it was a movement of social protest, which drew its inspiration as much from the primordial and still vital call of the prophets of Israel as from the slogans of European socialism; and it was prepared to identify itself with the fate of the Jews in all — and I mean all — aspects of that fate, the religious and worldly ones in equal measure.[32]

In this admirably balanced assessment (which is significant for what it does not contain, that is, apocalyptic territorial messianism, as for what it does), Scholem, while recognizing the role of the religious tradition, does not make it the dominant factor. To him Zionism was essentially a sociopolitical protest.[33] And in the judgment of many Jews, the Congress of Basel was important not primarily because it gave expression to a strictly religious hope for The Land, living and creative as that was, but because it also voiced a concern for the actual economic, political, and social distress and often despair of Jews in Europe; it was response not so much to a crisis in Judaism and to an endemic territorial theology as to the plight of the Jewish people.[34] To underestimate the secular character of much of Zionism and to overemphasize its undeniable religious dimensions is to lay oneself open to the temptation of giving to the doctrine of The Land a significance in much of Judaism that would be a distortion.

Our reference to Zionism in this essay dealing with David Roberts may well be deemed irrelevant. Was not Zionism later than his day — Herzl, the founder of Zionism, was not born until 1860 — how could it then be pertinent in any way? We have, however, deemed it well to recognize Zionism here because, although David Roberts was not directly touched by that later, developed movement, the world out of which it emerged was the complex

---

31. Ibid., 44.
32. Ibid.
33. Scholem, *Sabbatai Sevi*, 247.
34. Vital, *Origins of Zionism*, 375.

Jewish world with its concentration on The Land, among other things, which Roberts must, to some degree at least, have encountered.

In the third place, the witness of history, at first sight at least, might suggest that Eretz Israel has not been of the "essence" of Judaism to the extent that the literary sources and liturgies and observances of pious Jews and even the political activity of nonreligious Jews would suggest. Certain aspects of that history are pertinent. We have elsewhere indicated that there was a lack of any explicit appeal to the doctrine of The Land in the outbreak of the Maccabean revolt or the revolt against Rome in 66 c.e. This fact is striking.[35] Even more overlooked have been the expressions in the Maccabean period of protests against and opposition to the Hasmonaean rulers who had created an independent state.[36] These protests made the later attitudes of the Pharisaic leaders in coming to terms with Roman rule and in declaring the laws of The Land, wherever Jews dwelt, to be Law, less innovative than has customarily been recognized.[37] And at this point the nature of the rabbinic attitude across the centuries must be fully recognized. That the doctrine of The Land remained honored among the rabbis cannot be doubted. But despite the facts referred to in the preceding pages, after 70 c.e. until recent times it was a doctrine more honored in word that in deed. After 70 c.e. the powerlessness of Jews against the Roman authorities left the rabbinic leaders no choice other than submission and acquiescence to their divorce from The Land. This submission and acquiescence were to persist and mold the lives of the majority of Jews up to the present century and enabled the rabbis to come to terms with the loss of their temple, city, and The Land. As we have seen, protests in various forms against exile did not cease. Lurianic Qabbalah, for example, was a magnificent attempt to confront the curse of exile, and Sabbatianism in its historical context can be regarded as a desperate lunge at seizing the kingdom of God, which would lead to a return to Eretz Israel. But widely, both in Orthodox Judaism (by which is here meant the mainstream of Rabbinic Judaism) and in Reform Judaism in the United States and Western Europe, the question of The Land was eschatologically postponed either as an unacknowledged embarrassment or as a last or ultimate hope. Across the centuries most Jews have lived on the whims of the Gentile world: they have not been able to afford the risk of alienating their Gentile masters by giving practical expression to their visions of a territorial return to Eretz Israel. For most Jews, despite some brilliant exceptions, such visions were a luxury of Sabbath reading, dreams to be indulged in but not actively realized in daily

---

35. Davies, *Gospel and the Land*, 90–104.

36. See Isaiah 44:28; Ezra 1:1f.; 1 and 2 Chronicles; Josephus, *Antiquities* XII, 3:3, 138f.; *Antiquities* XIII, 13:5, 372f.; *Antiquities* XVII, 11:1, 299f.; Diodorus, *Bibliotheca Historica* 40:2. Cf. M. Stern, ed., *Greek and Latin Authors on Jews and Judaism* (Jerusalem, 1974), 185–86.

37. Scholem, *Sabbatai Sevi*, 31f.

life.[38] Instead, the rabbis emphasized that the Torah itself was to become a "portable land" for Jews; it could be obeyed everywhere and would constitute the center of Jewish religious identity everywhere.[39] Generally, Orthodox Judaism refused to indulge in political speculation and activity that might further a return to The Land but accepted instead an attitude of quietism. In one of the paradoxes of history, rabbis and apocalyptists were here at one: they both preferred to wait for a divine intervention, usually postponed to an indefinite future, to produce the return.[40] From a different point of view, Reform Judaism, in order to accommodate its faith to the nineteenth century and to make it comparable and compatible with Christianity, also refused to give to any particular place, "The Land," a special overwhelming significance. In brief, in most rabbinic writing up to the twentieth century and in some orthodox circles even up to the present, the significance of The Land, though never denied, has been transferred to the "end of days." Paradoxically, The Land retained its geographic character or actuality and was not always transcendentalized, though it was largely *de facto* removed from the realm of history altogether. And in Reform Judaism, The Land, again in some circles even up to recent times, was conveniently relegated to a secondary place; its geographic actuality was either sublimated or transformed into a symbol of an ideal society located not necessarily in Eretz Israel. Historically then, out of necessity since 70 c.e., the doctrine of The Land as a communal concern (it was often cherished by individual Jews) was largely dormant or suffered a benign neglect in much of Judaism.

What happened is apparent. In their realism the rabbis at Jamnia had triumphed over the Zealots of Masada. They recognized that the power of Rome was invincible: For them Jewish survival lay in sensible, because unavoidable, political submission and in obedience to the Torah in all aspects of life where this was possible. The law of the country where Jews dwelt became Law.[41] The paradigmatic figure was Johannan ben Zakkai, who had only asked of Vespasian permission to found a school where he could teach and establish a house of prayer and perform all the commandments — a spiritual center that accepted political powerlessness. For most of the rabbis after 70 c.e. exile became an accepted condition. For them discretion became the better part of valor. That it is to their discretion that Judaism owes its existence since 70 c.e. can hardly be gainsaid.

In the fourth place, exile itself is a factor that needs emphasis. David Vital

---

38. Ibid., 31 n. 9.

39. The phrase "portable land" I first heard from Louis Finkelstein; it was first used, if I recall correctly, by H. Graetz. The Talmud is sometimes called a "portable state."

40. See David Daube, *Civil Disobedience in Antiquity* (Edinburgh, 1972), 85–86.

41. The principle was *dina demalkwta' dina'*. See *T.B. Nedarim* 28a; *T.B. Gittin* 10b; *T.B. Baba Kamma* 113a–b; *T.B. Baba Bathra* 54b.

begins his work *The Origins of Zionism* with the sentence, "The distinguishing characteristic of the Jews has been their Exile." Bickerman wrote of the dispersion as follows:

> The post-biblical period of Jewish history, that is, that following Nehemiah . . . is marked by a unique and rewarding polarity: on the one hand, the Jerusalem center, and on the other, the plurality of centers in the Diaspora. The Dispersion saved Judaism from physical extirpation and spiritual inbreeding. Palestine united the dispersed members of the nation and gave them a sense of oneness. This counterpoise of historical forces is without analogy in antiquity. . . . The Jewish Dispersion continued to consider Jerusalem as the "metropolis" (Philo), turned to the Holy Land for guidance, and in turn, determined the destinies of its inhabitants.[42]

The fact of exile has been inescapable and extraordinarily tenacious and creative in the history of Judaism. The Talmud itself, like much of the Tanak, was formulated outside The Land. Surprisingly, Judaism did not produce a theology of exile on any developed scale until late.[43] But the presence of large bodies of Jews outside The Land, so that (until the twentieth century) the exiles became numerically and otherwise more significant that those who were in The Land, cannot but have diminished among many Jews the centrality of The Land and influenced their attitudes toward the doctrine concerning it. The conspicuous preeminence of the state of Israel in our time can easily hide the significance of the exile for Judaism throughout most of its history. But the theological preeminence of Jews outside The Land in Jewish history needs no documentation. Apart from all else, their significance in the very survival of Judaism must be recognized. The loss of the Temple and The Land, the centers of Judaism, could be sustained only because there were organized Jewish communities scattered elsewhere.[44] Disaster even at the center did not spell the end of Judaism but was offset and cushioned by its existence elsewhere. From this point of view, exile may be regarded as having been the historical condition for the survival of Judaism and Jewry. That this did not mean a radical decline of the significance of the primary center we shall indicate later.[45]

The four factors we have isolated above are to be further connected with what, in a previous study, we called cautionary considerations — the possible

---

42. Elias Bickerman, *From Ezra to the Last of the Maccabees: Foundations of Post-biblical Judaism* (New York, 1962), 3f.

43. See now, however, Thomas M. Raitt, *A Theology of Exile: Judgment and Deliverance in Jeremiah and Ezekiel* (Philadelphia, 1977) for a discussion of the development of this theme in the Tanak.

44. Cohen, *Zion in Jewish Literature*, 52.

45. Vital, *Origins of Zionism*, 1–20.

place of the "desert" as opposed to The Land in Judaism, the secondary role played by Abraham outside the Pentateuch, the transcendentalizing of The Land (pointing to a muted role for it) — which tend to curb the temptation to an excessive emphasis on the territorial dimension of Judaism. We refer the reader to that study. All these factors cannot be ignored.[46]

A Contradiction Resolved?
The Jews' Interpretation of Their Own History

Our treatment so far has pinpointed what appears to be a contradiction: The theology of Judaism in the main seems to point to The Land as of its "essence"; the history of Judaism seems to offer serious qualifications of this. Can the contradiction between the theology of Judaism and the actualities of its history be resolved? The Jews' understanding of their own history comes to terms precisely with this contradiction and resolves it in life, *solvitur ambulando.* What does this mean?

On the previous pages we appealed to history in support of the claim that exile as much as, if not more than, life in The Land has significantly marked Jewish history. The force of that appeal must not be belittled. In isolation, however, it is misleading, because in the Jewish experience, both religious and secular, exile has always coexisted with the hope of a return to The Land. Without that hope the Jewish people would probably have gradually disintegrated and ceased to be. They have endured largely because of the strength of that hope. Here the distinction between exile and simple dispersion is important. The two terms are easily confused. Statistics cannot be supplied, but many Jews throughout the centuries have chosen to live outside The Land voluntarily, and many still do. The dispersion as such is not exile. But in most periods Jews have had no choice and ultimately owe their place in the various countries of the world to the enforced exile of their ancestors. It is with these exiles, not simply with the dispersed, that we are here concerned. This notion of exile must be given its full weight and significance. That Jews outside Palestine conceived of their existence as that of exiles meant that they were still emotionally and conceptually bound to their home base, to Eretz Israel, wherever they were: they were not simply dispersed. As Gershom Cohen has urged, this was the fundamental reason that made possible the continuance of the link between dispersed Jews and Eretz Israel. The Diaspora had maintained the notion of its existence as a *galuth,* exile. "That is to say, by the time Palestine ceased to be the central Jewish community, its centrality had been so impressed upon the Jewish mind that it could not be uprooted."[47]

---

46. Davies, *Gospel and the Land,* 75–158.
47. Cohen, *Zion in Jewish Literature,* 48.

Many Jews have been sustained largely by the way in which they have traditionally interpreted their own history as revealing a recurring pattern of exile
and return. They have understood their existence (in the various countries
of their abode) as essentially transient or pilgrim; they have recognized that
they have had no abiding country anywhere but have always been en route
to The Land.

The scriptures point to the patriarchs in search of The Land; the settlement of The Land is followed by the descent (a necessary "exile") into Egypt,
followed by a return and the reconquest of The Land. Later there is another
exile to Babylon and again a return in the time of Cyrus. The Hellenistic period saw the rise of a vast dispersion — both voluntary and forced — and the
first-century revolt against Rome was followed by an exile that continued to
this century, again only to lead to a return. The pattern of exile and return,
loss and restoration, is constant across the sweep of Jewish history. Even the
so-called nonexilic exile of Jews in Moorish and Christian Spain, where Jews
had long enjoyed virtual integration into the societies in which they lived,
ended in disaster and a fresh dispersion. Jews have constantly been conditioned by the harsh actualities and interpretation of their history to think of
the return. The point is that the pattern of exile and return has been historically so inescapable that it has nurtured and underlined the belief that there
is an inseparable connection among Yahweh, His people, and His Land. In
Judaism, history has reinforced theology to deepen the consciousness of Jews
that The Land was always "there" — whether to be wrestled with in occupation or to return to from exile. As Professor Edmund Jacob has written,
"En effet, toute l'histoire d'Israel peut être énvisagée comme une lutte pour
la terre et avec la terre, comme le combat de Jacob était une lutte avec Dieu
and pour Dieu."[48]

In Jewish tradition the return could be conceived of in two ways. Nonreligious Jews in every age could interpret the return to The Land as a political
event, that is, as the restoration to Jews of political rights in their own land
denied after the collapse of the Jewish revolt in 70 c.e. (unrealistic as it must
have often seemed to non-Jews). Such Jews have often understood exile and
return in secular-political-economic terms. Not only secular Jews, but also
many of the rabbis, thought of the return in that way. The rabbinical leaders never recognized that the conquest of Eretz Israel by any foreign power
could be legitimized: the Romans were usurpers, their agents thieves. The
Land belonged to Israel because Yahweh had promised it to her: her right to
it was inalienable. So in the Mishnah it is regarded as legitimate to evade

---

48. "In effect, the entire history of Israel can be regarded as a struggle for The Land and with
The Land, as Jacob's wrestling was a struggle for God and with God" (Edmund Jacob, *Israel dans
la Perspective Biblique* [Strasbourg, 1968], 22).

the Roman taxes (*Mishnah Nedarim* 3:4). The ruling powers were to be given obedience but not cooperation — even in the interest of law and order. To the rabbis the return would involve control of The Land.

But to religious Jews much more was involved than this. To put it simply, to them just as exile was conceived of as the outcome of the wrath of God on a disobedient people, so too the return was to be the manifestation of His gracious purpose for them despite their past disobedience. From this point of view, the return was to be a redemption. What was primarily, if not always exclusively, of political significance to nonreligious Jews was of theological significance for the religious Jews.

This neat division between the religious and nonreligious Jews, like all such divisions, is misleading. Both categories were not so distinct; they interacted and were mutually stimulating as well as quite variegated. The concepts of the one permeated those of the other to make for infinite complexity. The secular thought in terms of return and the religious in terms of redemption ultimately; but because of the nature of the Tanak, the secular (or political) and the religious return and redemption often dissolved into each other. In the Zionist movement, secular, socialistic Jews constantly found themselves at home with the religious members in the movement who did not share their political views, but provided a common ambiance of thought on or sentiment for The Land.

Nevertheless, seeing the return in terms of redemption had certain discernible and definite consequences, as had seeing it in terms of the restoration of political rights. To the religious Jews, as previously indicated, the various exiles the Jewish people had endured were due to the will of God. He had intervened in history to punish by exile those disobedient to the commandments. So too, they argued, the return would be an act of divine intervention. The return would be an important aspect of the messianic redemption. As such it could not be engineered or inaugurated by political or any other human means: to force the coming of the return would be impious.[49] They best served that coming who waited in obedience for it: men of violence would not avail to bring it in. The rabbinic aloofness to messianic claimants sprang not only from the history of disillusionment with such, but from this underlying, deeply ingrained attitude. It has been claimed that under the rabbis Judaism condemned itself to powerlessness. But if such phraseology be used, it has also to be admitted that powerlessness was effective in preserving Judaism in a hostile Christendom and must, therefore, have had its own brand of power. And there is more. Orthodoxy did recognize the dependence of the return upon the divine initiative, but this did not prevent

---

49. E. E. Urbach, *The Sages: Their Concepts and Beliefs*, trans. Israel Abrahams, 2 vols. (Jerusalem, 1975), 1:649–92.

it from always retaining in principle that a certain human obedience could bring the initiative into play. And in Lurianic Qabbalah, for example, this connection was particularly active,[50] as in Rabbi Kuk.[51]

For the purpose of this essay, the significance of the attitude toward their existence in foreign lands and toward the hope of the return that I have ascribed to religious Jews is that despite their apparent quietism in the accep-tance of the Torah as a portable land — and this is only an *Interimsethik* — the hope for the return to Eretz Israel never vanished from their conscious-ness. They remained true in spirit to the territorial theology of the Tanak and of the other sources of their faith. Religious Jews generally, especially of the most traditionalist persuasion (except perhaps in modern Germany, where they often thought themselves to have been "at home"), have regarded any existing, present condition outside The Land as temporary. If not always pil-grims to it in a literal sense, they have always set their face toward The Land. This fidelity has in turn strengthened the continuing belief in the umbilical, eternal connection between the people of Israel and its Land and lent to that Land a sacred quality. In the experience of Jews, theology has informed the interpretation of history and history in turn has confirmed the theology.

In reflecting on the answer finally to be given to the question presented to us as to the place of The Land in Judaism, in the light of the evidence set forth here, an analogy from Christian ecclesiology suggests itself. In Roman Catholicism and high-church Anglicanism the distinction has often been drawn, in discussions of the apostolic episcopate, between what is the *esse* and the *bene esse* of the Christian church. Is this distinction applicable to the ways in which the mainstream of Judaism has conceived of The Land? Judaism has certainly been compelled by the actualities of history to accept exile as a permanent and major mark of its existence and as a source of incal-culable benefit. Has it implicitly recognized, despite the witness of its classical sources and, it might be argued, in conformity with much in them, that while life in The Land is the *bene esse* of all Jewish religious existence, it is not the *esse?* Moses desired to be in The Land so that he might have the possibility of achieving greater obedience to the Torah: That he did not enter was a great deprivation. But it was not fatal to his existence as a Jew. It is the greatest blessing to live in The Land, but living there is not absolutely essential. A Jew can remain true to his Judaism by the standards set by the sources as long as he is loyal to the Torah. He can continue in his faith outside The Land but not outside the Torah. Not The Land but the Torah is the "essence" of Ju-daism; it is, indeed, its relation to the Torah that gives holiness to The Land.

---

50. Scholem, *Sabbatai Sevi*, 15–22.

51. J. B. Agus, *Banner of Jerusalem: The Life, Time, and Thought of Abraham Isaac Kuk* (New York, 1946).

From this point of view it could be argued that The Land is the *bene esse*, not the *esse* of the Jewish faith.[52]

Yet one is uneasy with this analogy, and not only because the Torah itself and the Mishnah are so overwhelmingly concerned with The Land. The antithesis between *esse* and *bene esse*, conceptually valid as it may seem to be, does not do justice to the place of The Land. Because the term "essence" suggests the impersonal, it is as inadequate in dealing with The Land as it is in dealing with Christianity, as inadequate, for example, as Harnack's use of the notion of the "Essence of Christianity."[53] Néher and André LaCocque have pointed us to the personification of The Land in Judaism.[54] They go too far in ascribing an actual personalism to simile and metaphor and figurative language. But exaggerated as their claims may be, they do guard against impersonalism in understanding the role of The Land. The Land evokes immense and deep emotion among religious Jews: it is "La Terre mystique de l'Absolu." It presents a "personal" challenge and offers a "personal" anchorage. The sentiment (a term here used in its strict psychological sense) for The Land is so endemic among religious Jews and so constantly reinforced by their sacred sources, liturgies, and observances that to set life in The Land against life outside The Land as *esse* against *bene esse* is to miss the point. It is better to put the question in another way and ask: Does The Land lie at the heart of Judaism? Put in this more personal manner the question answers itself.

In another study we suggested that for Paul, as for many in early Christianity, life under the Torah and in The Land was transformed into life "in Christ," which became the Christian counterpart of the life in The Land of Judaism. Few would not agree that the heart of Christianity (I avoid the term "essence") is Jesus Christ. Similarly, many take the heart of Judaism to be the Torah. But to accept Judaism on its own terms is to recognize that near to and, indeed, within that heart is The Land. In this sense, just as Christians recognize the scandal of particularity in the Incarnation, in Christ, so there is a scandal of territorial particularity in Judaism. The Land is so embedded in the heart of Judaism, the Torah, that — so its sources, worship, and theology attest — it is finally inseparable from it. "Il faut . . . ne pas essayer de diviser des choses indivisibles."[55]

The scandal presented by a particular land is no less to be recognized than that provided by a particular person. One may interpret the relation between

---

52. Davies, *The Territorial Dimension of Judaism* (Berkeley, Calif., 1982; reprint, Minneapolis, 1991).

53. S. W. Sykes, "Essence of Christianity," *Religious Studies* 7 (December 1971): 291–306.

54. André Néher, "Israel, terre mystique de l'Absolu," in *L'Existence Juive* (Paris, 1962); André LaCocque, "Une Terre qui decoule de Lait et de Miel," *Revue du Dialogue*, no. 2 (1966): 28–36.

55. See chap. 1, n. 36, above for translation. Jean Juster, quoted in G. F. Moore, *Judaism in the First Centuries of the Christian Era: The Age of the Tannaim*, 3 vols. (Cambridge, Mass., 1927–40), 1:234. See also Davies, *Territorial Dimension of Judaism*.

Israel and The Land as a theological mystery or reject it simply as an unusually bizarre and irritating phenomenon. Many will find the crass materiality of the connection between Israel and The Land offensive to their mystical or spiritual sensitivities: others will find much to satisfy them in the emphasis of Judaism on the need to express itself in tangible, material societary or communal form in The Land.[56] Of its historicity in the Jewish consciousness or self-identity there can, in any case, be no doubt. To accept it as a fact of historical significance is not to justify it, but it is to begin to understand it and to respect it as an aspect of Judaism's doctrine of election. "S'il y a un peuple élu, il y a aussi une terre élu."[57] The discussion of The Land drives us to the mystery of Israel, that is, the eschatological purpose of God in His dealings with His people.

Christians and the Land

Our treatment of The Land in Judaism is over. How did David Roberts relate to the doctrine of The Land in Judaism? Because he was a Christian, we must touch briefly on the Christian response to that doctrine. The various aspects of the Christian response to it are foreshadowed in the New Testament. The data in the New Testament fall into two groups.

First, there are strata in the New Testament in which the Jewish understanding of The Land emerges in a critical or negative light. In one stratum (Acts 7) it was rejected outright. In other strata The Land is taken up into a nongeographic, spiritual, transcendent dimension. It becomes a symbol especially of eternal life, of the eschatological society in time and eternity, beyond space and sense. In such strata the physical entities as such — The Land, Jerusalem, the Temple — cease to be significant, except as types of realities that are not in essence physical. It is justifiable to speak of the realia of Judaism as being spiritualized in the Christian dispensation.

But second, there are other strata in which The Land, the Temple, and Jerusalem, in their physical actuality, are regarded positively; that is, in a certain way they retain a significance in Christianity. This arises from two factors — history and theology. The emergence of the Gospels witnesses to a historical and therefore geographic concern in the tradition, which retains for The Land its full physical significance. The need to remember the Jesus of history entailed the need to remember the Jesus of a particular land. Jesus belonged not only to time, but to space; and the space and places that he occupied took on significance, so that The Land continued as a concern in

---

56. Davies, *Territorial Dimension of Judaism.*
57. "If there is a chosen people, there is also a chosen land" (Werblowsky, "Israel et Eretz Israel," 376).

Christianity. History in the tradition demanded geography — a concern with the place and places where Jesus lived.

But a theological factor also helped to ensure this. Especially in the Fourth Gospel, the doctrine that the Word became flesh, though it resulted in a critique of distinct, traditional holy spaces, demanded the recognition that where the glory had appeared among men all physical *forms* became suffused with it. "We beheld His glory" had the corollary that *where* this had happened became significant. If we allow a diffused Platonic as well as apocalyptic dimension to Hebrews and the Fourth Gospel, then their authors believe in a sacramental process, that is, the process of reaching the truth by the frank acceptance of the actual physical conditions of life and making these a "gate to heaven." Such sacramentalism could find holy space everywhere, but especially where Jesus had been. The sacramentalism was later to inform the devotion to the holy places among many Christians throughout the ages.[58]

The witness of the New Testament is, therefore, twofold. It transcends The Land, Jerusalem, the Temple. But its history and theology demand a concern with these realities also. Is there a reconciling principle between these apparently contradictory attitudes? There is. By implication, it has already been suggested. The New Testament finds holy space wherever Christ is or has been: it personalizes "holy space" in Christ, who, as a figure of history, is rooted in The Land; He cleansed the Temple and died in Jerusalem and lends His glory to these and to the places where He was, but, as living Lord, He is also free to move wherever He wills. To do justice to the personalism of the New Testament, that is, to its Christocentrism, is to find the clue to the various strata of tradition that we have traced and to the attitudes they reveal: to their freedom from space and their attachment to holy places.

It is these attitudes, negatively and positively, that have informed the history of Christianity. *Acceptance* of the doctrine of The Land, *rejection, spiritualization, historical concern, sacramental concentration* — all have emerged in that history. I illustrate with a brevity that is distorting. Much modern theology, concentrating on demythologizing, tends to reject the realia of which we speak as anachronistic; medieval and much Puritan thought witness to their spiritualization; the archaeological intensity of much modern scholarship especially and much also of its literary criticism point to a historical concern centering in the quest of the historical Jesus; and in Greek Orthodoxy and in medieval theology, expressed in the history of pilgrimages to Palestine and in the Crusades, connected as these are with the motif of the imitation of Christ, the sacramentalism of which I write is a striking characteristic. To illustrate all this in depth is beyond the range of this essay. But one thing in the history of Christianity — I do not say Christendom — needs no illustra-

---

58. See Davies, *Gospel and the Land*, 366–76.

tion, so ubiquitous is it: its Christocentrism. In the end, where Christianity has reacted seriously to the realia of Judaism, whether negatively or positively, it has done so in terms of Christ, to whom all space and all places, like all things else, are subordinated. In sum, for the holiness of place, Christianity had fundamentally, though not consistently, substituted the holiness of the person: it has Christified holy space. I suggested that to be "in Christ" for Christians is to be "in The Land."

David Roberts and the Land

At this point we revert to the question asked at the beginning of this essay: Is there irony involved in Roberts's work? Let it be stated at once that the traditional understanding of the attitude of Judaism to art allows no room for irony here, because that faith, so it has long been asserted, was not concerned with the artistic expression of beauty. Typical of this traditional approach to Judaism and art is a trenchant chapter by Peter T. Forsyth, a Scottish theologian of the early years of this century. In his book *Christ on Parnassus*, Forsyth begins a chapter entitled "Hebrew Art and Religion" with the words: "The second commandment passes the death sentence on Hebrew Art. . . . Neither painter, sculptor, nor dramatist could live under the shadow of this stern law."[59] In his insistence on a lack of an artistic sense in the Jewish tradition, Forsyth expresses the academic orthodoxy of his time. As was then customary, he contrasted the Hebraic with the Greek tradition: the latter was conducive to art, whereas, so Forsyth asserted, the nature of Hebrew religion, of the Hebrew people, and of their country and history all led Jews away from artistic expression. For Forsyth, who, we emphasize again, was typical of scholarship up to his day, and who, as far as I am aware (there is no index to his book), never referred to him, David Roberts's priority and preeminence in the painting of The Land would occasion no surprise. For him, the Jewish artists' neglect of such painting was what we should expect. David Roberts's work should provoke no irony.

Not only Gentile scholars took the view represented by Forsyth. Kalman Bland has documented how Jewish thinkers, "simultaneously embroiled in socio-political warfare over the questions of Jewish emancipation, assimilation and cultic reform," also shared in this view. He cites Heinrich Graetz, the famous late-nineteenth-century Jewish historian, who "typifies all modern

---

59. The second commandment states, "You shall not make yourself a graven image or any likeness of anything that is in heaven above or that is in the earth beneath, or that is in the water under the earth" (Exod. 20:4). Forsyth adds as a footnote, "We have the same prohibition in the Koran and the same result in Islam; to say nothing of Scotland. English Puritanism was different." See Peter T. Forsyth, *Christ on Parnassus: Lectures on Art, Ethic, and Theology* (New York, n.d.), 43 n. 1.

scholars and theologians who first devised and then perpetuated a normative, aniconic, eternally verbal, ethical essence of Judaism. Eager to flee the natural and the visual in order to embrace the spiritual and the audial, they concocted chaste Hebraic ears and aesthetically seductive but morally questionable pagan eyes." Explicitly it was with paganism that Graetz contrasted Hebraism, but behind this contrast was the generally accepted contrast, in his day, of primitive (pagan) with advanced societies.[60]

But the contrast between Hebraism and Hellenism, as if they were two isolated, watertight compartments, has largely broken down,[61] and since the publication of E. R. Goodenough's *Jewish Symbols in the Greco-Roman Period* that contrast has been radically challenged in the realm of art also. Goodenough drew attention to the frescoes in the Dura-Europos Synagogue and to other phenomena pointing to a Jewish art. His immense work makes it less and less feasible to explain away — as so confidently does Forsyth and as has been customary among scholars — the decoration of the tabernacle and the Temple, the carved fruits and trees, flowers and the fresco.[62] It may be still premature to pronounce that Forsyth's view, that "there is no Hebrew Art," is dead and buried. The paucity of references to beauty in the Tanak is striking, although the social and political conditions have not always made it easy for Jews to be artistically preoccupied. But the evidence produced by Kalman Bland[63] that, as in the ancient classical period, so in the Middle Ages, Jews

---

60. Kalman P. Bland, "Medieval Jewish Aesthetics: Maimonides, Body, and Scripture in Profiat Duran," *Journal of the History of Ideas* 54 (1993): 535.

61. Davies, *Paul and Rabbinic Judaism: Some Rabbinic Elements in Pauline Theology*, 4th ed. (Philadelphia, 1980), vii–xii.

62. Forsyth, *Christ on Parnassus*, 44–45.

63. Bland, "Medieval Jewish Aesthetics." He refers to Jeremiah 3:19, Ezekiel, and Psalm 48:3, and to the grace after meals. In a private letter of 3 February 1996 he writes:

As I suspected, *Zion in Jewish Literature* (ed. A. Halkin) refers to several sources — biblical and rabbinic — that associate "beauty" with the Land of Israel. Page 19, for example, refers to Jeremiah (3:19) and Ezekiel. Page 23, for example, refers to Psalm 48:3. In Gershom Cohen's article, page 41, reference is made to Israel as a "beautiful" land and to an article by J. Guttmann where the term and its synonyms are discussed. For a hint at the *topos* in medieval poetry, see Dimitrovsky's discussion [in *Zion in Jewish Literature*] on pages 76–77. These references are merely the tip on an iceberg. The rabbinic Grace after Meals contains the blessing praising the Land and its beauty: "We thank You Lord, our God, for having bequeathed unto our ancestors a beautifully gracious (*Hemdah*), goodly (*Torah*) and ample (*Rehavah*) Land...." Such a quotidian bit of liturgy surely impressed on Jewish consciousness a sense that the land was beautiful.

I have taken the liberty of attaching some xeroxes of medieval Hebrew poetry to whet your appetite and to assure you that Israel was considered "beautiful" despite her desolation and despite the absence of her "children" during the Galut. (A quick check of the Concordance under Land, "Yafah," and "Hemdah" reassures me, too, that the midrash is filled with the same and that the medieval poets were treading familiar territory.) The xeroxes are taken from *The Penguin Book of Hebrew Verse*, edited and translated by T. Carmi. Page 223 has God describing Zion as a "delightful, beautiful plant." Page 314 has Israel, the Land, described as the beautiful maiden from Song of Solomon. Page 348, by Judah

were familiar with and engaged in all sorts of artistic work; the evidence in Cecil Roth's work, *Jewish Art: An Illustrated History*,[64] of a Jewish artistic concern down to the present time, and the evidence in Jerusalem in recent years, as at the activity in the Mishkenot Sheananim and also the Bezalel Institute for Art in the Hebrew University, Jerusalem — all call for very serious consideration and recognition. We eagerly await Kalman Bland's forthcoming study of Judaism and art. Nevertheless, it does still seem to us very pertinent to ask why Judaism did not provide a counterpart to David Roberts and whether it is not ironical that it is a Scottish Presbyterian who has done most artistic justice to The Land in painting.

One answer to this question has little to do with the artistic attitude of Judaism as such, but very much to do with the central concern of that faith. What was primarily important about The Land for Jews was not its physical nature or geographic character, its riches or its poverty, and not its landscape as such, whether beautiful or otherwise, but the utterly central fact that it was The Land promised or sworn by Yahweh to them, that it was the covenanted Land of a covenanted people. This concentration on the covenanted character of The Land along with the misguided interpretation of the second commandment, as not simply referring to idolatry but to all artistic expression, may have accounted for the tardiness of Jews in producing artistic representation of The Land in painting and otherwise and allowed a Gentile, David Roberts, to assume such a distinctive place as *the* artist of The Land, which, as a Christian, he called "the Holy Land."

This last sentence leads us to the character and intent of David Roberts's presentation of The Land. His biographer Katharine Sim, in *David Roberts R.A. (1796–1864)*, makes clear that he was interested in Judaism: he sometimes deliberately sought to live among Jews and was sympathetic to them.[65] But there is little evidence that his knowledge of Judaism was any more than could be garnered from his Presbyterian upbringing. That knowledge was probably exclusively biblical and Christian and untouched by the developments of Jewish thought on many matters, and especially, for our purpose, on The Land. The doctrine of The Land, which we have here attempted to present, would not have impinged upon him. He does not seem to have been theologically sensitive. Thus he showed little interest in the Islam of the Arabs whom he encountered. "Roberts himself," Sim writes, "made little attempt to understand Islam, and, almost worse though in ignorance — re-

---

Halevi, has no specific use of "beauty" but it is surely implicit in the poet's love for the very air, water, and trees of the land.

64. New York, Toronto, and London, 1961.
65. Katharine Sim, *David Roberts R.A., 1796–1864: A Biography* (London, 1984), 83, 130, 136.

viled those few courageous men who had penetrated the mask."[66] We can be fairly certain that the intricacies of Jewish thought were unknown to him. Nor should we expect any profound awareness of the Christian theological tradition, except insofar as he had been brought up in a simplistic biblical Sunday School tradition. The force of that tradition, however, we can illustrate from the most recent work by one of the leading American novelists, Reynolds Price. He writes of the influence of his early reading of the Bible upon him as follows:

> I am hardly alone in the world in saying that the central narratives of the Old and New Testaments — especially the four life stories called Matthew, Mark, Luke, and John — drew early at my mind and have kept their magnetism for me. In my case, their hold has lasted undiminished nearly six decades. Before I could read I often turned the profusely illustrated pages of *Hurlbut's Story of the Bible*, imagining what tales had produced such swarming pictures. By the age of eight, I had begun making drawings of my own from the knowledge I gained in reading the tales with my new-won literacy and yielding to the pull of their fresh unnerving actions — Abraham bent on butchering his Isaac, the boy David with the hacked-off head of a monstrous Goliath; or (strangest and most riveting of all) the birth of a unique glistening child in a strawy stable with attendant angels, shepherds, and Wise Men.
>
> ...I meant to learn to exert power as nearly strong and awful, as irresistible and fertile, as those old stories of ancient Jews and their endless trials. Mine would be stories that felt as near to the truthful ground as the ones I had learned in Genesis, Exodus, Judges, Samuel, Kings, or Matthew, Mark, Luke, and John. I wanted, over all else, to make new stories that might somehow share in those old stories' radiant will to change whole lives and alter the sun in its course if need be.[67]

Price is an artist in words. The Bible, and with it The Land, exerted the same influence on David Roberts in painting. That Roberts was extremely sensitive to the beauty of landscape is clear,[68] and his early experience in painting scenes for the theater had given him the training to deal with the landscape of The Land in paint. But just as the Bible itself does not concentrate on

---

66. Ibid., 24.
67. Reynolds Price, *Three Gospels: The Good News according to Mark, the Good News according to John, an Honest Account of a Remarkable Life* (New York, 1996), 1–2.
68. Sim, *David Roberts R.A.*, 13, 95, 117, 119, 120, 124, 130, 141, 150, 147, 153, 148 — scenery and smells.

the beauty of The Land, so too with Roberts. The landscapes he painted from memory from sketches on his return to England are generally "rough" and without detail; it was the buildings in the landscape that concerned him. Although, as we noted previously, he used the term "the Holy Land," it was not The Land as such, and its importance for Jews, that engaged Roberts, but the topoi — the places — where Christ, The Lord, had worked and to which He had lent His glory. Roberts — as Dr. Sarah Schroth, the curator of the Duke University Museum of Art revealed to me — was above all a topographical artist (and such artists are not high in the hierarchy of artists), and in his lithographs it is not so much The Land and its landscape as the historical places in The Land that engaged him — the places that Christ had touched. So too, the indigenous people of The Land, were they Jews or Palestinian Arabs, do not seem to have occupied him as an artist. The figures in his lithographs are stereotypical and formal. (He might justifiably — but anachronistically — come under the lash of Professor Edward Said.) His concentration was on the biblical places familiar to him from his Presbyterian boyhood. Although in later life he did not, as did Price, make the biblical stories and scenes the springboard for a sophisticated theological awareness and sensitivity, the same stories and scenes from the Bible inspired Roberts to produce the most influential representations of them in painting. Because he was so moved by the Bible, his lithographs of the Holy Land have continued to impress the mind of the West — indeed, of the world — as none other, be it Jewish, Christian, or pagan. If there is irony in Roberts's lithographs, it is this: it was a Christian artist, for whom The Land had become subordinated to a person, "life in Christ" having taken precedence over life "in The Land," and not Jewish artists, for whom The Land is part of the very nature of their faith, who has most served The Land in art. His lithographs on the whole confirm the assertion often made that whereas Judaism concentrated on "The Land," Christianity has concentrated on holy places in "The Land," which has, through them, become "the Holy Land."

However, in thus assessing the strictly religious aspect of Roberts's work certain considerations are pertinent. First, the nature of the journal of his journey, written by Roberts himself and printed in *From an Antique Land*, from which conclusions have been drawn, is such that it should be used only with the greatest caution. Roberts wrote as he traveled, when he was inevitably occupied with the very demanding, mundane concerns of the itinerary, camp life — the financial arrangements for guides, for dromedaries, for meetings with various authorities for permission to traverse the territories under their control, and for the supplies or provisions, not to mention the physical exertion involved, the frequent discomforts and even dangers encountered. On top of all this, as he went along, he had to prepare the sketches of scenes, which were to be developed later on his return to England.[69] The labor in all this was immense. And there is another consideration little noticed. Unlike some other famous travelers who kept journals of their journeys — for example, Charles Darwin in England and Meriwether Lewis in the United States — Roberts did not find it easy to write. Like many artists who painted he was not a literary person: his brush was his pen. Sim makes it clear that, from his early days, Roberts did not find writing congenial: he had difficulty even with spelling — a difficulty that persisted into his later life and about which he was very self-conscious.[70] One has only to compare the comments on various places made by his fellow traveler, John Kinnear, with those made by Roberts himself to recognize the greater facility in writing enjoyed by the former.[71] Recording, in writing, religious or theological reflections would not come naturally to such a person, and how much less likely would they do so under the circumstances of his journeying.

And then, second, a Scottish Presbyterian is not likely to have expressed his or her religion sensitivities and experiences too frequently and easily. The Presbyterianism of Scotland, as we noted before, was austere, reserved, and restrained. The enthusiasm of Methodism, for example — and here I am confirmed by a specialist on Methodism, Dr. Frank Baker — has never been much in evidence in Scotland. Although there were scattered Methodist churches in a few places, Edinburgh being noteworthy, Methodism did not find congenial soil north of the Tweed. Not surprisingly, therefore, expressions of piety and theology by Roberts are hard to come by: he did not wear his heart on his sleeve. Certain references in his journal might be taken to indicate a religious sensitivity, but this is largely repressed or unexpressed, as in his comments on coming to Jerusalem.[72]

But when all this has been recognized, the absence of theological or spiritual reflections in Roberts's journal remains noteworthy. Even in the passages referred to on his coming to Jerusalem[73] it is not its awesome history and religious significance, but the beauty of the city's surroundings, that stands out

---

69. A biographer writes: "[Roberts] seemed to have the faculty of photographing objects on his eye, for I have again and again been with him while he was sketching very elaborate structures or very extensive views, and he took in a large mass at one glance, not requiring to look again at that portion until he had it completed in his sketch" (James Ballantine, *The Life of David Roberts, R.A.* (Edinburgh, 1866), quoted in Sim, *David Roberts R.A.*, 67–68). The scenes of the Holy Land by Roberts, therefore, are not directly painted from that land, but filtered through his memory and his sketches.

70. Sim, *David Roberts R.A.*, 7. There are examples of misspelling by Roberts in his journal and examples in quotations from his journal that appear in Dr. Schroth's chapter in *Jerusalem and the Holy Land Rediscovered*. See n. 1 above for publication information.

71. See, for example, David Roberts, *From an Antique Land: Travels in Egypt and the Holy Land* (New York, 1989), 113, 119, on Hebron and on Gaza.

72. Roberts, *From an Antique Land*, 119, 120.

73. *Jerusalem and the Holy Land Rediscovered*, 119, 120. See n. 1 above. Parenthetical page references are to this volume.

as marked by him: "[T]he whole country [around Jerusalem]," he writes, "is in the pure budding beauty of spring. I cannot imagine why travelers represent it as arid or desolate or yet as being surrounded by mountains" (120). I counted only two references to "our Saviour" in the journal (133, 147), and one misses the sense that Roberts was walking "In His Steps," as did countless pilgrims, in any significant way. Even in the most religiously evocative places he only rarely (see pp. 140, 142) refers to the text of the Tanak or of the New Testament. For example, he does not connect the name of Samson with Gaza (112). He finds Jerusalem wretched ("surely there cannot be any city more wretched" [134]), and does not explicitly reflect on its history and importance. The mystique of Jerusalem, earthly and heavenly, eludes him.[74] The absence of a theological interest emerges also, not only in the lack of interest in Islam, which we noted previously, but even, on occasion, in a slight touch of cynicism. This crops up when he describes the ascent of Mohamet to heaven from the Mosque of Omar and in the treatment of Cana in Galilee.[75] That Roberts was unaware of Jewish traditions in any but the biblical mode appears from this treatment of Tiberias: "[T]he town," he wrote, "with 400 of its inhabitants was destroyed[....] Its present inhabitants are nearly all Jews who came here to die[....] They live in expectation of the reappearance of the Messiah and are supported by contributions made by their brethren in different parts of the world."[76] He does not seem to be aware of the movements by Jews to settle in The Land to which we referred earlier, nor does he note (unless there is an omission in his journal indicated by the ellipses in the text printed in *From an Antique Land*) that Judah the Prince, the codifier of the Mishnah, was buried not far from Tiberias (at Beth Shearim). On the same page he refers to what he calls *Saffet*, by which he presumably means Safed, "where," he writes, "it is expected by the Jews the Messiah is to reign for 40 years before entering Jerusalem...." Again there may be an indication of an omission in the text, but Roberts, to judge from the journal, was unaware of the immense significance of Safed in Jewish history, in the sixteenth century, as the center for Lurianic Qabbalah. It is not surprising, therefore, that he was almost certainly unaware of the agelong and very living doctrine of the inseparable, eternal connection between the people of Israel and The Land.

But this cannot be the final word. The considerations we have adduced in these last few pages make it precarious to look for theological or religious intentions and insights in the lithographs of the Holy Land by Roberts. Sim

---

74. That this mystique is vitally alive is clear from a recent statement by the distinguished philosopher Emil L. Fackenheim, "Fighting for Jerusalem Today," *Midstream* 42 (February–March 1996): 21–24. See also Davies, *Gospel and the Land*, 130ff.

75. Roberts, *From an Antique Land*, 136.

76. Ibid., 147.

makes it clear that his personal conduct was, indeed, admirable: it revealed an ingrained humaneness, which explains his sympathy with the burden of the Arabs, poor Arabs to him.[77] To judge from his history, he was especially quick to express gratitude, which has often been called the greatest of all the virtues, to all who helped him in any way from his earliest days in Scotland to the time when the monks so often helped him in the monasteries of the Holy Land. But it is essential to recognize that he did not go to that land as a pilgrim (the notice he takes of pilgrims is generally objective and even clinical as it is of religious phenomena in general); at best he shows no more than a detached religious involvement. Sim calls him a "Painter Pilgrim" — and the emphasis, we suggest, should be on the painter. And the image of the Holy Land that his paintings presents has become dominant in the minds of most. How far that image is a representation of what the Holy Land was actually like in his day we cannot know. His lithographs are concentrated not primarily on The Land as such. Roberts drew his landscapes from memory after he had returned to England; they are rough outlines lacking in detail. What Sir William Orpen called "the Rise of Landscape Painting," marked particularly by J. W. Turner and John Constable, did not seem to have touched Roberts, although he knew and admired Turner. Apparently, the Romanticism of those who painted the natural landscape was largely alien to him. Similarly a comparison of Roberts's lithographs with the paintings reproduced by Marcel Brion, for example, in *The Bible in Art: Miniatures, Drawings, Paintings, and Sculptures Inspired by the Old Testament*, indicates how much more painters in Europe had been engaged with the personages of the Bible — with Moses, David, Adam and Eve, the prophets, and so forth — than was Roberts, whose lithographs concentrate on places rather than persons. As he did not neatly fit into the rise of landscape painting, so he did not belong to the great tradition of European religious portraiture, although it had preceded him in Gainsborough, Romney, and others. He stands almost independently alone. As in the scholarship of Scandinavians in theology and other disciplines — from the northern limits of Europe and outside the main European centers of art influenced by and simultaneously reacting against these centers — the same geographic origin accounts for a distinctive quality about the work of this Scottish painter, which in a peculiar way has won for him a very special place in the painting of the Holy Land. Through his independent genius, despite his detached religious involvement, he made a dominating contribution to the mystique of the land that Jews call The Land and that, like other Christians, he him-

---

77. Sim, *David Roberts R.A.*, 7; see for example p. 87. In this essay it has not been possible to engage the question of what happens when the claims of Jews to The Land conflict with those of other inhabitants of The Land. See Davies, *Territorial Dimension of Judaism*, 122–32. See also Kenneth Cragg, *This Year in Jerusalem: Israel in Experience* (London, 1982).

self called the Holy Land. There is, then, a final twist of irony in that it is one — a topographical artist — often seen to have little of what is now called "the vision thing," that is, the awareness of distant horizons, who has most influenced the way in which the Western world thinks of the ancient land of Israel.

Part II

Paul and Judaism

Chapter 6

Paul and the Exodus

I wish to speak to the use of sacred tradition in the theology of the Apostle Paul. This sacred tradition comes to the apostle in two important streams: the scriptures of Israel and the words of Jesus. I shall treat aspects of this tradition under two headings: (1) the Christian dispensation as a new exodus, and (2) echoes of the Jesus tradition in the letters of Paul.

The Christian Dispensation as a New Exodus

There is much to indicate that a very significant part of the conceptual world in which Paul moved, *as a Christian,* was that of the exodus. It is clear that, as for Matthew and other New Testament writers, so for Paul, there was a real correspondence between the Christian dispensation and the exodus of Israel from Egypt. The redemption of the Old Israel was the prototype of the greater redemption from sin wrought by Christ for the New Israel. This has been much recognized in recent scholarship.[1]

One of Paul's most important passages relating to this subject, 1 Corinthians 10:1–10, reads as follows:

I should like to thank four people for their help in the publishing of this essay. First, I cannot sufficiently praise the care and imagination which Dr. Craig A. Evans, in collaboration with my old friend Dr. Shemaryahu Talmon, brought to the preparation of this chapter. I am also grateful for the very helpful comments of the Dr. D. C. Allison, and to Sarah Freedman for her ready and unfailing competence.

1. See, for example, P. Dabeck, "Siehe, es erschienen Moses und Elias," *Bib* 23 (1942): 175–89; E. Sahlin, "The New Exodus of Salvation," in A. J. Fridrichsen, ed., *The Root of the Vine: Essays in Biblical Theology* (Westminster, England: Dacre Press, 1953); R. Schnackenburg, "Todes- und Lebensgemeinschaft mit Christus: Neue Studien zu Rom. vi.1–11," *TZ* 6 (1955): 32–35; J. Manek, "The New Exodus and the Book of Luke," *NovT* 2 (1957): 8–23; H. M. Teeple, *The Mosaic Eschatological Prophet* (Philadelphia: Society of Biblical Literature, 1957); G. H. Williams, *Wilderness and Paradise in Christian Thought* (New York: Harper, 1962); D. Daube, *The Exodus Pattern in the Bible* (London: Faber and Faber, 1963); U. Mauser, *Christ in the Wilderness: The Wilderness Theme in the Second Gospel and its Basis in the Biblical Tradition,* SBT 39 (Naperville, Ill.: Allenson, 1963); and now especially the extraordinarily rich work of D. C. Allison, *The New Moses: A Matthean Typology* (Minneapolis: Fortress Press, 1993).

I want you to know, brothers, that our fathers were all under the cloud, and all passed through the sea, and all were baptized into Moses in the cloud and in the sea, and all ate the same supernatural food and drank the same supernatural drink. For they drank from the supernatural Rock which followed them, and the Rock was Christ. Nevertheless with most of them God was not pleased; for they were overthrown in the wilderness. Now these things are warnings for us, not to desire evil as they did. Do not be idolaters as some of them were; as it is written, "The people sat down to eat and drink and rose up to dance." We must not indulge an immorality as some of them did, and twenty-three thousand fell in a single day. We must not put the Lord to the test, as some of them did and were destroyed by serpents; nor grumble, as some of them did and were destroyed by the Destroyer.

The interpretation of the Christian life as a counterpart of the exodus is here made quite explicit; note especially that the experience of the New Exodus, like that of the first, demands the forsaking of immorality (1 Cor. 10:8); that is, the taking up of the yoke of Christ, although this is not expressly so stated. Again, Paul's understanding of the Eucharist is largely covenantal; it is for him the institution of the New Israel, the counterpart of the Old (1 Cor. 11:20–34).[2] This is reinforced in 1 Corinthians 5:7, where Christ is referred to as a Passover lamb slain for Christians, and in 1 Corinthians 15:20, where Christ is the first fruits. This last contains a side-glance at the ritual of the Passover; Christ is the first fruits of a new redemption. Out of the passages where Paul roots the imperative in the indicative (1 Thess. 2:10–11; 4:7, 8; 5:5–11; 1 Cor. 5:7; Gal. 5:1, 25; 2 Cor. 8:7; Rom. 6:2–4; Col. 3:1), two certainly, and a third possibly, are influenced by the thought of the Christian as having undergone a new exodus. This is so as we saw in 1 Corinthians 5:7, and the motif of freedom in Galatians 5:1 owes something to the motif.[3] Moreover, if our argument elsewhere be accepted that the Pauline concept of dying and rising with Christ is to be understood in terms of a New Exodus,[4] then another passage, Romans 6:2–11, from the six

---

2. See my *Paul and Rabbinic Judaism. Some Rabbinic Elements in Pauline Theology*, 2d ed. (London: SPCK, 1955; reprint, Philadelphia: Fortress Press, 1980), 250–54.

3. On this, see D. Daube, *The New Testament and Rabbinic Judaism* (London: Athlone, 1956), 282. The whole chapter on "Redemption" (see pp. 268–84) is illuminating.

4. Davies, *Paul and Rabbinic Judaism*, 102–8. The language of "dying and rising with Christ" in Paul, particularly in European and continental theology, has been traditionally explained in terms of Hellenistic Mystery religions, whose ideas influenced the early church, partly consciously and partly unconsciously. This traditional explanation was subjected to exhaustive examination by A. J. M. Wedderburn in his truly classic work, *Baptism and Resurrection: Studies in Pauline Theology against Its Graeco-Roman Background*, WUNT 44 (Tübingen: Mohr [Siebeck], 1987). He concludes that this language finds "no true parallel" in the soteriology of the mysteries (342). He turns instead to "the obvious parallel" in the Mishnaic text relating to the Passover, m. *Pesaḥ*. 10.5, and refers (p. 344) to my own work in *Paul and Rabbinic Judaism*, 102–4, where

referred to, also contains this idea of the Christian dispensation as a counterpart to the first exodus. Among the metaphors used by Paul to expound his experience in Christ is that of "redemption," which, we cannot doubt, was intimately bound up in his mind with the thought of the emancipation of the Old Israel from Egypt (Exod. 6:6; 15:13; Deut. 7:8; 15:15).[5] In 2 Corinthians 6:16 the presence of God in the temple of the New Israel, the church, is expressly understood, we may assume, as the realization of the promise made to Moses, as for example in Exodus 25:8 "And let them make for me a sanctuary that I may dwell in their midst," or again in Exodus 29:43–45: "There will I meet with the people of Israel, and it shall be sanctified by my glory; I will consecrate the tent of meeting and the altar...and I will dwell among the people of Israel, and will be their God." This is in agreement with the view that in 2 Corinthians the thought of Paul is largely governed by the understanding of the Christian life in terms of a new covenant (2 Cor. 3:1–18) and of the sojourn in the wilderness (2 Cor. 5:1–5). Moreover, the reference in 2 Corinthians 6:14 — "or what fellowship has light with darkness?"[6] reminds us that Christians for Paul are children of the day. Thus, in Colossians 1:12–13, we read "...giving thanks to the Father who has qualified us to share in the inheritance of the saints in the light. He has delivered us from the domination of darkness and transferred us to the kingdom of his beloved Son, in whom we have redemption, the forgiveness of sins." It is possible that here the exodus motif is again apparent in the use of the term "inheritance." In Deuteronomy this term is closely connected with the deliverance from Egypt,[7] and it may be that for Paul it also suggests the eschatological redemption, through the death and resurrection of Christ, parallel to that wrought at the exodus. Certainly the motif of "light and darkness" which occurs in the same passage suggests this. In 1 Peter 2:9, 10 this motif occurs in a context which recalls the exodus, and especially Exodus 19:4–6. In *m. Pesaḥ.* 10:5 we read in the Passover service:

---

this is discussed, and even more sympathetically to Jewish ideas of "corporate personality" in the references to Adam. See Wedderburn's rich discussion on pp. 342–48. He finds that while "Davies has rightly perceived the *Grundstruktur* of Paul's thought...Davies was wrong to specify these ideas as peculiarly connected with the exodus; rather they are basic ideas, ways of looking at things, to which the Jews had given classic expression in their Passover liturgy" (344 n. 9). It still seems to us that it was in that liturgy — with which Paul, as a Pharisee, must have been highly familiar — that he was most directly exposed to the ideas concerned, although the precise form of that liturgy in Paul's day eludes us.

5. Davies, *Paul and Rabbinic Judaism*, 268–75.

6. The use of the "darkness and light" motif in Paul can be connected perhaps also with the kind of dualism we find in the Dead Sea Scrolls; see S. Wibbing, *Die Tugend- und Lasterkataloge im Neuen Testament* (Berlin: Töpelmann, 1959), 61–63. On 2 Corinthians 3:1–18; 5:1–2, see Davies, *Paul and Rabbinic Judaism*, 106–8, 309–20.

7. The Greek verb "to inherit" (κληρονομεῖν) and its corresponding substantives have a long association with the exodus, the land of Canaan being the "inheritance" of Israel, as in, for example, Deuteronomy 4:20, 21, etc.

"Therefore we are bound to give thanks, to praise, to glorify, to honor, to exalt, to extol, and to bless him who wrought all these wonders for our fathers and for us. He brought us out from bondage to freedom, from sorrow to gladness, and from mourning to a festival day, *and from darkness to great light* and from servitude to redemption; so let us say before him the *Hallelujah*" (my emphasis). Specific references to darkness and light are clear in the Exodus story itself. In Exodus 10:21–23 we read: "Then the Lord said to Moses, 'Stretch out your hand toward heaven that there may be darkness over the land of Egypt, a darkness to be felt.' So Moses stretched out his hand toward heaven, and there was a thick darkness in all the land of Egypt three days; they did not see one another, nor did any rise from his place for three days; but all the people of Israel had light where they dwelt." The parallelism between Old and New Israel there may not be pressed, however, because the Old Israel did not strictly pass from darkness, although they were surrounded by it (Exod. 12:23). Nevertheless, the symbol of a passage from darkness to light was taken up by Deutero-Isaiah and employed to describe redemption (Isa. 42:16) — "I will turn the darkness before them into light, the rough places into level ground," a redemption which was a New Exodus. Paul in Colossians 1:12–14 may be governed by the same concept.

So far, however, we have only pointed to passages where the concept of exodus, as the type of Christian redemption, has been employed by Paul in a general sense. In many of the passages cited above as containing the New Exodus motif, while there is an appeal, implicit or explicit, to its consequences in good conduct, there is none to any specific commandment as such which characterizes the New Exodus. Are we then to conclude that it was in the character of the exodus, almost solely as deliverance, rather than as also imposing a demand, in the giving of the Law, that Paul found it pertinent for the interpretation of the gospel? In other words, did anything in his understanding of the New Exodus "in Christ" correspond to those events in the total complex of the exodus that transpired *particularly* at Sinai? It is our contention that there was, and that on grounds which may not be equally cogent but which are all worthy of attention. They constitute the second category of consideration which we mentioned above as specifically suggesting that the words of Jesus were important for Paul.

Echoes of the Jesus Tradition in the Letters of Paul

We begin with the assertion that it has been insufficiently recognized how frequently the Epistles of Paul echo the Synoptic Gospels, even as it has been too readily assumed that the apostle was indifferent to the Jesus of history, his works, and especially for our purpose, his words. Two factors are relevant: first, there is clearly traceable in the Epistles a process whereby reminiscences of the words of the Lord Jesus himself are interwoven with traditional material; and second, there is strong evidence that there was a collection of sayings of Jesus to which Paul appealed as authoritative. In this connection 1 Corinthians 7:25 is particularly instructive. The data we have provided in detail elsewhere; we here merely reiterate that the tables presented by Alfred Resch in his work *Der Paulinismus und die logia Jesu* demand serious evaluation.[8]

It might be observed that whereas Resch found 925 parallels with the Synoptic Gospels in nine Pauline letters, Victor Furnish found only eight which he believed could with any confidence be identified as dominical.[9] According to J. D. G. Dunn in a recent study, "that there can be such a disparity at once tells us how subjective the whole exercise has been and still is."[10] Some of the parallels discussed by Dunn include the following:

Rom. 12:14: *"Bless those who persecute you, bless* and do not *curse"*

Luke 6:27–28: "Love your enemies . . . *bless* those who *curse* you"

Matt. 5:44: "Love your enemies and pray for *those who persecute you"*

1 Cor. 13:2: "if I *have* all *faith* so as to move (μεθιοτάναι) *mountains"*

Matt. 17:20: "if you *have faith* . . . you will say to this *mountain,* 'Move from here to there and it will move (μεταβήσεται)' "

1 Thess. 5:2, 4: "You yourselves *know* well that the day of the Lord is coming like a *thief* in the night . . . you are not in darkness and that day will surprise you like a thief"

Matt. 24:43: "Know this that if the householder had *known* at what watch the *thief* was to *come,* he would have watched"

---

8. A. Resch, *Der Paulinismus und die logia Jesu in ihrem gegenseitigen Verhältnis untersucht,* TU 12 (Leipzig: Hinrichs, 1904). See Davies, *Paul and Rabbinic Judaism,* 136–38. Cognate to this field of study is Paul's usage of the Old Testament, both explicit and allusive. See the important work by R. B. Hays, *Echoes of Scripture in the Letters of Paul* (New Haven: Yale University Press, 1989), and discussion of this work in C. A. Evans and J. A. Sanders, eds., *Paul and the Scriptures of Israel,* JSNTSup 83, Studies in Scripture in Early Judaism and Christianity 1 (Sheffield: JSOT Press, 1993).

9. V. P. Furnish, *Theology and Ethics in Paul* (Nashville: Abingdon Press, 1968).

10. J. D. G. Dunn, "Jesus Tradition in Paul," in B. D. Chilton and C. A. Evans, eds., *Studying the Historical Jesus: Evaluations of the State of Current Research,* NTTS 19 (Leiden: Brill, 1994), 155–78. See also A. M. Hunter, *Paul and His Predecessors* (London: SCM Press, 1961), 47–51; D. C. Allison, "The Pauline Epistles and the Synoptic Gospels," *NTS* 28 (1982): 1–32; F. Neirynck, "Paul and the Sayings of Jesus," in A. Vanhoye, ed., *L'Apôtre Paul,* BETL 73 (Louvain: Peeters, 1986), 265–321.

1 Thess. 5:13: *"live at peace among* yourselves" (εἰρηνεύετε ἐν ἑαυ-τοῖς)

Mark 9:50: *"live at peace with* one another" (εἰρηνεύετε ἐν ἀλλήλοις)

Rom. 16:19: "I want you to be *wise* (σοφούς) in regard to what is good and *innocent* (ἀκεραίους) in regard to what is bad"

Matt. 10:16: "Be *wise* (φρόνιμοι) as serpents and *innocent* (ἀκέραιοι) as doves"

1 Thess. 5:6: "So then, let us not sleep as others do, but let us *keep awake* (γρηγορῶμεν) and be sober"

Matt. 24:42: *"Keep awake* (γρηγορεῖτε) therefore" (cf. Luke 21:34–36)

1 Thess. 5:16: *"Rejoice* (χαίρετε) at all times"

Luke 10:20: *"Rejoice* (χαίρετε) that your names have been written in heaven"

With the echoes of the teaching of Jesus in his epistles it must be assumed that Paul refers to a law of the Messiah.[11] This is not a mere overhang from a pre-Pauline Jewish-Christian legalism unrelated to the essentials of Paul's thought. In addition to what we have noted in another work, the evidence seems to suggest that the interpretation of the teaching of Jesus as a New Law was not necessarily aboriginal in primitive Jewish Christianity but only comes into prominence in later Jewish Christianity after the fall of Jerusalem in 70 c.e..[12] Nor again is the phrase "the law of Christ" to be explained away as a vague equivalent to an immanent principle of life like the Stoic law of nature.[13] Moreover, though there are places where Paul seems to understand the law of the Messiah as fulfilled in the law of love, this last also does not exhaust the meaning of the phrase. Almost certainly it is a comprehensive expression for the totality of the ethical teaching of Jesus that had come down to Paul as authoritative. Paul's vocabulary at several points

11. 1 Corinthians 9:21; Galatians 6:2. See Davies, *Paul and Rabbinic Judaism*, 142; C. H. Dodd, "Ἔννομος Χριστοῦ," in W. C. van Unnik et al., eds., *Studia Paulina in honorem Johannis de Zwaan* (Haarlem, Netherlands: Bohn, 1953), 96–110.

12. See M. Simon, *Verus Israel* (Paris: Éditions E. de Boccard, 1948), 100–103, whose treatment, however, also shows that there were anticipations of the later interpretation of Christianity as a New Law in the New Testament itself, for example, James 1:25; Galatians 6:2; Hebrews 7:12. The notion of a New Law is closely associated with that of a new people (see pp. 102–3); J. Daniélou (*Théologie du Judeo-Christianisme*, 2 vols. [Paris: Desclée, 1958], 1:216–18) notes how Christ became not only a New Law but the New Covenant.

13. C. H. Dodd, *The Bible and the Greeks*, 2d ed. (1935; Naperville, Ill.: Allenson, 1954), 37; the view is retracted in "Ἔννομος Χριστοῦ." See also H. Schürmann, "'Das Gesetz des Christus' (Gal. 6:2)," in J. Gnilka, ed., *Neues Testament und Kirche* (Freiburg: Herder, 1974), 282–300.

makes it clear that he regarded himself as the heir of a tradition of ethical, as of other, teaching, which he had received and which he had to transmit. He was the servant of one who had criticized the tradition of the fathers as obscuring the true will of God; he himself violently attacked the same tradition. Nevertheless, he turns out on examination to be the steward of a new tradition.[14]

The *content* of this tradition can be broadly divided into two groups:

1. That which deals with Christian preaching where the tradition is identified with the gospel or the apostolic message itself. The chief passages are as follows (my emphasis):

"For I *delivered* to you as of first importance what I also *received,* that Christ died for our sins in accordance with the scriptures, that he was buried, that he was raised on the third day in accordance with the scriptures, and that he appeared to Cephas, then to the twelve. Then he appeared to more than five hundred brethren at one time, most of whom are still alive, though some have fallen asleep. Then he appeared to James, then to all the apostles. Last of all, as to one untimely born, he appeared also to me. For I am the least of the apostles, unfit to be called an apostle, because I persecuted the church of God. But by the grace of God I am what I am, and his grace toward me was not in vain. On the contrary, I worked harder than any of them, though it was not I, but the grace of God which is with me. Whether then it was I or they, so we preach and so you believed" (1 Cor. 15:3–11).

"For I would have you know, brethren, that the gospel which was preached by me is not man's gospel. For I did not *receive* it from man, nor was I taught it, but it came through a revelation of Jesus Christ" (Gal. 1:11–12).

"As therefore you *received* Christ Jesus the Lord, so live in him, rooted and built up in him and established in the faith, just as you were taught, abounding in thanksgiving. See to it that no one makes a prey of you by philosophy and empty deceit, according to human *tradition,* according to the elemental spirits of the universe, and not according to Christ" (Col. 2:6–8).

2. Tradition concerned strictly with rules or orders for the Christian life, as in 1 Corinthians 11:2: "I commend you because you remember me in everything and maintain the *traditions* which you were taught by us, either by word of mouth or by letter." (See also 1 Cor. 7:10, 12, 40; 11:14; 1 Thess. 4:15.)

The *forms* of the terminology employed to describe the reception and

---

14. For what follows, see these pivotal works: O. Cullmann, "The Tradition," in A. J. B. Higgins, ed., *The Early Church* (London: SCM Press, 1966), 59–104; L. Cerfaux, "La tradition selon Saint Paul," in *Recueil Lucien Cerfaux,* 2d ed. (Gembloux, Belgium: Duculot, 1954), 253–82; H. Riesenfeld, *The Gospel Tradition and Its Beginnings* (Oxford: Blackwell; Philadelphia: Fortress Press, 1970); P. Neuenzeit, *Das Herrenmahl* (Munich: Kösel, 1960), 77–88; J. Waggenmann, *Die Stellung des Apostels Paulus neben den Zwölf* (Giessen, Germany: Töpelmann, 1926), 464–73.

transmission of all forms of the traditions in both groups 1 and 2, while they appear in Hellenistic sources,[15] almost certainly have their origin for Paul in a Jewish milieu. Note the following: "hold to the tradition" (1 Cor. 11:2; 15:2; compare Mark 7:18); "stand in the gospel which you have received" (1 Cor. 15:1; in the traditions, 2 Thess. 2:15). Most striking, however, is the use of "receive" and "deliver" (1 Cor. 11:2, 23; 15:3; 1 Thess. 2:13; 2 Thess. 2:15; 3:6; Gal. 1:9, 12; Phil. 4:9; Col. 2:6, 8), which translate the Hebrew *quibbel min* and *masar le* respectively.

Thus, the *terminology* used by Paul was customary in Judaism. Are we to conclude from this that he regarded the Christian tradition as similar in its nature to that handed down in Judaism, or was there an essential difference between them? In other words, is there a "rabbinic" element in the Pauline understanding of tradition, that is, the conception of a tradition of a pre-scribed way of life transmitted from "authority" to "authority"? The question revolves around Paul's understanding of the source of the Christian tradition with which he was concerned. And in the first group of material, mentioned above, the tradition is explicitly stated to have been derived, not from men but directly from God. In 1 Thessalonians 2:13 it constitutes the message *of God;* and while in 1 Corinthians 15:1–11 its exact source is not described, both in Galatians 1:11–12 and Colossians 2:6–8 the tradition is deliberately, and very forcefully, set over against the tradition of men. Thus, so far as the content of his gospel as such is concerned, that is if we may so express it, as kerygma, Paul insists that it was given of God himself, who was its sole source. However, while in 1 Corinthians 15:1–11 Paul does not describe the source of the tradition, he clearly presents it in non-Pauline terms,[16] in a form molded by the church probably at Jerusalem, so that in one sense he can be claimed to have received it from men. But this is true for him only of the form; the substance of the tradition was God, as his call was from God. While Paul could not but be aware of human agencies who had been at work in the precise formulation of the tradition containing his gos-pel, his emphasis was not on this aspect of the matter, which was entirely secondary. What intermediaries there were in themselves were not signifi-cant. Paul's emphasis was on the gospel as born of the divine initiative in Christ. As far, then, as what we may call the primary content of the kerygma was concerned, the tradition was not understood by Paul in a rabbinic man-ner. This is as true of 1 Corinthians 15:1–11, as of Galatians 1:11–12. Even though in 1 Corinthians 15:1–11 he might seem at first sight to be quot-ing authorities, as does *Pirke Aboth* 1:1–2, this is, in fact, not the case. The authorities in 1 Corinthians 15:1–11 are not teachers transmitting an inter-

---

15. J. Dupont, *Gnosis* (Paris: Gabalda, 1949), 59–60.
16. J. Jeremias, *The Eucharistic Words of Jesus* (London: SCM Press, 1966), 101–5.

pretation of a primary deposit, the one to another, but witnesses severally of a primary event. In *Aboth* 1:1–2 we find a chain of successive authorities; in 1 Corinthians 15:1–11 a series of "original" witnesses. The chronological sequence in *Aboth* denotes authorities increasingly removed from contact with the original deposit, and increasingly dependent on the preceding secondary authorities, but the chronological sequence in 1 Corinthians 15:1–11 is intended merely to describe the order in which the "immediacy" of the event was experienced by each witness; that is, it is not a rabbinic sequence. The source of Paul's gospel is God himself, who took the initiative in revealing himself in Jesus Christ, and, through his resurrection, created witnesses to Jesus Christ in the world. Thus Jesus Christ is not strictly the source of the kerygmatic tradition but its content: Jesus of Nazareth, crucified, buried, and risen is the primary deposit of the Christian tradition, given by God himself. In 2 Corinthians, Paul contrasts the Christian ministry with that of the Old Covenant, and it is of the highest significance that it is Paul himself, not Jesus, who is set in parallelism with Moses. Jesus is rather parallel to the Law, that is, the revelation granted to Moses. Jesus is not the first link in a chain of teachers, no new Moses, but rather a new "Law."[17]

As far, then, as those passages which deal with the kerygma as a tradition are concerned, Paul does not think of himself as a Christian rabbi dependent upon teachers, the first of whom was Jesus. But what of those in the second group isolated above, concerned with the tradition of teaching? Is there here another emphasis in which Jesus is thought of as a New Moses? In 1 Corinthians 10 the implication is unmistakable that Jesus is such: incorporation into Christ, the Rock, who is distinguished from the first Moses, is, nevertheless, parallel to that into Moses, and here the moral reference of the incorporation is made clear. The passages in which Paul cites the words of the Lord as authoritative would seem to support this implication. But here there is a complication. Paul in 1 Corinthians 10:1–11:1 uses the term, not Jesus, but Christ: elsewhere he speaks neither of a law nor of a word "of Jesus," but "of Christ" and "of the Lord." Is this significant? Oscar Cullmann thinks that it is. While recognizing that there were words *of Jesus* in the tradition, by concentrating his attention on a passage which we omitted from our classifications above, because it demands separate treatment, Cullmann comes to a striking conclusion. The passage concerned is the following in 1 Corinthians 11:23–24: "For I received from the Lord what I also delivered to you, that the Lord Jesus on the night when he was betrayed took bread, and when he had given thanks, he broke it and said, 'This is my body which is for you. Do this in remembrance of me.'"

---

17. Davies, *Paul and Rabbinic Judaism*, 149–50.

Here the source of a particular tradition — not, however, an ethical one — is declared to be "the Lord," which refers so Cullmann maintains, neither to God, the ultimate source of the kerygma, nor to the Jesus of history, but to the risen Lord. This can only be reconciled with the fact that we have previously noted, that Paul had received tradition from others, by claiming that the Lord, the exalted Christ, was himself the transmitter of his own words and deeds. Thus in 1 Corinthians 7:10, "Unto the married I command, yet not I but the Lord," *"it is the exalted Lord who now proclaims to the Corinthians, through the tradition, what he had taught his disciples during his incarnation on earth."*[18] Elsewhere, in Colossians 2:6, the Lord is the content of the tradition. The Lord is, therefore, both author and content of the tradition; the genitive in the phrase "the gospel of Christ," in Romans 15:19 and elsewhere, is a subjective genitive: "[T]he exalted Christ is Himself originator of the Gospel of which He is also the object."[19] While, as we noted above, the tradition is connected with the Jesus of history, Cullmann insists that we owe the tradition really to the exalted Lord. On 1 Corinthians 11:23 he writes: "The designation *Kyrios* not only points to the historical Jesus as the chronological beginning of the chain of tradition as the first member of it, but accepts the exalted Lord as the real author of the whole tradition developing itself in the apostolic church. Thus the apostolic *paradosis* can be set directly on a level with the exalted *Kyrios*."[20] The use of the aorist in 1 Corinthians 11:14 indicated how the exalted Lord who *now* commands in 1 Corinthians 7:10 and probably in 1 Thessalonians 4:15 is the same as the Jesus who walked on earth. "The exalted One Himself after His resurrection delivers the words which He has spoken." In this way, although Cullmann does not ignore the historical Jesus in this matter, he virtually relegated him to the background and elevated the *Kyrios* to supreme significance. It agrees with this that it is necessary for the exalted Lord to repeat what he had declared on earth. Moreover, Cullmann is thus able to connect the tradition with the activity of the Spirit, because the *Kyrios* is closely related to, if not identified with, the Spirit in Paul.[21] The conclusion is that tradition in Paul is opposed to the rabbinic principle of tradition in Judaism in two ways: "[F]irstly, the mediator of the tradition is not the teacher, the rabbi, but the *apostle* as direct witness; secondly, the principle of succession does not work mechanically as with the rabbis, but is bound to the Holy Spirit."[22] Cullmann refuses to treat the

---

18. O. Cullmann, *The Early Church: Studies in Early Church History and Theology*, ed. A. J. B. Higgins (Philadelphia: Westminster Press, 1956), 68. His emphasis.

19. Ibid., 69.

20. Ibid., 62.

21. Ibid., 70–72. See Davies, *Paul and Rabbinic Judaism*, 182, 196.

22. Cullmann, *The Early Church*, 72.

two groups of material distinguished above as different kinds of tradition: they are both to be understood as derived, as an undifferentiated whole, from the Lord, so that not only the key kerygmatic tradition that Paul received and transmitted, but also the didactic, is to some extent removed from the historical Jesus, and any analogy between Christian and Jewish tradition is obviated. Jesus as teacher, or Jesus as counterpart of Moses, has little significance for the tradition, but only Jesus as Lord. The Christ of Paul is not easily recognizable as the Jesus of the Mount, as Matthew understood him.

But is Paul so to be interpreted? Is the sharp distinction between the exalted Lord and the Jesus of history which Cullmann finds really present in Paul? Certain considerations are pertinent.

1. The exegesis of certain texts suggested by Cullmann is questionable. Thus in 1 Corinthians 7:10, 12, is it correct to interpret the verse to mean that the exalted Lord is now commanding (v. 10) or refusing to command (v. 12)? In 1 Corinthians 9:14 the past tense is used of a command of the Lord, and it is probable that the reference in the former two passages is also to a commandment given by Jesus in the past, which is in force in the present. When Shakespeare wrote of the pound of flesh, he did not mean Shylock to imply that the particular law referred to was there and then enacted, although he used the present tense. So too Paul in 1 Corinthians 7:10, 12 merely claims that a past commandment of Jesus is still in force.

Again the very passage on which Cullmann leans most, 1 Corinthians 11:23–26, points not to a distinction between Jesus and "the Lord," but to their identity. In 11:26 we read: "For as often as you eat this bread and drink the cup, you proclaim the Lord's death until he comes."[23] Clearly the "Lord's" death can only refer to the death of the historical Jesus, which probably takes the place in the "Christian Passover," or Eucharist, of the historical event of the exodus in the haggadah of the Passover. The Jesus remembered and proclaimed is also the present Lord and the Lord to come. Past, present, and future meet in the name "Lord," because "the Lord" is "Jesus." That very Holy Spirit to which Cullmann appeals in support of his position testifies to this very truth. While "no one speaking by the Spirit of God ever says 'Jesus be cursed!'" it is equally valid that "no one can say 'Jesus is Lord,' except by the Holy Spirit" (1 Cor. 12:3).

2. It has been claimed that Paul never refers to a word of Jesus as a

---

23. The force of "proclaim" here is "to make haggadah of it" — as was the exodus "proclaimed" in the Passover Haggadah. See Davies, *Paul and Rabbinic Judaism*, 252–53; G. B. Gray, *Sacrifice in the Old Testament* (Oxford: Clarendon Press, 1925), 395. For another approach, see Neuenzeit, *Das Herrenmahl*, 128–30.

commandment. This, however, is debatable.[24] In any case, the claim might be countered by the statement that nowhere does Paul regard the Spirit, the connection of which with "the Lord" Cullmann rightly emphasizes, as the source of ethical commandments, although it is that of moral power. The term "law" in Romans 8:2 ("For the law of the Spirit of life in Christ Jesus has set me free from the law of sin and death") denotes not so much commandments as "principle."

3. A factor which is not clear in Cullmann's discussion is the exact meaning which he ascribes to the term "Lord." Does he mean the "risen Lord" and the "exalted Lord" to refer to the same phenomenon? He uses the two terms apparently interchangeably and rather sharply separates both the risen Lord and the exalted Lord, whom he seems not to distinguish, from the historical Jesus. The improbability that this separation should be accepted appears when we set Paul's understanding of the didactic role of the Lord, as Cullmann understands it, over against the data in the rest of the New Testament. Mark's conception of the activity of the risen Lord we cannot certainly determine, either because the end of his Gospel has been lost, or, if he did finish it at 16:8, because he does not tell us anything about this activity. If we follow R. H. Lightfoot and others, and find in Mark 16:8 the expectation of an almost immediate *parousia* to be enacted in Galilee, then no didactic activity of the risen Lord can have been contemplated by Mark.[25] Clearly Mark cannot help us in our quest into the functions of the risen Lord. Matthew, however, is rich in significance just at this point. It is probable that for Matthew the resurrection is coincident with the glorification of Jesus as Lord. "All authority in heaven and on earth *has* been given to Him": the aorist tense in 28:18 is to be taken seriously. Jesus as risen is in heaven, that is, glorified. But the ethical instructions which he issues are identified with those which he had given to his own while on earth, and, we may assume, particularly those recorded in Matthew's Sermon on the Mount.[26] The Jesus of history has initiated an ethical *paradosis* which the glorified Christ reaffirms; the latter neither initiates the Christian *paradosis* nor repeats what, as the historical Jesus, he had previously delivered on earth: he needs merely to refer to the tradition of the latter.

When we turn to Luke there is a significant change. The risen Christ instructs his own (Luke 24:27, 44–49; Acts 1:6–8), although no explicit reference is made to any moral teaching he may have given. After forty days,

---

24. See the fuller discussion of this material in W. D. Davies, *The Setting of the Sermon on the Mount* (Cambridge: Cambridge University Press, 1964), 341–66.

25. R. H. Lightfoot, *Locality and Doctrine in the Gospels* (London: Hodder and Stoughton, 1938), 1–48; idem, *The Gospel Message of St. Mark* (Oxford: Clarendon Press, 1950), 80–97.

26. Lightfoot, *Locality and Doctrine*, 66–68 (on Matt. 28:16–20). He does not do justice to the didactic factor in the passage.

however, the risen Christ ascended into heaven, where he was glorified. Contact with him, of a direct kind such as had been theirs hitherto, is now denied his disciples until he comes again "in the same way as you saw him go unto heaven" (Acts 1:11). The risen Christ taught the things concerning himself (Luke 24:44–48) and gave commands (Acts 1:2) and spoke of the kingdom of God (Acts 1:3) — all of which possibly[27] *implies* ethical instruction — with a reference to what he had taught on earth. But the impression given is that the *glorified* Christ did not teach. This is the emphasis in Acts 2:32–36; 3:13–21, which reflect perhaps the earliest Christian preaching, and, by implication possibly, in Acts 13:30–31. On the other hand, in Acts 10:40–41 the resurrection alone is to the fore, there being no emphasis on any ascension. A didactic function is ascribed to the risen Christ. Luke would seem to confine teaching whether ethical or other to the latter. The Lord of glory is not directly available for such.[28] In the Fourth Gospel there is a reference to the ascension implied in 20:17, but mostly emphasis is laid on the risen Christ. Moreover, for John the real glorification of Jesus had already occurred in the crucifixion.[29] It follows that there is nothing in the Fourth Gospel comparable to Matt. 28:16–20 because, essentially, the resurrection could add nothing to the glory of the crucifixion. For John it is neither the risen Jesus nor the exalted Lord who exercises the task of teaching in the church, but the Holy Spirit, to which this function is not thus directly applied in Paul. The content of the teaching of the Spirit, however, is rooted in teaching already given by the historical Jesus. "But the counselor, the Holy Spirit," so we read, "whom the Father will send in my name, he will teach you all things, and bring to your remembrance all that I have said to you" (John 14:26).

For our purpose what is significant in all the above is that, however the relation between the risen Christ and the glorified or exalted Lord be conceived in the rest of the New Testament, whether in terms of ascension or not, the teaching ascribed to both figures always has reference to the teaching of the historical Jesus, both in ethical and other matters. The presumption, therefore, is that Paul also, unless he was quite removed from the main currents of the church, intended the same reference. This is particularly reinforced by the fact that Paul's understanding of the risen Christ seems to be closest to that of Matthew. He does not mention any Ascension, but only appearances of the risen Christ, who becomes the object of worship of the church. The

---

27. The exact content of the teaching in Acts 1:2–3 is difficult to assess. It is too precarious to claim on this basis that the risen Lord gave ethical instructions. But this does not invalidate the distinction we make in the text between the risen and glorified Lord in Acts.

28. In Matthew there is no statement on the ascension as such.

29. See, for example, John 17:1.

resurrection would appear to be for him the glorification.[30] That the glorified one was the risen Jesus would therefore have been central to Paul. That he called him the Lord does not mean that he was removed from the Jesus of history, with whom he is indeed identical.

4. This last leads us to what should never have been questioned, namely, that the term "Lord" stands in Paul for the historical Jesus in 1 Corinthians 11:23. The last phrase, "you proclaim the Lord's death until he comes," in 1 Corinthians 11:26 *must* refer to the historical Jesus, and any distinction between "the Lord" and "the Lord Jesus" in 1 Corinthians 11:23 is unlikely. In Acts 9:5, 13, 17, 27; 22:8, 19; 26:15, the risen Lord is made to refer to himself as Jesus, and "Lord" is used of Jesus 80, 18, 103, and 52 times respectively in Matthew, Mark, Luke, and John. Early Christianity thought of the historical Jesus as "Lord" and so did Paul.[31]

Paul then inherited and transmitted a tradition which has two elements, a kerygmatic and didactic. How are these elements related in his thought? Were they sharply differentiated, as Cerfaux holds, on being conceived as from God, and the other having its *point de départ* in the historical Jesus, so that there are two sources for the tradition? Or is Cullmann[32] justified in claiming that both elements issue from the risen or exalted Lord, who took the place of all Jewish *paradosis*? Cullmann makes too sharp a distinction be-tween the Lord as the source of all *paradosis*, and the historical Jesus as, at least, the source of the didactic *paradosis*. Cerfaux makes too rigid a distinc-tion between the two kinds of *paradosis*. But he does greater justice to the texts by giving due place to the historical Jesus as an initiator of one aspect of the tradition. Jesus as Lord and Jesus as teacher were both one for Paul. He may have dwelt more in his epistles on the former, but this is not because he did not recognize the significance of the teaching of Jesus, which to him was authoritative.

And this brings us to the final point, the possibility that for Paul the Per-son and the Words of Jesus had assumed the significance of a New Torah. In addition to the evidence for this supplied above, we refer to our treatment elsewhere.[33] The objections to this view have been many. But too much weight should not be accorded to the claim that, since Paul was indiffer-

---

30. It agrees with this that the resurrection of Christ is the inauguration of the New Age, not of an age preliminary to this; see Davies, *Paul and Rabbinic Judaism*, 285–320; and more recently D. C. Allison, Jr., *The End of the Ages Has Come: An Early Interpretation of the Passion and Resurrection of Jesus* (Philadelphia: Fortress Press, 1985; reprint, Edinburgh: T. & T. Clark, 1987).

31. For a balanced statement, see L. Cerfaux, *Christ in the Theology of St. Paul* (New York: Herder and Herder, 1959), 179–89, esp. 187–88.

32. On Cullmann's understanding of "the Lord," see *The Christology of the New Testament* (London: SCM Press, 1959), 195–97. Surprisingly he does not develop his understanding of the Lord as a designation of "the tradition" in this volume.

33. See Davies, *Paul and Rabbinic Judaism*, 147–76.

ent to the life of Jesus, he was also indifferent to his moral teaching. Nor need the absence of an explicit claim that Jesus is the New Torah be taken as decisive.[34] The same motives which may have led Paul to avoid the use of the term *Logos*, the fear of being misunderstood by Hellenists, may have led him to avoid the description of Christ as the New Torah, which might have been misleading in discussions with Jewish-Christian and Jewish opponents. Most serious is the objection that the concept of Christ as the New Torah contradicts Paul's radical criticism of the Law and his insistence on salvation as a free gift of grace in the Epistles. The Law is there conceived of as a preliminary, provisional discipline, whose term the coming of Christ has closed.[35] Indeed does not the Law for Paul come to fulfill functions ascribed by Judaism to Satan himself?[36] Thus, that Paul thought of Christ in terms of the Law is unlikely; more likely was he to view the Law in terms of Christ.

Full force must be given to these objections. But while, in ascribing to Paul the concept of Christ as the New Torah we are going outside Paul's *explicit* words or formulae, we are hardly going beyond his implicit intention, if we can judge this from his use of Jesus' words and life in his ethical exhortations and from his application to Jesus of those categories that Judaism had reserved for its highest treasure, namely, the Torah — that is, preexistence, agency in creation, wisdom. To be "in Christ" was for Paul to have died and risen with him in a New Exodus, and this in turn meant that he was to be subject to the authority of the words and person of Christ as a pattern. The historical circumstances of Paul's ministry, set as it was in a conflict against Judaizers, has given to this aspect of his interpretation of the Christian dispensation a secondary place, a fact further accentuated by the violence of Paul's persona, engagement with the Law in Judaism, not strictly as "Law" in the sense of moral demand only, but as a whole cultural or social system, which had the effect of cutting him off from the fascinating Gentile world.[37] But, though Paul attacked Judaizers and avoids referring to himself or to Christians as "disciples," at no point is he free from the constraint of Christ's example: he has as a Christian "learned Christ,"[38] and this we may understand in a twofold way. He has learned his words as formerly he did

---

34. Contrast at this point Cerfaux, *Christ in the Theology of St. Paul,* 274 n. 36; and W. Manson, in his review of my *Paul and Rabbinic Judaism, SJT* 1 (1948): 217–19, esp. 218–19.

35. I have summarized this in Davies, "Law in the New Testament," *IDB,* 95–192.

36. G. B. Caird, *Principalities and Powers* (Oxford: Clarendon Press, 1956), 41.

37. See C. H. Dodd, *New Testament Studies* (Manchester, England: University of Manchester Press, 1953), 72. That Luther's struggle over Law and gospel was also sociologically conditioned is noted by W. Joest, *Gesetz und Freiheit* (Göttingen: Vandenhoeck & Ruprecht, 1951), 135; and E. Benz, "Das Paulus-Verständnis," *ZRGG* 4 (1951): 289–91.

38. On the expression to "learn Christ" (Eph. 4:21), see William Manson, *Jesus the Messiah* (Naperville, Ill.: Allenson, 1943), 54.

those of the Torah,[39] and he has become an imitator of Christ,[40] as formerly he had doubtless been an imitator of Gamaliel. The process of learning in Judaism had a twofold aspect — the learning of teaching and the imitation of a life, that of the rabbi. The concept of the rabbi as living Torah and, therefore as the object of imitation, would be familiar to Paul, as it would have been to Philo,[41] who regards the patriarchs as living the Law before it was given. When Paul refers to himself as an imitator of Christ he is doubtless thinking of Jesus as the Torah he has to copy — both in his words and deeds. A passage in Romans 6:15–17 suggests the formative power of the teaching of Jesus in Paul's conception of the Christian life, and reveals his understanding of this teaching in relation to grace. It reads: "What then? Are we to sin because we are not under law but under grace? By no means! Do you not know that if you yield yourself to anyone as obedient slaves, you are slaves of the one whom you obey, either of sin, which leads to death, or of obedience, which leads to righteousness? But thanks be to God, that you who were once slaves of sin *have become obedient from the heart to the standard of teaching to which you were committed,* and, having been set free from sin, have become slaves of righteousness" (my emphasis).

The precise meaning of the words "have become obedient from the heart to the standard of teaching to which you were committed" in Romans 6:17 has been disputed. W. F. Beare's comment, however, is to be treated seriously. He finds Paul to be claiming that

> the Christian Didache, when it is followed with a wholehearted obedience, imparts to our lives a specific character and pattern, moulding them into the likeness of Christ. St. Paul speaks more often, it is true, of the power of the Spirit as the transforming influence in the Christian life; but it is quite wrong to imagine that he thinks of the leadings of the Spirit as a succession of formless impulses or vagrant illuminations. Here, in correlation with the call for obedience, he thinks naturally enough of the specific moral instruction in which the guiding of the Spirit is given concrete expression (Phil. 4:8–9). For all his faith in the Spirit, the apostle thinks of the Christian life as disciplined and ordered

---

39. This is implied in his use of the citation to which we have already referred.

40. 1 Corinthians 11; 1 Thessalonians 1:6; Philippians 2:5.

41. See my volume, *Torah in the Messianic Age and/or The Age to Come,* SBLMS 7 (Philadelphia: Society of Biblical Literature, 1952). It is not irrelevant to restate that the fact that the Law itself has a "personal" character for Philo; see Daniélou, *Théologie du Judeo-Christianisme,* 1:217. For Judaism, see my essay "Law in First Century Judaism," *IDB,* 89–95 (reprinted in Davies, *Jewish and Pauline Studies* [London: SPCK; Philadelphia: Fortress Press, 1984], 3–26); now see also E. P. Sanders, *Paul, the Law, and the Jewish People* (Philadelphia: Fortress Press, 1983); idem, *Jewish Law from Jesus to the Mishnah: Five Studies* (London: SCM Press; Philadelphia: Trinity Press International, 1990); idem, "Law in Judaism of the NT Period," *ABD,* 4:254–65; and Allison, *The New Moses,* 228–30, where Allison discusses the tradition of Moses himself as Torah.

in keeping with clear and concrete instruction given by precept and example. Such teaching is here conceived as the die or pattern which shapes the whole of the life which yields to it, in conformity with the will of God. No antithesis with the Law or with other (non-Pauline) "forms" is implied or suggested. He is thinking simply of the *didache* which belongs to the Gospel, the teaching concerning the way of life which is worthy of the Gospel of Christ, considered as a mould which gives to the new life its appropriate shape or pattern.[42]

The Christian life as Paul understood it was lived within a normative ethical tradition. This tradition is not an isolated deposit, however, but part and parcel of what Paul understands by the Christian dispensation, and, therefore, seen, not in opposition to grace, but as a concomitant of it. At no point is Paul without law (*anomos*); he is always with law (*ennomos*). To this extent Paul is at one with Matthew who also places the law of Christ in a context of the grace of Christ. This is nowhere clearer than in a section which is usually quoted in proof of the succor of Christ, but which also contains within itself the demand of Christ. "Come to me, all who labor and are heavy-laden, and I will give you rest. Take my yoke upon you and learn from me; for I am gentle and lowly in heart, and you will find rest for your souls. For my yoke is easy and my burden is light" (Matt. 11:28–30). The "yoke of Christ" stands over against the yoke of the Law. The upshot of all this is that Paul, who is usually set in antithesis to Matthew, would probably not have found the Matthean emphasis on the "law of Christ" either strange or uncongenial. He, too, knew of the same law, although the circumstances of his ministry demanded from him greater concentration on other aspects of the gospel.[43]

We may now sum up. In the light of the above, it can be urged that Paul had access to a tradition of the words of Jesus. This he had "received" and this he "transmitted"; to this, whenever necessary and possible, he appealed as authoritative, so that this tradition constituted for him part of the "law of Christ." Caution is, however, necessary in making this claim. Out of the Epistles as a whole, the passages where this emerges are few, and the use that the apostle made of a catechesis derived possibly from a non-Christian Hellenistic-Jewish tradition, into which he introduced few, if any, express words of Jesus, makes it doubly clear that he did not formulate a "Christian-rabbinic" casuistry on the basis of the words of Jesus that he had received. Whether the reason for the paucity of evidence in this matter is due to the historical fact that Paul during his ministry had to contend with "Judaizing"

---

42. F. W. Beare, "On the Interpretation of Rom. vi.17," *NTS* 5 (1959): 206–10. We should emphasize, as Beare does not, the role of the words of Jesus in the tradition. Beare refers to the other interpretations that have been suggested. We find his most plausible, with the qualifications mentioned.

43. Compare Cullmann, *The Early Church*.

tendencies, as was suggested above, is uncertain. Nevertheless, it is not going too far to claim that part of the being "in Christ" for Paul was standing under the words of Jesus. Paul, like Matthew, appealed to these words as authoritative. As for Matthew, so for Paul, there was a real correspondence between the Christian dispensation and the events of the exodus. The redemption of Israel from Egypt was the prototype of the greater redemption from sin wrought by Christ. Thus Christ for Paul also had the lineaments of a new and greater Moses. He shared with Matthew a common understanding of Christ and his words. Like Matthew, Paul too can speak of a law of Christ, partly, at least, composed of Jesus' words; he was governed by a tradition. Like Matthew, Paul too can speak of a law of Christ, partly, at least, composed of Jesus' words; he was governed by a tradition.[44]

---

44. The notion of Christ as the New Torah in Paul — a phrase which he himself never explicitly used — has been widely criticized. See E. P. Sanders, *Paul and Palestinian Judaism* (London: SCM Press; Philadelphia: Fortress Press, 1977), 479; studies by S. Westerholm, in P. Richardson and S. Westerholm, eds., *Law in Religious Communities in the Roman Period: The Debate over Torah and Names in Post-biblical Judaism and Early Christianity*, Studies in Christianity and Judaism 4 (Waterloo, Ontario: Wilfrid Laurier University Press, 1991), 54–55, 80–85; F. Thielman, *From Plight to Salvation: A Jewish Framework for Understanding Paul's View of the Law in Galatians and Romans*, NovTSup 62 (Leiden: Brill, 1989), 11. Allison (*The New Moses*) is more sympathetic. For my attempt to accept criticisms and respond to them also, see my "Canon and Christology in Paul," in Evans and Sanders, *Paul and the Scriptures of Israel*, 18–39, esp. 35–39; and my *Paul and Rabbinic Judaism* (4th ed.), xxvii–xxxviii, where I deal with the work of James A. Sanders in his *Torah and Canon* (Philadelphia: Fortress Press, 1972) (see pp. xxviii–xxx), and of E. P. Sanders, xxix–xxxviii, the former being more sympathetic or receptive than the latter. In a seminar John Barclay made it clear that in Galatians 6:2, in his judgment, it is unwise too quickly to turn to the rabbinic parallel for the "law of Christ." See also his rich work, *Obeying the Truth: A Study of Paul's Ethic in Galatians* (Edinburgh: T. & T. Clark, 1988).

Chapter 7

Paul and the Law:
Pitfalls in Interpretation

Because of its importance not only in his epistles and in other parts of the New Testament but also in the encounter between Roman Catholicism and Protestantism, the treatment of the Law by Paul has been and is one of the most discussed subjects in Christian theology and particularly in New Testament studies. In the course of this discussion Paul's view has frequently been misunderstood. Before we consider this matter, two preliminaries have to be noted. To begin with, there are few strictly "legal" discussions in Paul. This is highly significant. Of necessity our treatment of the Law in the apostle's writings has to be only tangentially legal and has to be centered in his understanding of the nature of the life "in Christ," by which all aspects of life, including the legal are, for him, to be informed. The concentration of the new life "in Christ" is of the essence of Paul's approach to the Law, which comes not to be dismissed by him but transposed to a new key. As will appear, Paul related all law to religion.

And then, it is important to note that the term "Torah," or Law, has for Paul a broad range of meanings, at least four of which have to be borne especially in mind: first, commandments (*mitzwoth*) which have to be obeyed; second, the accounts of Israel's history and the prophetic and wisdom literature; third, in connection with the figure of Wisdom, the cosmic function of Torah in creation and redemption; and fourth, Torah as the expression of a total culture, the whole of the revealed will of God in the universe, nature, and society. Neglect of the complexity of Paul's view of Torah has led interpreters, concentrating on one aspect to the exclusion of others, to oversimplify his response to it. We shall try to indicate certain considerations that should be operative in any adequate discussion of Paul and the Law by pointing out pitfalls in interpretation which have led to distortion.[1]

First, there has been a tendency to treat Law as if it simply meant commandment. Many Protestant theologians especially, but not only they, have

---

1. This is an abbreviated version of a paper which appeared in *The Hastings Law Journal* 29, no. 6 (1978): 1459–504, and is used with the permission of the editors.

often misunderstood Torah as commandment (*mitzwoth*) and interpreted the
Jewish tradition as one requiring obedience to the commandments as the
ground of salvation. This diminution of the scope of Torah has had momentous historical consequences. The traditional Protestant interpretation of the
Pauline polemic against the Law in Judaism and Jewish Christianity is familiar
and need not be repeated here,[2] but it has so colored the minds of Protestants and even Catholics that it has been difficult for them to give the Law its
due place in the corpus of revelation.[3] The doctrine of justification by faith,
with its corollary of the inadequacy of the Law, has been taken as the clue to
Paulinism. The appeal of that doctrine and, to many, its truth for a broken
and sinful humanity is altogether natural and should be fully recognized, but
it should not be allowed to govern our interpretation of Paul as a historical
figure. The traditional picture of Paul as suffering from pangs of conscience
under the Law has recently been severely criticized and dismissed.[4] The dismissal cannot be unqualifiedly accepted, but even if pangs of conscience and
moral scrupulosity are universally human and Paul experienced them too, it
would be wrong to make this the source of his criticism of the Law. Paul refers
to himself as blameless under the Law and in his own conscience (Phil. 3:6).

Torah in Judaism, moreover, is always seen in the context of God's gracious action. The exodus precedes Sinai (Exod. 20:1–2). The duties of the
Decalogue arise out of a deliverance, a deliverance of the unworthy. The
precedence of grace over Law in Israelite religion persisted, despite some neglect, in Judaism. The Law and the recognition of the need for obedience to
it are not the means of salvation for Judaism but the consequences or accompaniment of it. True, the commands of the Law are often isolated in Judaism
and their covenantal ground in the grace of God muted, but the relation of
the demands to the grace of God in freeing Israel from Egypt was not severed.

Thus the opposition of the Law to grace which has marked so much of
Protestantism, grounded as it is in individualism, that is, in the emphasis on
the sinner standing alone before the awful demands of God, is a distortion of
Paul. And it is well to note that, although a profundity, Paul was not a peculiarity in the early church. His understanding of Christian experience was
widespread. The primitive church understood its experience to be convenan-
tal in character and parallel to that of the Jewish people. The emergence of
the church was, if not the emergence of a New Israel,[5] at least the entrance

---

2. E. P. Sanders, *Paul and Palestinian Judaism* (1976), is a brilliant and massive contribution,
the true assessment of which will necessarily be a long time in coming. See also D. Patte, *The
Faith of the Apostle to the Gentiles: A Structural Introduction to Paul's Letters,* forthcoming.

3. F. J. Leenhardt, *Two Biblical Faiths: Protestant and Catholic* (1964).

4. K. Stendahl, *Paul among Jews and Gentiles* (1976), is especially associated with this view.
See W. D. Davies, "Paul and the People of Israel," *NTS* 24 (1977): 4–39, esp. 24–29.

5. P. Richardson, *Israel and the Apostolic Church* (1969), argues that the designation of the
church as the "New Israel" did not occur until Justin.

of Israel on a new stage of its history; and the structure of early Christianity is in at least some respects modeled upon, or grows out of, the structure of Judaism. This means that the Law is as integral to the gospel of the New Testament as it was for the Old.[6] Thus Paul's background in early Christianity, no less than in Judaism, demands that we cease to interpret his relation to the Law solely in individualistic or moralistic terms and recognize that Pauline Christianity is not primarily an antithesis to Law.

To do so is, however, difficult. Between us and Paul stands the Protestant Reformation. Moreover, Paul's conviction that Jesus was the Messiah led to a radical reassessment of current messianic ideas and a vivid contrast between the new order in Christ and the old order under the Law. His sharp antitheses are familiar. From his earliest epistle on, Paul lashed out unrestrainedly at certain Jews. Two things, however, should be borne in mind in assessing Paul's violent criticism. First, the discussion of Judaism and Jews in Paul is intramural. It is criticism of the faith, Law, institutions, and worship of Judaism not from without, but from within. Though differentiated in some respects, Christians were not separated from Judaism. Indeed, prior to 70 C.E., Christianity probably did not exist as a separate religious movement.[7] Second, the Judaism of which Paul was a part was a remarkably fluid and tolerant phenomenon. The Qumran sectarians bitterly attacked the authorities in Jerusalem and cut themselves off from their fellow Jews, but did not thereby see themselves as forsaking Judaism. Even the assertion that Jesus was Messiah was not for Paul tantamount to a rejection of Judaism, or the founding of a new religion, but rather expressed the profound conviction that the final expression and intent of Judaism had been born.[8]

Why has recognition of this fact been so difficult and tardy? Apart from the weight of scholarly tradition and conservatism, two historical factors are important. On the one hand, the catastrophic effects of the Jewish War led Jamnian Judaism to close its own ranks against dissidents and elevate Torah as *the* way of Jewish life. This, and the reaction among Jews and Christians, contributed most to the emergence of what we call Christianity as a distinct religion.[9] But Paul pre-dated Jamnia, and the post-70 separation must not be read back into his time. On the other hand, after Paul's death his letters were read mainly by those who little understood Judaism and were incapable of recognizing their setting in a family dispute. The intensity, and at times feroc-

---

6. One of the most illuminating developments in Old Testament studies has been the rehabilitation of the Law. For an account see W. Zimmerli, *The Law and the Prophets: A Study of the Meaning of the Old Testament* (1965), and R. E. Clements, *Prophecy and Covenant* (1965).

7. See E. Trocmé, "Le Christianisme primitif, un mythe historique?" in *Études théologiques et religieuses*, Revue Trimestrielle (Montpellier, France, 1974), 1:19.

8. The parallel with the seventeenth-century messiah, Sabbatai Svi, is instructive. See W. D. Davies, "From Schweitzer to Scholem: Reflections on Sabbatai Svi," *JBL* 95 (1976): 529–58.

9. See W. D. Davies, *The Setting of the Sermon on the Mount* (1964), 256–315.

ity, of Paul's discussions with his contemporaries were endurable when *intra muros*. But once removed from that setting they took on a radically different look. In time, though the process was slow, what was a disruption among Jews came to be spelled out as the denigration and rejection of Judaism and of the people of Israel as a whole.

Isolation of the Law
from Paul's Messianic Situation

What has been written has by implication pointed to the second pitfall: that of isolating Paul's concept of Torah from the total messianic situation in which he believed himself to be living. It is clear from Acts and the Epistles that the Law was the point at which Paul met with violent opposition, and it has been easy to suppose that this was the ultimate ground for opposition to him. It was not his messianic beliefs, for Judaism was hospitably tolerant of messianic claimants, but his acceptance of Gentiles without observance of the Law, which passed the limits of Jewish tolerance. But to state the matter thus unqualifiedly is misleading. The immediate cause of Jewish opposition may have been the Law, but Paul's controversial view of the Law was inextricably bound up with the significance which he ascribed to Jesus as Messiah and with the challenge this issued to all the fundamental symbols of Jewish life. To isolate the criticism of the Law from the total messianic situation, as Paul conceived it, is both to exaggerate and to emasculate it. The criticism of the Law was derivative, a consequence of the ultimate place Paul ascribed to Jesus as Messiah.

The messiahship of Jesus was crucial for Paul. He often uses "Christ" as a personal name and not as a title, but he did not thereby empty it of "messianic" connotations.[10] That Jesus was Messiah had momentous consequences, for a messianic movement had to come to terms with the Law. Moreover, Paul's reinterpretation of the Law in relation to Christ took place in a world where the role of Torah in the present and the future was a burning issue. Despite the firmly entrenched belief that the Law was perfect, unchangeable, and eternal, some expected that in the Messianic Age difficulties in the Law would be explained, some commandments changed, and, in later rabbinic passages, that a new Torah would be instituted or the old one abrogated.[11] And in the first century, as before and after,

10. See N. A. Dahl, *The Crucified Messiah and other Essays* (1974), 37–47; A. T. Hanson, *Studies in Paul's Technique and Theology* (1974), 13.

11. Davies, *Sermon*, 109–90; J. Jervell, "Die offenbarte und die verborgene Tora: Zur Vorstellung über die neue Tora im Rabbinismus," *ST* 25 (1971): 90–108; P. Schäfer, "Die Torah der messianischen Zeit," *ZNW* 65 (1974): 27–42; H. Schürmann, "Das Gesetz Christi (Gal. 6:2): Jesu Verhalten und Werk als Letztgültige Sittliche Norm nach Paulus Neues Testament und Kirche," *Pastoral Aufsatze*, B.6 (Leipzig, 1974), 95–102.

the content and character of the Law was a matter of intense debate as is shown by Qumran and the debates between the Houses of Hillel and Shammai.

Two epistles, in particular, discuss this matter. In Galatians 3–4 Paul organizes the history of his people into three epochs: from Abraham to Moses; from Moses to Christ, in whom the promise to Abraham is fulfilled; and the third epoch, introduced by Christ, of true sonship in liberty (Gal. 4:3f.; 5:13), a new creation (Gal. 6:5). This radical rewriting of history is Paul's own and gives an eschatological significance to Jesus from which Paul interprets the Law (cf. 1 Cor. 10:11; 2 Cor. 5:17). In Romans, Paul presents a similar, but not identical, analysis of history: from Adam to the Law, a lawless era when transgressions were not imputed (Rom. 4:15; 5:13); from Moses to Christ, when Law reigned and transgressions were imputed (Rom. 4:15); and from Christ onward, when the writ of the Law no longer ran (Rom. 7:6; 10:4).

Thus the proximate cause of Paul's persecution, his view of the Law, points to an ultimate cause, his Christology, which was at the beginning a messianology. In fact, given his Jewish view of the Law, ranging from commandment to an all-encompassing cultural environment and agent of creation, it was only a messianic event of revelatory and cosmic significance that could have induced Paul to reassess the Law as he did.

Failure to Recognize Variety and Change

The third pitfall results from the attempt to treat Paul's view of the Law systematically, making indiscriminate use of his writings without regard to their variety. This attempt to construct a monolithic view of Paul seriously misinterprets him.

In Galatians, where he confronts Judaizers and behind them the Jews, Paul views the Law with the cold eyes of an antagonist. To be under the Law is to be under a curse (3:10); the Law is inferior, given later than the promise, and delivered by angels (3:10–20); to obey the Law is to submit to the elemental and evil cosmic spirits (4:3, 9).[12] The positive function of the Law, as a custodian (3:19f.), is recognized only grudgingly. The coming of Christ frees men from the curse and tutelage of the Law (2:21; 3:13, 19; 5:11), so that at best it was a beggarly, passing phenomenon. Christians live under the Spirit and in freedom (5:13), bound to a law of the Messiah, the law of love (6:2).[13]

---

12. Bo Reicke, "The Law and the World according to Paul," *JBL* 70 (1951): 259–76.

13. The term "law" in Galatians 6:2 is not to be radically differentiated from the concept of command, or *Torah*, as if it means simply principle or norm rather than demand. See Davies, *Sermon*, 353.

At Corinth, Paul encountered both Jewish-Christian opponents[14] and enthusiasts. In response to the latter he called for restraint and a behavior
governed by his own example (1 Cor. 4:16; 11:1) or that of Christ himself
(2 Cor. 8:9). There is here, for Paul, a Christian "way" or "law," informed
by universal Christian practice (1 Cor. 4:17; 11:16; 14:34). Whereas at Anti-
och (Gal. 2:11f.) Paul ignored the scruples of Peter and others, thus ignoring
the claims of the weaker brother, in 1 Corinthians he urges consideration for
them. He can even say that "keeping the commandments of God is everything" (1 Cor. 7:19) which, while not a reference to Mosaic commands, does
show that Christian liberty does not free men from commandments. And in
2 Corinthians, where he may have faced different opponents, he comes to
understand Christian life as life in a covenant, and covenant includes demand or law (2 Corinthians 3). The Christian is also constrained by the
love of Christ (2 Cor. 5:14f.) which, while not a commandment, is a qualification of unrestricted freedom. To Christians in Galatia, Paul would have
appeared to be an antinomian, but to those in Corinth a disciplinarian if not
an incipient legalist!

In Romans, unlike Galatians, Paul is careful to recognize that the Law is
holy, righteous, and good (7:12, 16), spiritual (7:14), rooted in God (7:22, 25;
8:2, 7), designed for life (7:10), authoritative (7:19), and that it counts as one
of the privileges of Israel (9:4). While some arguments about the Law echo
Galatians, in Romans Paul approaches the Law not as if he were viewing it
clinically, from outside, but experientially, from the inside. He does consider
that Christ is the end of the Law (10:4), the Law, that is, as a means of salvation, but he also gives reasons for this conclusion. The Law was intended to
give life (Lev. 18:5), but was unable to do so (Rom. 3:23). It had, in fact, the
opposite result from that intended (4:13; 7:13). Romans 7, which is probably a defense of the Law, reveals the problem. The problem is sin, which
makes the intrinsically good Law serve its own intrinsically evil ends. The
Law reveals sin (3:20), incites it (7:5), indeed brings sin to life, for apart from
the Law sin is dead (7:8–9). What was good in itself becomes a power for
evil. How is the Law diverted from its original purpose? Not, as in Galatians,
because of connections with the "elemental spirits," but because of the weakness of "the flesh." The power of sin and the weakness of the flesh collude to
frustrate the purpose of the good and holy Law.

The treatment of Law in Romans is thus different from that in Galatians.
The one is written in the white heat of controversy and the other, perhaps
because Paul's view did not prevail in Galatia and because he desired the
support of the Christians in Rome,[15] is more conciliatory. In Romans he pro-

---

14. P. Vielhauer, "Paulus und die Kephaspartei in Korinth," *NTS* 21 (1974–75): 341–52.

15. Cf. J. Jervell, "Der Brief nach Jerusalem: Über Veranlassung und Adresse des Römerbriefs,"

vides a more positive estimate of the Law even while he still strikes against it. A more subtle and restrained Paul appears. To ignore this, and to present his view of the Law as monolithic, is to misunderstand him.

Neglect of Explicit Moral Demands in the Epistles

We have previously connected Paul with early Christian life in general and with the communal aspect of Christian life and we shall do so again. Here we are more concerned with the more directly personal aspects of life in Christ as it is related to the *Torah*.

First, quite simply, Paul places the demands of the Torah in the light of Christ. For him, the way of the Law gives place to the law or way of Christ. Torah became concentrated in the person of Jesus Christ and its demands informed by the *agape* and, indeed, the very presence of Christ.[16] But what exactly does this mean? First, that the moral life of the Christian bears constant reference to, or is molded by, the actual life of Jesus of Nazareth.[17] Second, moral teaching has its point of departure not only in the ministry of Jesus, but also in his resurrection. The resurrection was not only a triumph of life over death but also of forgiveness over sin; it was an expression, if not the expression, of God's grace.[18] Third, the mode of the presence of this risen Lord was life in the Spirit, who was the inspiration of the prophets of old, the mark of the new age, and the basis of a new morality (Gal. 5:22; 1 Corinthians 13). Thus for Paul, Christian morality had its point of reference in the life, resurrection, and living Spirit of Jesus. Putting it geometrically, this was the vertical relation of Christians with the living Lord.

For Christian morality this has three dimensions. First, that those "in Christ" appropriate and share in Jesus' death and resurrection, so that their moral life is rooted in what they are, new creations in Christ. The moral imperative rests on the indicative.[19] Second, there is the element of imitation in

---

ST 25 (1971): 61–73; U. Wilckens, *Rechtfertigung als Freiheit: Paulusstudien* (1974), 110–70. Contrast K. P. Donfried, "False Presuppositions in the Study of Romans," *CBQ* 36 (1974): 332–55.

16. W. D. Davies, *Paul and Rabbinic Judaism* (1948), 147f.

17. Apart from some such assumption, the preservation of the tradition about the words and works of Jesus in the Gospels is difficult to understand. Even granted that much of that tradition is a creation of the primitive community, its attachment to the figure of Jesus is itself significant. On Paul and Jesus, see now the article of Dale C. Allison, Jr., "The Pauline Epistles and the Synoptic Gospels: The Pattern of the Parallels," *NTS* 28 (1981–82): 1–32.

18. To connect the resurrection with morality is not usual, but it is implicit in 1 Corinthians 15:7f. Note also that the first appearances were to Cephas and the Twelve who had betrayed Jesus. We must assume that Paul knew the tradition about the betrayals.

19. On the "Indicative-Imperative" motif in Paul see V. P. Furnish, *Theology and Ethics in Paul* (1968), 242. Like Furnish, I, too, find the work of M. Goguel especially original and provocative. See M. Goguel, *The Primitive Church* (1964).

which the life of Jesus becomes the model for moral living. The importance of this theme in early Christianity has been variously assessed, but for Paul, at least, it is an undeniable one (1 Cor. 11:1; Rom. 15:3; 2 Cor. 10:1).[20] Third, the Christian life always has an eschatological dimension, which for Paul is most clearly expressed in his apostolic calling. True, his apostolic conscious-ness may have been more intense than in most, but all Christians believed they were caught up in the counsel of God. Christian morality is rooted in a "lively hope" (1 Pet. 1:1) even as it is informed by the earthly Jesus. It is governed by a memory and an anticipation.

But if there was a vertical dimension of Christian life for Paul there was also a horizontal, or human, societal one. Paul knows nothing of solitary re-ligion or individual morality, but rather sees the Christian firmly based in a community. A communal emphasis is probably at the root of Paul's "Christ mysticism," which issued not in a "flight of the alone to the Alone," but in the building up of the church.[21] Along with rationality (1 Cor. 12:8; 14:1f.; Rom. 12:2) and respect for personal integrity (Philem. 15–16), Paul sets forth the building up of the church as *the* criterion of Christian action (Rom. 14:21; 1 Corinthians 12–14).

Paul also emphasizes specific moral teaching, sometimes reminiscent of Jesus' words (e.g., Rom. 12:14/Matt. 5:43; Rom. 12:17/Matt. 5:39f.; Rom. 13:7/Matt. 22:15–22, etc.), sometimes quoting them directly (1 Thess. 4:15–16; 1 Cor. 7:25). The central command, however, which is the fulfillment of the Law and the principle of cohesion in the Christian community, is the command to love (Rom. 13:8–10; 1 Cor. 8:1, 13; Col. 3:14). In addition, for specific moral teaching Paul could call upon both Jewish and Hellenistic sources, the latter perhaps mediated by the Jewish Diaspora. Thus in Paul, as in early Christianity in general, not only are the absolutes of Jesus do-mesticated, but the domestic virtues of the world are also appropriated. That Paul could borrow freely from non-Christian sources suggests that he saw a continuity between the moral awareness of Christians and the non-Christian world, and this in turn was in all probability based on his view of creation.[22] For Paul the good life is the truly natural life. Morality is rooted in creation.

---

20. Furnish, *Ethics*, 217f., discusses the matter acutely and with a wealth of bibliographical detail, though in my view he separates too sharply the historical Jesus and the Son of God, or *Kurios*, thereby making the myth govern the history rather than the history the ground of the myth. I prefer to think of the history as given in the ministry of Jesus and fashioned and transmitted, rather than created, by the church.

21. This is one of the important insights of A. Schweitzer, *The Mysticism of Paul the Apostle* (1931), 105. But caution is necessary in accepting Schweitzer; see Davies, *Rabbinic*, 98 n. 7.

22. See W. D. Davies, "The Relevance of the Moral Teaching of the Early Church," in *Neo-testamentica et Semitica: Studies in Honour of Matthew Black*, ed. E. E. Ellis and M. Wilcox (1969), 30–49.

Conclusion

By looking at the historical meaning of *Torah*, the messianic context, and the developing theological framework within which Paul worked, we have sought to call in history to readjust the balance of traditional interpretations of his response to the Law.

The antithesis between Law and grace which governs much Christian, especially Protestant, thinking would have been alien to Paul. There is little doubt that for him Torah was an expression of divine grace. Despite the violent criticisms of the Law that Paul reiterates in his polemical epistles, always there remained in his gospel a demand. The demand, that of *agape*, could be interpreted as even more austere than that of the multitudinous *mitzwoth*, or commandments, of the *Torah*. "In Christ" Paul stood under a new Sinai requiring of him universal *agape* such as that called for in the Sermon on the Mount and elsewhere in the New Testament, the infinite demand of the "Law of Christ." But this did not mean that he was indifferent to those actualities and intricacies of existence that called for careful legal discrimination, refinement, and casuistry. Daube[23] has shown how in dealing with such human problems as marriage Paul stopped short of following the legal logic of his messianic absolutism and squarely faced the social realities of his day. No less than were the Pharisaic sages who taught him, he too was prepared to make concessions to the complexities of the order of society in which he found himself and to human weakness and sinfulness.[24] He was no fanatic unprepared to bend. Under the constraint of the very Christ whom he had called "the end of the Law," he was ready to be "all things to all men."[25] This required, as we have seen, sensitivity in moral direction. Nor again, convinced as he was of standing in the final messianic period of history and, indeed, of participating in the very inauguration of the "end of the days," was Paul indifferent to the tradition of his people, moral or otherwise. He was no antinomian; for him the Christian dispensation was the fulfillment and the annulment of that tradition. Distrust of all law, such as is frequently expressed in our time in the counterculture and elsewhere, and which Protestantism, especially in its Lutheran form, has often fostered, finds no support in Paul.

Notwithstanding this, Paul presents us with a radical and inescapable challenge. Paul sits lightly to certain specific commandments, and while he elsewhere retains others they do not play an important, and certainly not

---

23. D. Daube, "Pauline Contributions to a Pluralistic Culture: Re-creation and Beyond, Jesus and Man's Hope," in *Jesus the Hope of the World*, ed. D. G. Millar and D. Y. Hadidian (1971), 223–45.

24. D. Daube, "Concessions to Sinfulness in Jewish Law," *JJS* 1 (1959): 10f., discusses this motif in rabbinic law.

25. On 1 Corinthians 9:20 see D. Daube, *The New Testament and Rabbinic Judaism* (1956), 336–41; H. Chadwick, "All Things to All Men," *NTS* 1 (1954–55): 261–75.

an independent, part in his thinking. He brings the legal tradition of his fathers before the judgment seat of the *agape* of Christ and thereby achieves an immense and penetrating simplification of it. Moreover, the cause of this simplification, which is at the same time an intensification, is the personalizing of the concept of Torah by identifying it with Christ. Such notions challenge not only the concept of Torah in Paul's day but also the concept of law in the more restricted sense as it refers to modern legal systems. The problem of rigidity and ossification when laws are treated as absolutes, the oppressive weight and complexity of inherited precedent in legal traditions, and the tendency of the Law to become depersonalized are all matters which Paul's response to Torah sheds light on.[26] Of course, to move from Torah in the sense in which Paul understood it to law as it is understood in modern Western societies requires a leap of the imagination. The direct transference of Pauline categories to modern legal systems is inadmissible, not only because the concepts of law are different but also because Paul lived in the fervor of a messianic situation marked by intense eschatological expectation. Moreover, the primary point of comparison between Christianity and any other legal system, as between Christianity and Judaism, lies not in the absolute demands that characterized the early Christian movement in its first fine careless rapture, but in the latter developments within Christendom that culminated in canon law. Even with these caveats, however, Paul's insights give us much cause for reflection.

There is one further challenge from Paul. Related to this is an apparently paradoxical situation in which society, at least in the West, finds itself. On the one hand, under the impact of the developments of scientific technology, society is faced with perplexities and opportunities that are, apparently, new, and for which there seems to be no direct guidance from the past. On the other hand, this coexists with the sense, born this time of psychological and sociological sophistication and of the irreducible particularity of history, that there are entrenched historical traditions and age-old developments in law, as in other spheres, which hold a dead staying hand over things. There is a fatalism in law, as part of a wider fatalism, which tends to paralyze the belief in the possibility of change. In such a situation Paul is particularly challenging. The closing words of Michael Grant's biography of Paul are apposite:

> The historian's characteristic view that everything which happens has evolved from existing historical tendencies and trends would have seemed to him to be disproved by what, in fact, had happened: the redemptive death of Jesus Christ. Whether one agrees with him or not — Jews, for example, do not — that Christ's death was this total reversal of

---

26. For fuller discussion of these points see the article in *The Hastings Law Journal* (n. 1 above), 1459–504.

everything that had taken place hitherto, at all events Paul's general attitude, insisting that such totally world-changing occurrences *can* take place, seems plausible, defensible and right in our own day; the years which lie immediately ahead of us are likely to confirm the cogency of Paul's viewpoint even more insistently.[27]

Paul assumed that the entrenched and oppressive religious, social, political and legal structure of his day, what he refers to perhaps as τὰ στοιχεῖα τοῦ κόσμου, can be decisively challenged and transformed. Certain continuities he honored, including continuity in law, but he did not allow these to strangle the emerging new creation which he had embraced in Christ. Perhaps it is this daring belief in the possibility of a new beginning — in Law, as in other things — a beginning for him inseparable from Christ, which is Paul's most challenging legacy to mankind.

---

27. M. Grant, *Saint Paul* (1976), 197–98 (emphasis in original).

Chapter 8

A Pauline Allegory
in a French Context

In a recent contribution[1] I ventured to make a suggestion as to the force of the allegory of the two olives in Romans 11:13–24. Paul used that allegory in addressing Gentile Christians who were falling into anti-Judaism.

The context demands that the olive in Romans 11:17 be a cultivated one, as over against a wild olive (ἀγριέλαιος) mentioned in 11:17. Certain (τίνες) of the branches of the tree of the people of Israel have been lopped off (11:17). The use of the term "certain" is noteworthy. Whereas the translation "certain" suggests a minority, Paul here intends that the majority in Israel be understood as unbelieving and that most or a considerable number of the branches have been cut off. The use of "certain" points to Paul's sensitivity in referring to the unbelief of his people and of their having been cut off as a result.[2]

From what have the unbelieving Jews been cut off? It cannot be that they have been cut off from the Jewish people considered as an ethnic entity. They are still Jews. The branches broken off (the use of the passive verb ἐξεκλάσθησαν indicates the action of God Himself), then, are those Jews who have refused to be part of Israel conceived as the remnant that has believed in Christ. The cultivated olive in 11:17 stands for the community of Christian believers, the church, at first composed of Jewish Christians of the root of Abraham. In cutting themselves off from these, or in refusing to believe, the Jews were cutting themselves off from the life of the root as Paul understood it, although they still remained Jews after the flesh. Paul expresses himself laconically and clumsily. As the text stands, the Gentiles (the wild olive) who believe are grafted by God into or among (ἐν αὐτοῖς [11:17])[3] the branches lopped off so that they share in the cultivated olive.

---

1. W. D. Davies, "Romans 11:13–24: A Suggestion," in *Paganism, Judaïsme, Christianisme, Melanges Offert à Marcel Simon*, ed. M. Philonenko (Paris: E. de Boccard, with Univ. des Sciences Humaines de Strasbourg, 1978), 131–44.

2. Johannes Munck, *Christ and Israel: An Interpretation of Romans 9–11* (Philadelphia: Fortress Press, 1967), 123–24.

3. The Greek ἐν αὐτοῖς ("among them") must refer to the branches lopped off. As Ernst

The horticultural process is unthinkable, and Paul himself admits that it is unnatural (11:24). But the apostle's intent is clear. Through their acceptance of the gospel the Gentiles have been ingrafted into the People of God, the olive tree. And this olive tree — by the very principle of solidarity to which Paul had appealed in 11:16 — is continuous with the root of Abraham, so that through incorporation "in Christ" the Gentiles share in the root which is Abraham, as 11:18 indicates.

But Paul is anxious to insist that the priority always lies with Abraham and the Jewish people. Now that they were counted among the People of God, Gentile Christians were tempted to regard themselves as superior not only to the Jews, who had been lopped off, but also to Jewish Christians, whom they already outnumbered (11:18). Paul confronts this emerging Gentile arrogance head on.

He refers deliberately to the Gentile Christians as a wild olive. The condition of the Gentiles is that of wildness: they are, for Paul, not "cultivated." Over against Israel, even Israel after the flesh, they have not undergone an equal divine discipline. In Romans 9:4, Paul enumerates the benefits of being a Jew simply by natural descent. To his mind the privileges of the Jews had been the means of producing the cultivated olive which could bear fruit. However, Gentiles constitute a "wild olive" which by nature, be it noted, never produces oil. The Gentiles in being engrafted into the Jewish root contribute nothing. Perhaps it is the necessity of bringing this out forcefully that explains Paul's use of the symbol of the olive rather than the more customary symbol of the vine. The wild vine does produce wild grapes; the wild olive produces nothing useful.[4]

The Gentiles through Christ have now, indeed, been made partakers of the People of God and share in the benefits that spring from its root, Abraham. But this does not eliminate the priority of the Jews in that root. Paul tells the Gentiles: "It is not you who bear the root, but the root bears you" (11:18). The Jewish root is a necessity to Gentile Christians; they cannot live without it. All Gentile boasting over Jews is ruled out.

In 11:19, Paul meets still another Gentile misconception. Some Gentile Christians had the idea that the branches which had been broken off, that is,

---

Käsemann rightly insists (*An die Römer*, HNT 8a [Tübingen: J. C. B. Mohr, 1973], 296) it cannot mean "instead of." Paul is not dealing with the processes of nature, but with the astonishing activity of Divine Grace. The attempts made to find horticultural parallels to the grafting here described do not convince! See Munck, *Christ and Israel*, 128–30 (Excursus 3: "The True Olive Tree and the Wild Olive Tree"). The most thorough discussion is still that of Myles M. Bourke (*A Study of the Metaphor of the Olive Tree in Romans XI*, Studies in Sacred Theology, 2d ser., no. 3 [Washington, D.C.: The Catholic University of America, 1947], 65–111).

4. As far as I am aware, the first to point out that the wild olive does not bear fruit was Gustav Dalman (*Arbeit und Sitte in Palästina*, 6 vols. [Gütersloh: C. Bertelsmann, 1928–39], 1:680). See further Munck, *Christ and Israel*, 128–30.

the unbelieving Jews, had suffered this fate by divine purpose in order that the Gentiles might be engrafted into Israel. The implication is that God had, in fact, "favored" Gentiles over Jews, who were thereby regarded as inferior. Against this the apostle insists that the responsibility for the unbelief of the Jews rests squarely on themselves, not on divine preference for Gentiles. It was not that God had rejected the Jews. Rather the Jews themselves had chosen not to believe. The Gentiles had not been grafted into the olive because of any superior virtue on their part. In fact, they had not produced spiritual fruits. They were a wild, fruitless olive. The sole reason for their engrafting was their belief (11:19–20). So too, just as with the Jews who had not believed and were lopped off, those Gentiles who were now engrafted through their belief could also lose that status through disbelief. Gentile Christians, therefore, have no ground for claiming any superiority over Jews whether believing or unbelieving. Gentile Christians no less than Jews cannot count on any privilege: God deals with Gentile and Jew alike. In fact, since Jews were by nature related to the root, while Gentiles are not, the probability that those Jews who had been "lopped off" could be re-engrafted into the olive was more likely than that Gentiles should have been grafted into it in the first place. The privileges of Jews are real privileges, although they cannot be the ground of their acceptance.

Outside the confines of the symbols of the olive and the wild olive, but not unrelated to them, Paul announces a special mystery which should rein the arrogance of Gentiles. The unbelief that has befallen Israel is temporary. When what Paul calls "the fullness of the Gentiles" has been brought into "Israel," then all Israel, that is, the totality of the Jewish people, will be saved (Rom. 11:25–26). To justify this position Paul appeals to God's irrevocable election of the Jews and to the merit of their fathers (זְכוּת אָבוֹת).[5] In the end, both Gentiles and Jews are included in God's mercy, which is as wide as the world.

The symbols of the cultivated olive and the wild olive are used by Paul, then, in his efforts to formulate a philosophy of history, if we may so put it, which would acknowledge the place of the Jewish people in the Christian dispensation. At the very least we may claim that — altogether apart from Christ — Paul regards Jews as spiritually "cultivated" and the Gentiles as "underprivileged." To be of the root of Abraham physically was a privilege. The Jewish people were, in this regard, more fortunate than Gentiles. In 9:1–5

---

5. This probably is to be taken as a technical phrase. See Solomon Schechter, *Some Aspects of Rabbinic Theology* (London: Macmillan, 1909), 170–98; Arthur Marmorstein, *The Doctrine of Merits in Old Rabbinic Literature*, Jews' College London, Publication 7 (London: Oxford University, 1920; New York: Ktav, 1968), 37–107. See W. D. Davies, *Paul and Rabbinic Judaism: Some Rabbinic Elements in Pauline Theology*, 3d ed. (New York: Macmillan; London: SPCK, 1971), 268–73.

Paul expresses both his yearning for the salvation of his own people and his awareness of the advantages of the Jewish people.

The question of the relative importance of Gentiles and Jews in civilization, which, as we shall see, occupied Voltaire, Paul did not directly discuss. He was not, as a Jew, narrowly opposed to Hellenistic culture in all its forms — some of these he adopted as in 1 Corinthians 5:1; 11:13–14; he recognizes what is fitting for all men (Rom. 1:28). His habitat as an apostle was mostly the Hellenistic world; he knew its languages well.[6] He could be a Greek to the Greeks (1 Cor. 9:19–23). Such a person could not have had a "racist" view of the Greeks and Romans as inferior. When he insisted that he was a Hebrew born of Hebrews (Phil. 3:5), he was not speaking antithetically to criticize or reject Hellenism, but pointing to a tradition in which he was rooted and of which he was proud, because to that tradition belonged the spiritual privileges to which we have already referred. As a Christian, Paul did not think of Gentiles as inferior to Jews because of their race, but only because they were outside what he regarded as a superior religious tradition.[7]

It was the Jews' participation in that tradition that led Paul to ascribe to them a mysterious role in the history of mankind which enabled him to insist that Israel had a function even after Christ had appeared. In the *Festschrift* for Marcel Simon I suggested that Paul's allegory of the olive and the wild olive is doubly deliberate. It points not only to his high estimate of Israel but also to his low estimate of the spiritual attainments of the Gentiles. The true olive is a symbol of culture represented by Jewish tradition in its strictly Jewish and Christian expression.

While writing for the Simon *Festschrift*, my examination of the cultivated olive as a symbol for the Jews led me to ask how Paul's estimate of the Jewish people had fared in the thought of two French writers whose highly significant engagement with the Jews has much occupied me. In the thought of

---

6. A great classicist, Ulrich von Wilamowitz-Moellendorff, sees in Paul's writing "a classic of Hellenism" (*Die Griechische und Lateinische Literatur und Sprache*, 3d ed. [Leipzig and Berlin: B. G. Teubner, 1912], 232 [=*Die Kultur der Gegenwart* 1/8, ed. P. Hinneberg]). One of the most salutary changes in recent studies of the first century is the recognition that there was no rigid separation between the Hellenistic and Jewish worlds. See especially Martin Hengel, *Judaism and Hellenism: Studies in Their Encounter in Palestine during the Early Hellenistic Period*, 2 vols. (Philadelphia: Fortress Press, 1974), and Davies, *Paul and Rabbinic Judaism*, 1–16.

7. The question of the relation of Paul to culture is difficult. His main contacts were not with the higher intellectual currents of the Greco-Roman world but more with the religious which, to judge from his epistles, took on a gnostic cast. See Hans von Campenhausen, "Faith and Culture in the New Testament," in *Tradition and Life in the Church: Essays and Lectures in Church History* (Philadelphia: Fortress Press, 1968), 19–41; idem, "The Christian and Social Life according to the New Testament," in *Tradition and Life*, 141–59; also W. C. van Unnik, "The Critique of Paganism in 1 Peter 1:18," in *Neotestamentica et Semitica: Studies in Honour of Matthew Black*, ed. E. Earle Ellis and Max Wilcox (Edinburgh: T. & T. Clark, 1969), 129–42. It is interesting to read Raïssa Maritain's description of the Sorbonne in the light of von Campenhausen; see Raïssa Maritain, *We Have Been Friends Together: Memoirs* (New York: Longmans, Green & Co., 1945), esp. 60–78.

the first, Paul played a very important role, whereas in that of the other the apostle was an object of contempt. I refer to Jacques Maritain and Voltaire.

Jacques Maritain and the Jews

For many reasons (for example, the influence of his wife Raïssa, a Jewess who became, like him, a convert to Catholicism) Jacques Maritain was agonizingly — an adverb used advisedly — concerned with the people of Israel. Writing at a time when anti-Semitism overshadowed Western Europe, he found in Paul's Epistle to the Romans especially a scriptural ground on which he could stand to oppose the horror and from which he could expound what he conceived of as the "mystery" of the existence of the people of Israel. He refused the facile explanation of that existence in terms of race, nation, or people, and preferred Paul's characterization of it as a "mystery." He did not enlarge upon the apostle's precise use of that term but did give his full assent to Paul's recognition of Israel as irrevocably elect.[8]

To appreciate the thrust of Maritain's insistence on "The Mystery of Israel," certain attitudes toward the Jews among the French have to be borne in mind. Brought up in a distinguished Protestant family but converted to Catholicism, Maritain inevitably encountered in his life and in his studies an attitude toward the Jews which had become largely endemic in Roman Catholicism and the main currents of Protestantism. The criticism of Judaism which had accompanied the birth of Christianity, at a later date feeding on certain cultural and economic factors, developed into the fear of and hatred toward Jews to which the medieval period in Europe witnesses. Medieval anti-Jewish attitudes had persisted both in Tridentine Catholicism and in Protestantism. The majority of the clergy before the French Revolution were purveyors of what might be termed medieval anti-Judaism.[9] These attitudes to which we refer were not seriously challenged until this century and especially Vatican II. Waiving the question of whether the term "anti-Semitism" with its racial connotations can legitimately be used of these attitudes, and granting the occasional presence of Christian clergy who sought to champion the Jews, it is impossible to deny that traditional Christian anti-Jewish attitudes in Europe did nothing to dispel the climate within which anti-Semitism, properly so-called, could and did develop. Maritain was sadly and acutely aware of this. He knew those traditional Christian prejudices which had thrust Jews outside the mainstream of civilization because they were alleged

---

8. Jacques Maritain, "The Mystery of Israel," in *Ransoming the Time* (New York: Charles Scribner's Sons, 1941), 147–49.

9. See Arthur Hertzberg, "Churchmen and the Jews," in *The French Enlightenment and the Jews* (New York: Columbia University Press; Philadelphia: Jewish Publication Society of America, 1968), 248–67.

to be a people who had deliberately placed themselves outside salvation. And yet it was not with this traditional anti-Judaism that Maritain was directly engaged.[10] Rather he was concerned with two positions, one political and the other religious.

Maritain wrote his work *Le Mystère d'Israël* in 1937, when it was still possible in a France nauseated by anti-Semitic trends, "to consider the Jewish problem in a purely philosophical, objective and dispassionate manner."[11] But even at that date, as Maritain points out, there was a political liberalism in which it was possible to conceive of a "decisive solution" to the Jewish question. He does not enlarge upon the phrase "decisive solution."[12] But it seems clear that he refers to that long-standing "liberal" tradition which saw in the emancipation of Jewry and the increasing recognition of their rights a means toward their complete assimilation and silent disappearance as a distinct people. This liberal tradition insisted that the existing conditions and character of the Jews had been created by the persecutions from which they had suffered, that it was necessary to "enlighten" them, that this enlightenment would gradually lead to their assimilation. But by the time *Le Mystère d'Israël* had been translated into English in 1941, the situation had ominously changed: the thought of a new kind of solution had appeared. The precise date at which the doctrine of "the final solution" emerged in Germany and was deliberately pursued and implemented is not here important. By 1941, if not earlier, Maritain was aware of it. He writes of the "anti-Semitic nightmare spreading like a mental epidemic even among some groups of democratic people."[13] It is against both the liberal political quest for a "decisive solution" and the more barbaric Nazi threat of a "final solution" that Maritain responded:

> Israel is a mystery. . . . If Saint Paul is right, we shall have to call the *Jewish problem* a problem *without solution* — that is, until the great reintegration foreseen by the apostle, which will be like a "resurrection from the dead." To wish to find, in the pure, simple, decisive sense of the word, a *solution* of the problem of Israel, is to attempt to stop the movement of history.[14]

---

10. The main elements in the traditional anti-Judaism were (1) the crucifixion of Jesus by the Jews, (2) the dispersion as a proof of the merited punishment of Jews and of the divinity of Christ, (3) the continued existence and persistent misery of the Jews as a theological necessity. These emerge conveniently, for example, in Pascal (*Pensées*, Édition nouvelle revue sur les manuscrits et les meilleurs textes avec une introduction, des notes et un index analytique par Victor Giraud [Paris: C. Crès et Cie, 1924], nos. 571, 601, 619, 620, 638, 675, 640).

11. Maritain, *Ransoming the Time*, 141.

12. Ibid., 149.

13. Ibid., 141.

14. Ibid., 149.

On the purely human, political plane, Maritain — as Paul in Maritain's view had insisted — urges that there is no "solution" to the Jewish problem.[15] The Jew is here to stay. We must not simply learn to "tolerate" him as a "squalid nuisance" (a horrible phrase used in this connection) but to coexist with him in grateful appreciation.

Maritain points to what makes it impossible to ignore the presence of the Jew. There is above all his intensity. The presence of the Jew in any society ensures tension.

> The solution of a practical problem is the end of tension and conflict; the end of contradiction, peace itself. To assert that there is no solution — in an absolute sense — to the problem of Israel is to ensure the existence of struggle.[16]

Or again:

> Israel is here — Israel which is not of the world — at the deepest core of the world, to irritate it, to exasperate it, to *move* it. Like some foreign substance, like a living yeast mixed into the main body, it gives the world no quiet, it prevents the world from sleeping, it teaches the world to be dissatisfied and restless so long as it has not God, it stimulates the movement of history.[17]

Or again:

> Often despite itself, and at times manifesting in various ways a materialized Messianism, which is the darkened aspect of its vocation to the absolute, the Jewish people, ardently, intelligently, actively, give witness, at the very heart of man's history, to the supernatural. Whence the conflicts and tensions which, under all kinds of disguises, cannot help but exist between Israel and the nations.
>
> It is an illusion to believe that this tension can disappear (at least before the fulfillment of the prophecies). It is base — one of those specimens of baseness natural to man as an animal (be he an Arab, and himself the lineage of Shem, or a Slav, or a Latin, or a German...) and a baseness of which Christianity alone can, to the degree that is truly lived, free mankind — to wish to end the matter by anti-Semitic violence, whether it be of open persecution, or politically "mitigated." There is but one way, and that is to accept this state of tension, and to make the best of it in each particular case, not in hatred, but in

---

15. That Paul knew of the Jewish "problem" appears from Romans. See W. D. Davies, "Paul and the People of Israel," *NTS* 24 (1977–78): 4–39.

16. Maritain, *Ransoming the Time,* 149.

17. Ibid., 156.

that concrete intelligence which love requires of each of us, so that we may agree with our companion — with our "adversary" as the gospel says — quickly while we are with him on the way; and in the awareness that "all have sinned and have need of the glory of God" — *omnes quidem peccaverunt, et egent gloria Dei.* "The history of the Jews," says Leon Bloy, "dams the history of the human race as a dike dams a river, in order to raise its level."[18]

Or again:

> I have already said that Israel's passion is not a co-redemptive passion, achieving for the eternal salvation of souls what is lacking (as concerns application, not merits) in the Saviour's suffering. It is suffered for the goading on of the world's temporal life. In itself, it is the passion of a being caught up in the temporal destiny of the world, which both irritates the world and seeks to emancipate it, and on which the world avenges itself for the pangs of its history.[19]

The price paid by Israel for its life as "a goad," or as Bloy's dike that raises the river in history, has been high. The persecution of the Jews is the price of their peculiar contribution and status as elect. The matter is illuminatingly, though laconically, stated by Maritain as follows:

> It has been said that the tragedy of Israel is the tragedy of mankind; and that is why there is no solution to the Jewish problem. Let us state it more precisely: it is the tragedy of man in his struggle with the world and of the world in its struggle with God. Jacob, lame and dreaming, tireless irritant of the world and scapegoat of the world, indispensable to the world and intolerable to the world — so fares the wandering Jew. The persecution of Israel seems like the sign of the moments of crisis in this tragedy, when the play of human history almost stops at obstacles that the distress and moral weakness of nations cannot surmount, and when for a new start it demands some fresh horror.[20]

To the political liberals offering a decisive solution and the National Socialists offering a final solution, Maritain opposes the Pauline doctrine: Israel is the chosen olive tree.[21]

But Maritain faced a less obvious religious criticism of his interpretation of Paul as justifying the continuance of Jewry. Most "enlightened" Christians had approached the Jewish question from the religious angle somewhat as

---

18. Ibid., 168.
19. Ibid., 177. Is there not here a strange "dualism" in Maritain's position?
20. Ibid., 151.
21. Ibid., 183.

follows. The emphasis of Judaism is on the One God. The service of Him just because God is One and there is no other, must within itself contain universality and should have led to the search for a universal community. But historically Judaism remained concentrated on Israel. The gospel offered it a choice: was it prepared to become a truly universal religion? Judaism rejected that challenge and despite the large humanism of many of its sages, chose to become an essentially closed society. Fortunately Christianity has carried on the values of its Jewish heritage. It follows there is no *raison d'être* for the continuance of Judaism. Christians could justifiably welcome the disappearance of Jewry on religious grounds. Christians who held such a view were far removed from the advocates of a "decisive solution" or a "final solution." But they usually did ignore the history of Jews since the first century and refused to take seriously the continuing presence and mystery of Israel in the world.[22]

Maritain opposes these liberal Christian views as he did the politically liberal and Nazi ones. Drawing upon Romans 9–11, he asserts that there is a continuing *necessity* for the existence of the Jewish people. Not only are they now to be subjected to a "final solution" by annihilation or to a "decisive solution" by assimilation, but to consider them as religiously irrelevant, as did liberal Christians, was a denial of the Christian scriptures themselves. What is now the cultivated olive, the community of believing Christians, is of the same root as the nonbelieving Jews. Like Paul, Maritain insists that without its Jewish root the Christian community itself cannot live. The covenant of the Jewish people with God is eternally valid; they still have a function even in the Christian dispensation (Rom. 11:1, 2).[23]

But, over against the interpretation of Paul advocated by Maritain, it has been urged that, in fact, there is implicit in Paul himself an attitude toward Jews which ultimately requires their absorption, both by assimilation into the general society and by the Christian community itself. Does not Paul look forward to a time when all Jews will be saved and *ipso facto* lose their identity? Does he not too envisage at the End the cessation of Israel after the flesh? On the basis of Romans 9–11, on which Maritain rested his case, even Paul has been declared an "anti-Semite."[24] Such an astounding charge requires a careful examination and definition of terms.

---

22. This position was probably most forcefully expressed by Arnold Joseph Toynbee, *The Study of History*, 12 vols. (London, New York, and Toronto: Oxford University Press, 1954–61), 5:74–75; 8:580–83.

23. See Jacques Maritain, *La Pensée de Saint Paul* (New York: Longmans, Green & Co., Editions de la Maison Française, 1944), 141: "A travers toutes les vicissitudes de son exil et de l'histoire du monde Israël reste toujours le peuple de Dieu — frappé mais toujours aimé à cause de ses pères." [Across the vicissitudes of its exile and the history of the world, Israel always remains the people of God — afflicted but always beloved as the children of their fathers.]

24. So Rosemary Radford Ruether, *Faith and Fratricide: The Theological Roots of Anti-Semitism* (New York: Seabury Press, 1974), 95–107, esp. 104: "Paul's position was unquestionably that of

In the nineteenth- and twentieth-century sense in which the term anti-Semitism has come to be used, as denoting a hatred toward Jews on the grounds of their racial inferiority, it cannot apply to Paul. The justification for rejecting any anti-Semitism in the strict sense in Paul is that Romans 9–11 makes clear that the root of the cultivated olive, the true Israel, is Abraham, the father of the Jewish people. If we should use racial terms at all, and this seems dubious, the descent of the Jews from Abraham immediately makes anti-Semitism in any racial sense impossible for Paul. Maritain expresses himself more convolutedly: "The ingenious anti-Semites who vituperate 'Jewish racism' forget that the first one responsible for the concept of an elect race, that concept being taken at its pure source, is the God of Abraham, of Isaac, of Jacob, the God of Israel — *your* God, dear Christians who turn yourselves against the chosen olive tree into which you were grafted."[25]

But what of the more subtle charge that the Pauline hope for the End demands the end of the Jews as Jews? Does he reveal what might be called an eschatological anti-Semitism? Simply to point to Paul's expressions of concern for his own people (9:1–5; 10:1) as making such a charge unthinkable is not enough. Maritain is aware of the need to face the charge squarely. What mainly concerns him is the continued role of Jews in history. Like the cultivated olive, that is, the believing Christian community, the Jewish people also, born of the same root, remains to stir and to sustain mankind, although in a different way from that of the church, to the End. Moreover, Maritain insists that the nature of the final salvation of all Jews, as Paul understands it, safeguards their identity. One could have wished Maritain to have been as explanatory at this very crucial point as he is emphatic. He writes:

> But when Jewish people as such shall convert itself and pass under the Law of the new covenant, it will be within its own ancient privileges, extending to all peoples in accordance with the very universality of the Church, and transfigured in accordance with the truth of the spirit, that, in joining itself to the Gentiles in one single field, *it will find itself received anew.*[26]

---

anti-Judaism"; p. 107: "[Paul] enunciates a doctrine of the rejection of the Jews (rejection of Judaism as the proper religious community of God's people) in the most radical form, seeing it as rejected not only now, through the rejection of Christ, but from the beginning. The purpose of Paul's "mystery" is not to concede any ongoing validity to Judaism, but rather to assure the *ultimate vindication of the Church.* If the Church is the eschatological destiny of Israel, then this truth must finally win out by having the 'Jews' themselves testify to it. They must admit finally that it is not through Torah, but through faith in Jesus as the Christ, that they are intended to be saved" (her italics). Ruether does not sufficiently distinguish anti-Semitism and anti-Judaism. She uses both terms apparently interchangeably. See my "Paul and the People of Israel" (n. 15) for a critique of her position.

25. Maritain, *Ransoming the Time,* 183.
26. Ibid., 186. Italics added.

Or again:

> And as for the extraordinary promise concerning the future conversion
> of Israel according to the flesh, does it not indicate for this people, as
> God's people, an astounding and permanent prerogative?[27]

This is Maritain's understanding of Paul. No one has sought to do greater justice to that apostle's care for his own people. That he truly interpreted that
care we do not doubt. But that the final engrafting of all Israel onto the cultivated olive, in the mind of Paul, would not be the abandonment of its identity
but its reinterpretation on a higher level, requires a more detailed and subtle
treatment of Romans 11:25ff., in particular, than Maritain provides. He is,
unfortunately, more emphatic at this point than he is explanatory.

Throughout his treatment, Maritain makes abundantly clear his Roman
Catholic *point de départ*. His central emphasis in his understanding of the
mystery of Israel is on its sacred, theological, or supernatural character. The
elect olive is what concerns him. It is very significant that he nowhere refers
to the symbol of the wild olive, bearing no fruit, as denoting the Gentiles.
"Israel" for him was and is the astounding interweaving of the natural and
the sacred, of the supernatural and the temporal: its case was unique. But
unique as Israel is, Paul enabled the French scholar to appeal to the profound, indeed essential, continuity of the Christian faith with Judaism and of
the church with the people of Israel. This meant that for Maritain Jews were
not "outsiders" in the Christian dispensation who had to be assimilated or an-
nihilated, but part of the very root and continuing life of Christendom. Israel
had introduced into Western civilization a supernatural order, which gave it
meaning. Salvation was and is from the Jews (compare John 4:22). Although
Maritain does not dwell on the symbol of the wild olive for the Gentiles, the
implication of his position is that that symbol is an appropriate one.

Voltaire and the Jews

The contrast with another tradition in France leaps to the eye. One might
have expected Maritain, in insisting on the necessity for the full recognition
of the people of Israel, while primarily resting on scripture, to have appealed
also to the tradition of the French Enlightenment. Would not its emphasis on
tolerance and universalism have furthered that acceptance of Jews on their
own terms that Maritain desiderated? The emancipation of the Jews in the
French Revolution had generally been understood as the fruit of the enlightened *philosophes*. They insisted on a rationality and tolerance extending even

---

27. Ibid., 187–88.

to Jews. Their enlightened attitude was conveniently reinforced by the financial prudence which led eighteenth-century France to recognize the benefits that Jewish capital would bring. In the Enlightenment a philosophic and an economic climate combined to make a more humane attitude to Jews acceptable and even necessary. And yet Maritain makes no appeal to this. The reason is not far to seek. The record of the Enlightenment on the Jewish question is not unambiguous.[28] That ambiguity surfaces most strikingly in its most luminous figure, Voltaire.

It is not for an outsider to Voltairean studies, even one intensely involved in the question concerned, to settle the problem of Voltaire's attitude to Jews. Aubery refuses to be intimidated by those who find it anti-Semitic. He admits that, as are all born into Christendom, Voltaire was inevitably touched by that disease even as he urged the brotherhood of man. Beginning with a quotation from Voltaire's own works, Aubery writes: "'Oublions nos querelles,' 'le monde entier n'est qu'une famille les hommes sont frères; les frères se querellent quelque fois; mais les bons coeurs reviennent aisément.' (M.XXIX. 582) Ces phrases de Voltaire . . . expriment une idée sur laquelle, à son habitude, il revient sans cesse."[29] Aubery insists, "En réalité ni antisémite ni philosémite Voltaire s'est toujours efforcé de juger les Juifs avec équité."[30] Voltaire, he suggests, treated Jews with irony and demystified them, but except insofar as he had inherited the endemic anti-Semitism of Christendom,[31] he

---

28. See especially Hertzberg, *The French Enlightenment and the Jews*; Fadien Lovsky, "L'Antisémitisme Rationaliste," in *Antisémitisme et Mystère d'Israel* (Paris: Albin Michel, 1955), 261–300. For a different view, see Pierre Aubery, "Voltaire et les Juifs: Ironie et démystification," in *Studies on Voltaire and the Eighteenth Century*, ed. Theodore Besterman (Geneva: Institut et Musée Voltaire Les Delices, 1963), 24:67–79; Paul H. Meyer, "The Attitude of the Enlightenment towards the Jews," in Besterman, *Studies on Voltaire and the Eighteenth Century*, 26:1161–1206.

29. "'Let us forget our quarrels,' 'the whole world is only a family, brothers who sometimes quarrel among themselves; but good hearts come easily.' These phrases of Voltaire . . . express an idea on which, according to his custom, he ceaselessly returns" (Aubery, "Voltaire et les Juifs," 24:73).

30. "In reality, neither an anti-Semite nor a sympathizer with Jews, Voltaire always strove to judge Jews with equity" (ibid., 24:71).

31. That the anti-Semitism of the Enlightenment is the residue of Christian influences has been used to explain the traces of it in Voltaire and others, who could not escape Christian contamination. Thereby the Enlightenment is exculpated. Related to this is the claim that Voltaire's attacks on the Old Testament and on Jews are motivated by his concern to attack Christianity, as was Hitler's "final solution." In the eighteenth century as in the twentieth, Christianity was too well established to be attacked directly. The wiser course was to attack it through its supposedly weaker progenitor, Judaism. This in turn points to a factor which must be fully recognized. Voltaire and other critics of the establishment were not facing paper tigers. When they attacked the established order in church and state, they risked severe punishment and even death. See, for example, Hugh Trevor-Roper, "The Historical Philosophy of the Enlightenment," in Besterman, *Studies on Voltaire and the Eighteenth Century*, 27:1667–87. It is not easy to condemn Voltaire for attacking Christianity through Judaism. But, even *if* he did so, his motives, though not justifiable, are not incomprehensible. His position was fraught with insecurity. See John McManners, *Reflections at the Deathbed of Voltaire: The Art of Dying in Eighteenth-Century France*, an inaugural

cannot be charged with that prejudice. His virulent attacks on Jews are on those of the ancient world not on those of his own time; a rigid distinction must be made between these two categories. "Il prend bien soin de distinguer entre la grossièreté, la barbarie des anciens Hébreux et les moeurs de ses contemporains juifs."[32] But apart from the natural tendency of minds in the least inclined to anti-Semitism — and such minds do not lend themselves to refinements historical or otherwise[33] — to ignore such a distinction deliberately, it would be difficult not to be influenced in the direction of anti-Semitism by such sentences as the following by Voltaire: "N'est-il pas clair (humainement parlant, et ne considérant que les causes secondes) que les Juifs, qui espéraient la conquête du monde, ont été presque toujours asservis, ce fut leur faute? Et si les Romains dominèrent, ne le méritèrent ils pas par leur courage et par leur prudence? *Je demande très humblement pardon aux Romains de les comparer un moment avec les Juifs.*"[34] The underlined words would jump across any chronological distinctions! Voltaire closes his article on "Juifs" in *Dictionnaire Philosophique* as follows: "Enfin vous ne trouverez en eux qu'un peuple ignorant et barbare, que joint depuis longtemps la plus sordide avarice à la plus détestable superstition, et à la plus invincible haine pour tous les peuples qui les tolèrent et qui les enrichissent. Il ne faut pourtant pas les brûler."[35] Such irony is always difficult to assess; it so easily passes over into cynical cruelty.

It is not surprising, then, that there are others who do not deal so gently with Voltaire. They find that his tolerance and generosity did not extend to the Jews. Anti-Semitism is one of the rare Christian errors he did not condemn.[36]

---

lecture delivered before the University of Oxford on 21 November 1974 (Oxford: Clarendon Press, 1975). Others have pointed to Voltaire's unfortunate personal experience with Jews as a source of his anti-Judaism. On exposing the anti-Christian origin and character of Hitler's anti-Semitism, see Maurice Samuel, *The Great Hatred* (New York: A. A. Knopf, 1940), and W. D. Davies, "Chosen People: The Approach to Antisemitism," *The Congregational Quarterly* (London) 26, no. 4 (October 1948): 327–41.

32. "He takes great care to distinguish between the incivility, the barbarity of the ancient Hebrews, and the morals of contemporary Jews" (Aubery, "Voltaire et les Juifs," 24:71).

33. See Jean-Paul Sartre, *Anti-Semite and Jew* (New York, 1965), 17–54 (=*Réflexions sur la Question Juive* [Paris, 1946]).

34. "Isn't it clear (humanly speaking, and only considering secondary causes) that the Jews, who hoped to conquer the world, have almost always been enslaved, which has been their own fault? And if the Romans became dominant did they not merit it by their courage and their prudence? *I humbly apologize to the Romans for comparing them, even for a moment, with the Jews*" (François Marie Arouet de Voltaire, "Questions sur les Conquêtes des Romains et leur décadence," in *Essai sur les moeurs et l'esprit des nations et sur les principaux faits de l'histoire depuis Charlemagne jusquà Louis XIII*, ed. René Pomeau, 2 vols. [Paris: Garnier frères, Classique Garnier, 1963], 1:183). Italics added.

35. "Finally, you will find them nothing but an ignorant and barbarous people, who have long combined the most sordid avarice with the most detestable superstition, and the most invincible hatred for all peoples who tolerated and enriched them. Nevertheless, it is not necessary to burn them" (Voltaire, "Juifs," in *Dictionnaire Philosophique, Oeuvres Complètes de Voltaire*, new ed. [Paris: Garnier frères, 1879], 521).

36. Lovsky, "L'Antisémitisme Rationaliste," 263.

That he was only thinking in negative terms of Jews in the distant past and not of his contemporaries seems to be contradicted by the ridicule with which he met the proposition made in Great Britain in 1753 that Jews should be given citizenship. Whether or not Voltaire himself should be regarded as an anti-Semite, his treatment of the Jews certainly could and did provide ammunition for anti-Semites in later years. In *Essai sur les moeurs* Voltaire writes:

> Vous êtes frappés de cette haine et de ce mépris que toutes les na-tions ont toujours eus contre les Juifs: c'est la suite inévitable de leur législation; il fallait, ou qu'ils subjuguassent tout, ou qu'ils fussent écrasés. Il leur fut ordonné d'avoir les nations en horreur (Deut. 7:16). ... Ils gardèrent tous leur usages, qui sont précisément le contraire des usages sociables; ils furent donc avec raison traités comme une nation opposée en tout aux autres; les servant par avarice, les détestant par fanatisme, se faisant de l'usure un devoir sacré.[37]

The denigration of ancient Jews in the article "Juifs" (section 4: "Réponse à quelques objections") in the *Dictionnaire Philosophique* is clear: in number inferior; they massacred the inhabitants of Palestine whose land they took; their law was cruel; their military prowess dubious; Solomon had wealth and concubines but no timber or workers for the Temple; Judah and Israel hated each other; they borrowed an alphabet in Babylon; learned little from the Babylonian sages ("Il paraît que les Juifs apprirent peu de chose de la science des mages: ils s'adonnèrent aux métiers de courtiers, de changeurs, et de fripiers, par là ils se rendirent nécessaires, *comme ils le sont encore*, et ils s'enrichirent" [italics added]);[38] only the worst party returned to Israel from Babylon; they had internal dissensions; the Jews loved money more that the Temple ("L'esprit séditieux de ce peuple se porta à de nouveaux excès: son caractère en tout temps était d'être cruel, et son sort d'être puni").[39] Only their fecundity preserved them ("Les Juifs ont regardé comme leurs deux grands devoirs: des infants et de l'argent").[40] Militarily they were ineffective; they had no navy; they had no industry; their government was as ineffective

---

37. "You are struck by this hatred and contempt that all nations have always had against the Jews: this is what inevitably follows from their own Law; it was necessary either to subjugate them totally or entirely to crush them. They have been commanded to abhor all nations (Deut. 7:16). . . . They keep all their own customs, which are precisely the opposite of socially acceptable customs; they were then with reason treated as a nation opposed in everything to all others; rather they serve the nations with avarice, detesting them fanatically, to make usury their sacred duty" (Voltaire, *Essai sur les moeurs*, 2:64).

38. "It seemed that the Jews learned little of the wisdom of the East. They devoted them-selves to the professions of courtier, money changers, and tailors, so as to render themselves indispensable, *as they still are,* and to enrich themselves."

39. "The seditious spirit of this people reached new heights: their character had always been cruel, and their lot to be punished."

40. "Jews regarded as their great duties to have children and to make money."

as their military discipline; their philosophy was negligible ("Celui que aurait mangé du boudin ou du lapin aurait été lapidé, et celui qui niait l'immortalité de l'âme pouvait être grand-prêtre");[41] it was nothing noble like their horror of idolatry that caused them to be hated but their cruelty to those whom they conquered. "Les Hébreux ont presque toujours été ou errants, ou brigands, ou enclaves, ou séditieux; *ils sont encore vagabonds aujourd'hui sur la terre, et en horreur aux hommes, assurant que le ciel et la terre, et tous les hommes, ont été créés pour eux seuls.*"[42]

Small wonder in the light of such assertions that Labroue, an anti-Semite during the occupation of France in the forties, wrote: "Notre antijudaïsme d'État s'inspire si peu de prosélytisme confessionel qu'il trouve sa référence la plus décisive dans la tradition Voltairienne."[43] Hitler himself, through Frederick II, it has been asserted, drank from Voltairean springs.[44] To understand how the Enlightenment could spawn or feed anti-Semitism, we should consider two aspects of it present in Voltaire.

First, to the rationalist seeking for a universal, ordered society, the very existence of the Jews, who challenged him with what seemed to be irrational claims, was itself irrational. The *philosophes*, like some later Christian liberals, found a scandal in the particularity of the Jews; they refused to fit into a rational universe.[45] The attacks of Voltaire on Christianity and on the Jews again and again emphasize the sheer irrationality of the two faiths.[46] In the world of the Enlightenment a chosen people was anathema.

But second, equally offensive to Voltaire would have been the notion that the Gentiles were a wild olive as Paul had held. His attitude to Jews is bound up with his understanding of Western civilization. *Mutatis mutandis,* his attitude could be taken as the exact opposite to that of Paul (Voltaire's treatment of whom is consistently more unfavorable than his treatment of Jesus)[47] and to that of Maritain. For Paul, as later for Maritain, the olive, "the Israel of

---

41. "Those who ate sausage or rabbit were stoned, and those who ridiculed the immortality of the soul became high priests."

42. "Hebrews have almost always been either outcasts or thieves or ghettoized or seditious. *They remain vagabonds today on the earth, abhorred by men; they feel assured that heaven and earth and all humankind have been created for them*" (Voltaire, "Juifs," 512–20). Italics added to final quotation.

43. "Our state-sanctioned anti-Judaism is inspired less by the proselytism of the confessional (i.e., the church) than by its most decisive source, the tradition of Voltaire (Henri Labroue, *Voltaire antijuif* [Paris: Documents contemporains, 1942], 8, quoted in Lovsky, "L'Antisémitisme Rationaliste," 267). Lovsky, however, recognizes Labroue's tendentiousness and the questionableness of some of his citations. Aubery ("Voltaire et les Juifs," 24:70–71) dismisses Labroue.

44. Lovsky, "L'Antisémitisme Rationaliste," 267.

45. Aubery ("Voltaire et les Juifs," 24:68) quotes Voltaire's *Sermon des Cinquantes,* 1762, "La Religion doit être conforme à la morale, et universelle comme elle."

46. See especially, Peter Gay, ed., "Introduction," in *Voltaire's Philosophical Dictionary* (New York: Basic Books, 1962), 3–52, esp. 35–52.

47. A. J. Bingham, "Voltaire and the New Testament," in Besterman, *Studies on Voltaire and the Eighteenth Century,* 24:203.

God," ultimately deriving from a Semitic root, provided for a salvific agent in history, whereas the wild olive, signifying the Gentile world, was spiritually fruitless. For Voltaire on the other hand, the Semitic tradition was despicable. To him the people of the Bible suffered from an unreasonable and extreme pride: "C'était, il faut avouer, un chétif peuple arabe sans art et sans science, caché dans un petit pays montueux et ignoré...il ne fut connu des Grecs que du temps d'Alexandre, devenu leur dominateur, et ne fut-apperçu des Romains que pour être bientôt écrasé par eux dans la foule."[48] Hertzberg describes Voltaire's outlook as follows:

> At the very heart of the whole of Voltaire's outlook there was, as André Maurois has seen, a vision of universal history that was constructed in opposition to the orthodox one of Bossuet. Voltaire did not see the Jews and biblical history as central; he looked back to pagan, Greco-Roman antiquity as the golden age. Then there had been true philosophy and culture. This would have been ruined by the advent of Christianity. In his own mind Voltaire was a Cicero *redivivus* who had come to recreate that world. The glory of the new age of enlightenment would be that Europe would be restored to its true foundations.[49]

In short, the wild olive was the Jews, the cultivated olive the Greeks and Romans.

> The nucleus of Voltaire's views of the Jews, however, amounts to this: there is a cultural, philosophical, and ethnic tradition of Europe which descended, through the human stock of that continent, from the intellectual values that were taught by the Greeks. Those were in turn carried to all the reaches of the European world by the Romans. This is the normative culture of which Voltaire approved. The Jews are a different family, and their religion is rooted in their character. Christianity is the Jewish religion superimposed on people of a different world, both ethnically and culturally. It is somewhat better than Judaism because it has been affected by the nature of those who have adopted it and by their earlier, healthier tradition. It is possible to redeem Europe by reviving its attachment to its own fundamental nature and tradition. European men can be freed effectively of Christianity because Christianity is here a longstanding infection; it is not one of the foundations of the European spirit, deriving from its character. The case of the Jews is radically

---

48. "This was, it must be acknowledged, a pitiful Arabic people without art or science, hidden in a small mountain range of an ignored country...unknown by the Greeks who, since the time of Alexander, became their oppressor, and unknown by the Romans, among whom they soon disappeared in the crowd" (Voltaire, *Chrétien-contre six Juifs* 1776 M. XXIX, p. 504).

49. Hertzberg, *The French Enlightenment and the Jews*, 299. Compare Gay, "Introduction," 12–13.

different. Being born a Jew and the obnoxiousness of the Jewish outlook
are indissoluble; it is most unlikely that "enlightened" Jews can escape
their innate character. The Jews are subversive of the European tradition by their very presence, for they are radically other, the hopelessly
alien. Cure them of their religion and their inborn character remains.[50]

The interpretation of the Enlightenment as a taproot of modern anti-
Semitism is beyond our competence adequately to assess. The incalculable
liberating influence of the Enlightenment is not in question.[51] Maritain's own
critical exegesis of Paul's epistle would hardly have been possible without it.[52]
But at least an interrogatory conclusion does seem justified. In some of its
expressions, did the Enlightenment fail in its treatment of the Jews as did the
Christian tradition (both in its orthodox and liberal expressions) which it so
critically dismissed? And did that unenlightened failure in the end have even
more disastrous consequences than Christian anti-Judaism? Can it be that
Voltaire was a link in Western intellectual history between the anti-Judaism
of classical paganism and the anti-Semitism of our age?[53]

The aim of this brief and inadequate treatment has been to indicate that
a thinker who took Paul seriously in Romans 9–11 found an antidote to an
anti-Semitism, which, in the judgment of many, had been present in the most
distinguished representative of the Enlightenment in France who had not
found Paul congenial.[54]

---

50. Ibid., 306–7.

51. But see John Hallowell, ed., *From Enlightenment to Revolution/Eric Voegelin* (Durham, N.C.:
Duke University Press, 1975).

52. Meyer, who recognized anti-Semitism especially in the later Voltaire, quotes a Jewish
writer, Isadore Cohen, commemorating the centenary of his death in 1878 ("The Attitude of the
Enlightenment toward the Jew," 26:1177–78): "Si Voltaire nous a été funeste, la voltairéianisme
nous a été éminemment utile...le bien qu'il a fait — bien inestimable — en déracinant la
tyrannie ecclésiastique, en minant les principes de l'Inquisition, en éteignant la flamme des
bûchers, lui a survécu. C'est là le plus clair de son oeuvre, et les méprises ou les petitesses
de ses appréciations sont effacées par la grandeur des résultats que lui doit la civilisation." [To
us Voltaire has become distressing, but Voltairianism has been eminently useful.... The good he
did accomplish — inestimable good — in laying bare the roots of ecclesiastical tyranny, in under-
mining the principles of the Inquisition, in extinguishing the flame of the butchers — this has
survived him. This is the most estimable of his work, and the faults or pettiness of his valuations
are erased by the grandeur of the results that he has left to civilization.]

53. Hertzberg, *The French Enlightenment and the Jews*, 10. He goes so far as to consider Voltaire
a precursor of Hitler.

54. Unfortunately the excellent chapter by Bernard E. Doering in his work *Jacques Maritain
and the French Catholic Intellectuals* (Notre Dame and London: University of Notre Dame Press,
1983), 126–67, came too late for use in this chapter.

Part III

The Jewish Background
of the Gospels

Chapter 9

A Different Approach to Jamnia: The Jewish Origins of Matthew's Gospel and Messianism

Professor Louis Martyn has put us all deeply in his debt by drawing attention — strikingly, with great imaginative originality — to the radical break between Johannine Christianity and Jamnian Judaism. However, the very effectiveness of his work has perhaps overshadowed other less dramatic reactions to Jamnian Judaism among Christians. The Gospel of Matthew in particular, it might be urged, points to an encounter and engagement with that Judaism more nuanced, and less polarized perhaps, than that dealt with by Professor Martyn. The consideration of the Matthean reaction to Judaism at Jamnia, therefore, may help to fill in something of the background — contemporary but possibly distant rather than immediate — of the developments in Johannine circles.

The term "messianism" in the subtitle needs careful definition since it can easily be confused with "Christology." Is Matthew's "messianism" a Christology? Traditionally in Christian theology, in its strict sense, the term "Christology" designates the doctrine about the way in which God became man "in Christ" — that is, the mode or, if one may so crudely put it, the mechanics of the Incarnation in Christ. Recently, an Oxford scholar has urged that the Messiah was regarded as a divine or divinely begotten being in some passages in Jewish sources. However, most of the evidence of those sources points unambiguously to the Messiah as being purely human. Is the same true of Matthew's understanding of Jesus?

Certain verses have been taken to indicate that God became man in Jesus, his Son, in the story of the virgin birth in 1:18–25. But that story begins with τοῦ δὲ Ἰησοῦ Χριστοῦ ἡ γένεσις οὕτως ἦν ["Now the birth of Jesus Christ was thus..."] not with τοῦ δὲ υἱοῦ τοῦ θεοῦ ἡ γένεσις οὕτως ἦν ["The birth of the Son of God was thus..."], and the role of the Son of God Christology in the strict sense so emphasized by Professor Kingsbury[1] in

---

1. See especially Jack D. Kingsbury, *Matthew: Structure, Christology, Kingdom* (Philadelphia:

171

his influential and important studies is not foremost in the birth narratives
as a whole, and this should warn us against overemphasizing its significance.
Similarly, to read any later Trinitarian significance into the Spirit in Matthew
is unjustifiable. In the virgin birth narrative the "spirit," a term neuter in
Greek and feminine in Hebrew, is best understood in terms of the invasive
power of God; there is no suggestion of the Spirit as the Second Person of a
Trinity. But what of 1:23: ἰδοὺ ἡ παρθένος ἐν γαστρὶ ἕξει καὶ τέξεται υἱόν,
καὶ καλέσουσιν τὸ ὄνομα αὐτοῦ Ἐμμανουήλ, ὅ ἐστιν μεθερμηνευόμενον
μεθ᾽ ἡμῶν ὁ θεός?[2] There are those who have taken Matthew to equate Jesus
with God in this verse. (See John 1:1–5; 20:28.) This view appears as early
as Irenaeus (*Adv. Haer.* 3.21.4: "Carefully, then, has the Holy Ghost pointed
out, by what has been said, His birth is from a virgin, and His essence, that
He is God [for the name Emmanuel indicates this].") In recent scholarship,
many have placed 1:23 in parallel with 28:20. It is claimed that the words,
"Lo, I am with you," at the end of the Gospel most naturally refer to God
and recall the presence of God in Jesus in 1:23. The argument is that μετά
with the genitive in Matthew usually means "in company with." But usually,
in Matthew, God is referred to as being "in heaven" (2:9). To be "with men"
would be more appropriate to the Son than to God, the Heavenly Father: the
Son has here in 1:23 become God with us.

But all these considerations (and they are not very cogent) do not out-
weigh the others. Apart from 1:23, even if by implication there, Matthew
never refers to Jesus as God, as is the case with most of the New Testament.[3]
If Matthew has intended to identify Jesus with God, we should have found in
1:23 Ἐμμανουήλ...ὁ θεὸς μεθ᾽ ἡμῶν ["Emmanuel...God with us"] rather
than μεθ᾽ ἡμῶν ὁ θεός ["God with us"]. Here the order of words makes ὁ
θεός adverbial. The passage is not a statement of the Incarnation — that is,
it is not strictly christological — although in a general sense it does indicate
that for Matthew in Jesus' coming God's Spirit has become uniquely present
among men. The Trinitarian formula in the canonical text in 28:19–20 poses
such textual difficulties that it cannot be taken to invalidate the rejection of
a strictly christological aspect in the messianism of Matthew. The most that
could be claimed is that the messianism of Matthew offers an inchoate Christology, its raw materials as it were. Matthew's use of the term "Lord" for Jesus,
important and possibly primary as it is, does not invalidate our position.[4]

We can now turn to the origins of the teaching about Jesus, the Messiah,

Fortress Press, 1975), esp. p. 75, and *Jesus Christ in Matthew, Mark, and Luke* (Philadelphia:
Fortress Press, 1981), 64–78.

   2. "Behold the young woman will be pregnant and she will bear a son, and they will call him
Emmanuel, which having been translated means God with us."

   3. The use of *egō eimi* in 14:27 is still problematic.

   4. For details, see Kingsbury, *Matthew* and *Jesus Christ in Matthew, Mark, and Luke.*

in Matthew. But before we do so three other preliminary notes are necessary. First, we take Matthew to have been a Jew who had accepted the Christian belief that Jesus was the Messiah. Everything points to his having been a sophisticated sage, possibly a trained Pharisee, rooted in Judaism, although familiar with the Hellenistic mentality and language. Hellenism and Judaism had deeply intermingled in Matthew's day, but it is to the Jewish sources that we most naturally turn for the signs of his thoughts. "Messianic" ideas in the form of an expectation of a future deliverer were not peculiar to Judaism, but they were certainly prominent in the first-century Jewish world, and Hellenistic and other parallels, though interesting, are peripheral to our purpose: They cannot be allowed to govern our exegesis.

A second preliminary is that the title of this chapter speaks of origins in the plural. We are not seeking a single origin. If we were, our task would be concentrated in the historical Jesus of Nazareth. The ultimate origin of Matthew's messianism is the historical Jesus and the impact he had on those who first believed. He is the *fons et origo* of Matthew's messianism. In this sense, there is one origin to it, whether Jesus himself claimed to be Messiah or not. The elusiveness of that one origin, however, we need not emphasize.

Third, we can here only deal with broad central aspects of our theme. We cannot follow every twist and turn in the origins of Matthew's messianism. Because of this we shall concentrate on the beginnings of Matthew's Gospel, the prologue — that is, chapters 1 and 2. Fortunately much that is most pertinent in the rest of the Gospel is there foreshadowed. To examine the prologue will provide a guide to most — though, as we shall see, not all — of Matthew's emphases and because the prologue is replete with quotations and allusions to their origins also.

What, then, are the broad outlines of Matthew's messianism and what are the origins?

The New Creation

We begin where Matthew began. His messianism is from the beginning cosmic in scope: The coming of Jesus is comparable to the creation of the universe. The evidence is clear in the first verse. Scholars have treated Matt. 1:1, βίβλος γενέσεως Ἰησοῦ Χριστοῦ υἱοῦ Δαυὶδ υἱοῦ Ἀβραάμ ["a record of the generations of Jesus Christ, son of David, son of Abraham..."], as introducing either the genealogy in 1:2–17 or the genealogy and the virgin birth in 1:2–25; or 1:2–2:23 down to the coming of Jesus in Nazareth; or, again, the whole section from 1:1 down to 4:16, which ends with the settling of Jesus in Capernaum before he began his ministry. But as early as Jerome, the first verse was also referred to the entire Gospel: It is a title for the whole of the Gospel of Matthew. The word γένεσις was understood to mean either "genesis" or "history." This seems to us to be the intent of Matthew in this first verse; it is twofold, at least. In the first place he quite deliberately begins his Gospel with the words βίβλος γενέσεως to suggest a parallel with the first creation described in Genesis 1 and 2, and a parallel with the creation of the universe and Adam and Eve, on the one hand, and the new creation brought by Jesus, the Messiah, on the other. In using the term βίβλος, which is anarthrous, he is doubtless following prophetic, didactic, and apocalyptic conventions. The evidence is abundant.[5] But there is more to it than this. Matthew intends his βίβλος γενέσεως to recall the first book of the Tanak. The title "Genesis" had already been given to the first book of the Tanak in the earlier manuscripts of the LXX and other sources. But when I wrote *The Setting of the Sermon on the Mount* I had not proved that it was used when Matthew wrote. However, Dale C. Allison has referred to passages where Philo uses "Genesis" for the first book of the Tanak. The word "genesis" in Matthew 1:1 would, we conclude, naturally evoke that book. Jesus is the initiator of a new creation parallel to the first: the genitive in 1:1 is subjective.[6] We might speculate further. Like the Hebrew text at Genesis 1:1, so Matthew 1:1 begins with the letter *beth* or *beta*. Later sages made much of the initial *beth* in בראשית in Genesis 1:1. Some interpreted it as indicating "blessing" (ברכה), some (because *beth* is the numerical "2") as connoting two worlds of space and time. One interpretation claimed that the first letter was *beth* because *beth* is not circular and, therefore, closed, but open-ended. The creation is open-ended and looks to the future (see *Gen. Rab.* 1:10 on Gen. 1:1). Did such speculation, which is not dateable, but is apparently early,[7] influence Matthew to begin his Gospel with *beta*? Such speculation, fantastic to us, would have been congenial to Matthew.

But even if this significance assigned to the initial *beta* is too speculative, there is much in Matthew besides the initial words to suggest a new creation. It has been claimed with some degree of probability that the role of the Holy Spirit in the virgin birth in 1:18 recalls the activity of the Spirit at the creation in Genesis 1. Matthew takes up from Q the reference to the Spirit of God descending as a dove on Jesus at his baptism in Jordan in 3:16. There have been differing interpretations of the dove, but the most probable is that which points to the new creation motif. The calming of the raging sea in 8:23–27 recalls passages in the Old Testament (Job 38:8–11; Ps. 89:9), indicating God's cosmic control. The discussion of divorce in 19:3–9 directs

---

5. See the examples in W. D. Davies and Dale C. Allison, Jr., *The Gospel according to St. Matthew: A Critical and Exegetical Commentary, I–VII*, ICC (Edinburgh: T. & T. Clark, 1988), 149–53.

6. See W. D. Davies, *The Setting of the Sermon on the Mount* (Cambridge: Cambridge University Press, 1964), 67–72.

7. In the passage referred to, the speculators, introduced by R. Jonah in R. Levi's name, were probably widespread.

Matthew's hearers to Genesis 1 and 2. As the synoptic parallels to some of
the passages referred to indicate, Matthew was not alone in the New Testament in thinking in this way. There were Jewish Christians before him who
had thought so. The relationship between Matthew and the Pauline epistles
is unresolved, but certainly Paul had understood the Christian dispensation
in terms of new creation and Jesus in terms of the Last Adam. It was he who
may have been the first to develop the interpretation of Jesus as the Last
Adam. One of the direct sources of Matthew — Mark — implies the new
creation probably in its use of ἀρχη τοῦ εὐαγγελιοῦ ["the beginning of the
gospel"] in its very first verse and in the evocation of Adam in its account
of the temptation. The prologue of the Fourth Gospel is no stranger to the
notion of a new creation. Jewish and other Christians before and after Matthew were familiar with it (see *Barnabas* 6). Its ultimate source is clear: it is
Judaism.

Gunkel long ago established the parallelism between the cosmic beginnings in Genesis and the anticipated messianic beginnings: as he put it, *Urzeit*
parallels *Endzeit*. This is given prominence in Matthew from the very first
words of his Gospel. The interpretation of Jesus as the Messiah who inau-
gurates a new creation is fundamental for him. He embraced the conviction
explicitly expressed in 4 Ezra 7:30, but with a long history before his day, that
with the coming of the Messiah the world would once again be "as it was in
the beginning." As did the sages, he connected the beginning, the *rēshīth* of
Genesis 1:1, with the Messiah, and accepted the principle τὰ ἔσχατα ὡς τὰ
πρῶτα ["the last things (are) as the first"], that messianism has a cosmic dimension. Jesus sets in motion a γένεσις, a new creation. I emphasized that
the title of this lecture refers to origins, but there is a caveat to be uttered:
There is one origin — in the inaugurator of the new creation, Jesus.

A scientific analogy may help here. Modern physicists and astronomers
have sought to find a common center from which the totality not only of this
universe but of all universes is to be derived. Through intricate mathematical
calculations they have been able to locate this center in space and time. They
concluded that there was a kind of ball of fire that originally exploded. There
was a "Big Bang," an explosion, at or of this central core, from which all else
has evolved. For Matthew, we may argue, Jesus as Messiah was comparable
with this "Big Bang" in that he explosively inaugurated a new creation.

The Son of David

But the matter is not so simple. According to most scientists perhaps, we
cannot go behind the "Big Bang" to any space or any time. Unimaginable
as this is to common sense, before the "Big Bang" there was no space and
there was no time; these are concepts relative only to the "Big Bang." Space

and time came into being only in relation to each other with or as a result of the "Big Bang," which has no origin or origins. To speak of any purpose or will of God behind the "Big Bang" is inadmissible. Oddly enough some of the rabbinic sages *mutatis mutandis* said the same of the beginning of Genesis 1:1. "Just as the *beth* is closed at the sides but open in front, so you are not permitted to investigate what is above and what is below, what is before and what is behind." This is explained in *b. Hag.* 11a as referring either to space or time or both" (*Gen. Rab.* on 1:1 p. 9).[8]

But for Matthew's understanding of Jesus, as the inaugurator of the new creation, things are different. Certainly he is the Big Bang so to put it. But he emerged at a particular time and space and he has an origin and origins. Much as Matthew by implication emphasized the newness of the Messiah, Jesus is no novelty for him, and the centrality of his initiatory power connects him with a past in time and space. We can and must go behind him to the history of his people in time and to the land of Israel in space. The very term "Messiah" is incomprehensible without that people and their understanding of their own existence and of the world's.

Again we turn to the title of the Gospel. The term βίβλος γενέσεως does not refer only to the creation in Genesis 1:1. As elsewhere in Matthew, one word or group of words can have more than one connotation and function. So here, βίβλος γενέσεως refers not only to Genesis 1:1 but also forward to the genealogy of Jesus. The term γένεσις in 1:18 refers to the birth of Jesus, and it can also refer to the history or life of Jesus. βίβλος γενέσεως recalls the first creation and past history and simultaneously points forward to the emerging new creation and new history, and Matthew finds in the first creation and in the past history of God's people, Israel, the type or pattern of events in the life of Jesus and his people, the church.

Let us first look at the genealogy particularly, but also at the whole of

---

8. I am aware of the dangers of using analogies from scientific theories in the discussion of literary and theological themes. The scientific theories deal with "tangible," physical actualities. Their use as metaphors in such studies as the present one can obliterate the difference between their subject matter and the metaphorical. I had thought of the analogy between the new creation and the prologue of Matthew and the Big Bang theory before reading a brilliant essay by George Steiner on "Some Black Holes," *The Bulletin of the American Academy of Arts and Sciences* 41, no. 2 (1987): 12–28. In words he ascribes, in imagination, to Sir Karl Popper, had Popper been present at the lecture, Steiner writes, "Don't mix up the momentary sound use of metaphor by exact sciences with what it is they are really doing or looking for" (26). However, Steiner's other words deserve quotation even more, that "there are certain moments in history and culture when convincing metaphors and compelling images in the arts, in philosophy, and in the exact and applied sciences seem strangely congruent, when the force of these metaphors is such that they bend gravitationally the light of sensibility... on its passage out of highly specialized areas into the more diffuse but vital centers of feeling and thought" (26). The same awareness emerges in a remarkable passage in Walter Benjamin ("Some Reflections on Kafka," in *Illuminations*, ed. Hannah Arendt [New York: Harcourt, 1968], 142). Possibly for us to *feel* as Matthew felt about the advent of Jesus into the world, nothing would be more helpful than an initiation, however superficially and amateurishly, into modern scientific discussion of cosmology.

chapters 1 and 2. Matthew inherited the belief endemic to Judaism that the creation embodied a divine intention and that God is the Lord of history. God is divinely sovereign over all things. History is in the hands of God, the sphere of his purposeful activity. Looking for redemption, to use Luke's prologue (2:38), rose out of this belief: Messianism for Matthew is simply the corollary of the Jewish certainty about God — that God was responsible for creation and committed to history and, if so, committed not only in the past but in the future — hence the messianic hope. In fact, for Matthew history had a messianic pattern. Each stage of Jewish history suggested the Messiah to him. The pattern leading to Jesus, the Messiah, is threefold. Each of the three stages is constituted of fourteen generations. From Abraham to David, the king in 1:2–6; from David to the deportation to Babylon and the exile (vv. 7–11); from the exile to Jesus — in each of these divisions were fourteen generations. This is expressly stated in Matthew 1:17. According to the tradition of *gematria*, well established in first-century Judaism, fourteen, as a number, spells the name of David. By explicitly pointing to "fourteen" in 1:17, Matthew indicates that history is messianic in form and leads to Jesus as the Messiah. Objections raised to the use of *gematria* in the genealogy are not cogent, as I have argued elsewhere. There is precedence for the use of it in 1:1–7 in Genesis 46:8–27, where it occurs in a genealogy. Knowing that the Old Testament listed fourteen names from Abraham to David, Matthew probably set himself to look for fourteens and constructed his own Davidic messianic genealogy on this pattern. In his text the name David stands immediately before the genealogy, is placed in the fourteenth spot in the genealogy itself, and twice at its conclusion. At the fourteenth spot David is uniquely honored with the title "King": τόν βασιλέα. The very first name after Ἰησου Χριστοῦ in 1:1 is David.

Historically the term "Son of David" as a standard messianic title is attested in the rabbis in *b. Sanh.* 97a–98a and may already be present in the *Pss. of Sol.* 17:21–35 in the first century B.C.E. It developed out of Old Testament passages such as Isaiah 11:10 (the root of Jesse) and Jeremiah 23:5; 33:15. By the first century it had become the dominant Jewish expectation. Possibly the shortcomings of the non-Davidic Hasmonaeans furthered the process that led to this. The messianic king "who was to come" was perceived as a Son of David who would fulfill the promises of 2 Samuel 7:16, where the prophet Nathan is commanded by God to tell David: "Your family shall be established and your kingdom shall stand for all time in my sight, and your throne shall be established forever" (2 Sam. 7:16, author's translation). Already before Matthew wrote, Christian circles recognized the Davidic connections of Jesus (Rom. 1:3–4; see also Acts 2:29–36; 13:22–23; 2 Tim. 2:8; Rev. 5:5; 22:16). But of all New Testament writers it is Matthew who most emphasizes that Jesus is of Davidic ancestry. "Son of David" occurs nine times in

Matthew, over against three times in Mark; it never occurs in Luke. It was apparently Matthew's most characteristic designation for the earthly Jesus, the Messiah. In the prologue — which refers to Bethlehem, the city of David (2:8, 16) — there is a clear intent to set forth Jesus as qualifying, through his father Joseph (1:16), as the royal Messiah of the Davidic line. It agrees with this that in the genealogy in 1:2–17, unlike Luke in 3:31, Matthew traces the descent of Jesus through Solomon, a son of David, who later became famous as a mighty healer, exorcist, and magician (Josephus, *Ant.* 8:45–49). It is significant that Matthew precisely connects Jesus as Son of David with healings and exorcisms (9:27; 12:23; 15:22; 20:30–31).

So far we have noted two aspects of Matthew's messianism: it affirms a new creation, and it traces a pattern in history that leads to the emergence of a Son of David as Messiah. In all this he draws upon the Tanak and traditions within Judaism. But one thing already makes it clear that he draws upon both selectively. In view of the reference to Genesis one would expect a parallel to be indicated between Jesus and Adam in the genealogy, as was the case with Luke. One scholar has found Adam to be the key to the chiasmus he finds in 1:1–16.[9] But, although Adam probably is in Matthew's mind, as in Mark's in the temptation narrative, the name is not found in the genealogy and does not appear even once in Matthew's Gospel. Paul was probably an innovator here, but Matthew, even if he knew of Paul's thought, ignores it. His concentration is on the divine activity in so guiding history as to lead to Jesus as Son of David. Matthew's thought smacks of "determinism." History seems inevitably to have led to Jesus as Messiah. But it is a "determinism" that allows for human error and perversity. Persons are always free to dispute and thwart the divine purpose at least temporarily. As in the Joseph saga, humans may mean evil and do it, and God may mean it for good (Gen. 5:20), so in Matthew's genealogy there are sinners, but they subserve the divine purpose. Matthew is Pharisaic in his understanding of the paradox that everything is determined and free will given (*Aboth*), and for him the determination of history is messianically aimed. The emergence of Jesus, the Son of David, is its climax.

The Son of Abraham

In all that we have said about the Son of David, it is clear that Matthew has drawn upon the kingship ideology of ancient Israel. This was grounded on that of the ancient Near East, and Mowinckel urged that this was the source of the messianic idea as it emerged in Jewish sources, the Tanak and

---

9. See Peter F. Ellis, *Matthew: His Mind and His Message* (Collegeville, Minn.: Liturgical Press, 1974).

the extracanonical literature. Notice that the Davidic messianic hope was essentially a hope of and for Israel: it was inextricably ethnic. As 2 Samuel 7 makes clear, the choice of David as king had been inextricably bound in the tradition to the choice of Israel as God's people. In 2 Samuel 7:23 David asks:

> And thy people Israel to whom can they be compared? Is there any other nation on earth whom thou, O God, hast set out to redeem from slavery to be thy people? Any other for whom thou hast done great and terrible things to win fame for thyself? (Author's translation)

In the Hebrew tradition on which Matthew drew, messiahship had grown out of a particular people's history. It could be read exclusively in terms of that people's history — it involved Israel's peoplehood and territory and history. The source and condition of the messianic yearning that Matthew had indicated were the words, "I will be their God and they will be my people." There was and is in the Jewish messianic hope what Kenneth Cragg has called the perspective of an "inherent privacy." It was the hope of God's own chosen.[10] With this "privacy" — or, to use the more usual term, "exclusiveness" — Matthew had to come to terms. He does so in the very first verse by asserting that Jesus is not only the Son of David, but also the son of Abraham. Here the meaning of "Son of Abraham" is probably dual. First, Jesus is Son of David and, through him, he is personally and biologically the Son of Abraham; he is Son of Abraham as are all Jews whose father is Abraham. The term "Son of Abraham" is not to be taken automatically as "messianic." In Matthew 1:1 it certainly means that Jesus is one of Jewish blood or one worthy of the father Abraham. But, second, it may also be that "Son of Abraham" is here a messianic title or, at least, is messianic in intent. Outside Matthew, in Luke (1:30–33, 55, 69–73; Acts 3:25; 13:23) the promises concerning the seed of David and the seed of Abraham are brought together. Paul takes Jesus to be of the seed of Abraham (Gal. 3:16). And in the Tanak, Jeremiah 33:21–22, and later in the Targum on Psalm 89:4, Genesis 17:7, the promise to Abraham and his seed is associated with 2 Samuel 7:12 (the promise to David and his seed). The first verse of Matthew, then, means not only that Jesus is Messiah as Son of David — indicating the fulfillment of the strictly private Jewish hope — but also as the Son of Abraham. What does this signify?

The figure of Abraham in Jewish tradition needs scrutiny. He is certainly, like David, of the highest significance for the Jewish people as such. It was with him that God had made a covenant with Israel (Genesis 12, 15). In the *Testament of Jacob* 7:22 he is the "father of fathers." Descent from him constituted the ground for membership in the Jewish people (4 Ezra 3:13–15). Thus as a Son of Abraham Jesus is in Matthew 1:1 an Israelite indeed, a true

---

10. See K. Cragg, *The Christ and the Faiths* (Philadelphia: Westminster Press, 1986), 99.

member of the people of Israel. Matthew makes him bring to its culmination the history that began with Abraham; the genealogy underlines his Jewishness. But there is another side to Abraham and his significance. He had a particular relevance to those who were not Jews by birth — that is, to those not within the covenant made between God and Israel through him. God had called Abraham before God had established the covenant, before there were Jews. Another way of stating this is to claim that by birth Abraham was a Gentile, and the covenant that God had initiated through him was to be a blessing not only to Jews but to all nations (Gen. 12:3; 18:18). Abraham came to be portrayed as the father of all nations as well (Gen. 17:5; 1 Macc. 12:19–21). The promise to Abraham could, therefore, be exploited to further the Jewish mission. One Tannaitic sage saw in him the first proselyte (*b. Hag. 3a*). Paul, therefore, could naturally use the figure of Abraham as the true father of all who have faith, both Jews and Gentiles (Rom. 4:1–25; Gal. 3:6–29).

Likewise Matthew, in 8:11–12 and in 3:9 possibly and in 1:1, appeals to an Abrahamic strain in Judaism itself to serve his Gentile interests. Franz Rosenzweig defined Judaism as a life one possesses by birth in "the eternal self-preservation of procreative blood . . . through shutting the pure spring of blood off from foreign admixture. . . . Descendant and ancestor are the live incarnation of the eternal people, both of them for each other. . . . We experience our Judaism with immediacy in elders and children."[11] We suggest that, while Matt. 1:1 includes Jesus, as Messiah, in the people of Israel by calling him the Son of David and a Son of Abraham, at the same time by calling Jesus the son of Abraham, Matthew intends to redefine that people to include Gentiles. And just as the motif of the new creation reemerged in the prologue in the story of the virgin birth (1:18–25), and the significance of the Son of David is pointed to 1:2–17, so too the evocation of the Gentiles in the term "Son of Abraham" in 1:1 finds confirmation in the introduction into the genealogy itself of women of foreign origin — Tamar, a Canaanite, or an Aramaean; Rahab, a Canaanite; Ruth, a Moabitess; and Bathsheba, a Hittite; and in the story of the Magi. In thus connecting Jesus, Son of David, the king of the Jews, with the Gentile Abraham, Matthew was not innovating. In some sources Abraham was regarded as a king, and the advent of the Messiah was to witness the incoming of the Gentiles.[12] There were elements in Jewish apocalyptic as well as in the Old Testament that provided a hope for the final redemption of Gentiles. Doubtless Matthew was aware of these, and doubtless they were being neglected in the renewed apocalypticism after

---

11. Franz Rosenzweig, *The Star of Redemption,* 2d ed. (Boston: Beacon Press, 1970), 341, 346.

12. For the evidence, see W. D. Davies, *Jewish and Pauline Studies* (Philadelphia: Fortress Press, 1984), 381.

70 C.E. And so he called Jesus, the Son of Abraham, one who was relevant to the crisis in Jewish-Gentile relations, which three centuries of the exposure of Jews to Hellenism had produced, the Savior of the world "not only of Israel." Was he not opposing the narrow exclusiveness of the nationalism of his day, even after the collapse of Jerusalem, in calling Jesus the Son of Abraham?

The Greater Moses

We now go beyond the title and the genealogy in the prologue to another figure or presence that the birth narratives in chapters 1 and 2 evoke quite unmistakably, though not explicitly, for the interpretation of Jesus, that of Moses. In his genealogy Matthew does not mention Moses at all as being among the ancestors of Jesus. The reason is simple. In the part of the genealogy that covers the period up to the exile, Matthew largely follows the genealogy provided for him in 1 Chronicles. Up to 1:13 he copies an Old Testament genealogy. All the names in 1:13–15 occur in the LXX. But after this, for the five hundred years between Zerubbabel and Joseph, the father of Jesus, Matthew has only nine names. The names in 1:2–6 occur in 1 Chronicles 1:28, 34; 2:1–15 (see also Ruth 4:18–22). The name of Moses is not in these passages, and Matthew — while innovative in the formulation or pattern of his genealogy — does not choose to depart from the substance of the scriptures where he is drawing upon them, and so he also omits Moses, or rather does not insert his name. However, the influence of the figure of Moses in Matthew's interpretation of Jesus as Messiah has long been recognized, although in different degrees. The evidence is clear. Here I note only the bare bones.

1. The infancy narratives recall the circumstances at the birth of Moses, especially as recorded in Josephus, and the *Liber Biblicarum Antiquitatum*. I note only the peril at the births of Jesus and Moses, from Herod and the Pharaoh respectively, the exile of both into Egypt, and the flight at night.[13]

2. The events in chapters 3 and 4, immediately following the birth narratives, recall the story of the exodus from Egypt. The baptism of Jesus at the Jordan is parallel to the passing of Israel through the Red Sea. The sojourn for forty days in the desert to fast and to be tested is comparable with the forty years of Israel's wandering in the wilderness, where Israel was tempted. As Israel was tempted by the worship of the golden calf, so Jesus was tempted to idolatry. The temptations of Jesus are a reliving of the temptations of Israel and are understood by Matthew in the light of Deuteronomy 8:2–3.

---

13. For the evidence, see R. E. Brown, *The Birth of the Messiah* (Garden City, N.Y.: Doubleday, 1977), 111–16.

3. Following on chapters 3 and 4 comes the Sermon on the Mount. Probably most scholars have seen here a delineation of Jesus as a New Moses, giving his new Torah from a new Sinai. For many reasons, not the least of which was the desire not to read into Matthew what was congenial, I long resisted this direct parallel with Mount Sinai in favor of a parallel with Mount Zion, which von Rad taught us to consider as the mount of the assembly of the nations and of which Jeremias wrote so approvingly. After examining every mountain scene in Matthew, Donaldson comes to the conclusion that in Matthew "the mountain motif is a device used by the evangelist to make the christological statement that Christ has replaced Zion as the center of God's dealings with his people: in him all the hopes associated with Zion have come to fruition and fulfillment."[14] This fits into the deterritorializing of Judaism in much early Christianity, but it overlooks two things: the data to which I have elsewhere referred, pointing to a well-marked Mosaic motif in Matthew, and the very convincing data pointed out by D. C. Allison, regarding the nature of the introduction to the Sermon on the Mount and its conclusion.[15] First, after Jesus has gone up to the mountain, from which he gives his "sermon," he sits down on it. His "sitting" has suggested to commentators that Jesus here simply assumes the role of a teacher. Teachers and sages and rabbis and others sat when they taught. In 5:1–2 Jesus has his *yeshiba* (*yeshiba* means "sitting") (see Sir. 51:23). But this does not go far enough. Matthew 5:1–2 recalls Deuteronomy 9:9 (which may well have been alluded to in 4:2). Deuteronomy 9:9 reads: "When I went up to the mountain to receive the tables of stone, the tables of the covenant which the Lord made with you, I remained on the mountain forty days and forty nights; I neither ate bread nor drank water." The Hebrew word translated "remained" in the RSV is *wā'ēšeb* from *yāšb*. To this verb the BDB gives three meanings. The second and third are "remain" and "dwell," but the first is "sit." The Jewish sages made much of this. In *b. Meg.* 21a we read:

> One verse says, "And I sat in the mountain" [Deut. 9:9], and another says, "And I stood in the mountain" [Deut. 10:10]. Rab says: He [Moses] stood when he learnt and sat while he went over [what he had learnt]. R. Ḥanina said: He was neither sitting nor standing but stooping. R. Joḥanan said: "Sitting" here means only staying, as it says, "And ye stayed in Kadesh many days" [Deut. 1:46]. Raba said: The easy things [he learnt] standing and the hard ones sitting?

The same text appears in *t. Sotah* 49a. The verb *wā'ēšeb* was, then, ambiguous. The dating of the rabbinic texts is uncertain, but some sages took

---

14. T. L. Donaldson, *Jesus on the Mountain*, JSNTSup 8 (Sheffield: JSOT Press, 1985), 200.

15. See D. C. Allison, *The New Moses: A Matthean Typology* (Minneapolis: Fortress Press, 1993), 172–80.

Deuteronomy 9:7 to refer to Moses *sitting* on Mount Sinai, as Jesus according to Matthew did on the mount of the sermon. Matthew not only knew
the Hebrew text of the Tanak involved, but he was probably also acquainted
with the Jewish exegetical traditions about it. This is further indicated by another simple datum. Jesus in 5:1–2 "goes up to the mountain." The Greek is
simple: ἀνέβη εἰς τὸ ὄρος. This phrase occurs in the LXX twenty-four times:
eighteen of these are in the Pentateuch, and most refer to Moses. The phrase
ἀναβαίνω εἰς τὸ ὄρος occurs in Deuteronomy 9:9.

But further, the close of the sermon also recalls Moses on Sinai. In 8:1
we read: "When he had gone down from the mountain..." This is a redac-
tional verse. The Greek is καταβάυτος δὲ αὐτοῦ ὑπὸ τοῦ ὄρους. This is
identical to the LXX(A) at Exodus 34:29 of Moses' descent from Sinai (see
Exod. 19:14; 32:1, 15). The construction cited occurs only once in the LXX
(LXX[B] has 'εκ for ἀπο). The beginning and closing of the sermon linguistically recall Moses on Sinai. I have elsewhere indicated that the figure of
Moses lurks behind the Matthean Jesus in other passages outside the sermon
and the prologue; they cannot be discussed here. We can safely assert that
the figure of Moses had drawn into itself messianic significance for Matthew
and that his Jesus and his messianism have inescapable Mosaic traits. Even
11:27–30, usually interpreted in terms of Ecclesiasticus 51, almost certainly
should be understood in terms of Moses.[16] He refers to Exodus 33:12–13,
where there is reciprocal knowledge between God and Moses, which Jews
took to be exclusive. This is implicit in the context in Exodus (see 33:7–11,
17–23); Deuteronomy 34:10 makes it explicit. Paul reveals echoes of Exodus
33:12–13 in 1 Corinthians 13:12–13, and Allison finds the Exodus passage to
be the background of 11:27. In addition, the reference to "rest" in 11:28 has
its parallel in Exodus 33:14, and Exodus 33:12–13 sheds light on the order
of the mutual knowledge presented: The order of "the Father knows the Son
and the Son knows the Father" in 11:27 may have been influenced by the
fact that God's knowledge of Moses comes first in the Exodus passage. Finally, the attribution of meekness to Jesus (11:29) has its parallel in Moses'
characterization in Judaism. Numbers 12:3 reads: "Now the man Moses was
very meek" (πραυς σφόδρα in the LXX). If Allison be followed — and his
case is strong — there is no need to go outside the exodus tradition to any
Hellenistic Jewish syncretism, to the Dead Sea Scrolls, to the mystical philosophical literature of the East, or to the Wisdom tradition to account for
11:27–30, as Professor Suggs has so forcefully urged.

Up to this point we have noted four strands in the messianism of Matthew.
First, it is informed by the interpretation of Jesus in terms of a new creation.

---

16. D. C. Allison has made this convincingly clear in "Two Notes on a Key Text: Matt. 11:25–
30," *JTS* 39 (1988): 477–85.

Second, it is Davidic. Matthew drew upon the kingship ideology of the ancient Middle East, which Mowinckel long ago argued was the source of the messianic idea. Third, there is the Mosaic strand: Jesus is the greater Moses, who has wrought a new exodus, and brought a new Law — that is, Matthew's messianism drew upon the tradition of the exodus, which Joseph Klausner had emphasized as the determinative element in messianism, and had drawn to itself creation motifs. Then, fourth, there is the Abrahamic strand, which had struggled to break through the privacy of the Davidic and exodus traditions to reach out to the larger world. But here I must issue a warning. The differentiation of these four strands I have suggested in Matthew is almost certainly too clear. As in much modern science, our messianic models tend to a conceptual clarity that belies the "fuzziness" of all the data with which we have to deal. The strands I noted are in fact inseparable; they intermingle and are evoked not in isolation but all together sometimes in apparent confusion. They combine to produce a complexity of messianic presentation that belies the clarity and simplification of our neat divisions. Of one thing we can be certain: All the strands have their ground in the Tanak. I have noted elsewhere Matthew's familiarity with the Tanak. The formula quotations, which are from his hand and not drawn from a distinct preexistent source, alone establish that he knew the Hebrew Bible as well as the LXX. There is other massive evidence for this, but as has already appeared and will later appear, it was not the MT and the LXX in their isolation or textual nudity nor in their historical context that he knew. He knew them as they were understood and interpreted in the Judaism of his day. The Apocrypha and Pseudepigrapha and other Jewish sources here claim their inescapable due.

This leads to at least two other dimensions of Matthew's messianism that are most important. I can only touch upon them here. Matthew applies the title Messiah to Jesus of Nazareth, a person who had endured the most ignominious and painful death, crucifixion — a form of death the Jews especially regarded as being under the curse of God. Nor was the suffering of Jesus confined to the cross. It was foreshadowed with trials at his birth; the political opposition of King Herod; the calumny of his origin; the temptation narrative, which points to his encounter with unseen powers of evil and Satan; and the constant opposition from religious leaders. To use another scientific metaphor, Matthew has throughout fused the messianic with suffering. The crucified Messiah seems a contradiction in terms; it constitutes a fusion. Was it a revolution?

It has often been claimed that it was, that Judaism knew nothing of a suffering Messiah. I would like here to refer to my discussion in *Paul and Rabbinic Judaism* and to note in addition certain facts.[17] Apart from the pres-

---

17. W. D. Davies, *Paul and Rabbinic Judaism*, 4th ed. (Philadelphia: Fortress Press, 1980), 264.

ence of the great enigma of Isaiah 53 — so important for Matthew — in the Tanak, I suggest that the presentation of Jesus as the Greater Moses probably carries within itself the notion of suffering. Moses certainly knew suffering — in the flight from Egypt as a refugee and fugitive and in the suffering with and for his people in the wilderness, where he faced the difficulties of idolatry and rebellion. Moses was a man of sorrow and was acquainted with grief. Not surprisingly some scholars saw his lineaments in Isaiah 53. The first redeemer was a suffering redeemer. So, too, the prophets, especially Jeremiah, were suffering figures. Not surprising and not unrelated to all of this is the high evaluation of suffering in Judaism. The difficulties in connection with the place of Isaiah 53 in Matthew and in the rest of the New Testament, I can only refer to, but the fact that the Suffering Servant of Isaiah 53 informed Matthew's view of Jesus can hardly be denied.

And then there is the enigma of the meaning of the Son of Man and his relation to the Messiah. Some scholars have traced the figure to Ezekiel, others to Enoch, others to Daniel 7. The debate continues, even though some have refused to contemplate a definite figure, the Son of Man, but simply a personal reference in the term. We prefer to look at Daniel 7 as determinative for Matthew. In that passage also the Son of Man is a suffering figure. For our purposes what needs to be emphasized is that for the sources of Matthew's messianism we have to consider not only the Tanak, but also the Apocrypha, the Pseudepigrapha, and extracanonical sources.

With these bare statements we must leave the role of suffering and of the Son of Man in Matthew. Nor can I here deal with the alleged influence of the Wisdom tradition. Some concluding thoughts are in order. We have emphasized that the origins of Matthew's messianism essentially, informed as it was by the ministry of Jesus of Nazareth, are in the Old Testament as it was understood and interpreted in his day. The Old Testament was his chief quarry both in Hebrew and Greek. But now we have to recognize that his use of it, while governed by the interpretations of it current in his own day, was very selective. He took over much from the Jewish traditions; he cast off much. In two areas especially he may have abandoned or neglected what he found in Judaism. First, it is not clear that he retains the political territoriality of Jewish messianism. Second, he ignores the priestly elements in the messianic hope. That he did not embrace the territorialism of Judaism is consonant with his emphasis on Abraham and the Gentiles. Despite 19:27, he is not governed by Jewish privacy. Moreover, his distance from the discredited Zealots and the apocalyptic fervor that was probably reemerging in his day would reinforce his aloofness from territorialism. Similarly his indifference to priestly elements in messianism, which could be speculatively exploited by Christians and were (as, for example, in the Epistle to the Hebrews), is also understandable. His dialogue was with Pharisaism. The Temple was in ruins;

the priesthood had become unnecessary and survived only in the shadow of Pharisaism. In the dialogue with Judaism in its Pharisaic form, Matthew was immediately and chiefly concerned with the messianic Torah — a notion at least inchoate in first-century Judaism — and the greater Moses. There were elements, not obviously significant in the ministry of Jesus, that would have naturally fostered the notion of Jesus as priest in Matthew, but given the climate after Jamnia, which was not conducive to this, they were either over-looked or ignored. Nevertheless, despite its emphasis on the new creation, Matthew's messianism, because of its restraint, is not utopian, but restorative. This is largely because its sources are not simply the Jewish tradition in the Tanak, the Apocrypha, and the Pseudepigrapha, but the actualities, political and religious, of the situation he faced after the collapse of Jerusalem and the rise of Rabbinic Judaism. The necessity to formulate a parallel attraction to Pharisaism at Jamnia was among the factors that led to his presentation of a New Moses with a new messianic Torah. The necessity to break the chrysalis of an increasingly privatized Judaism brought forth the Abrahamic emphasis. The presentation of the Son of Man as judge and of the Suffering Messiah, whose words are in the Sermon on the Mount, was possibly not unrelated to a desperate recrudescent, triumphalist apocalyptic, which was finally to lead to Bar Kokba.

At the same time, Matthew's messianism was paradoxical. He was aware of the demands of Judaism and deliberately honored them through the empha-sis on Jesus as Son of David. Simultaneously, at a time when many Christians were doubtless tempted to revert to Judaism, he also preserved the radical newness of the gospel in terms of the new creation. In sum, any treatment of the origins of Matthew's messianism must recognize three dimensions at least: the actuality of the messianic ministry of Jesus; the illumination brought to the presentation of that messianic ministry from Jewish sources in the Tanak, the Apocrypha, and the Pseudepigrapha; and the political and religious conditions within which the messianism of Matthew came to be formulated. This last element, the context, does not *determine* the content of Matthew's messianism; Jesus and Judaism did that. But we suggest that it does help to *define* the forms in which he presents it. Perhaps this is the best point at which to refer to a most significant final aspect of Matthew's messianism.

Messianism, as Gershom Scholem reminded us, often born of disillusion and despair, has its dark side. It can lead to unrealistic, visionary enthusiasms that prove destructive. Doubtless much in early Christian messianism was of this nature. Paul had to combat it, and even more did Matthew have to shy away from it. In my work *The Setting of the Sermon on the Mount* I traced a *gemaric*, cautionary note in Matthew in which he tempered the radicalism of the early Christian movement and began to adapt its more perfectionist, ex-treme expressions to the actualities. There is evidence, pointed out especially by Kingsbury, that Matthew's church was probably more comfortably situated than those in which Mark and Paul found themselves and that Matthew was better prepared than Christian enthusiasts to come to terms with the well-to-do and to adapt the tradition. How far early Christian thinking was under the constraint of the disappointment caused by the postponement of the *parousia* is in dispute. Matthew at any rate seems to have come to terms with that postponement and seems to contemplate a future on earth for the church of an indefinite duration, although he retains the sense of urgency. In such a situation his messianism becomes tempered, not to say modified. His emphasis on the commandments of Jesus as the Greater Moses is not unrelated to this, as are those aspects of his Gospel that might be labeled as traces of early Catholicism. As compared with that of many early Christian enthusiasts, the messianism of Matthew is rabbinically sober: it is Mosaic. Matthew pricks the balloons of enthusiasts by fashioning a messianism in which the figure of Moses is as prominent as the figure of David, and the figure of the Son of Man is especially, perhaps, in judgment. His messianism, in short, is a corrective messianism, corrective of excesses and illusions within the Christian community, as it was corrective, in the light of Jesus, of the messianic hope in the Jewish tradition. More messianism, Matthew seems to be saying, is not enough, and in this does he not paradoxically stand near to the rabbis at Jamnia?[18]

---

18. On messianism in Matthew, see W. D. Davies and Dale C. Allison, Jr., *The Gospel according to St. Matthew*, ICC 3 (Edinburgh: T. & T. Clark, 1997), 718–21.

Chapter 10

Aspects of
the Jewish Background
of the Gospel of John

At the time when Rudolf Bultmann was finding connections between the Fourth Gospel and Gnosticism, C. H. Dodd also turned both to Hellenistic sources, especially the *Hermetica,* and to Jewish sources, publishing his great work *The Interpretation of the Fourth Gospel* in 1953. This volume can be regarded as the full flowering of the emphasis on Hellenism in New Testament study. In this sense it marks the end of an era. But *The Interpretation of the Fourth Gospel* also shows "the encroachment of the Semitic on New Testament scholarship — an encroachment that has grown ever stronger — so that it also reflects new beginnings. [C. H. Dodd's writings] are a mirror of the transition which has marked our time from a predominantly Hellenistic to a more Semitic approach to the New Testament. In him one world was already dying and another struggling to be born."[1] I now connect this transition with a young B.D. student who was among the members of my earliest classes at Duke University in the fifties and later became for many years my colleague there, Dr. D. Moody Smith.

The subject assigned to me is the Jewish background of the Fourth Gospel. To be dealt with at all adequately, this theme needs to be divided into three sections. There is, first, the world of Jewish belief and practice which formed part of the general background, that is, the cultural and religious hinterland of the author of the Fourth Gospel (henceforth called John): the inherited furniture of John's mind, the unexpressed religious and other assumptions which governed him consciously and unconsciously, the "Common Judaism" described by E. P. Sanders. Then, second, there is the immediate foreground of John's mind, the specific conditions and developments within Judaism at the time when he wrote, which we conveniently call the period of "Jamnian Judaism." This has proved to be particularly important for the

---

1. W. D. Davies, "In Memoriam: Charles Harold Dodd, 1884–1973," *NTS* 20 (1973–74): i–v.

understanding of the Fourth Gospel. We are justified in making this clear distinction between background and foreground because, with most scholars, we assume that John's Gospel was written around the end of the first century — the time of Jamnian Judaism — by a Jew, who had become a Christian.

There is also a third aspect to the theme: that is, what can be called John's immediate inner "domestic" foreground, that is, the conditions which he faced within his own community of Jewish (and possibly other) Christians. Some of these were fully committed to Jesus and his followers and prepared to establish an existence separate from the main body of Jews and Judaism; others were not prepared to take such a step. Only scholars immersed in Johannine studies can deal adequately with this aspect; we do not feel competent to do so. Our treatment, therefore, cannot but be more generalized than this third aspect demands,[2] and must be confined to the first two backgrounds noted above. We must crave the reader's indulgence. We recognize that there is necessarily much interpenetration among background and foreground and John's domestic world. The reader will also be aware that this very brief treatment is necessarily reductionist; for example, we do not touch upon possible Samaritan influences upon John.

The Jewish Background

When I first read John's Gospel, I discovered to my amazement that its Greek, which seemed at first encounter the easiest in the whole of the New Testament, was the most difficult to translate. The vocabulary of John is simple, but there is always a strange twist in the structure of his sentences, especially in his use of relative clauses, which makes translation difficult. I soon realized that this is so because the Greek of John was more influenced by Semitic (Aramaic) usage than that of any other New Testament documents. C. F. Burney,[3] like C. C. Torrey, went so far as to claim that the Gospel of John was first written in Aramaic and that, as we now have it, it is a translation. Few have been convinced of this, but it is evident that John thought as a Jew. The Greek he wrote was influenced by a Hebraic-Aramaic idiom and connotation.

---

2. Raymond E. Brown, *The Community of the Beloved Disciple* (New York: Paulist Press, 1979), and J. Louis Martyn, *History and Theology of the Fourth Gospel*, rev. ed. (Nashville: Abingdon Press, 1979), are particularly important here. For a summary statement, see R. A. Culpepper's excellent study, "The Gospel of John and the Jews," *The Review and Expositor* 84 (1987): 273–88, esp. 281–82.

3. *The Aramaic Origin of the Fourth Gospel* (Oxford: Clarendon Press, 1926); so also C. C. Torrey, *The Four Gospels: A New Translation* (New York and London: Harper, 1933), and idem, *Our Translated Gospels: Some of the Evidence* (New York and London: Harper & Brothers, 1936).

In the recent reaction against the overemphasis on the Hellenistic in favor of the Semitic in New Testament studies, it is easy to underestimate and, indeed, overlook the deep interpenetration of the Hellenistic and Semitic worlds to which we referred above. Jean Daniélou[4] used the term "Jewish-Christian" of those Christians who expressed their thought in terms borrowed from Judaism. In this sense, as in others recognized by Daniélou, John was a Jewish Christian. This is why the studies of Adolf Schlatter, C. H. Dodd, David Hill, George Caird, and of the contributors to Kittel's famous *Wörterbuch* — to name only a few — still illumine the vocabulary of John; they were all very sensitive to this phenomenon. To understand John it is necessary to listen to him with two pairs of ears as it were. As every bilingual person knows, bilingualism easily deceives. And John's bilingualism does so in favor of finding either a Hellenistic or a Hebraic-Aramaic connotation (or perhaps both) in his very same words. This was what led C. H. Dodd to find the *Hermetica* so ubiquitously present in John, while M. Philonenko saw Essenism in so many documents. But there can be no doubt in the light of studies since Dodd that by far the dominant element in the tradition John inherited was the Judaism of his people: this formed the ultimate background on which he drew.[5]

To describe this background in detail is impossible here. The first century in the history of Judaism was one of transition. By that time, Persian, Greek, and Roman influences had left their mark on Judaism to make it varied, complex, and fluid. The recognition of this has been reinforced by two developments in the scholarship of this century. First, in the past, a rigid distinction was drawn between Judaism in Palestine, uncontaminated to any considerable degree by Gentile influences, and the Judaism which developed outside Palestine, which had assimilated much from the Greco-Roman culture within which it grew. There has now developed a greater appreciation of the extent to which Judaism had been for a long period, certainly since the time of Alexander the Great, subject to Hellenistic influences. Archaeologists have revealed in the synagogues of Palestine a considerable Greek influence; rabbis have been discovered to have tasted Greek culture, and it has been claimed that even their exegetical methods are adaptations of Greek tradi-

---

4. *The Theology of Jewish Christianity*, ed. J. A. Baker, History of Early Christian Doctrine before the Council of Nicea 1 (London: Darton, Longman & Todd, 1964), 9.

5. Dodd's treatment of the words of the Gospel of John is, for the reasons indicated, still extremely important. An example of the interpenetration to which we refer was offered by Martin Buber in a memorable seminar at Princeton University. He took the Greek words in John 3:8, πνεῦμα πνεῖ ("wind [or 'spirit'] blows"), to be a direct reference to the Spirit of God being "on the face (פני) of the waters" in Genesis 1:3: the πνεῖ of John, as Buber argued, being a transliteration into Greek of the Hebrew פני. Readers may find this improbable, but only a Hebrew scholar such as Buber could "hear" the text in this dual way. We all can now so hear it, but only after he had pointed this out.

tions. In the realm of ideas, on immortality, anthropology, and, possibly, time, and in the sphere of institutional life of the synagogue, Greek influences and terminology are traceable. Nor must the regular intercourse between the diaspora Jews and Palestine, and especially Jerusalem, be forgotten. This meant that Palestinian Judaism was not closed to diaspora ideas and habits. On the other hand, despite the greater ease with which Greco-Roman forces could impinge upon the Judaism of the Diaspora, the real contacts which the latter maintained with Judaism at its cultural and religious center in Palestine, the maintenance of the annual half-shekel tax for the support of the Jews, and the visits from the emissaries sent from Jerusalem to the Diaspora — all these meant that Judaism everywhere preserved an unmistakable unity which found expression in the ubiquitous synagogue, which was both a sign and cause of this unity. Thus, Philo of Alexandria agreed in crucial matters with the rabbis of Palestine, and it is strikingly significant that the Jews of the Diaspora were prepared to substitute Aquila's rough Greek translation of the Old Testament for the LXX partly in order to retain a text more in accord with rabbinic exegesis. Thus the division of first-century Judaism into distinct Palestinian and Hellenistic compartments has broken down.[6]

But there is, second, another development not unconnected with this. Since 1947 we have been in possession of the manuscripts called the Dead Sea Scrolls. While there is still no unanimity about their place and date of origin, so that we must use them very cautiously, most scholars have regarded them as pre-Christian and emanating from a sect possibly akin to that of the Essenes, whose faith was an extreme form of Pharisaism. While the Dead Sea Scrolls are not as revolutionary as was at first claimed, they have reinforced what we have just written: there were Greek books discovered in the "library" of the legalistic community that was centered at Qumran (though the presence of Greek books does not necessarily mean their acceptance). The Dead Sea Scrolls also support the recent tendency to emphasize that the Judaism of the first century was far less monolithic and more complex and changing than previous scholars had supposed. Like the language of the time, which the Scrolls have revealed to be in process of development, so too the religion.

Can we find a common element or conjoined common elements shared by all forms of Judaism of the period? With caution we can disentangle these elements but with the caveat that, taken in isolation, they are at best abstractions. In other words, any common element that might be identified was variously clothed by the several groups which constituted first-century Judaism. But there were certain basic assumptions which we can discern: belief in the one

---

6. For bibliographical details, see the introduction in Davies, *Paul and Rabbinic Judaism*, 4th ed. (Philadelphia: Fortress Press, 1980), v–xii. Martin Hengel's great work has abundantly confirmed and established the point of this paragraph.

God, the one People of His choice, the one Land; the one Law which connected the people, The Land and God, and obedience to whose Law governed
the future; and a hope for the future in that Land, an eschatological hope.
These assumptions constituted much of the substance of the Jewish tradition
that John inherited, but they were not distinct or consciously separated. They
were rather a cluster of assumptions, mutually interacting. Each in its turn,
at different periods, could become prominent or suffer eclipse as compared
with the others. Conjoined, they were the furniture of John's mind. They are
here separately listed only for academic convenience: none of them was an
"island." The relative importance of each of these elements has been much
discussed: was there a hierarchy of "values" in Judaism? For our immediate
purpose, we emphasize again that the elements we noted separately are all
integrally interrelated.[7] E. P. Sanders's definition of this Judaism as "covenantal nomism" has been widely accepted.[8] Apart from other important studies,[9]

---

7. On all this, see W. D. Davies, "Reflections on the Nature of Judaism," *Revue d'Histoire et
de Philosophie Religieuses* 75 (1995): 85–111.

8. See his *Paul and Palestinian Judaism: A Comparison of Patterns of Religions* (Philadelphia:
Fortress Press, 1977). We hesitate quite fully to endorse "covenantal nomism" because it perhaps
needs to recognize, more clearly and sufficiently, the "territorial dimension" — the place of The
Land. Sanders's definition runs as follows: "The 'pattern' or 'structure' of covenantal nomism is
this: (1) God has chosen Israel and (2) given the law. The law implies both (3) God's promise to
maintain the election and (4) the requirement to obey. (5) God rewards obedience and punishes
transgression. (6) The law provides for means of atonement, and atonement results in (7) maintenance or re-establishment of the covenantal relationship. (8) All those who are maintained
in the covenant by obedience, atonement, and God's mercy belong to the group which will be
saved. An important interpretation of the first and last points is that election and ultimately
salvation are considered to be by God's mercy rather than human achievement."

9. The works of Jacob Neusner have been especially important. See also the English translation of Emil Schürer, *The History of the Jewish People in the Age of Jesus Christ*, revised and
edited by G. Vermes et al. (1897–98; Edinburgh: T. & T. Clark, 1973–87); the brief treatments
by Lawrence H. Schiffman, *From Text to Tradition: A History of Second Temple and Rabbinic Judaism* (Hoboken, N.J.: Ktav, 1991); and studies by Lee I. A. Levine ("The Age of Hellenism:
Alexander the Great and the Rise and Fall of the Hasmonean Kingdom") and Shaye J. D. Cohen ("Roman Domination: The Jewish Revolt and the Destruction of the Second Temple") in
Ancient Israel: A Short History from Abraham to the Roman Destruction of the Temple, ed. Her-
shel Shanks (Washington, D.C.: Biblical Archaeological Society, 1988), 177–204 and 205–35,
respectively. The developments after 70 C.E. outlined above have been questioned: the "myth"
of Jamnia has been dismissed as having no historical grounds. The case against it has been
brilliantly stated by Philip S. Alexander in the chapter, "'The Parting of the Ways' from the
Perspective of Rabbinic Judaism," in *Jews and Christians: The Parting of the Ways* A.D. 70–135,
ed. James D. G. Dunn, The Second Durham-Tübingen Research Symposium on Earliest Christianity and Judaism (Tübingen: J. C. B. Mohr [Siebeck], 1992), 1–26. However, we emphasize
(see below, under "The Jewish Foreground") that for convenience we use the term "Jamnia"
of the process that eventually led to the fully developed later Rabbinic Judaism. That process
was gradual and not completed until the third century. It produced discussion and activity such
as is adumbrated in John's Gospel: doubtless there were initial, preparatory expressions of this
process which John encountered and reflects. But scholars, accustomed to the leisurely discussions of "ideas" rather than to the more immediately demanding need for action in situations
of social crisis, perhaps tend to underestimate the degree to which the kind of crisis that faced
Jewry after 70 C.E. demanded immediate response, and that gradualism in such a situation can be
overemphasized. See "Retrospect," in W. D. Davies and D. C. Allison, *A Critical and Exegetical*

readers can now fortunately turn to Sanders's truly magisterial work *Judaism, Practice, and Belief, 63* B.C.E.–66 C.E.[10] to give substance to the assumptions we have noted, and to the activities and the hopes — messianic and other — that they engendered. In this essay we only list these fundamentals of the content of John's Jewish background, because his immediate foreground calls for more pointed attention. We can only reiterate here that John did not encounter Jesus and his movement with a *tabula rasa* but with a mind enriched by the wealth of the Jewish religious tradition. Professor D. Moody Smith has himself sought to indicate how fully aware John was of that tradition.[11]

The Jewish Foreground

What, then, of the immediate Jewish foreground of John? We have pointed to the theological complexity of that Judaism, although we did not dwell on the fissiparous, divisive sectarianism which that complexity had spawned. Apart from the Pharisees, there were the Sadducees, the Essenes, the members of the Qumran community, "apocalyptists" of various types, the Zealots, Sicarii, the Fourth Philosophy, the Samaritans, Therapeutae, Christians, and there was also diaspora Judaism. But the events that culminated in the fall of Jerusalem in 70 C.E. and those that ensued therefrom were of crucial significance in the history of Judaism. Some have claimed that they transformed it.[12] After 70 C.E. under the initial leadership of Johannan ben Zakkai, the Pharisees became the dominant (though not the sole) surviving group, and it was they who were to lay the foundations for the more concentrated and homogeneous rabbinic Judaism of later times. Our sources do not allow us to trace and date developments with strict exactitude, but the essential characteristics, activity, and achievement of "Jamnia" are clear. We strongly emphasize that the term "Jamnia" is here used not for that location, nor for any precise definite date of any "council," but for the whole complex process of transformation to which we have referred.[13]

Commentary on the Gospel according to St. Matthew, vol. 3, ICC (Edinburgh: T. & T. Clark, 1997), and the balanced statements by Douglas R. A. Hare, *The Theme of the Persecution of Christians in the Gospel according to St. Matthew,* SNTSMS 6 (Cambridge: Cambridge University Press, 1967), 48–56, esp. 54–56. D. M. Smith refers to "the initial certainty that Johannine Christians felt threatened by expulsion from the Synagogue (9:22; 12:42; 16:2)" ("Representation of Judaism in the Gospel of John," forthcoming). We concur.

10. London: SCM Press; Philadelphia: Fortress Press, 1992.

11. Smith, "Representation of Judaism in the Gospel of John."

12. See especially Jacob Neusner, "The Formation of Rabbinic Judaism," ANRW 11.19.2 (1979): 3–42; also Shaye J. D. Cohen, "Yavneh Revisited: Pharisees, Rabbis, and the End of Jewish Sectarianism," in *Society of Biblical Literature 1982 Seminar Papers,* ed. K. H. Richards (Chico, Calif.: Scholars Press, 1982), 45–61; and idem, "The Significance of Yavneh: Pharisees, Rabbis, and the End of Jewish Sectarianism," HUCA 55 (1984): 27–53.

13. Failure to recognize that we use the term "Jamnian" for the whole "process" of the emergence of Rabbinic Judaism, strictly so-called, has led to criticism of our position, which is beside

This process was symbolized in the character and work of R. Johannan ben Zakkai, who first gathered at Jamnia the scholars who survived the revolt of 66–70 c.e. against Rome. Owing to the paucity and confusion of our sources, there can be no complete biography of this key figure. But three forces seem to have molded him. First, under the influence of the great and gentle Hillel, his teacher, he became — in a positive, almost aggressive way — a man of peace. He opposed the policy of armed revolt against Rome from the beginning. When war finally came, his experience of it merely confirmed Johannan in his pacifism. At the appropriate moment, he decided to leave the doomed city to found a school in Jamnia where Judaism could preserve its continuity. His attitude to the war had set Johannan over against the apocalyptic-zealot visionaries and sectarians who had plunged his people into destruction. Although it is important to note that he did not abandon apocalyptic hopes, not fiery zeal but patient attention to the immediate task of obedience to the Law was always Johannan's aim. It continued to be such after 70 c.e., when he sought to lead his people away from fiery, futuristic fantasies to the actualities of the present. Thus the study and application of the Torah with a view to defining the task next to be done was his policy.

Second, the earthly, rabbinic sobriety of R. Johannan had been probably reinforced by his early experience in Galilee, which was prone to the charismatic and the apocalyptic. Reaction against unrealistic, uninformed enthusiasm, which he encountered in Galilee,[14] had increased Johannan's reverence for the learning of the schools. But there remains a third factor in his development. The relationship between Pharisaism and the priesthood in first-century Judaism can be easily misunderstood: it was one of both acceptance and rejection. On the one hand, the sacrificial system and the priesthood were ordained in the Law and, therefore, to be honored. But, on the other hand, there was much in the priesthood that Pharisees could not but condemn and which created friction between the priests and the Pharisees, who were essentially purists. This was aggravated because Pharisees sometimes presumed to instruct the priesthood in their interpretation of

---

the point. Similarly, the use of the term "council" for the deliberations among the sages after 70 c.e. has been clouded by unconscious parallels drawn between what went on after 70 c.e. among the sages and the more formalized and structured "councils" of later Christianity. There was no "Council of Jamnia." See Davies and Allison, "Retrospect," in *The Gospel according to Saint Matthew.* The complexity of the transition period from 70–135 c.e. is summarized by N. T. Wright, *The New Testament and the People of God,* vol. 1: *Christian Origins and the Question of God* (Minneapolis: Fortress Press, 1992), 161–66, ("Judaism Reconstructed [a.d. 70–135]"). Wright's view that "early Christianity, claiming the high ground of Israel's heritage, was first and foremost a movement that defined itself in opposition to paganism and only secondarily in opposition to mainline Judaism itself" (165) needs more consideration than space allows here. Is it acceptable?

14. For the relationship between Galilean and Judean Judaism, see Martin Goodman, in *The Cambridge History of Judaism,* vol. 3, forthcoming; and Francis Xavier Malinowski, "Galilean Judaism and the Writings of Flavius Josephus," (Ph.D. diss., Duke University, 1973).

the Law. It is not surprising, therefore, that a predominantly lay Pharisaism found itself opposed to the priesthood in fact although it accepted it in principle. Johannan ben Zakkai shared in this opposition. Over against charisma, apocalyptic vision, and priesthood, he set the Torah and the sages; alongside, if not over against the Temple, he set the House of Study. He carried these emphases with him to Jamnia.

Thus both nurture and experience had determined that the leader of Judaism after 70 C.E. should be a man of the Law and the synagogue and of peace, of the present duty rather than the future hope, of "study" more than "sacrifice." It was he who placed his stamp on the deliberations of the sages after 70 C.E. as they faced the problems of reconstruction. By the time that Johannan was followed as leader by Gamaliel II, the foundations had been gradually and truly laid for the ultimate triumph of Pharisaic Judaism, and they were reinforced by the latter.

Two inextricable dangers confronted the Pharisaic leaders after 70 C.E., namely, disintegration within Judaism itself and the contemporaneous, insidious attraction of forces from without, that is, of paganism in general and, especially, of Christianity and Gnosticism in some form or other. Under these circumstances a policy of consolidation and exclusion was the only sane one, and, in the light of what we have written above, it was to be expected that this was the policy which their rabbinic sobriety dictated to both Johannan and Gamaliel. Opposing extreme apocalyptic fervor, priestly pretensions, and unrealistic quietism or romanticism, they faced the present with the realism of the Law to be applied: under their leadership the Torah became central.

As always, the process of consolidation also demanded certain "pruning." In the first place, serious rivals to the dominant Pharisaic elements within Jewry itself had to be eliminated. The Zealots had been largely "liquidated" by the war; so too the Essenes were decimated, and, although Essenism did not die in 70 C.E., it was not subsequently aggressive enough to constitute a menace. It was, however, necessary to deal with the Sadducees. The sages saw to it that Sadduceanism was discredited: they made a "dogma" of the resurrection from the dead, belief in which was denied by the Sadducees, who thus automatically became heretics.[15] The sages, whom we assume to have been, at the least, predominantly Pharisaic, also asserted their authority over the calendar. They gradually transferred to the synagogue a part of the ritual of the Temple in such a way that the dignity of the congregations outside the Temple was to be honored: any pretensions to priestly superiority over the congregation were denied. Legislation was passed also concerning gifts and offerings normally due to the Temple so as to assert the authority of the sages over that of the priests.

---

15. See *Mishnah Sanhedrin* 10:1.

The Pharisees forged further links between the actual worship of the synagogue and the defunct Temple. Whenever possible they aimed at concentrating in the synagogue forms previously associated with the Temple, so that these forms would continue to evoke memories of the latter. The Temple had always been a symbol of the unity of Jewry, and thus the synagogue could constantly serve after 70 C.E. to preserve that unifying significance. Thus the Pharisees made changes in the use of the *lulav* ("palm branch") in the Feast of Tabernacles and introduced the priestly blessing from the Temple into the liturgy of the synagogue. Rabban Gamaliel II revised the Passover Haggadah to include references to the Passover sacrifice at Jerusalem and prayers for the restoration of that city and its sacrificial system. In the same spirit the sages standardized and unified the details of the synagogue's traditional service of worship. The same concern for unity led to a concentration on the problem of the canon and in the same period to the institution of the rabbinate, which legitimized the Pharisaic leaders as the guarantors of the tradition against the excesses of sectarians and charismatics.

In the second place, the Pharisaic sages also sought to do away with dissension among themselves, especially that between the Houses of Hillel and Shammai. The Mishnah reveals the efforts of the Pharisees to minimize the differences between these two houses. They feared that those differences, which occasioned deep personal bitterness, might lead to the creation of "two laws," a conception which would have insinuated a divided loyalty, a disastrous disunity, at the very heart of Judaism. Apart from this, the interpretation of the Law in the first century had been in a chaotic state and for the sake of unity the Pharisees saw the need to codify it. The developments which culminated in the codification of the Mishnah of Rabbi Judah the Prince, about 220 C.E., had their insistent beginnings in the period of Jamnia: codification and modification of the legal tradition was in the Jamnian air. This was part of the Pharisaic response to the need for unity and for adaptation to changed conditions.

In addition to consolidating Judaism internally, the sages were also called upon, thirdly, to preserve it from enemies without. Consolidation was inseparable from exclusion. We are here particularly concerned with the fear of the subversive influence of Christianity which may have influenced the sages. Some scholars have sought to minimize, if not to deny, any such fear on the ground that Judaism was so engrossed in its internal problems that it overlooked or deliberately ignored the incipient menace of Christianity. Others have contrasted the active opposition to the latter which Judaism offered in the second century with its comparative unconcern about it in the first. Thus, for example, although Christians had already in the first century interpreted the fall of the Temple as a punishment on Jewry for their rejection of Christ, it is only in the second that the rabbis reveal a polemical interest in that event. But, while it is true that bitterness increased as the second century came, there was conflict before this, and there are unmistakable signs that the sages were not uninfluenced by the rising significance of Christianity.

Interest in the canon was, partly at least, a reaction to Christianity. It is clear that the dispute as to whether the scriptures "rendered the hands unclean," that is, were to be treated as "holy," went back to the period before the war, as appears from *Mishnah Yadaim* 4:6. But the attempts at fixing a canon have been claimed to reflect the need to counteract certain influences — the heresy of the Sadducees, the futuristic fantasies of apocalyptists, the speculative aberrations of Gnosticism, and, from the Pharisaic point of view, the equally dangerous quietistic illusions of Christianity. As Christianity produced a literature, Judaism had to look more guardedly to its own. In *Mishnah Sanhedrin* 10:1 the "external books" — the prohibition of which occurs in a context dealing with heresy — have been interpreted as "heretical," particularly early Christian writings.[16] But Ginzberg[17] urged that "external" here did not mean "heretical," but merely noncanonical, and that the prohibition intended applied, not to private, but to public reading. It is exceedingly unlikely that Jewish synagogues would have been in danger of reading Christian writings in public, so that the prohibition can hardly have applied to them. Similarly the predominant view that "the books of the *minim* [heretics]" in such passages as *Tosepta Shabbat* 13:5 and *b. Gittin* 45b, etc., can be regarded as Christian has been challenged. The pith of the argument for the customary view — that the reference is to Christian writings — is twofold. (1) The term *minim* can include Jewish Christians; (2) in *b. Shabbat* 116a, apparently an early passage, there is a specific reference to the Gospels, in the phrase *awen gilion* ("blasphemous marginalia") and in *Tosepta Yadayim* 2:13 and *Tosepta Shabbat* 13:5 the term *gilionim* again suggests the Gospels. But Kuhn's arguments[18] are convincing that the books of the *minim* refer to scriptural, that is, Old Testament, texts written and used by heterodox Jewish groups such as that at Qumran. While the term *minim* used of such groups included Jewish Christians, it only later came to denote groups outside Jews, and especially Gentile Christians. Moreover, *gilionim* refers quite simply to

---

16. *Mishnah Sanhedrin* 10:1 reads as follows, in Danby's translation: "All Israelites have a share in the world to come, for it is written, '*Thy people also shall all be righteous, they shall inherit the land for ever, the branch of my planting, the work of my hands that I may be glorified*' [Isa. 60:12]. And these are they that have no share in the world to come: he that says there is no resurrection of the dead prescribed in the Law [some texts omit these last four words], and he [that says] that the Law is not from Heaven, and an Epicurean [one opposed to the rabbinical teachings]. R. Akiba says: Also he that reads the heretical books. [literally, 'external books,' which Danby understands as 'books excluded from the canon of Hebrew Scriptures']."

17. Louis Ginzberg, "Some Observations on the Attitude of the Synagogue towards the Apocalyptic-Eschatological Writings," *JBL* 41 (1922): 115–36.

18. K. G. Kuhn, "Giljonim und sifre minim," in *Judentum, Urchristentum, Kirche: Festschrift für Joachim Jeremias*, ed. Walther Eltester, BZNW 26 (Berlin: Töpelmann, 1960), 24–61.

the margins of Torah scrolls, while *awen gilion* cannot be a transliteration of *euaggelion* ("good news"), which has a plural in α: *gilionim* can hardly have been formed out of *euaggelia*. Moreover, *b. Shabbat* 116a is too late, despite its mention of early authorities, to be used for the Jamnian period. The outcome of Kuhn's work is to make us more cautious in connecting the fixation of the canon at Jamnia directly with the Christian Gospels and writings, despite the impressive list of scholars who have urged this.

Nevertheless, Kuhn's understanding of the *minim*, as including Jewish Christians, leaves the door open for the view that the fixation of the canon at Jamnia was not unrelated to the awareness of a growing Christianity, as was the later codification of the Mishnah to the growing authority of the New Testament. The changes in liturgy and religious practice introduced by the sages in the Jamnian period make this clear. While the deliberate attention paid to these matters was largely stimulated by the need for liturgical and other unity within Judaism, it also revealed anti-Christian concern. One of the liturgical developments especially was the reformulation of the chief prayer of the synagogue, called the *Tefillah* or *Amidah*, so that it came to constitute eighteen benedictions. A petition (the *Birkath ha-Minim*), the twelfth benediction — either against heretics, including Jewish Christians, or against heretics and specifically Jewish Christians — was introduced into the *Tefillah*, at what exact date we cannot ascertain. But it was probably between 85 and 90 C.E. This *Birkath ha-Minim* makes it clear that the sages regarded Jewish Christians as a menace sufficiently serious to warrant a liturgical innovation. It worked simply, but effectively, as follows. In the synagogue service a man was designated to lead in the reciting of the *Tefillah*. As he approached the platform, where the ark containing the scrolls of the Law stood, the congregation rose. The leader would recite the benedictions, and the congregation, finally, responded to these with an "Amen." Anyone called upon to recite the *Tefillah* who stumbled on the twelfth benediction could easily be detected. Thus the *Birkath ha-Minim* served the purpose of making any Christian or other "heretic" who might be present in a synagogal service conspicuous by the way in which he recited or glossed over this Benediction.

Largely similar in its intent to isolate Jewish Christians was the use of the ban at Jamnia. This again involved the assumption that the *Beth Din* ("house of judgment," or court of law) in that place had taken to itself the status of the Sanhedrin, because it meant the reintroduction of a usage which, before the war, had been controlled by that body. There can be no doubt that R. Eliezer, one of the most important figures at Jamnia after the withdrawal of Rabbi Joḥannan ben Zakkai, had, either before or after his banishment, been in such communication with Christians that their tradition was known to him. And it is also clear that the reason for the frequent use of the ban by Rabban Gamaliel was his fear of dissentients, among whom were Jewish

Christians, against whom, as against others, the *Birkath ha-Minim* was aimed. In this connection, it cannot be sufficiently emphasized that the sages were frequently in contact with Jewish Christians.[19] Justin Martyr's *Dialogue with Trypho* 16.4 refers almost certainly to the *Birkath ha-Minim*, although the reference in 138.1 cannot simply be to the *Birkath ha-Minim*, which was not strictly a law: we have no other evidence for such a law. However, the main point is clear: by the end of the first century the synagogue had adopted an attitude of isolation from and opposition to Jewish Christians in the interests of its own integrity. It did this, possibly if not probably, by the significant liturgical change in the use of the *Birkath ha-Minim*, by the use of the ban, and, possibly, by a legal enactment whose precise date and character is lost to us.[20]

In view of the data given above, it is arguable that, when John was writing, the Judaism that any Jewish Christian faced was very dynamic: it was vigorously adjusting to the new conditions prevailing among Jewry after 70 c.e. It was not only a reacting Judaism, but one actively engaged in proselytizing and presenting its case against the encroachments of the Christian and other movements. The view that after 70 c.e. Judaism ceased to be missionary cannot be substantiated: it continued to be such until the fifth century.[21] John had to come to terms with a militant Judaism. The recognition of this "foreground" illuminates much in his Gospel. Are there other pointers to this vigorous Jamnian Judaism in that document? We note the following possibilities.

1. It appears from a simple glance at the demography of his Gospel that it was the Pharisaic sages with whom John had to deal. Most of first-century Judaism had been marked by a multiplicity of sects, but gradually after 70 c.e. it was the Pharisees who best survived and, in time, became dominant. The

---

19. See W. D. Davies, *The Setting of the Sermon on the Mount* (Cambridge: Cambridge University Press, 1964), 276–78.

20. Whether we trace a concern to combat Christianity elsewhere in the liturgy is discussed in Davies, *The Setting of the Sermon on the Mount*, 279–82, where the Jamnian emphasis on the *Shema* in the life of Jewry and in the synagogal service, on the *Tefillah* (phylactery), and on the *Mezuzah* (doorpost scroll) is noted as possibly having had a polemic anti-Christian intent, as had the withdrawal of the Decalogue, the *Mezuzah*, and the *Tefillah* from the synagogue service. On the *Birkath ha-Minim* see William Horbury, "The Benediction of the *Minim* and Early Jewish-Christian Controversy," *JTS* 33 (1982): 19–61; Steven T. Katz, "Issues in the Separation of Judaism and Christianity after 70 c.e.: A Reconstruction," *JBL* 103 (1984): 43–76; Reuven Kimelman, "*Birkath ha-Minim* and the Lack of Evidence for an Anti-Jewish Prayer in Late Antiquity," in *Jewish and Christian Self-Definition*, vol. 2: *Aspects of Judaism in the Greco-Roman Period*, ed. E. P. Sanders with A. I. Baumgarten and Alan Mendelsohn (Philadelphia: Fortress Press, 1981), 226–44, 391–403.

21. The view that after 70 c.e. Judaism from necessity became isolationist was contested by Marcel Simon, *Verus Israel: A Study of Relations between Christians and Jews in the Roman Empire (135–425)*, Littman Library of Jewish Civilization (New York: Oxford University Press, 1985), esp. 272, and recently by L. H. Feldman, "Proselytism by Jews in the Third, Fourth, and Fifth Centuries," *JJS* 24, no. 1 (1993): 1–58. See also Robert L. Wilken, *John Chrysostom and the Jews: Rhetoric and Reality* (London and Berkeley: University of California Press, 1985).

multiplicity of the sects referred to in the Synoptic Gospels reflects the situation when the sources on which they drew and those Gospels themselves were written. The same is true of John; he too reflects his own historical situation. Whereas in the earlier first century there existed Pharisees, Sadducees, the scribes, Essenes, the sectarians at Qumran, Zealots, Sicarii, the members of the Fourth Philosophy, Samaritans, Therapeutae — many of whom (scribes, Sadducees, Pharisees, Herodians, Zealots) are mentioned in the Synoptics — in the Gospel of John most of these groups do not appear. They no longer existed, having been largely eliminated in the revolt against Rome, 66–70 C.E. In John's Gospel "the Jews" are usually directly equated with Pharisees. The foreground of John, then, would seem to be that of Pharisaic Jamnia.[22]

2. In a study of the Sermon on the Mount, we suggested that the Gospel of Matthew was among other things a response to Jamnian Judaism. That John also points to Jamnian activity was suggested by Martyn in his important study *History and Theology in the Fourth Gospel*. He had earlier urged that the twelfth benediction, the *Birkath ha-Minim* of the *Tefillah*, was reformulated in order to make it easier to detect Jewish Christians and other sectarians, whom the sages wanted to exclude from the synagogue service. The version of the *Tefillah*, or eighteen benedictions, found in the Cairo Genizah is as follows: "For apostates let there be no hope. And let the arrogant government be speedily uprooted in our days. Let [the Nazareans = Christians] the *minim* [heretics] be destroyed in a moment." The Cairo Genizah text contained only the word *minim* (heretics), but possibly Samuel the Small (80–90 C.E.) revised this older form by the addition of the word *notzrim* (Nazareans), in order to include Jewish Christians. The passage in John 9:22 (see also 12:42), Martyn urged, is to be understood in the light of the *Birkath ha-Minim* — the twelfth benediction. Not all have been convinced, as Martyn has recognized.[23] However, whether or not the exact form of the twelfth benediction was changed by the addition of "the Nazareans" in order explicitly to include "Christians" among the *minim*, it still seems to us historically probable that the sages at Jamnia were aware of the "menace" of the Christian movement and that among the *minim* whom they sought to exclude from the synagogue were Jewish Christians who were attending those synagogues.

Assuming, then, that John, at the very least, was caught up in events which ultimately led to the formulation of the *Birkath ha-Minim*, even though

---

22. See Shaye J. D. Cohen, *From the Maccabees to the Mishnah*, Library of Early Christianity (Philadelphia: Westminster Press, 1987), 224; and idem, "The Significance of Yavneh."

23. Martyn, *History and Theology in the Fourth Gospel*, rev. ed., *passim*. See also D. M. Smith, "Judaism and the Gospel of John," in *Jews and Christians: Exploring the Past, Present, and Future*, ed. J. H. Charlesworth with F. X. Blisard and J. S. Siker (New York: Crossroad, 1990), 76–96, esp. 85–88.

the exact date of its formulation eludes us, can we detect other data in his Gospel that confirm his engagement with Jamnian Judaism? We can here only very cursorily suggest a few pertinent aspects of the Fourth Gospel.

3. John, it has been claimed, in presenting the "signs" which Jesus gave through miraculous events, drew upon a special source. Fortna[24] and Martyn[25] have taken this source to have been a kind of text used in the synagogue for missionary preaching aimed at Jews — "that they may believe that Jesus is the Christ, the Son of God, and that believing they may have life in his name" (John 20:31). However, it seems clear that the use of miracles in the original source on which John drew, if such existed, was altogether simpler than the use ascribed to them by John. The "signs" of John are not simply miraculous wonders; they are pointers to a truth beyond themselves. John makes a miracle a "sign," a point of departure for a dialogue or discourse in which he sets forth a truth of the gospel. For example, in 6:1–58, the feeding of the five thousand is expounded in terms of the manna given to the people of Israel in the wilderness: not through Moses, but in Jesus comes the eternal life — the living bread. In 11:1–53 the sign, the raising of Lazarus from the dead, is followed by the discussion of the resurrection of the dead. There are indications that John is aware of the dangers of concentrating on the merely miraculous. In 4:48, for example, in response to an officer who pleaded with him to cure his son, Jesus asks: "Will none of you ever believe without seeing signs and wonders?" Nevertheless, unlike the synoptic writers (see Mark 8:11–12), John regards "the signs" as legitimate pathways to belief (2:11; 2:23), although they do not always achieve their aim (12:37). In 1:51 the implication is that greater "signs" than the one concerning Nathanael can appropriately be anticipated. Into the intricacies of the discussion concerning the signs-source in recent scholarship we cannot enter here. It is pertinent that John drew upon and elaborated a written or oral tradition of miracles to provide evidence that Jesus was the expected Messiah of Judaism.

If John did elaborate and reinterpret a previously existing signs-source written to convince Jews by interpreting the miracles, is it possible that he was aware of the rejection of "simple" miracles by the sages? While retaining his "miracles" as "signs," did he partly at least lend them a new, more sophisticated signification in order to undercut the rabbis' objection to "miracles"? In short, does the elaboration of "signs" by John suggest that he has one ear open to the sages, who in order to counteract the Christian use of miracles to establish the claims of Jesus rejected the validity of "the miraculous"? Exaggeration is easy at this point. The rabbis may have rejected miracles because

24. Robert T. Fortna, *The Gospel of Signs: A Reconstruction of the Narrative Source Underlying the Fourth Gospel*, SNTSMS 11 (London: Cambridge University Press, 1970).

25. See Martyn, *History and Theology in the Fourth Gospel*.

miracles were so commonplace as to be insignificant. But, though caution is in order, there can be little doubt that the use of miracles to legitimize Jesus as the Messiah, such as we find in John, engaged the sages. A. Guttmann long ago made this clear.[26] The rejection of miracles and of the *bath qôl* ("daughter of a voice" = heavenly voice) by the sages was almost certainly a reaction against their use by early Christians. The matter, however, is complex. Is it possible that John in using the reinterpreted miracles of a possibly early, simpler "Book of Signs" was reacting at least partially, as we suggested, to the criticisms by the Jamnian sages, or was it that the Jamnian sages were reacting to John and the Christian evidential use of miracles? In either case Jamnian Judaism and Johannine Christianity were mutually reacting. The full scope of their mutual reaction we cannot trace within the limits of this article. Here we can only note that John seems anxious to avoid specific reference to a *bath qôl* in his dealing with the baptism of Jesus in 1:29–34, and that in 12:27–33 (see especially vv. 30–31) his treatment of the voice out of heaven implies caution. Was he aware of the Jamnian critique of the *bath qôl?*

4. We make only one further suggestion by way of an illustration of this possible mutual reaction. It concerns the attitude of John to the geographic or territorial dimension of Judaism as the Jamnian sages — like other Jews in other ages — so emphatically embraced it. In *The Gospel and the Land: Early Christian and Jewish Territorial Doctrine*,[27] we provided evidence that John was markedly concerned with "holy space." The Hebrew scriptures, the Midrash, the Midrashim, the Talmud, and the liturgies that Jews have constantly celebrated and the observances they have kept across the centuries all point to the Land of Promise, Eretz Israel, "The Land," as uniquely related to the deity as established in Jewish tradition. A recent study by B. Halpern-Amaru, *Rewriting the Bible: Land and Covenant in Postbiblical Jewish Literature*,[28] gives further evidence from *Jubilees*, *The Testament of Moses*, and the works of Philo and Josephus that in their concern for the Land of Promise, the authors of these documents, who were roughly contemporary with John, rewrote and reinterpreted the biblical sources in Genesis dealing with the covenant and containing the references to the promised land. Those documents reveal how their authors were each influenced by their several historical settings and by their contemporary interests, and how, under the impact of those settings and interests, they all reinterpreted differently the tradition they had received. The complexity and difficulty of the understanding of The Land in the postexilic period we had already indicated in *The Gospel and the Land*,

---

26. See Alexander Guttmann, "The Significance of Miracles for Talmudic Judaism," *HUCA* 20 (1947): 363–406; see also Davies, *Paul and Rabbinic Judaism*, 374–75.

27. (Berkeley: University of California Press, 1974; reprint, Sheffield, England: JSOT Press, 1994), 234–88.

28. Valley Forge, Pa.: Trinity Press International, 1994.

and Halpern-Amaru's work has greatly increased our awareness of that complexity. It is now clear that the question of The Land was as living a concern in the "intertestamental" period as it came to be in the rabbinic period.

However, it has been suggested that after 70 C.E. many Jews were tempted to leave The Land to escape its onerous, devastated conditions, and the sages at Jamnia were especially concerned about opposing emigration. Thus, they initiated a deliberate policy of extolling the virtues of The Land. The need to encourage Jews to remain in it became urgent. The emigration of Jews to neighboring countries, especially to Syria, threatened to depopulate The Land. For example, Rabbi Eliezer the Great (Ben Hyrcanus, 80–120 C.E.), in order to protect Palestinian agriculture, wanted to subject Syrian agriculture to all the requirements of tithing and of the sabbatical year, so as to make it less attractive for Jewish farmers to emigrate to Syria. Rabbi Gamaliel II (80–120 C.E.) shared in the same purpose, though in a less extreme manner.[29] We have elsewhere urged that the economic was not the only cause for The Land's glorification,[30] but the other causes do not directly concern us here. Suffice it to note that many factors after 70 C.E. conjoined to enhance that glorification.

In two ways at least we connect both the concentration on the centrality of the Law as the "portable land" of Jews in Rabbinic Judaism, and the simultaneous emphasis on The Land as the only sphere for the truly full life of Jews — their *bene esse* — with emphases in John's Gospel.

We previously referred to the exploitation by John of a possible signs-source, oral or written, to reinforce the centrality of Jesus. There were other ways in which he made clear that Jesus' Person had replaced the Torah as "the ultimate" for Jews, as for all people. From the prologue on, the christological emphasis in his Gospel is unmistakable. That emphasis was strictly "personal." But the "personal" bears in itself "the universal": the "personal" in itself challenges any form of particularism such as that centered in the Torah and in The Land. The Jamnian sages would find John's christological emphases a menace. Is it merely accidental that while John is careful to make Moses, as the mediator of the Torah, subordinate to Jesus as the Christ,[31] *Pirke Aboth*, in the very first verse, makes it emphatically clear that it was through Moses that the Torah came? The first word of the *Aboth* is "Moses" ("Moses received the Law from Sinai . . ."), just as the first verse of John points to the Logos as incarnate in Christ.

At the same time, the elevation of holy places in Judaism and of The Land by the sages, we suggest, might have reinforced John's marked concentration

---

29. See *Mishnah Ḥallah* 4:7–8.
30. Davies, *The Gospel and the Land*, 56–60.
31. John 1:17, etc.

on the person of Christ. Although unlike Paul he does not so freely engage in proof from scripture, and although we cannot directly pinpoint his dismissal of the Pharisaic emphasis on The Land, implicit in his christological emphasis is such a dismissal. The force of this dismissal must be measured against the background of that living engagement with The Land to which we pointed in our work and which Halpern-Amaru has further documented.

Moreover, one aspect of the doctrine of The Land is, possibly, directly countered by John. The gift of the Holy Spirit, which plays a notable part in John's Gospel, was, like the gift of prophecy and of the resurrection of the dead, connected by some sages with The Land (*Mekilta Pisha* 1 on Exod. 12:1–13:16). We have elsewhere tried to show how the experience of the Holy Spirit was tied to The Land and occurred, according to some, only in The Land.[32] Is it possible that in his interpretation of the Holy Spirit, John is reacting to the territorial limitation of the Spirit which was exercised by Jamnian Pharisaism? Was his pneumatology, like his Christology, at least partly sharpened by his reaction against Jamnian influences, that is, the concentration of the sages on the Torah and The Land? The words in 3:8 ("The wind [spirit] blows where it wills; you hear the sound of it, but you do not know where it comes from, or where it is going. So with everyone who is born from spirit" [NEB]) were spoken in response to "one of the Pharisees named Nicodemus, a member of the Jewish Council" (3:1). They take on added significance when set over against the territorial boundary set to the activity of the Spirit by Pharisaism: for John that activity embraces the whole of creation and yet can dwell "in the humble heart."[33] Similarly in the prologue at 1:11, if the term τὰ ἴδια ("his own") includes The Land, as some commentators suggest, is not its thrust sharpened in the light of the Pharisaic emphasis on the significance of The Land? That Land had rejected the Lord of Glory. So too the theme of the replacement of holy places in John, which is unmistakable, gains force when set against the Pharisaic emphasis.[34] The poignancy of that emphasis itself must, in turn, be understood in the light of the fall of Jerusalem and the devastation of The Land in the revolt against Rome. To point to Jesus, the Christ, as the replacement of the fallen Temple and of the sacred holy places, like Bethel, as does John, at a time when the war against Rome had deprived Jews of their Land and Temple and desecrated their holy places so that their loss was constantly and painfully present, was to touch a most raw nerve. John lived in a postwar world, when traditional geographic and

---

32. Davies, "Reflections on the Spirit in the *Mekilta*: A Suggestion," in *Jewish and Pauline Studies* (Philadelphia: Fortress Press; New York: SPCK, 1984), 72–83.

33. See Buber's connection in n. 5 above.

34. On this see Davies, *The Gospel and the Land*. The following commentators note that τὰ ἴδια in John 1:11 may refer to the land of Israel: B. F. Westcott, Theodor Zahn, G. H. C. Macgregor, J. H. Bernard, Raymond E. Brown, and Rudolf Schnackenburg.

other loyalties had been violated. His theme of "replacement" was, therefore, peculiarly sensitive and challenging and could not but provoke resentment. Nor must it be overlooked that John wrote when the failure of Jewish Christians to join in the revolt against Rome had made them a source of contempt and hatred for their Jewish kinsmen. Jewish Christians were "quislings," supplying comfort to the enemy. As Dale Allison and I have pointed out in our commentary on Matthew,[35] the emphasis on love of the enemy and on reconciliation in that Gospel, in the Sermon on the Mount, and elsewhere is partly due to its author's reaction to the atrocities of the revolt. We suggest that, likewise, John's emphasis on the gift of peace — not as "the world giveth" — in his Gospel finds its sharpest outlines when set over against the horror of that revolt. Oddly enough, both the sages and John, opposed as they were, enjoined on their followers the same theme — the importance of unity, reconciliation, and peace. They were both children of a war-torn world, and the horror of strife had burnt into their bones, as it had into Matthew's.

The reaction of Jewry to John's Christian challenge — its replacement of Torah and The Land by the Person of Christ — could have been nothing but sharp and bitter. Is it this that, in part at least, explains that antagonism toward Jews in John which has led to the charge that he was "anti-Semitic"? To examine the use of the phrase οἱ Ἰουδαῖοι, "the Jews," in John is not possible here. The views of Malcolm Lowe[36] that the term means "Judeans," of von Wahlde that it signifies a handful of highly placed officials,[37] and of Bultmann that it is an "archetypal symbol of the sinfulness of humankind"[38] have all been examined by Ashton and found not altogether satisfactory.[39] Given the pointers that I have tried to indicate (implicit rather than unambiguously explicit though they be), does not the antagonism of Jamnian Pharisaism to the growing Christian movement provide at least in part the reason for John's pejorative use of "The Jews"? Limitations of space do not allow us to do justice to this complex question, but we can suggest that the Jamnian/Christian context needs further consideration because it constituted the foreground of John.

So far we have emphasized the Pharisaic foreground of John. Ashton, in his very important study *Understanding the Fourth Gospel*,[40] has reminded us of the apocalyptic world to which John belonged, and since the days of Johannes

---

35. Davies and Allison, *The Gospel according to Saint Matthew*, vol. 1, *passim*.

36. Malcolm Lowe, "Who Were the ΙΟΥΔΑΙΟΙ?" *Novum Testamentum* 18 (1976): 101–30 (here, 106–7).

37. Urban C. von Wahlde, "The Johannine Jews: A Critical Survey," *NTS* 28 (1982): 33–60.

38. Rudolf Bultmann, *The Gospel of John: A Commentary* (Philadelphia: Westminster Press, 1971), 86.

39. John Ashton, *Studying John: Approaches to the Fourth Gospel* (Oxford and New York: Clarendon Press, 1994), 5–36.

40. (Oxford: Clarendon Press; New York: Oxford University Press, 1991), 381–401.

Weiss and Albert Schweitzer the eschatological (apocalyptic)[41] dimension of early Christianity, including that of John, has been fully recognized. But while Ashton's emphasis is a healthy corrective to any diminution of the apocalyptic elements in John, the dichotomy between the apocalyptic and the Pharisaic or rabbinic cannot be pressed, as it once was.[42] The Pharisees of Jamnia, despite their suspicion of "extremism" among early Christians and others, could themselves embrace the apocalyptic. Akiba found Bar Kokba to be the Messiah: Sage and seer could and did coexist in the same person. Judaism was not rigidly compartmentalized between the Pharisaic and apocalyptic. John was familiar with both worlds. It was not messianism as such that the sages objected to but the Christian variety of it. Moreover, the Pharisees and the Christians were alike in that they were both often leery of the excesses of the apocalyptic. The "eschatology" of early Christianity, it might be argued, was reductionist, as was that of the Pharisees.[43] By reductionist we mean that it was not as elaborate and complex as much found in the apocalyptic sources. Moreover, the concentration of eschatology in the Person of Christ in John, to which C. H. Dodd pointed us in his emphasis on the "realized eschatology" of the Fourth Gospel, naturally led to reductionism in the sense indicated.[44] It could be claimed that in John eschatology or apocalyptic in large part has been engulfed by Christology.

Here Scholem's understanding of the development of any radical messianic movement (such as early Christianity in its relationship to Judaism) illumines the place of John as he encountered Jamnian Judaism. It is important to recognize the stage at which John penned his Gospel in the development of Christianity in its relationship to Judaism. The Gospel created a crisis of tradition within Jewish messianism. This messianism, in which conceptions of an ideal world, of the restoration of the Davidic kingdom, of the centrality of The Land, and of Jerusalem were combined with those of the day of the Lord and the last judgment, was a recognized aspect of Jewish revelation and tradition. Belief in a future redemption had become domesticated within the tradition of Judaism with little discomfort to that tradition. Hopes for a redemption either by the restoration of Israel and the world to a primordial or primeval condition, that is, in a restorative sense, or by the ad-

---

41. On the distinction between eschatology and apocalyptic we cannot here enlarge, nor on what C. H. Dodd taught us to call·"realized eschatology" in John. See Dale C. Allison, *The End of the Ages Has Come: An Early Interpretation of the Passion and Resurrection of Jesus* (Philadelphia: Fortress Press, 1985), 51–61.

42. See Davies, "Preface to the Fourth Edition," in *Paul and Rabbinic Judaism*, xxvi, and idem, "Apocalyptic and Pharisaism," in *Christian Origins and Judaism* (New York: Arno Press, 1973), 19–30.

43. For reductionism in Paul, see Davies, "Pauline and Jewish Christianity according to Cardinal Daniélou: A Suggestion," in *Jewish and Pauline Studies*, 164–71.

44. See again Allison, *The End of the Ages Has Come*, 51–61.

vent of a kind of utopia, which represents "the conception of redemption as a phenomenon in which something emerges which has never before existed, in which something totally new is unmistakably expressed," could coexist. Scholem continues:

> Of course, those restorative and utopian elements in the messianic idea could exist side by side *as long as it was simply a hope that was projected into the distant future, an affirmation of faith that corresponded to no real experience.* As long as the messianic hope remained abstract, not yet concretized in people's experience or demanding a concrete decision, it was possible for it to embody even what was contradictory without the latent contradiction being felt.... Messianism could take over even a conservative attitude and in this way become part of the tradition. Messianic *activity,* however, could hardly do this. The moment that messianism moved from the realm of affirmation of faith, abstract doctrine, and synthesizing imagination into life and took on acute forms, it had to reach a point where the energies that lay dormant in these two elements would emerge into conflict with each other — the conflict of the tradition of the past version versus the presence of redemption.[45]

For Paul the conflict to which Scholem refers had not yet been resolved; it was still brewing. It was not clear in Paul's day whether Christian "messianism" would demand an utterly radical break with the tradition of Judaism. It could be taken as an interpretation of the Jewish tradition, and rooted in the Jewish scriptures. This could be the reason for Paul's constant engagement with the Law. Christian messianism had initiated the crisis, but Paul had not fully resolved it. John, on the other hand, assumes that the true meaning of the Jewish tradition — of the Law — was to be found in its witness to Jesus the Messiah. But he still engaged in the interpretation of the Law in a midrashic fashion, and Martyn may be going too far in claiming that "John employs a form of midrashic discussion in order to terminate all midrashic discussion."[46] The temptation is to think of John as having been a development beyond Paul. But it may be wiser to think of the differences between Paul and John as different responses to Judaism at different points in the conflict between early Christianity and its mother faith. Again, it was not simply that John, a Jewish Christian, was concerned with Jews and Jewish Christians only and had to be concerned with them, whereas Paul was the apostle to the Gentiles and therefore had to focus on the Law which separated Jews and Gentiles; nor simply that the sages, like John himself, had come to see more clearly and unambiguously than Paul had that there would

---

45. G. Scholem, *The Messianic Idea in Judaism and Other Essays on Jewish Spirituality* (New York: Schocken Books, 1971), 51–52 (italics added).

46. Martyn, *History and Theology in the Fourth Gospel,* 128.

have to come a parting of the ways and were, at the least, engaged in that process which eventually would lead to the *Birkath ha-Minim*. The center of the sages' concentration had shifted to the claims of Jesus of Nazareth, which, now that so many Gentiles had so obviously embraced Jesus, was taken with a new seriousness by the sages. The Christian movement was no longer merely speculative but had tangible consequences. Until the success of the Gentile mission — a visible fact, not merely a speculation — had emerged, the sages could have regarded early Christianity as a passing phenomenon. But the church's missionary activity had changed the situation. In their response to it, they could no longer minimize the seriousness of the Christian challenge. It was at this particular juncture, when the sages had come to realize more fully the importance of the Christian movement as a critical challenge, that John wrote, and in this light are his christological and other emphases, to which we previously referred, to be understood.

The prologue of John's Gospel reveals these emphases: the counter-Pharisaic, the christological, and the deterritorializing. There Christ has become the Word, the Light, the Life — attributes which the sages applied to the Torah, the Wisdom of God. But in a very illuminating essay, Culpepper urged that the center or pivot of the prologue is not primarily in its Christology, but in 1:12b: "And he gave them authority to become the children of God." Not even "the incarnation nor the witness of the community that 'we have beheld his glory' would have enduring meaning were it not for the result of the confession of the incarnation. He gave [us] authority to become children of God." Culpepper continues, "[B]y claiming the designation 'the children of God' the Johannine community was identifying itself (or perhaps more broadly all Christianity) as the heir to a role and standing which Israel had abdicated by her failure to receive the Son of God. This was a subject of considerable dispute between the Johannine school and 'the Jews.' "[47] In an essay to which we previously referred, along with Torah, The Land, and the Messiah as basic elements in Judaism, we named the People of Israel.[48] Recently Arthur Hertzberg has claimed that "the essence of Judaism is the affirmation that the Jews are the chosen people; all else is commentary."[49] Exaggerated though this may be, it was true of first-century Judaism that there was for the sages a "privacy" in the relation of Jews to the divine which is difficult to deny. It was a challenge to this "privacy" which the success of the Pauline mission had raised, and which John resolved in 1:12b by re-

47. R. A. Culpepper, "The Pivot of John's Prologue," *NTS* 27, no. 1 (1980–81): 1–31 (here, 31).

48. See the discussion above and Davies, "Reflections on the Nature of Judaism."

49. See A. Hertzberg, *The Condition of Jewish Belief: A Symposium Conducted by the Editors of "Commentary" Magazine* (New York: Macmillan, 1966), 90.

defining the term "children of God" to include among God's chosen people whosoever "believed" in Jesus.

In sum, John engaged all the essential elements in the Judaism of his day, to which we have pointed, and challenged them in the name of Christ. Unfortunately, though understandably, the challenge led to bitterness toward Christians among Jews and toward Jews among Christians. It was this bitterness which constituted the context which engendered that vivid, foreboding sense of "crisis," inescapable in John, to which C. H. Dodd pointed.[50] The yearning of Paul for the acceptance of Jesus by his own people (Romans 9–11) and the anxious ambiguity of Matthew about the relationship between his church and the Jewish people[51] have given way, in the Fourth Evangelist, to a more radical opposition and judgment — although John can still assert that "salvation is of the Jews" and does not include all Jews, including himself, among "The Jews."[52]

---

50. Dodd, *The Interpretation of the Fourth Gospel*, particularly 352–53. And see John 3:19; 5:22, 24, 27, 29, 30; 7:24; 8:16; 12:31.

51. See Wright, *The New Testament and the People of God*, 1:98–102; R. T. France, *Matthew: Evangelist and Teacher* (Grand Rapids, Mich.: Academic Books, 1989), 206–41, on "Matthew and Israel" (esp. the last paragraph); and the rich treatment by Jean-Claude Ingelaere, "Universalisme et Particularisme dans l'Évangile de Matthieu: Matthieu et le Judaïsme," *Revue d'Histoire et de Philosophie Religieuses* 75 (1995): 45–59.

52. Dr. D. C. Allison, Jr., read the typescript of this chapter; I am very grateful for his helpful criticism and comments. I also thank Sarah Freedman for her unfailing competence.

Part IV

An American
Interpretation of Judaism

Chapter II

Israel, the Mormons,
and the Land

Mormonism is a most complex phenomenon. It arose out of a twofold matrix: Christianity and America. The duality of its origin pervades it. But through Christianity it goes back to an even more ultimate matrix: to Judaism and the Israelite religion. Through Christianity, Mormons came to be connected with the Jews. Their response to the Hebrew people and their land has been truly amazing. And it is with this response that we are here concerned. For the sake of clarity, I shall divide my essay into three parts. Part 1 deals with Mormonism as a return to Israel, Part 2 with Mormonism as the restoration of Israel, and Part 3 with Mormonism as the reinterpretation of Israel. In that last section we shall concentrate on The Land.

Mormonism as a Return to Israel

The early Mormon leaders were steeped in the Old Testament scriptures. Some of them undertook to learn Hebrew that they might understand the scriptures better. All their writings either draw upon or reflect the Old Testament. Like the early Christian church, they used what might be called collected testimonia, particularly those derived from Deutero-Isaiah. But whereas the early Christian church drew predominantly on the Prophets and Psalms and neglected Leviticus, the Mormon leaders also appealed to the passages in the Old Testament dealing with the priesthood. Although there is no direct dependence on Leviticus, Levitical motifs reemerge in Mormonism with more frequency than in the New Testament. This, then, is the first strong link between Mormons and Israel: they share common scriptures in what we usually call the Old Testament.

But the link is closer. Those scriptures were interpreted in such a way as to find in the People of Israel the physical ancestors of the Mormon people. It was natural for Paul to regard Abraham and Moses as his ancestors, and he even went so far as to call them the fathers of Corinthian Gentile Christians (1 Cor. 10:1). But the apostle hardly thinks of this as a physical, biolog-

213

ical connection between Israel and the Gentile church: the connection is spiritual.

The Book of Mormon goes further. It claims that certain Jews were fugitives from the land of Israel at the time of the captivity of Zedekiah, which is now dated in 587 B.C.E., and came to the Western world, that is, the Americas, their land of promise across the sea. Indeed, the manifest theme of the Book of Mormon is the arrival and settlement of Hebrews in the Americas before the Christian era. The American Indians were descended from one of these fugitives, Laman, who rebelled against the father-leader Lehi. This rebellion caused the Lamanites, the ancestors of the American Indians, to be cursed with a dark skin. Into the details of the Book of Mormon we need not enter. The point is that Mormons believe themselves to be Israelites in a literal sense and also to be closely related to the Indians, who are also physically descended from Israelites. The Mormons, then, are a continuation of what the fathers of the Christian church were to come to call the old Israel. But for Mormons there is no old Israel. They simply regard themselves as Israel in a new stage of its history (the process of "adoption" often referred to by Mormons cannot be discussed here).[1]

If we compare the Mormon attitude to Israel with the attitudes expressed in the early Christian church, certain similarities and contrasts appear. Among certain Jewish-Christian groups, who were later opposed by the dominant currents in the church, there were doubtless many who retained an emphasis on the biological or physical continuity between themselves as Christians and the Jewish people, or Israel. But such Jewish Christians (if they existed in any number), for reasons we cannot discuss here, ceased to be historically important. We do not find in the New Testament any insistence on any possible biological or physical or genealogical continuity between Christians and Jews. In fact, in some documents, Israel after the flesh is denigrated.[2] Instead we may roughly distinguish three attitudes. In some documents we find the notion that the gospel is simply a form of Judaism, in others that it is the antithesis of it, and in still others that it is the fulfillment of it.[3] Only in the writings of Paul do we have an emphasis on the continuity

---

1. The significance of the adoption of Mormons into the people of Israel over against what he regards as our overemphasis on the genealogical or physical relationship between Mormons and Israelites was urged on me by Professor Louis Midgley. But in the current concordances to the Book of Mormon and the Doctrine and Covenants there is no item under the term "adoption." According to D&C 84:34 the members of the two Mormons priesthoods become the seed of Moses and of Abraham, but in D&C 103:17 the Mormons as a whole are "the children of Israel and of the seed of Abraham." To Brigham Young, Mormons were "my people Israel," D&C 136:22. But here the word "adoption" is missing.

2. This theme cannot be carefully considered here. See W. D. Davies, "Paul and the People of Israel," *NTS* 24 (1977): 4–39.

3. See W. D. Davies, *The Gospel and the Land: Early Christianity and Jewish Territorial Doctrine* (Berkeley: University of California Press, 1974), 400–401.

of the church with Israel and a recognition of the significance of its role in history that is in any way comparable with what we find in Mormonism. But in Paul also the continuity to which he points has nothing to do with biological or genealogical continuity. In this he too differs radically from what we find in Mormonism.

Here, then, in its understanding of its physical continuity with Israel (so that Mormons can regard themselves as physically related to Israelites and to the Indians of the American continent, who were originally Israelites), Mormonism offers what seems to be a novel treatment of what we might call the Jewish question. It is as far removed from anti-Semitism and even anti-Judaism as it can be. There is instead what one might almost call a pro-Semitism as expressed for example in appendix 18 of James E. Talmage's *The Articles of Faith*. There we read: "[T]he destruction of Jerusalem by the Romans . . . witnesses that every nation that fought against Israel, or in any way oppressed them, passed away."[4] Contrast this with the almost standard New Testament understanding of the fall of Jerusalem. That document regards that event as a due and just punishment for the Jewish people who were held responsible for the putting of Jesus to death by the Romans. I do not know how the Mormon interpreters reconcile their position with this interpretation given by the New Testament. Certainly they do not, as it has been claimed, deny that the New Testament — whether rightly or wrongly

---

4. James E. Talmage, *The Articles of Faith* (Salt Lake City: The Church of Jesus Christ of Latter-day Saints, 1947), 514. The whole passage reads as follows:

. . . Time will show the same general result from the destruction of Jerusalem to the millennium. The Prophet Isaiah, speaking of the time when the Lord should favor Israel, said, "All they that were incensed against thee shall be ashamed and confounded: they shall be as nothing; and they that strive with thee shall perish" (41:11). "I will feed them that oppress thee with their own flesh; and they shall be drunken with their own blood" (49:26). "I have taken out of thine hand the cup of trembling, even the dregs of the cup of my fury; thou shalt no more drink it again: but I will put it into the hand of them that afflict thee; which have said to thy soul Bow down, that we may go over." — A *Compendium of the Doctrines of the Gospel*, by Elders Franklin D. Richards and James A. Little, pp. 228, 229.

3. *Israel among the Nations* — "When we reflect that it is thirty-two centuries since the enemies of Israel began to oppress them in the land of Canaan, that about one-third of the time they were a people in that land they were more or less in bondage to their enemies; that seven hundred years before the coming of Christ the ten tribes were scattered throughout western Asia; that we have no record that any have as yet returned to the land of their inheritance; that nearly six hundred years before Christ the Babylonish captivity took place, and that, according to the Book of Esther, only a part of the Jews ever returned, but were scattered through the one hundred twenty-seven provinces of the Persian empire; that Asia was the hive from which swarmed the nomadic tribes who over-ran Europe; that at the destruction of Jerusalem by the Romans the Jews were scattered over the known world; we may well ask the question, Does not Israel today constitute a very large proportion of the human family?" — *Compendium*, Elders F. D. Richards and James A. Little, p. 89.

does not concern us here — sometimes does place on Jews responsibility for the Roman crucifixion.[5]

There is also the same difference in attitude toward the dispersion of the Jews. Both in Pharisaic Judaism and in early Christianity there is little attempt to find any blessing in the exile of Jews from their homeland in Palestine. There is a remarkably strange absence of any developed theology of exile in Judaism. Passages regarding the exile as having atoning value are few; rather, that event is regarded as an undesirable disaster. The exiled life is a squalid life.[6] So too in early Christianity the dispersion of the Jews, greatly increasing after the fall of Jerusalem, was regarded as punishment for their rejection of Jesus. Later Christendom (I hope that I may be allowed here to distinguish Christianity from Christendom) found the Jews everywhere a problem. Christians first tolerated them in their midst if they became converts; they then later proceeded to find Jews intolerable and placed them in ghettoes. And in the twentieth century they went even further. In some quarters it was tacitly preferred that Jews should not exist at all, and "the final solution" of their annihilation, which culminated in the Holocaust, was offered and pursued.

As compared to this, the Mormon attitude toward Jews is extremely refreshing. But it presents problems of a historical character. To name only two, there is the historical problem caused by the understanding of the Lamanite-Indian relationship and the presence of Jews in pre-Christian America; and related to all this, apart from the doctrine of "adoption," there is the difficulty of finding a verifiable physical genealogical connection between Jews and such obviously British and Scandinavian figures as peopled the early Mormon movement.[7] But leaving aside the grounds on which Mormonism founded its pro-Semitism, its reality is clear and fresh. The tone as much as the substance of the words of Mormon leaders concerning Jews[8] is miles re-

---

5. It is striking, however, that in the passages where the cross emerges in the Book of Mormon and in the Doctrine and Covenants the Jews are not explicitly mentioned as responsible for it; rather, the cross is dealt with in broad terms. See 1 Nephi 11:33 and 3 Nephi 27:14. It is surprising how few references to the cross occur in the Book of Mormon. In the index to the Doctrine and Covenants no item entitled "cross" occurs. But in D&C 18:11 and 35:2 there is again no specific reference to the role of Jews in the crucifixion but concentration on the suffering of Christ for all men. All this may be significant as pointing to the absence of any anti-Judaism in Mormonism.

6. See Davies, *The Gospel and the Land*, 120 n. 113.

7. This historical problem will be familiar to students of Mormonism. It arises from two causes. First, there is the strictly factual or historical connection of Israelites with the Americas in the pre-Christian era, and second, arising from and bound up with this, the question of the nature of the visions reported by Joseph Smith and the literary genre of the Book of Mormon. Should the contents of the latter be taken as historical, or does not the Book of Mormon rather belong to the genre of the apocalyptic and pseudepigraphical literature? These two immense problems can only be indicated here.

8. See n. 4 above. Mormonism is millennial: the Jews will be gathered at the end of the days, as will their relatives the American Indians. See 1 Nephi 10:3, 14; 2 Nephi 3:5; 10:50–59;

moved from the climate which made possible the Holocaust in our time, a climate not often opposed and even fostered by the Christian tradition.

It agrees with this benign attitude toward the Jewish dispersion that Mormons hold that in the last days, while the Jews will be gathered at Jerusalem, the Israelites on the new continent — the American Indians and Mormons — will come to Zion built here in this land by the members of the Mormon Church. This has been a continuous part of Mormon doctrine (D&C 29:7; 45:43, 57:1).

This emphasis on the continuance of Israel up to the end of history introduces us to a theme which is dividing New Testament scholars very radically at this time.[9] The geographic and physical actuality of the redemption or return of Jews to Zion as developed in the Mormon tradition has no parallel in the New Testament. It is possible that Jewish Christianity and even some early fathers retained such a hope.[10] But the one nearest to Mormons in spirit, if not in substance, at this point is Saint Paul.

To sum up, then, Mormonism, like most radical movements, is conservative. It first is a return: it follows the French notion of "return" and gathering: *recueillir pour mieux sauter.* The Mormons regard themselves as Israel — in some sense physically or genealogically so. And in many points of doctrine, while they differ from the New Testament as normally interpreted, they offer salutary emphases, even though it might be argued that they do so for debatable reasons. But they go even further: they regard themselves not only as returning by descent to Israel, but as reliving the life of Israel in their own lives. This brings us to the second point of our paper. Mormonism is a restoration of Israel.

Mormonism as the Restoration of Israel

The emergence of Mormonism, as far as I am aware, has seldom been characterized in terms of messianism: Joseph Smith did not regard himself as the Messiah, nor was he so regarded by his followers, although he was given an eminent status. Nevertheless, to anyone familiar with messianic movements, the parallels with Mormonism are striking. Similarly there are features of

---

20:22; 21:12; 25:11; 3 Nephi 16:4, 5; 20:11–19, 28, 29, 33, 46; 21:1, 22, 29; Mormon 5:14; Ether 13:10, 11.

9. See Davies, "Paul and the People of Israel," where the views of Rosemary Radford Ruether and Krister Stendahl are discussed. For a trenchant rebuttal of Ruether, see John M. Oesterreicher, *The Anatomy of Contempt: A Critique of R. R. Ruether's "Faith and Fratricide,"* The Institute of Judaeo-Christian Studies Paper no. 4 (South Orange, N.J.: Institute of Judaeo-Christian Studies, Seton Hall University, 1975).

10. The evidence has not been garnered but reference may be made to J. Daniélou, *Theologie du Judéo-Christianisme,* vol. 1: *Histoire des Doctrines Chrétiennes Avant Nicée* (Tournai, Belgium: Desclée & Cie, 1958). A careful reading of Daniélou from this point of view is profitable.

Mormonism which recall the apocalyptic and pseudepigraphic literature. I recall the shock with which, on turning from a study of the Sabbatian messianic movement, I recognized the same features in Mormonism — enthusiasm, repentance, a vivid anticipation of the end, and the dual roles of Sabbatai Svi and Nathan of Giza, strangely repeated — *mutatis mutandis* — in those of Joseph Smith and Brigham Young.[11]

In a broad sense, therefore, I do not think it misleading to think of Mormonism as a kind of messianic or eschatological movement; it regarded itself as a millennial movement. This illumines the aspect of it with which we now deal — that of restoration. Ever since Hermann Gunkel wrote his famous study, *Schöpfung und Chaos in Urzeit und Endzeit,* it has been recognized that eschatological movements are governed to a large extent by the notion that the end of creation and of history or the goal of history is to be like its beginning: the Greek phrase for this is *ta eschata hôs to prôta,* meaning "The last things are as the first." In Jewish apocalyptic it is expressed as *kᵉgô'êl achrôn kᵉgô'êl r'ishôn;* or "The last Redeemer is as the first Redeemer."[12]

This principle was very operative in Mormonism (although, let it be repeated, Joseph Smith was not viewed as a Messiah).[13] It has been pointed out that Mormonism did not accept the doctrine of the fall of Adam as introducing among his posterity a *crippling* inability to do the good. Here it is nearer to Christian tradition in its mainstream than to Judaism.[14] But, as Dr. Nibley has illumined for us, Mormonism does recognize an "ecclesiastical" fall as in a lesser degree does Protestantism generally.[15] In a loose way Mormons may be compared with Rudolf Sohm and Adolf Harnack at this point. They hold that the early Christians "did not retain the kingdom of God after the second century of the Christian era; that from that time to the present, they have had no more authority to administer Christian ordinances than Apostate Jews; and that all their forms and ordinances, and ministrations, are an abomination in the sight of God." This is "the great Apostasy of

---

11. The classic volume for all this is G. Scholem, *Sabbatai Svi: The Mystic Messiah, 1626–76,* now excellently translated into English by R. J. Zwi Werblowsky (Princeton: Princeton University Press, 1973).

12. On this see H. J. Schoeps, *Theologie und Geschichte des Judenchristentums* (Tübingen: Mohr, 1959).

13. To judge from the Doctrine and Covenants, Joseph Smith was chosen for the work of the Lord, D&C 3:9; ordained an apostle, 20:2; was seer, translator, prophet, elder as well as apostle, 21:1; 124:125. He was to be the sole receiver of revelations, 28:2; he received a heavenly vision and conversed with Christ, 76:1–14. But though like Christ it was necessary that he seal his testimony with his blood, 136:39, at no point is he designated Messiah. He witnesses to the latter. Nothing reveals the distinction between Joseph Smith and the Messiah more than that he was commanded to repent, 5:21; 93:47; and the claim that if he did not abide in the Lord, another would be sent for in his stead, 35:18; compare 3:9–11. The Lord in 35:18 is undoubtedly Jesus, but he is also the Lord God. See 35:1–2; 34:1.

14. Compare Davies, *The Gospel and the Land,* 396–98.

15. Hugh W. Nibley, in personal correspondence.

the Christian Church," which commenced in the first century.[16] Mormonism is an attempt to go behind the corruption of this "ecclesiastical" fall and to restore a kind of primordial Jewish pre-Christian communion between man and God, to reestablish Christ's church, and at the same time to reenact the life of the Israel of God. This was to be not simply a restoration of Hebrew ideals but also a restoration of the Hebrew institutions and experience. This restorative tendency is found in the New Testament itself, and clearly in the Dead Sea Scrolls and elsewhere, but it is especially marked in Mormonism. Let us substantiate this under the following headings.

First, Mormons came to see themselves as a part of a renewed Israel, born in a covenant of "the children of Israel, and of the seed of Abraham," led by one like unto Moses (D&C 103:17).[17]

Second, this Israel was in the wilderness, as was the former Israel: it has been called out of the wilderness (see D&C 5:14; 33:5).[18] Joseph Smith, the one like unto Moses, received commandments as did Moses. True, the com-

---

16. See Thomas F. O'Dea, *The Mormons* (1957; Chicago: University of Chicago Press, 1975), 134. According to John A. Widtsoe, *A Rational Theology* (Salt Lake City, 1915), as cited by O'Dea, "For seventeen centuries these falsehoods continued. Such is the religion 'of the papal, Greek, and Protestant Churches of the nineteenth century.... Instead of having apostles, prophets, and other inspired men in the church now, receiving visions, dreams, revelations, ministrations of angels, and prophecies for the calling of officers, and for the government of the church — they have a wicked, corrupt, uninspired pope, or uninspired archbishops, bishops, clergymen, etc., who have a great variety of corrupt forms of Godliness, but utterly deny the gift of revelation, and every other miraculous power which always characterized Christ's Church.'" On the notion of a fall in the history of the church in Sohm and Harnack, see my "A Normative Pattern of Church Life in the New Testament," reprinted in *Christian Origins and Judaism*, ed. W. D. Davies (London: Darton, Longman & Todd, 1962), esp. 202–5.

17. The idea of the eternity of covenants in Mormonism made any supersession of the old covenant by the new (that is, any fundamental demotion, let along destruction, of the old covenant) utterly uncongenial. Also unacceptable was the notion of the old covenant as merely promissory of or preparatory to a new, as in the New Testament. Compare O'Dea, *The Mormons*, 136. But the doctrine of the everlasting covenants is not always clear. The last covenant of baptism ordained by Joseph Smith causes "all old covenants to be done away with" and yet this new covenant was from the beginning. The passage in D&C 22:1–4 reads as follows:

> Behold, I say unto you that all old covenants have I caused to be done away in this thing; and this is a new and an everlasting covenant, even that which was from the beginning.
> Wherefore, although a man should be baptized an hundred times it availeth him nothing, for you cannot enter in at the strait gate by the law of Moses, neither by your dead works.
> For it is because of your dead works that I have caused this last covenant and this church to be built up unto me, even as in days of old.
> Wherefore, enter ye in at the gate, as I have commanded, and seek not to counsel your God. Amen.

18. D&C 5:14: "And to none else will I grant this power, to receive this same testimony among this generation, in this the beginning of the rising up and the coming forth of my church out of the wilderness — clear as the moon, and fair as the sun, and terrible as an army with banners." D&C 33:5: "And verily, verily, I say unto you, that this church have I established and called forth out of the wilderness."

mandments of Moses did not enable anyone to enter by the straight gate, and Joseph Smith contrasts his covenant with that of Moses; nevertheless, the president, Joseph Smith, was to be like Moses. In D&C 28:2 we read: "But, behold, verily, verily, I say unto thee, no one shall be appointed to receive commandments and revelations in this church excepting my servant Joseph Smith, Jun., for he receiveth them even as Moses." Here there is an unambiguous endorsement of Moses. Contrast the tentativeness and ambiguity with which Moses is often surrounded in the New Testament, as for example in John 1:17.

Third, like Israel of old, Joseph Smith and his people are pilgrims marching to a promised land, the center of which is a Zion, a New Jerusalem. As Abraham, Isaac, Jacob, and Joseph had prospered in this world as part of and as a result of their covenant with God, so would the new chosen people (who early thought of themselves as spiritual and, as we saw, even literal descendants of the old) prosper under the new covenant. As in Judaism the city of Zion came to be regarded as the quintessence of the totality of the land, so in Mormonism. As for Zion, the City of Holiness, Joseph Smith claimed to have found a reference to it in papyri containing a story older than that found in Genesis. This city — the City of Holiness, even Zion, the city of Enoch — "was to return to earth to dwell amid the holy city to be built by the Mormons."[19] (See Moses 7:62–63.)

Fourth, just as in the Old Testament and Judaism, Zion — that is Jerusalem — was to be a kind of world center to which the scattered peoples of Israel (more strictly, of Judah — that is, Jews descended from that tribe) were to return, so also the Zion envisioned by Mormonism was to witness a return of all other Israelites from whom Mormons came or into whom they had been "adopted." All this means that the millennialism of the prophetic and the apocalyptic traditions of Judaism was taken over by the Mormons.[20]

This reference to the prophetic and apocalyptic makes clear that apocalyptic was one strong aspect of the matrix of Mormonism. But this was not its only matrix. It has been customary to put prophecy and apocalyptic over against the Law, as its antithesis. This notion dominated the work of R. H. Charles, who edited the Apocrypha and Pseudepigrapha. Recent scholarship has corrected this false antithesis.[21] The prophets have now been seen to be directly dependent at many points on the priestly tradition. It is striking that, by another route, the priestly tradition has also come into its own in Mormonism. Part of the restorative aspect of Mormonism was the reintro-

---

19. On this section see O'Dea, *The Mormons*, 134–315.

20. On Zion, see D&C 63:24, 36; 103:20; 45:71; 66:11; 62:4; 64:30; 101:20, 70, 74; 133:12; 84:2.

21. See, for example, "Apocalyptic and Pharisaism," in my *Christian Origins and Judaism*, 19–30.

duction of the importance of priesthood: the Aaronic priesthood and that of Melchizedek came to be revived or reintroduced into the Mormon community. There is an endemic anticlericalism in Mormonism from its beginning: in true democratic fashion it has emphasized the active participation of all the members in the religious life of the community. But simultaneously it has also combined this with a developing concept of the priestly office. The movement developed a lay priesthood elaborately organized into two orders or subdivisions; the lower, called the Aaronic or Levitical priesthood, is believed to have been restored through the ordination of Joseph Smith and Oliver Cowdery in 1829 at Harmony, Pennsylvania, under the hands of an angel, who announced himself as John, the same that is called the Baptist in the New Testament.[22] The higher or Melchizedek priesthood is believed to have been restored through the miraculous intervention of Peter, James, and John, at a time which is uncertain.[23] As in ancient Israel, priests are ordained by the laying on of hands.

It is not necessary to enlarge further here on the priesthood except to reiterate that it is part of a wider restorative process in the life of Israel. Part of the same process can be seen in the numerical aspects of the Mormon organization. Some numbers like that of the ninety-six members of the council of elders (D&C 107:89) suggest no biblical parallel that I am aware of, but the use of the number 70 for the elders who are called to be traveling missionaries and of the number 12 for the council, under the direction of which they work (107:23, 25), recall not only the Twelve and Seventy of the Gospels but the twelve tribes and the twelve patriarchs and the seventy elders of the Old Testament in the period of the wilderness (Exod. 24:1; Num. 11:16). The priestly tradition of the Old Testament, so long separated from the prophetic and the apocalyptic in much Christian interpretation of the Old Testament

---

22. D&C 13: "Upon you my fellow servants, in the name of Messiah I confer the Priesthood of Aaron, which holds the keys of ministering of angels, and of the gospel of repentance, and of baptism by immersion for the remission of sins; and this shall never be taken again from the earth, until the sons of Levi do offer again an offering unto the Lord in righteousness."

23. D&C 68:19; 107:18; 124:123. D&C 84:14–19 reads as follows:

Which Abraham received the priesthood from Melchizedek, who received it through the lineage of his fathers, even till Noah;

And from Noah till Enoch, through the lineage of their fathers;

And from Enoch to Abel, who was slain by the conspiracy of his brother, who received the priesthood by the commandments of God, by the hand of his father Adam, who was the first man —

Which priesthood continueth in the church of God in all generations, and is without beginning of days or end of years.

And the Lord confirmed a priesthood also upon Aaron and his seed, throughout all their generations, which priesthood also continueth and abideth forever with the priesthood which is after the holiest order of God.

And this greater priesthood administereth the gospel and holdeth the key of the mysteries of the kingdom, even the key of the knowledge of God.

and of Judaism, is given a new attention and respect in Mormonism and reunited with these. Here it is tempting to think that Mormonism — apparently so essentially a child of New World Protestantism and so suspicious of the great Evil church[24] — at first glance and very paradoxically is more akin to Catholicism than to the Protestantism within which it arose.

But there are other elements of restoration. In particular the reference just made to the patriarchs is here highly important. Mormonism held that covenants were eternal and so revived the polygamous marriage which most, though not all, the patriarchs of the Old Testament had practiced. It justified polygamy in terms of the patriarchs. Plural marriage, then, which constituted at one point a central aspect of the worldview of Mormonism and a symbol of its separateness and of its innovative character, was in fact an aspect of its restorative thrust.[25] It was even suggested later (although never officially) that there was polygamy in the New Testament and that Jesus had married Mary and Martha.[26] The account of the revelation leading to polygamy makes the restorative purpose clear. Here again it is not germane to our purpose to enlarge upon this aspect of Mormonism except insofar as it illumines the continuity of Mormon practice with that of ancient Israel and points clearly to the restorative tendency in Mormonism. The familial emphasis in modern Mormonism, which has now officially abandoned polygamy, belongs to the same emphasis.[27]

Time does not allow us to enlarge further upon this attempt to recapitulate or to restore the life of ancient Israel in the Mormon community. Let it only be stated that the emphasis on the geographic dimension of the Jewish life and hope to which we shall soon devote our attention also belongs to this category of the "restorative." But the geographic dimensions of Mormonism — its materiality — illustrate not merely its principle of restoration but — and very vividly and concretely — its principle of reinterpretation. Thus we turn next to our third section: Mormonism as reinterpretation.

---

24. O'Dea, *The Mormons*, 34.

25. D&C 132:37, 38, 40. O'Dea, *The Mormons*, 139, quotes Parley P. Pratt, *Key to the Science of Theology* (Liverpool and London, 1855), 163:

> It was a law of the ancient Priesthood, and is again restored, that a man who is faithful in all things, may, by the word of the Lord, through the administration of one holding the keys to bind on earth and heaven, receive and secure to himself, for time and all eternity, *more than one wife.*
>
> Thus did Abraham, Isaac, Jacob, Moses, the Patriarchs and Prophets of old.

See also Orson Pratt, *The Bible and Polygamy* (Salt Lake City, 1874).

26. T. B. H. Stenhouse, *Rocky Mountain Saints* (London, 1874), 485.

27. D&C, "Official Declaration" by Wilford Woodruff, 24 September 1890. This was endorsed on 6 October 1890 by the man who would become the next president of the Church of Jesus Christ of Latter-day Saints, Lorenzo Snow.

Reinterpretation or Transference in Mormonism

So far we have emphasized the continuity in Mormon existence — continuity especially with the Jewish people. Continuity between Judaism and the Christian faith is present very markedly in parts of the New Testament, but this is even more emphasized in Mormonism. We now turn in our last section to the discontinuity in Mormonism. This discontinuity arises not so much out of the rejection of the Judeo-Christian tradition as out of its reinterpretation. In the particular aspect of Mormonism with which we shall now be concerned, that is, the territorial, it involves what we can call the transference of categories or their radical redirection.

It is no accident that it is in the territorial dimension that reinterpretation and discontinuity are most marked. In social and religious arrangements the memory of the usages of the people of Israel could be normative and regulative. Given the stance of Mormonism, they were naturally copied. But in territorial matters emulation was not so easy; in fact, it was in any direct manner impracticable, if not impossible. Here the actualities of the American experience of the Mormons become actively significant. But to understand this, certain aspects of the self-understanding of Israel in the Old Testament have to be recalled.

First, the God of Israel, although peculiarly related to Israel as his chosen people, remained the God of heaven and earth. Even in the Israelite context, there was a cosmic, a this-worldly, earth-encompassing dimension to his being and purpose. The Redeemer of Israel was the Creator. Creation and redemption were inseparable. This meant that the material world, not only the so-called spiritual world, was his concern. This cosmic materialism, if we may so express it, of the God of Israel is much emphasized in Mormonism, which refuses to make any sharp distinction between the material and the spiritual. For example, the human body is important, the *physical* earth and *physical* actualities. Mormonism, on one side, is as highly materialistic as it can be, as is essential Christianity always.

But this further helps to explain why the land of Israel was as important to the people of Israel as the Old Testament claims it to have been. It was the land of promise in the life of Israel. (I am not so certain that the emphasis on the land of Israel as especially belonging to God himself is as emphasized in Mormonism.) And the quintessence of the land was Jerusalem, Zion.

In agreement, then, with its "material" emphasis, if I may so put it — an emphasis which paradoxically did not, as it did in Israelite religion, preclude an equally emphatic "otherworldliness" — Mormonism took over the notions of the inseparability of cosmic renewal and human spiritual renewal and also the notion of a promised land and a promised city. Mormons may be defined as a people in search of a land and a city which, indeed, like the Jews in the case of Jerusalem and Eretz Israel, they do distinguish.[28]

But where was their promised land? Like many cultures, the Mormon culture had to find a center for its promised land. In Judaism, Israel is the center of the world, Jerusalem is the center of Israel, and the Temple, resting on the Rock on and around which all the universe was built, is the center of Jerusalem. We find in Mormonism a quest for this center. But the quest becomes an American one, even while Jerusalem remains the center for Jews (of Judah, that is, strictly Judaite Jews). For Mormons — the other Israelites — the promised land becomes this side of the world, the Americas. And the center? In ancient Israel, there were many centers at first — Bethel, Shechem, Samaria, until finally Jerusalem reigned as the *centrum mundi*. So too in Mormonism. The movement from the beginning to Kirtland, Ohio, was a search for the center and its temple. Later Missouri, and Nauvoo in Illinois, gained that honor, and finally, Zion was built in Salt Lake City. As I read the sources, however, Missouri remained the *centrum mundi par excellence,* despite the actuality of Salt Lake City and the temple there.[29] But be this as it may, there is, then, a very marked territorial dimension to Mormonism. It took literally the territorial prophecies of the Old Testament, appropriated the Old Testament claim that occupancy and permanence in the promised land were dependent on the keeping of the commandments, and wherever it went insisted that the Temple was necessary to hold back the overwhelming chaos that can break out if it is neglected. The territoriality of Judaism is reinterpreted by Americanizing it. The new reality of America imposed itself on the scriptural substructure of Mormonism. This land of America superseded the memory of the land of Israel in the Mormon mind even when that mind remained true to that memory and nourished itself upon it.

Does not Mormonism radically depart from Christianity in all this? Yes and no. In the New Testament there are several ways in which the territorialism of Judaism and Jewish apocalyptic is dealt with: by rejection, spiritualization, historicization, sacramental concentration.[30] Possibly in Jewish Christianity, whose sources are largely lost to us, the centrality of the land of Israel and of Jerusalem was retained. There is some evidence that this was so.[31] In this case there is again a point of contact between Mormonism and Judaism through Jewish Christianity. But does not Mormonism, in retaining so much of the literal interpretation of the apocalyptic tradition, depart from the main elements of early Christianity which either ignore, spiritualize, sacramentalize, or historicize the land and Jerusalem? It seems so.

---

28. On The Land, that is, Eretz Israel, in Judaism, see my work *The Gospel and the Land.*
29. D&C 52:42; 57:1, 2; 62:6. Independence, Missouri, was the *centrum mundi.*
30. See the conclusion to Davies, *The Gospel and the Land.*
31. See above, n. 10.

And yet there are factors we must recognize. First, there is the comparative ease with which Mormons, at immense cost, were able to transcend place. They moved from Kirtland, to Missouri, to Nauvoo, to Salt Lake City. They were never tied to a place but remained sojourners and pilgrims. One striking fact illustrates the essential importance of this. When Brigham Young was faced with the threat of federal troops being sent to take over the land of Utah and the city the Mormons built, what did he do? He did not declare an open city to save the city and the state as the French declared Paris an open city in World War II. Instead he decided to abandon the city of the federal troops and declared a policy of "scorched earth."[32] Place was not the ultimate concern, but the community. This means that already during the lifetime of Brigham Young himself space was subordinated to the covenanted people, to time. Mormons have had centers in Ohio, Illinois, and Missouri, but they left them all and made a home in Utah; and they were prepared to leave that.

There is another factor pointing to this transcendence of territory. Wherever Mormons have taken over a new missionary field, they have first sanctified it and declared it holy unto the Lord. But this implies that all places have become open to the Divine Presence. The widespread missionary thrust of Mormonism, although always centered in Zion[33] in Utah, has the effect of dissipating its territorial intensity. Temples are now being built in far-flung places. As a result geographic concentration must necessarily wane. And coincident with this is the same spiritualizing of the concept of the land and Jerusalem as we found in early Christianity. The words of Thomas O'Dea in connection with the building of a first temple in Switzerland deserve quotation: "[I]t testifies to the first stage in the separation of the Mormon notion of Zion and the gathering from a definite piece of land and from the New World. A more abstract, more spiritualized conception of the gathering, in which a Mormon way of life is seen as possible without physical removal to and residence in a Mormon community in America, is developing."[34] If so, then Mormonism is approaching more nearly to the main development of territorial theology in the main Christian bodies; that is, it is gradually becoming deterritorialized and approaching more closely to the thought of an ancient hymn:

> Jesus, where'er thy people meet
> There they behold thy mercy seat,
> Where'er they seek thee thou art found,
> And every place is hallowed ground.

32. O'Dea, *The Mormons,* 102
33. From the early Utah days the Mormons considered Utah as Zion. They planned eventually to return to Missouri, the ultimate capital of the Zion which would include all of the American continent.
34. O'Dea, *The Mormons,* 118.

> For Thou within no walls confined,
> Inhabitest the humble mind.
> Such, ever bring Thee where they come
> And, going, take Thee to their home.

In this it seems that Mormons and other Christians can join. Joseph Smith is himself reported to have said that Zion is where are "the pure in heart."[35]

Summary

To recapitulate very crudely: Mormonism asserts its continuity with Israel even genealogically. It *returns* to the roots of Judaism and Christianity in Israel. It also *restores* the forms of Israel that it regards as having been corrupted by both religions through a kind of "ecclesiastical" fall. Its substructure and its structures are in the Old Testament and the New Testament. But it also reinterprets and accommodates or transfers ancient forms, in a very remarkable way, to an American setting and mode. Mormonism is the Jewish-Christian tradition in an American key.

Finally, I hazard a suggestion. Mormonism arose in a place and time when many utopian, populist, socialistic ideas were in the air. It gave to these a disciplined, organized American outlet and form: what it did was to re-Judaize a Christianity that had been too much Hellenized. But note that parallel with this American movement was a European movement, Marxist Communism, which also, from one point of view at least, was a protest against the false spiritualization of a too much Hellenized Christianity that had neglected its Judaic roots — a protest in judgment.[36] Let it be clear. We do not claim that there is any direct contact between Mormonism and Marxist Communism. But the former is the American expression of many of the same forces that led in Europe to Marxism. Mormonism certainly injected, and I hope will continue to inject, into the American scene the realism of Judaism and thus challenged a too-Hellenized Christianity to renew its contact with its roots in Israel. Is it too much to hope that by mutual interaction both Mormonism and traditional Christianity can be instructed, and even corrected and possibly changed?

---

35. D&C 92:21: "Therefore, verily, thus saith the Lord, let Zion rejoice, for this is Zion — THE PURE IN HEART; therefore, let Zion rejoice, while all the wicked shall mourn." Compare D&C 101:18. Nevertheless, Mormons retain the hope of a territorial "gathering" of Israel in the future.

36. See Davies, *The Gospel and the Land*, 385–89, esp. 388.

Chapter 12

The Mormon "Canon"

Uniqueness is always hard to substantiate: Christians, Jews, and Gentiles have been related in many varied and complex ways. But there seems to be no parallel to the way in which Mormons — while claiming to be Christians — assert as well that they are genealogically connected with Jews and that they are therefore physically a rediscovered, restored, and reinterpreted "Israel." As far as I am aware they constitute a very special, if not unique, case of Christians among Jews and Gentiles since by implication they have redefined all three of these terms.[1] We here reflect on one aspect of Mormon life: their fixation of their own "canon."[2]

The attitude of the Church of Jesus Christ of Latter-day Saints, or the Mormons, to scripture is unusual — undeniably radical if not unique. Certain factors govern the way in which Mormons have been led to their formation of their own canon of scriptures which is both similar to and different from Protestant, Roman Catholic, and Orthodox canons of scripture.

There can be no question that Mormons regard themselves as Christians. They affirm that they have Jewish roots and belong to and emerge within the tradition which is rooted in the OT and the NT. Both Testaments are explicitly stated to be canonical for them. The *Articles of Faith* of the Mormon Church were published on 1 March 1842, twelve years after the organization of the church, as "The Wentworth Letter."[3] The eighth article reads: "We believe the Bible to be the word of God as far as it is translated correctly." By the term "Bible" is meant the Hebrew Bible and the NT. The Apocrypha, accepted as canonical by the Roman Catholic Church but about which the Greek Orthodox Church is ambiguous, is not canonical but is nevertheless valuable. The prophet Joseph Smith, the founder of Mormonism, is reported to have prayed to know whether the Apocrypha contained God's holy word.

---

1. See W. D. Davies, "Israel, the Mormons, and the Land," in *Reflections on Mormonism, Judaeo-Christian Parallels* (Provo, Utah: Brigham Young University Press, 1978), 79–97. Reprinted above as chapter 11.

2. The term "canon" as applied to Mormonism is not without difficulty. That is why I have placed the term "canon" in quotation marks in the title and introduction. Hereafter these marks are omitted, except where otherwise necessary.

3. In *Times and Seasons* 3 (1842): 706–19.

On 9 March 1833, at Kirtland, Ohio, he received the following reply by revelation: "Verily thus saith the Lord unto you concerning the Apocrypha. There
are many things contained therein that are true, and it is mostly translated
correctly. There are many things therein that are not true, which are in-
terpolations by the hands of men" (D&C 91:1–2; see below, p. 233, for an
explanation of this abbreviation). For this reason it was decreed by Joseph
Smith that it was not necessary that the Apocrypha should be translated
again (D&C 91:3), and it did not become a part of the Mormon canon.[4]

The Bible as the Mormons knew and spoke of it was the English translation known as the King James Version (KJV), published in 1611. But in
the eighth *Article of Faith,* already cited, the Bible is accepted as canonical
only "as far as it is translated correctly." This qualification is important. On
15 October 1843, Joseph Smith declared that "I believe the Bible as it read
when it came forth from the pen of the original writers. Ignorant translators, careless transcribers, or designing and corrupt priests have committed
many errors."[5] This is not surprising. Earlier, in June 1830, Joseph Smith had
already reported that God had revealed to him that many things had been

---

4. On the Apocrypha, see the fascinating article by J. M. Ross, "The Status of the Apocrypha," *Theology* 82 (May 1979): 183–91. I am indebted to the (unpublished) paper of one of
my students, Father Dimitri Cozby, on "Orthodox Christian Views of the Disputed Books of the
Old Testament," in which bibliographical data are given. He confirms

> the dominating view among Orthodox theologians in that the disputed books rightfully
> belong in the OT and are in some sense divinely inspired, but that they are to be distin-
> guished from the books of the short canon. The precise implications of this distinction
> are not spelled out, however, though it does not apparently preclude their reading in pub-
> lic worship as well as for private edification. One should also remember that this position
> lacks official sanction and universal acceptance and is questioned by Orthodox theolo-
> gians of repute. Regarding terminology, both "deuterocanonical" and *"anagignoskomena"*
> seem to be acceptable designations, but the latter is perhaps preferable due to its Patristic
> origin.

Truman G. Madsen, professor at Brigham Young University, in a private note of 20 June 1985
and orally, reminds me, however, that "considerable care was taken to include the Apocrypha
with the biblical materials placed in the cornerstone of the Nauvoo Temple. And Joseph Smith
is reported to have said of the Apocrypha that " 'it required much of the Spirit' to discern the
truths within it." See Edward L. Stevenson, *Reminiscences of Joseph the Prophet* (Salt Lake City:
private publication, 1893). Madsen goes on to say:

> The declaration that "there are many things contained therein [the Apocrypha] which
> are true and it is mostly translated correctly" has been sometimes extended by Mormons
> to apply to other extra-canonical materials. With the Dead Sea Scrolls came the dis-
> covery that *many biblical books* have earlier Hebrew and Aramaic texts. The question
> has been raised again "Are they scripture or important supplements?" Typically, Mormons
> deny such volumes canonical status while tending to the view that in some cases they
> precede and in others echo authentic biblical materials. They are sympathetic to the view
> that many extra-canonical writings may reflect inspired source materials.

5. In *The History of the Church of Latter-day Saints,* second edition with introduction and
notes by B. H. Roberts (1902; Salt Lake City: Deseret, 1964), 6.57 (henceforth *HC*). The *HC* is
the history of Joseph Smith, the prophet, by himself.

taken from the words that Moses himself had written, but that some of these were to be recovered. The OT, as it stands, is therefore lacking in many ways. Convinced that he was inspired by the spirit of the ancient prophets, Smith believed that he could seek to detect by the gift of discernment what was not in accordance with the Spirit in the Bible and also recognize that much that was originally in it had been either taken away from it or lost.

This conviction lies behind the claim to his having had an early divine commission to revise the Bible. In D&C we read of a revelation given at Kirtland, Ohio, on 7 March 1831. This revelation concerning the future repeats much of the apocalyptic teaching of the NT. It reaches a point where the following words occur: "And now, behold, I say unto you, it shall not be given unto you to know any further concerning this chapter, until the New Testament be translated, and in it all these things shall be made known; Wherefore I [God] give unto you [Joseph Smith] that ye may now translate it, that ye may be prepared for things to come" (D&C 45:60–61). The implication was that the KJV as it stood was regarded as inadequate. Accordingly (under the guidance of revelation) Smith began to revise the Bible. The exact date when he began this revision is not known. Presumably it was begun after 7 March 1831, but was interrupted, because on 1 December 1831, Smith recorded that "I resumed the translation of the scriptures, and continued to labor *in this branch of my calling* with Elder Sidney Rigdon as my scribe." There are references to this work of revision in his revelations recorded for 16 February 1832, 8 March 1833, and 6 May 1833. Smith called his work of revision that of "translation." The work was carried on intermittently till July 1833. The Book of Genesis was first revised in the fall and winter of 1830. After 7 March 1831, Smith began the NT and after this resumed work on the OT. By 2 July 1833, most of the revision was completed but revisions and alterations continued up till Smith's death in 1844. An edition of Joseph Smith's Bible (i.e., the Bible, the KJV which he used) was published in 1867, and in 1944 a "New Corrected Edition" appeared.[6] This latter contained only a few adjustments and changes. In probably only 352 verses does the edition of 1944 differ from that of 1867. The Mormons think of Smith's version of the biblical texts he translated as "inspired," but it has never been accepted as canonical as a whole, although the revision of Matthew 23:39 and Matthew 24 was so accepted.[7]

---

6. The most significant changes in the Joseph Smith translation are now footnoted in the new (1979) Mormon edition of the KJV. The lengthiest additions are presented in a separate section of the appendix. Their net effect is threefold: (1) to trace the messianic and christological understanding of various OT texts to an earlier date than most scholars allow; (2) to resolve contradictions or conflicting readings; and (3) to clarify the timebound and obscure passages (so T. G. Madsen).

7. See Milton R. Hunter, *The Pearl of Great Price* (Salt Lake City: Bookcraft, 1951), 43–46.

So far we have noted the biblical contents of the canon of the Mormon Church. Our discussion revealed acceptance and criticism of the Christian canon as normally understood in Protestantism and largely in Roman Catholicism and Orthodoxy. The criticism centered on the character of the KJV as a translation that required revision and as a corruption of God's original revelation caused by ignorance or deliberate priestly intent. Emphasis seems to be put most on omissions from what God originally had revealed.[8] Not surprisingly, then, the Bible was revised although the KJV retained preeminence. Equally it is not surprising, since the Bible was regarded as inadequate, that the Mormon Church claimed to have had further revelations which are to be taken as scripture. In the first place, these revelations are those believed to have been given to Smith at various intervals. We may now surmise those documents, in addition to the NT and the OT (without the Apocrypha), are regarded as canonical in Mormonism.

There Is, First, the Book of Mormon[9]

Responding to words in James 1:5, and troubled by the war of words and tumult of opinions among the religious denominations of his day, Joseph Smith retired to the woods to ask wisdom of God. His petition was answered. On 21–22 September 1823,[10] two heavenly personages appeared to him. According to Smith, they were the Father and the Son. They advised him to join no denomination but to prepare himself for a great task. There followed a series of reported revelations. These included the miraculous discovery and translation of a set of gold plates.[11] Joseph Smith claimed that they were revealed to him by the counsels of Moroni, an angel, who identified himself as the son of Mormon, the original compiler of the plates. After four years of trial and temptation, on 22 September 1827, Joseph Smith was given charge of the

---

8. See on this especially the provocative article by Hugh W. Nibley, "The Forty-Day Mission of Christ — The Forgotten Heritage," *VC* 20 (1966): 1–24.

9. The Book of Mormon is regarded by Mormons as a divinely inspired record covering generally the period of 600 B.C.E. to 400 C.E., made by the prophets of the people who inhabited the Americas centuries before Christ. In Mormon belief, this record was made known to Joseph Smith by Moroni, the last of those pre-Columbian prophets on the American continent, and was translated by Smith. In the judgment of Krister Stendahl "the laws of creative interpretation by which we analyze materials from the first and second Christian centuries operate on and are significantly elucidated by works like the Book of Mormon and by other writings of revelatory character." He insists that "such authentic writing should not be confused with spurious gospel forgeries, many of which are discussed in *Strange Tales about Jesus* (Philadelphia: Fortress Press, 1983)." See Krister Stendahl, *Meanings: The Bible as Document and as Guide* (Philadelphia: Fortress Press, 1984), 99. This judgment calls for scrutiny: we find it more provocative than convincing.

10. See James E. Talmage, *A Study of the Articles of Faith* (1890; Salt Lake City: The Church of Jesus Christ of Latter-day Saints, 1976), 255.

11. Moroni revealed that the plates were buried in a hill, called Cumorah or Ramah near Palmyra in western New York State, not far from Joseph Smith's home.

plates. A portion of these plates he then claimed to have translated as the Book of Mormon. It was published in 1830. The Book of Mormon purports to be a history of pre-Columbian America (from 600 B.C.E. to 400 C.E.), its settlement by some Hebrews, and their subsequent destiny and apostasy. The translation was made possible by means of two special stones set in rims to which a breastplate was attached. This instrument was called the "Urim and Thummin" — a term which refers to certain elements in the accoutrements of the high priest in the OT (Exod. 28:30; Lev. 8:8; Deut. 38:8; Ezra 2:63; Neh. 7:65). In time Joseph Smith, through the instruction of the heavenly personage, showed the plates to his close associates — Oliver Cowdery, Martin Harris, and David Whitmer. These three men signed a sworn affidavit declaring "with words of soberness, that an angel of the Lord came down from heaven, and the engravings thereon." Later eight other witnesses swore that "Joseph Smith, the translator of this work, has shown unto us the plates of which hath been spoken, which have the appearance of gold, and as many of the leaves as the said Smith has translated we did handle with our hands; and we also saw the engravings thereon." They added that they had "seen and hefted" the plates: they did so with "words of soberness." According to Mormons all eleven of these first witnesses remained steadfast in their testimony until they died.[12]

According to the eighth of the *Articles of Faith*, Mormons believe the Book of Mormon to be the word of God. "The elders, priests and teachers of this church shall teach the principles of my gospel, which are in the Bible and the Book of Mormon, in which is the fullness of the gospel" (D&C 42:12). The Book of Mormon "contains the truth and the word of God" (D&C 19:26). It was recognized, however, that, like the Bible, the Book of Mormon also was a translation, not the original text.[13] Thus the original text itself was an abridgment of a more original record. At this point the contents of the Book of Mormon need not detain us. It is made up of fifteen books, one being a kind of editorial note. In all, in the current edition of the Mormon Church, it contains 522 pages. Nor again need we seek to "explain" the Book

---

12. As far as I am aware, the fact that — apart from Smith himself — the witnesses numbered exactly eleven has escaped comment. Can it be that there is here a contrast and parallel intended with "the Twelve" who formed the inner circle of the disciples of Jesus in the NT? One of the Twelve did not remain steadfast, so that the effective witnesses were eleven. Perhaps Smith himself was the twelfth. See 1 Corinthians 15:5, where the Greek text of Nestle gives "the Twelve" (τοῖς δώδεκα), but some manuscripts — D*, G, and Latin and Syriac versions — read eleven (τοῖς ἕνδεκα). Did the risen Lord appear to Judas? The textual evidence favors reading "the Twelve" — as does the theology of the early church. There is no evidence to support this conjecture and it must remain only such.

The constraint of evidence had led several encyclopedias to reverse their earlier allegations that the three witnesses "later denied their testimony." See R. L. Anderson, *Investigating the Book of Mormon Witnesses* (Salt Lake City: Deseret, 1981), 67–78.

13. Note especially the full title as given in Talmage, *Articles of Faith*, 257f.: *The Book of Mormon: An Account Written by the Hand of Mormon upon Plates Taken from the Plates of Nephi.*

of Mormon, as has been done, in terms of a pious fraud or forgery, or of psychological or historical causes. All such explanations do not affect believing Mormons, who claim the Book of Mormon to be revealed truth. It was therefore canonized and regarded as the direct fulfillment of the prophecy of Isaiah 29:4. It is a parallel testimony with that of the Bible in fulfillment of Ezekiel 37:16–19.[14] Joseph Smith has brought the restored dispensation of the fullness of time anticipated by Paul in Ephesians 1:9, 10.[15]

The *Pearl of Great Price*

In addition to the OT and the NT and the Book of Mormon, there are other documents regarded as canonical which have been gathered into one volume called *The Pearl of Great Price: A Selection from the Revelations, Translations, and Narrations of Joseph Smith, First Prophet, Seer, and Revelator to the Church of Jesus Christ of Latter-day Saints.*[16]

1. *The Book of Moses* in eight chapters, giving visions revealed to Joseph Smith in June 1830. These visions are in part derived from Smith's revision of Genesis. While chapter 1 was not from the Book of Genesis, chapters 2–8 were revelations received while Smith was "translating" or revising the book (see *HC* 1:98–101); chapter 6, verses 45–68, and chapter 7 are an extract from the prophecy of Enoch.

2. *The Book of Abraham.* According to Smith, this is derived from two rolls of papyri from the "catacombs of Egypt" sold to the Mormons at Kirtland, Ohio, in July 1835 by one Michael Chandler. It purports to be the history of Abraham written by Abraham with his own hands in "characters of hieroglyphics" (*HC* 2:236).

3. The revised form of Matthew 23:39 and chapter 24, as "translated," that is at some points reworded and in some verses expanded, by Joseph Smith.

4. *Extracts from the History of Joseph Smith, the Prophet.*

5. *The Articles of Faith of the Church of Jesus Christ of Latter-day Saints.*[17]

---

14. Talmage, *Articles of Faith,* 20–21.

15. Ibid., 21. Timothy L. Smith has argued that the appeal of the Book of Mormon in the first generation, to converts as to inquirers, was essentially its confirmation of the biblical witness of Christ. Its role as supplementary scripture was, he concludes, secondary. He adds that no doctrine of any prominence in the Book of Mormon is without biblical precedent. See Timothy L. Smith, "The Book of Mormon in a Biblical Culture," *Journal of Mormon History* (1982): 3–21. One hesitates to confirm this view without further examination.

16. Salt Lake City: The Church of Jesus Christ of Latter-day Saints, 1979.

17. The *Articles of Faith* are in the *Pearl of Great Price* but, according to T. G. Madsen, "neither Joseph Smith nor his successors viewed the Articles of Faith as scriptural or even as 'creedal' in

We have given the contents of the *Pearl of Great Price* in the edition published at Salt Lake City by the church in 1979. Another section reads *The Doctrine and Covenants of the Church of Jesus Christ of Latter-day Saints, Containing Revelations Given to Joseph Smith, the Prophet, with Some Additions by His Successors in the Presidency of the Church.* (The French translation speaks of a *choix*, a selection from the revelations.) The edition of 1979, when compared with the previous editions of 1833, 1876, 1879, and 1921, shows change. In earlier editions, from 1851 to 1902, a hymn called "Truth," known familiarly as "Oh Say, What Is Truth," appeared. It was then dropped (section 77 of the D&C first printed in *Times and Seasons* in 1844) and was first included in the 1876 edition of the D&C.[18]

So far we have dealt with documents that have already been given canonical status by the Mormon Church. In addition to those already indicated, certain other writings of the Mormon Church, composed of utterances which have continued into the present, are esteemed as scripture. In D&C 68:2–4 we read:

> And, behold, and lo, this is an ensample unto all those who were ordained unto this priesthood, whose mission is appointed unto them to go forth — And this is the ensample unto them, that they shall speak as they are moved upon by the Holy Ghost. And whatsoever they shall speak when moved upon by the Holy Ghost shall be scripture, shall be the will of the Lord, shall be the mind of the Lord, shall be the work of the Lord, shall be the voice of the Lord, and the power of God unto salvation.

This revelation indicates the brethren may speak without being "moved upon by the Holy Ghost." But when they do so speak (when moved upon by the Holy Ghost), their words become scripture. How was it to be determined whether a particular speech or writing were by the Holy Ghost? Two criteria were to be observed. One is expressed by Brigham Young as follows:

status. For Joseph Smith, creeds were to be viewed as 'suggestive' not 'as setting up stakes' and were not to rank as scripture" (personal correspondence; see n. 4 above). One of the *Articles of Faith* (the eighth) says "many great and important truths are yet to be revealed." Madsen finds here an official statement "to assure that neither the Articles of Faith nor the canon is final if that means complete."

18. On all this, see Hunter, *Pearl of Great Price*, 240–48. Concerning the prophecy of Enoch, Matthew Black, who has written on *1 Enoch*, orally informed me that he finds no trace of its influence in the Mormon texts. But see also J. H. Charlesworth, "Messianism in the Pseudepigrapha and the Book of Mormon," in *Reflections on Mormonism* (Salt Lake City: Publishers Press, 1978). As a parallel in the Enochic corpus, George Nickelsburg has called my attention in correspondence to 4QEnGiants 8:3: *prsgn lwh' tny[n]* ("the copy of the sec[on]d tablet"; J. T. Milik, *The Books of Enoch* [Oxford: Clarendon Press, 1976], 314–15). Nickelsburg has also noted the idea in *Jubilees* 8 and the Nag Hammadi treatise *The Three Steles of Seth*.

Were your faith concentrated upon the proper object, your confidence unshaken, your lives pure and holy, everyone fulfilling the duties of his or her calling according to the Priesthood and capacity bestowed upon you, you would be filled with the Holy Ghost, and it would be as impossible for any man to deceive and lead you to destruction as for a feather to remain unconsumed in the midst of heat.[19]

I am more afraid that this people have so much confidence in their leaders that they will not inquire for themselves of God whether they are led by Him. I am fearful they settle down in a state of blind self-security trusting their eternal destiny in the hands of their leaders with a reckless confidence that in itself would thwart the purposes of God in their salvation, and weaken what influences they could give to their leaders, did they know for themselves, by the revelations of Jesus, that they are led in the right way. Let every man and woman know, by the whispering of the Spirit of God to themselves, whether their leaders are walking in the path the Lord dictates, or not.[20]

In these passages the burden of proof for the "scriptural," that is, canonical character of any utterance, is placed upon the hearer. A Mormon knows whether another Mormon has spoken "when moved upon by the Holy Ghost" when he himself is moved upon by the Holy Ghost in response to his brother's words.

But Joseph Smith had previously provided another criterion. According to D&C 18:1–4, citing a revelation given in early June 1829 through Smith himself to the elders of the church at Kirtland, Ohio:

1. Now behold, because of the thing which you, my servant Oliver Cowdery, have desired to know of me, I give unto you these words:

2. Behold, I have manifested unto you, by my Spirit in many instances, that the things which you have written are true; wherefore you know that they are true.

3. And if you know that they are true, behold, I give unto you a commandment that you rely upon the things which are written;

4. For in them are all things concerning the foundation of my church, my gospel, and my rock.

Here the reference to what Cowdery had written is to the Book of Mormon. When Joseph Smith urges reliance on "the things that are written" it means

---

19. *Journal of Discourses* (Liverpool: R. D. and S. W. Richards, 1854–56), 7:2.
20. Ibid., 9:150.

the Book of Mormon. Cowdery and, by implication, all Mormons were not to rely on their own ideas or concepts. The written word was also stressed later on 7 June 1831, through a revelation to Smith at Kirtland, Ohio. Certain people — Joseph Smith, Sidney Rigdon, John Corrill, John Murdock, Hyrum Smith, Jr. — are to journey "preaching the word by the way, saying none other things than that which the prophets and apostles have written and that which is taught them by the Comforter through the power of prayer" (D&C 52:9; cf. 52:36). They are to go two by two (cf. D&C 52:10) presumably so that individual utterances — among other things — might be "checked." One test for prayer, speech, and humility is given in D&C 52:15–18 — obedience to the ordinances (cf. D&C 6:9). Another test of the spirit is understanding (D&C 50:12–24), and further, the Spirit of Truth witnesses to itself; it is received by the Spirit of Truth in the hearer (D&C 50:14–19; cf. 50:31). The operative verses are:

> Therefore, why is it that ye cannot understand and know, that he that receiveth the word by the Spirit of truth receiveth it as it is preached by the Spirit of truth? Wherefore, he that preacheth and he that receiveth, understand one another, and both are edified and rejoice together. And that which doth not edify is not of God, and is darkness. That which is of God is light; and he that receiveth light, and continueth in God, receiveth more light; and that light groweth brighter and brighter until the perfect day. (D&C 50:21–24)

In the passages cited, the discussion of how words uttered in the present could be taken for scripture applied to missionaries in the early days of the church (though there is no indication that these words were therefore to be written down, so that the term "scripture" is ambiguous). Later the same privilege was extended to other utterances which were not strictly missionary. Persons of the First Presidency and the Quorum of the Twelve were commissioned with a special calling and gift. These — prophets, seers, and revelators — had a special spiritual endowment in connection with their teaching of the people. Subject to the authority of the president of the church, this group had the "right, power, and authority" to declare the mind and will of God to his people. Only to this group is this special gift given. Over and above them stands the president of the church, who has further, special endowment. He is The Prophet, The Seer, The Revelator. He alone has the right to receive revelations for the people either new or "corrective" of previous revelations. He alone can give authoritative interpretations of scriptures that are binding on the church. He alone can change the doctrines of the church. He alone is the mouthpiece of God to his people in the sense that he alone can declare to and for the entire church the mind and will of God. Anyone seeking to act in any such matters, unless authorized by the president to do so, can be known to be out of order and not to have been moved by the Holy Ghost. See D&C 20:1–4 for the commissioning of Joseph Smith and Oliver Cowdery as first and second elders of the Mormon Church; 20:9–12 for the inspiration and confirmation of the translation of the Book of Mormon by men and angels "proving to the world that the holy scriptures [here the Bible and Book of Mormons are meant] are true and that God does inspire men and call them to his holy work in this age and generation, as well as in the generations of old, thereby showing that he is the same God yesterday, today and forever, amen" (D&C 20:11).[21] However, the elevation of the president[22] did not make it impossible for him on rare occasions to teach and preach when he had not been "moved upon by the Holy Ghost" (*HC* 5:265). Asked if a prophet was always a prophet, Smith quickly affirmed that "prophet was a prophet only when he acted as such" (see *HC* 5:265; 2:302).

The processes whereby the added scriptures of Mormonism came into being we can only touch upon. There have been various approaches to the experience of Joseph Smith which led to the Book of Mormon. Abnormal psychology and sociological pressures have been appealed to for explanation. As we noted earlier, for our present purposes such attempts are not important because, however explained, believing Mormons took the experience of Joseph Smith as valid communications from God: they were of divine origin. But this did not preclude much consideration of the style and structure of the messages of Smith.

Particular emphasis was placed on the first vision to Smith. In Moses 1:9–10 (given years after Smith's first theophany), Smith recounts the experience of Moses on Mount Sinai. After his experience of being in the presence of God, and after that presence had been withdrawn from him, "as he was left to himself, [Moses] fell to the earth. And it came to pass that it was for the space of many hours before Moses did again receive his natural strength like unto man; and he said unto himself: 'Now, for this cause I know that man is nothing, which thing I had never supposed.'" It is sometimes said that Smith seems to have reenacted this experience in his own first and later visions. After the third visit of "the personage," from beyond at his bedside, the "heavenly messenger" who revealed to him the location of the plates from which the Book of Mormon was to emerge in translation, he writes that "I found my strength so exhausted as to render me entirely unable. . . . I fell helpless to the ground, and for a time was quite unconscious of any thing."[23] But caution is necessary. There is no direct parallel with the biblical account of Moses' experience on Sinai. There is in the *Origin of the Book of Mormon*

---

21. For the kerygma, see D&C 20:21ff.; 107:7, esp. 107:18, 64–67, 91–92 (the comparison with Moses); 115:19 (on loyalty to the president, 117:13); 124:125 (but see also 124:126).

22. On which see D&C 90:1–4; 107:8, 64–67, 91–92; 124:123; HC 11:477; 6:363.

23. Preface to the Book of Mormon, *Origin of the Book of Mormon*, unpaginated.

no reference to Moses falling to the ground. On the contrary, it is the exulta-
tion of Moses in the presence of the Lord that is emphasized: his face shone.
On the other hand, in Exodus, Moses cannot be allowed to see the "fullness
of the glory" of God. But there is no such restraint in the account Smith gives
of the visit of Moroni. Smith's fear soon left him after Moroni first came, but
there is little of the Promethean character of the biblical Moses in the Smith
of this vision.

More similar to that of Smith is the outcome of the revelation recorded
in Daniel 8. This ends in 8:26–27 as follows: "And the vision of the evening
and the morning which was told is true; wherefore shut thou up the vision;
for it shall be for many days. And I Daniel fainted, and was sick certain days;
afterward I rose up, and did the king's business" (KJV). Paul's vision near
Damascus was more violent than that of Smith. According to Acts 9:3f., Paul
fell to the ground and was blinded by the light of the vision for three days,
during which he took no food or drink (cf. Acts 22:6–11). Reference is sometimes made to parallels with the account of the Transfiguration (Mark 9:2ff.
and parallels). But the only common element is the reference to the light
on Jesus' face. The references to the fear of the disciples, and to their falling
on their faces, are not parallel to anything in the *Origin*. One might conclude that the account of Smith's vision owes little to the biblical tradition
except for the use of certain forms that have become traditional in the description of visions.[24] For the conventional visionary language, the reader is
referred to a rich discussion of the parallels between the accounts of Paul's
conversion and materials in the Pseudepigrapha and the OT.[25] The account
of Smith's version is more extensive than those of the Bible and possibly the
Pseudepigrapha, but the same phenomena emerge in Mormon visions or revelations as in the biblical and pseudepigraphic documents, for example, voices
(*1 Enoch* 5:10; D&C 88:1; 76:1–66). The Spirit, unless by implication only,
is surprisingly absent from the first vision; but note references to the Spirit
in D&C 8:1. In this passage the revelation is connected with understanding
and meditation as well as with the Spirit. In D&C 8:2–3 the mind and the
heart are the media, through the Holy Ghost, of revelation or the spirit of
revelation (cf. D&C 110:1–4). One manner of revelation as experienced by
Smith is described by Parley Parker Pratt.[26]

The belief that there are books in heaven which record (1) registers of
actual Israelite citizens with a right to temporal blessedness and also (in Dan.

---

24. Richard L. Bushman, in his *Joseph Smith and the Beginnings of Mormonism* (Urbana: University of Illinois Press, 1984), chap. 1, shows that the first visions were part of Joseph Smith's
familial and environmental setting.

25. See Johannes Munck, *Paul and the Salvation of Mankind*, trans. Frank Clarke (London:
SCM Press, 1959), chap. 1.

26. See the appendix at the end of this article.

12:1) to an immortality of blessedness, and (2) the record of good and evil deeds, emerges clearly in the OT and the Pseudepigrapha and in later rabbinic sources. These documents also contain the notion of heavenly tablets containing God's plans (laws?), for example, Exodus 25:9, 40; Daniel 10:21 ("what is written in the Book of Truth"). Here the context refers to "future events which have already happened." The convention of heavenly tablets presenting divine mysteries is, then, an ancient and well-established one. It was revitalized powerfully by Joseph Smith. The currents by which the convention had reached him, apart from the OT and the Pseudepigrapha, we probably cannot trace. It may be significant that the first translation of *1 Enoch* from the Ethiopic was published in 1821, just before the rise of Joseph Smith to prominence, and that references to heavenly tablets in that work may have contributed to the form that Joseph Smith's vision assumed. Another pseudepigraphic work, *The Book of Abraham*, which became part of the Mormon canon, is declared to have been translated by Joseph Smith from "some ancient Records that have fallen into our hands from the catacombs of Egypt" (HC 2:235–351).[27]

The Mormon canon, then, is made up of biblical and nonbiblical documents and of utterances recognized as under the influence of the Spirit. What is the relative weight attached to these various components of the canon? The answer has been clearly given. As we have seen, appeal to the writings in the detection of the presence of the Spirit in given utterances is emphasized. But the presidents of the Mormon Church have made it clear that primacy is to be given not to the written words from the past, however sacred, but to the living word of God. The following quotation from Wilford Woodruff needs no comment:

> I will refer to a certain meeting I attended in the town of Kirtland in my early days. At that meeting some remarks were made that have been made here today, with regard to the written word of God. The same principle was presented, although not as extensively as it has been here, when a leading man in the church got up and talked upon the subject, and said: "You have got the word of God before you here in the Bible, Book of Mormon, and Doctrine and Covenants; you have the written word of God, and you who give revelations should give revelations according to those books, as what is written in those books is the word of God. We should confine ourselves to them." When he concluded, Brother Joseph turned to Brother Brigham Young and said, "Brother

---

27. Is it without significance that William Blake, the great visionary, died in 1827, and that the decade in which Joseph Smith saw visions saw also the appearance of some of Blake's work of vision and of the reinterpretation and correction of the Christian tradition? As far as I am aware, this question has not been posed. Did the *Zeitgeist* favor visions?

Brigham I want you to take the stand and tell us your views with regard to the written oracles and the written word of God." Brother Brigham took the stand, and he took the Bible, and laid it down; he took the Book of Mormon, and laid it down; and he took the Book of Doctrine and Covenants, and laid it down before him, and he said: "There is the written word of God to us, concerning the work of God from the beginning of the world, almost, to our day." "And now," said he, "when compared with the living oracles those books are nothing to me; those books do not convey the word of God direct to us now, as do the words of a Prophet or a man bearing the Holy Priesthood in our day and generation. *I would rather have the living oracles than all the writing in the books*." That was the course he pursued. When he was through, Brother Joseph said to the congregation, "*Brother Brigham has told you the word of the Lord, and he has told you the truth.*" ... The Bible is all right, the Book of Mormon is all right, the Doctrine and Covenants is all right, and they proclaim the work of God and the word of God in the earth in this day and generation until the coming of the Son of Man; but the Holy Priesthood is not confined particularly to those books, that is, it did not cease when those books were made.[28]

In a conference report for April 1955, Marion G. Romney states: "There are other prophets who will talk to you during this conference.... [They] are prophets as much as any men who ever lived upon the earth have been prophets. I plead with you to hear their voices.... These men will preach and teach the gospel of Jesus Christ as he himself defined it." The implication is that the written canon can be subordinated to the present experience of being "moved upon by the Holy Ghost." Harold B. Lee, eleventh president of the church, states the position without ambiguity and deserves quotation.

Sometimes we get the notion that if it is written in a book, it makes it more true than if it is spoken in the last general conference. Just because it is written in a book does not make it more of an authority to guide us. President John Taylor goes on with this same idea and explains why *the scriptures of the past are not sufficient for us today:*

"The Bible is good; and Paul told Timothy to study it, that he might be a workman that need not be ashamed, and that he might be able to conduct himself aright before the living church [there is that word "living" again], the pillar and ground of truth. The church-mark, with Paul, was the foundation, the pillar, the ground of truth, the living church, not the dead letter. The Book of Mormon is good, and the Doctrine and Covenants, as land-marks. But a mariner who launches into the

---

28. Wilford Woodruff, *Conference Report* (October 1897): 22–23.

ocean requires a more certain criterion. He must be acquainted with heavenly bodies, and take his observations from them, in order to steer his barque aright. Those books are good for example, precedent, and investigation, and for developing certain laws and principles. But they do not, they cannot, touch every case required to be adjudicated and set in order.

"We require a living tree — a living fountain — living intelligence, proceeding from the living priesthood in heaven, through the living priesthood on earth. . . . And from the time that Adam first received a communication from God, to the time that John, on the Isle of Patmos, received his communication, or Joseph Smith had the heavens opened to him, it always required new revelations, adapted to the peculiar cir-cumstances in which the churches of individuals were placed. Adam's revelation did not instruct Noah to build his ark; nor did Noah's rev-elation tell Lot to forsake Sodom; nor did either of these speak of the departure of the children of Israel from Egypt. These all had revelations for themselves, and so had Isaiah, Jeremiah, Ezekiel, Jesus, Peter, Paul, John, and Joseph. *And so must we, or we shall make a shipwreck.*"[29]

I do not know a stronger statement, and I have gone back enough generations to quote a prophet. I might have said the same thing myself in the same language, and you, because you have more faith and are better grounded in believing in a living oracle today, perhaps, would have believed. But I have gone back enough generations to President Taylor so that probably it has more "epical" authority than if I had said it in my own language today. But you see the point that he makes.[30]

The Mormons' need for living adaptability and flexibility in the present created a need for present revelation and ensured the priority of living prophets as they are "moved by the Spirit" even over the written scriptures.

This leads to the question of how the emergence and development of the Mormon canon compares and contrasts with the process of canonization in early Christianity. Certain contrasts leap to the mind.

First, then, the Mormon canon is far larger than the traditional Christian one. Apart from the OT and NT, the Mormons have canonized the Book of Mormon (522 pages), the Doctrine and Covenants (270 pages), and the *Pearl of Great Price* (60 pages), a massive amount of materials — not as large as the Bible but of considerable size. This volume itself is certainly far larger than the NT — the traditional specifically Christian part of the canon. Cer-

---

29. Quoted in Harold B. Lee, *Stand Ye in Holy Places* (Salt Lake City: Deseret, 1974), 34. Italics added.

30. Harold B. Lee, "The Place of the Living Prophet, Seer, and Revelator" (address to Seminaries and Institutes of Religion Faculty, Brigham Young University, 8 July 1964), 9.

tain factors may account for this. The initial experience of Joseph Smith, which gave birth to Mormonism, was in the form of a revelation of *documents* to be translated. This committed Mormonism from the beginning to a substantive addition to the traditional canon. The Book of Mormon became a basic document of Mormonism far more immediately than did the NT to the early church. Similarly, the form of Joseph Smith's experience of successive revelations demanded their preservation in writing, as did the form of the revelations given to subsequent presidents of the Mormon Church. Eventually these also had to be recorded in written form because most of them were originally spoken. Contrast with all this the simple fact that Jesus never wrote anything. (He is simply recorded to have written on the sands once, John 9:6–8.)[31] No known document of revealed truths and histories and commandments came from his hands. Moreover, apart from the Book of Revelation (1:10, 19), no document in the NT claims to have been written at the direct command or dictation of the deity. In this sense Mormonism is a far more "bookish" movement than other movements in Christianity from the beginning. That is of its essence.

The "bookishness" in itself gave an impetus to a rather speedy development of a canon in Mormonism. The canon begins to be defined in the very earliest stages of the history of the movement. With this speed went a certain readiness to add to the canon with considerable flexibility and a readiness to subordinate past "canonical" documents to the present experience of revelation under the Spirit. Contrast again the slow and checkered fixation of the canon of the NT. It was not finally fixed until the end of the fourth century. Moreover, although the church fathers had pondered and elaborated on the faith, their important letters and utterances did not achieve canonization. The need for restraint in the early church governed the limitation of the canon, whereas the need for flexibility in Mormonism led to its expansion comparatively more freely and more rapidly. There is here a paradox. The early church, beginning without a revealed book (apart from the OT), only gradually sought a book, the NT, to be its "rule" or "canon." The Mormon Church, on the other hand, beginning with the Bible and a complete revealed book, comparatively quickly added many more "revelations."[32]

---

31. T. G. Madsen explains: "Catholicism distinguishes biblical theology from sacred tradition. Since the Vatican Council, both are regarded as 'historically conditioned.' For the Mormons the living word of the living leadership may *become* sacred tradition. But it only becomes *canon* by the double process of prophetic presentation and common consent" (personal correspondence; see n. 4 above).

32. In the NT, women are among the witnesses to the significance of the birth of Jesus and to the empty tomb (Mark 16:1f.; Luke 23:55–24:11; 24:22; Matt. 28:1–10; John 20:1–10). In John 20:11–18 a woman, Mary Magdalene, sees the risen Jesus. At first sight, such a role for women does not appear in the accounts of the revelations to Joseph Smith in the Mormon tradition, i.e., they are not presented as witnesses. But T. G. Madsen insists that Mormon women (e.g., Joseph's wife Emma) were witnesses to many of the origin-events of the church and were immediately

Is there an explanation for this? Perhaps it lies in the attitude of the early church and of Mormonism to the traditions within which they respectively emerged. One suggestion is that the criticism of Mormonism by the major churches of Christendom — Protestant and Roman Catholic — with whom the Mormons had to react was initially far more violent than was the criticism of the early Christian movement by Judaism. The need for self-definition and, therefore, for the canonization of certain texts, was more immediately felt by Mormons than by early Christians. It should not be overlooked that early Christians lived in a milieu and at a time before the appearance of "cheap" printing, while the nineteenth century in the United States was a period when religious tracts of all kinds were abundant, so that the publishing of and concentration on religious documents was not only easier but more usual and expected than in the first and subsequent centuries during which NT came to be fixed.[33]

Second, we offer a general reflection, prompted by the history of the Samaritans. The Samaritans chose to accept only the five books of Moses (that is, the Pentateuch) as their canon, excluding all else. But the Samaritans exercised little if any influence upon either Judaism or the pagan world around them. Unlike the early church, which did wrestle with the question of adding new documents to the OT, and spread into the Gentile world, the Samaritans remained in the small region of Palestine and gradually became more and more numerically diminished. Is there, one may ask, a correlation between the smallness of the Samaritans' canon and their very limited influence? The Mormons, by way of contrast, have today dispersed to traverse the entire world. Is their canon, ever augmented, a sign or a symbol of the vitality and inclusiveness of their faith? What began as a small American sect has become worldwide in its range and influence.

Third, it is necessary to state that the Mormon view that the OT has been corrupted has its parallel among certain Jewish Christians of the first centuries of the Christian era.[34] Schoeps has maintained that certain Jewish-Christian sects claimed that ideas in the primitive Jewish tradition concerning

---

given voting or "sustaining" rights with the men in all matters of church leadership. A woman, Sister Mary Whitmer, was privileged to see the plates of the Book of Mormon. See *LDS Biographical Encyclopedia*, compiled by Andrew Jensen (Salt Lake City: Deseret, 1901), 1:283. And women were made joint heirs with men to all the blessings of the gospel including the higher blessings of the temple.

33. On the fixation of a canon as a function of self-definition, see James A. Sanders, *Torah and Canon* (Philadelphia: Fortress Press, 1972). For the most important factor influencing the extent to which the Jewish group could change the Torah, see p. 90.

34. See Hans Joachim Schoeps, *Theologie und Geschichte des Judenchristentums* (Tübingen: Mohr-Siebeck, 1949), 148–87. Particularly important is now the (unassessed) approach of Ben Zion Wacholder (*The Dawn of Qumran: The Sectarian Torah and the Teacher of Righteousness* [Cincinnati: Hebrew Union College Press, 1983]) to the attitude of the sectarians to the written Torah.

the Temple, sacrifice, and the cult had been changed when the Bible was assembled. On this point the Mormons — perhaps without being aware of it — revert to a Jewish criticism of the OT left behind and neglected by the Christian tradition. It should be emphasized, therefore, that the notion that the Bible is corrupted is not peculiar to Mormons.

Fourth, Mormon utilization of nonbiblical documents is not unique. We have stated that for the Mormons the extrabiblical tradition has become as important as the biblical writings. *Mutatis mutandis*, one finds a similar development in rabbinic Judaism, for which the oral tradition — *torah shebe'al peh* — has sometimes been even more important than the OT.[35] Without overstatement, one may claim that for rabbinic Judaism the oral tradition preserved in the Mishnah, and developed later in the Talmud and elsewhere, has become the rule of life for religious Jews. The relation between the Mishnah and the OT is one of the most difficult questions in Judaism. There are knowledgeable Jews who emphasize that the oral law developed independently of the OT. See, for example, the work of Ellis Rivkin, who writes: "The Mishnah when set alongside the Pentateuch starkly reveals not a logical progression, but a quantum jump. *By any measure the Mishnah is incongruent with the Pentateuch.*"[36] In Rivkin's view there are between the Mishnaic system and the Pentateuch profound discontinuities that are the result of a Pharisaic revolution. At this point the Mormons are like the rabbinic Jews: in a veritable revolution — like that of the Pharisees — they elevate their own tradition above the Christian and Jewish canons. Although that tradition is plastic, as is the rabbinic, it is arguable that the links between the OT and the Doctrine and Covenants with *The Pearl of Great Price* of the Mormons are perhaps better preserved than the links between the Tanak and the Mishnah.

However, as we saw, the new revelations received by the Mormons were written down immediately. The rabbis, on the contrary, chose very deliberately not to write down the oral law until the second century c.e. Perhaps the reason why the Mormons wrote the revelations and commandments of Joseph Smith immediately was simple. For them it was not necessary to establish their oral tradition against the Pentateuch through a long period, as it was for the Jews, because in Christianity the OT had already been subordinated to the NT. It was against the Christian churches of their time, not against the scriptures, that the Mormons sought to establish their identity. To do this they needed to compose new scriptures.

But, finally, one may ask whether one may truly use the word "canon" to describe all the scriptures that the Mormons have accepted as revelation

---

35. On this see W. D. Davies, *Jewish and Pauline Studies* (Philadelphia: Fortress Press, 1984), 14, where I cite *m. Sanh.* 11:3.

36. Ellis Rivkin, *The Hidden Revolution* (Nashville: Abingdon Press, 1978), 223. Italics added. See also Davies, *Jewish and Pauline Studies*, 10–14.

and the future scriptures which they are likely, on their theological premises, to adopt as such. The word "canon" implies that there is a list of books, fixed or set in order and authorized, and accepted by a religious community as the norm for its own understanding of itself. For such a community the truth has already been given in the selected scriptures. Revelations received after a canon has been fixed serve simply to explicate the same canon: they are in accord with that canon, not revolutionary or independently revelatory. For Saint Paul, for example, the gospel had been given "according to the scriptures," that is, according to the canon of Judaism. Subsequently in Protestantism and Catholicism and Orthodoxy every interpretation of the gospel is understood to be according to the scriptures (*kata tas graphas*). Paul's own letters could eventually become canonical because they, too, were understood not to contradict the scriptures. But for the Mormons the scriptures of the Bible are apparently subordinated to the revelations given to Joseph Smith and to the succeeding presidents of the church.[37]

It agrees with this that in their theological writings, the Mormons seldom speak of their "canon" but of what they call "the Standard Works of the Church."[38] In the indices to their work one does not often find the word "canon." One may translate the phrase "standard works" by "classical writings" or by "definitive works." In a dictionary of the Bible,[39] published by the Mormons in 1979, there is a treatment of the word "canon," but even that account emphasizes the notion of a progressive revelation.[40] That notion is in tension with the definition of a canon in the strict sense. This is why Mormonism must be represented as a radical movement, despite its continuity within Judaism and Catholicism. The issue raised by the attitude of Mormons to their "canon" is fundamentally this: at what point does the notion of progressive or continuous revelation, as they understand it, fall outside "the limits of tolerance" of those churches that submit themselves to the traditional canon — Protestant, Roman Catholic, or Orthodox? Mormons have

---

37. This notion is not to be confused with that of the apostolic succession in Roman Catholicism. That doctrine is primarily concerned with the preservation of the continuity of the tradition, whereas the presidents in Mormonism are not only agents of continuity but more perhaps of newness of revelation.

38. Talmage, *Articles of Faith*, 7.

39. "Bible Dictionary with Explanatory Notes and Cross-References to the Standard Works of the Church," in *The Holy Bible (Authorized KJV)* (Salt Lake City: The Church of Jesus Christ of Latter-day Saints, 1979), 519–792.

40. T. G. Madsen comments on this as follows: "Mormons are often characterized as Biblical literalists and even as verbal infallibilists. Both characterizations are misleading. The initial Mormon acknowledgment of translational and transmissional error has already been noted. In addition, writers within the standard works themselves, including the Book of Mormon, speak of the faults and the mistakes of men" (personal correspondence; see n. 4 above). Stendahl observes that to say this of and in a sacred book strengthens rather than weakens respect ("The Sermon on the Mount and Third Nephi in the Book of Mormon," in *Meanings*, 101). Joseph Smith himself made clarifying revisions in most of the documents he himself wrote or translated.

raised acutely the question of the nature of revelation within the Jewish and Christian traditions: is "revelation" to be controlled by a fixed canon or is it open to development and even revision in terms of subsequent "revelations"? Progressive and continuous revelation is certainly an attractive notion, but equally certainly it is not without the grave danger of so altering or enlarging upon the original revelation as to distort, annul, and even falsify it. This is the fundamental question which all the more traditional Christian communions and, indeed, the NT itself, pose to Mormonism.[41]

Appendix

Elder Parly P. Pratt (speaking of the revelation, now printed as section 50 of the Doctrine and Covenants, given in May 1831) describes how the prophet worked when receiving revelations. He says:

> After we had joined in prayer in his translating room, he dictated in our presence the following revelation: — (Each sentence was uttered slowly and very distinctly, and with a pause between each, sufficiently long for it to be recorded, by an ordinary writer, in long hand).
>
> This was the manner in which all his written revelations were dictated and written. There was never any hesitation, reviewing, or reading back, in order to keep the run of the subject: neither did any of these communications undergo revisions, interlinings, or corrections. As he dictated them so they stood, so far as I have witnessed; and I was present to witness the dictation of several communications of several pages each. . . . [42]

It seems clear that on this occasion there was no audible voice, though the opening sentence of the revelation reads: "Hearken unto me, saith the Lord your God." However, President B. H. Roberts points out that when

---

41. Another question faces Mormonism more acutely than other Christian communions. The tradition of connecting revelation with divinely commissioned and divinely inspired and even written stones or documents has been questioned radically in recent discussion. The revelation to Moses as recorded in the OT can hardly be taken literally as an event in which the divine handed over or dictated to Moses Ten Commandments written on stone. Aetiological and liturgical elements are now recognized to have entered into the presentation of what is understood to have happened. The account of the giving of the Torah *witnesses* to the revelation of God on Sinai in the experience of Israel but is not to be taken literally. However, Mormonism demands that the account of the announcement and discovery of the Book of Mormon by Joseph Smith be taken factually and literally, not merely as an attempt, necessarily inadequate, to witness to a revelation. It must be asked whether in Mormonism conventional modes of describing revelation found in the OT and the Pseudepigrapha have been so literally taken over as fact as to give a facticity to what was intended as symbolic. As noted, other communions face this difficulty, but it is peculiarly contemporary and acute in Mormonism.

42. Parley P. Pratt, Jr., ed., *Autobiography of Parley Parker Pratt* (Salt Lake City: Deseret, 1938), 62.

some of the early revelations were published in the Book of Commandments in 1833, they

> were revised by the Prophet himself in the way of correcting errors made by the scribes and publishers; and some additional clauses were inserted to throw increased light upon the subjects treated in the revelations, and to paragraphs added, to make the principles or instructions apply to officers not in the church at the time some of the earlier revelations were given. The addition of verses 65, 66 and 67 in section xx of the Doctrine and Covenants is an example.[43]

At Montrose, Iowa, in August 1842 (there is some uncertainty as to the exact date), the prophet, attending a Masonic ceremony, prophesied that the saints would be driven to the Rocky Mountains and declared events incident to the move. Brother Call describes this scene as quoted in his bibliography by Tullidge, as follows:

> Joseph, as he was tasting the cold water, warned the brethren not to be too free with it. With the tumbler still in his hand he prophesied that the Saints would yet go to the Rocky Mountains; and, said he, this water tastes much like that of the crystal streams that are running from the snow-capped mountains. We will let Mr. Call describe this prophet scene: "I had before seen him in a vision, and now saw while he was talking his countenance change to white; not the deadly white of a bloodless face, but a living brilliant white. He seemed absorbed in gazing at something at a great distance, and said: 'I am gazing upon the valleys of those mountains.' This was followed by a vivid description of the scenery of these mountains, as I have since become acquainted with it. Pointing to Shadrach Roundy and others, he said: 'There are some men here who shall do a great work in that land.' Pointing to me, he said, 'There is Anson, he shall go and shall assist in building up cities from one end of the country to the other, and you,' rather extending the idea to all those he had spoken of, 'shall perform as great a work as has been done by man, so that the nations of the earth shall be astonished, and many of them will be gathered in that land and assist in building cities and temples, and Israel shall be made to rejoice.'[44]
>
> "It is impossible to represent in words this scene which is still vivid in my mind, of the grandeur of Joseph's appearance, his beautiful descriptions of this land, and his wonderful prophetic utterances as they emanated from the glorious inspirations that overshadowed him. There was a force and a power in his exclamations of which the following is

---

43. HC 1:173 n.
44. Note here the equation of Mormons with "Israel."

but a faint echo. 'Oh the beauty of these snow-capped mountains! The cool refreshing streams that are running down through those mountain gorges!' Then gazing in another direction, as if there was a change of locality: 'Oh the scenes that this people will pass through! The dead that will lay between here and there.' Then turning in another direction as if the scene had changed: 'Oh the apostasy that will take place before my brethren reach that land!' 'But,' he continued, 'the priesthood shall prevail over its enemies, triumph over the devil and be established upon the earth, never more to be thrown down!' He then charged us with great force and power, to be faithful to those things that had been and should be committed to our charge, with the promise of all the blessings that the Priesthood could bestow. 'Remember these things and treasure them up. Amen.' "[45]

---

45. In Edward W. Tullidge's *Histories,* vol. 2: *History of all the Northern, Eastern, and Western Counties of Utah and Also the Counties of Southern Idaho, with a Biographical Appendix . . . and . . . a Commercial Supplement* (Salt Lake City: Press of the Juvenile Instructor, 1889), 271ff. HC 7:85 n.

Epilogue

"Mystical Anti-Semitism" Reconsidered

In the field of historical inquiry, accepted patterns of thought often interfere with new empirical research. The conceptual equipment a historian brings to explore unknown terrain may just be unsuited for the task and serve to distort rather than delineate the contours of his topic. The proper understanding of many a new subject has been long delayed by an instinctive application of well-worn notions that make it difficult to approach the subject at hand without blinders. Should those notions about the past also be in error, the difficulty in studying a new topic is twice compounded. It may thus take sometimes a generation or two before historians are able to free themselves from the straitjacket of earlier conceptualizations in order to conduct their research in terms dictated by the subject itself. — Ismar Schorsch[1]

If there exists a cure for Judeophobia, the age old malady of Christendom, it lies not in the suppression of symptoms but in their exposure to the light. — Frank E. Manuel[2]

In a volume bearing the striking if not sensationalist title *The Satanizing of the Jews: Origin and Development of Mystical Anti-Semitism,*[3] Joel Carmichael, the editor of *Midstream,* has presented a very wide-ranging, yet succinct and clear survey of a phenomenon he calls "Mystical Anti-Semitism." This phenomenon, he finds, came into being because early Christian theologians ascribed to "The Jews" the central role in the crucifixion of Jesus of Nazareth. Interpreting Jesus as the Son of God, they came to see his destroyers, "The Jews," as satanic. This was natural: in the Jewish tradition, especially as revealed in the Apocrypha and Pseudepigrapha, but also in other sources, there

---

1. "On the History of the Political Judgment of the Jew," The Leo Baeck Memorial Lecture 20 (New York: Leo Baeck Institute, 1976).

2. *The Broken Staff: Judaism through Christian Eyes* (Cambridge: Harvard University Press, 1992), 1.

3. New York: Fromm International, 1992. I am grateful to Professors D. C. Allison, Kalman Bland, and Arthur Hertzberg for helpful comments on this chapter. But I am solely responsible for the views here expressed.

248

was held to be a fundamental opposition between God and Satan.[4] And so in opposing Jesus, God's Son, "The Jews" had played a satanic role: in taking the side of the devil they had themselves became "demonic." Because they came to be so understood by early Christian theologians, Carmichael asserts that "The Jews" came to be seen in a dual vision.

On the one hand, since they had fulfilled a satanic role in opposition even to the incarnate deity, "The Jews" were *ipso facto* seen to have an immense significance: they had not simply opposed a human being, Jesus — a prophet and the Messiah — but God Himself. Their daring in opposing the very deity implied that "The Jews" had extraordinary power. But at the same time, a second vision interposed itself, that of actual Jews, often living in abject poverty and social and political powerlessness, despised and rejected by those around them — a people whose insignificance Realpolitik could always assume. Hence arose a paradox, that of Jews, a people often pitifully weak, but seen to have even cosmic power as "The Jews." This ironic and tragic paradox could have arisen for one reason only: the cosmic significance Christian theologians ascribed to "The Jews" blinded them to the all too obvious historical weakness of Jews. (Carmichael assigns to Christian theologians almost the exact counterpart of the "blindness" Paul had ascribed to his fellow countrymen (see Rom. 11:7, 25; 2 Cor. 3:14; 4:4). Their blindness induced Christian theologians to find in "The Jews" a dreaded, eerie, awesome, threatening power and an uncanny, unnerving mystery. This utterly paradoxical attitude, Carmichael forcefully and untiringly emphasizes, was born of Christian theology: it arose only with the emergence of Christianity. And it is this unreasoned and unreasonable paradoxical attitude that Carmichael designates as mystical anti-Semitism. He very clearly distinguishes this mystical anti-Semitism from the kind of customary friction and hostility which Jews — like other ethnic, especially minority, groups — have known before and after the first century. It is *sui generis*.[5]

---

4. See now E. Pagels, *The Origin of Satan* (New York: Random House, 1995). But it is precarious to trace Satan — as he came to be understood in later centuries — solely to the Old Testament. See N. Cohn, "Le Diable au Coeur," *New York Review of Books*, 21 September 1995, 18–20, who also points to the Zoroastrian influences. On this see M. Boyce, "Persian Religion in the Achemenid Age," in *Cambridge History of Judaism* (Cambridge: Cambridge University Press, 1984), 1:279–309.

5. The unusual use of the term "mystical" demands explanation. By it Carmichael means that Christian theology has lent to the hatred of Jews "an outsize dimension," which "identifies the Jews with a concept beyond themselves." This, along with its intensity and duration, has given to mystical anti-Semitism ("the Longest Hatred") its unique character — as Carmichael puts it, "a special tincture." Carmichael does not notice that "the outsize dimension" to which he refers had already been formulated by Jews themselves; they had themselves elaborated the timeless cosmic myth about Jews before it was later appropriated by many of the church fathers and turned against the majority of Jews. In reviewing positively Steven T. Katz's great work *The Holocaust in Historical Context*, vol. 1: *The Holocaust and Mass Death before the Modern Age* (New York: Oxford University Press, 1994), in the *American Historical Review* 100 (Decem-

According to Carmichael, this kind of anti-Semitism generated, informed, and has sustained what Maurice Samuel long ago taught us to call "The Great Hatred," which has cursed, as it has baffled, Jews themselves since the first century: it turned Jews into "The Jews," possibly as early as the Fourth Gospel.[6] For with the acceptance of the Christian faith as the religion of the Roman state in the fourth century, this mystical anti-Semitism came to provide a continuing conceptual and organizational backdrop to Western European civilization, down to the very present. How and why could it have so continued? Because, urges Carmichael, the continuance of this attitude toward "The Jews" became a necessity for Christian theology itself. His argument is complex. In Carmichael's mind it turns upon a change which the Apostle Paul's understanding of Jesus underwent in the theology of the early church. As for most of the earliest New Testament writers, so for Paul also, Jesus, albeit the Messiah, had been a human figure who had inaugurated the kingdom of God. This kingdom was soon to find its final establishment in an order in which for Paul "all Israel," along with the believing Gentiles, would be saved (Rom. 11:26).[7] Thus the salvation of Jews was ultimately assured. However, as Paul's thought exerted its influence and evolved (note the verb "evolve" here: it is Carmichael's term),[8] early Christian theologians wrought a change. From the beginning Paul had understood Jesus not solely as a human figure, but also as a supernatural being. In the theology of the early church

ber 1995): 1526b, Gavin Langmuir writes: "[Katz] asserts that the Church Fathers, by situating Jews mythically and taking them as 'metaphysical markers,' made them both other and unreal (*The Holocaust*, 255–63). He overlooks the fact that the Jews had much earlier situated themselves mythically, transformed themselves and their god into 'metaphysical markers,' come to view Gentiles as others and been viewed by Egyptians and Romans as intolerant and other." The same applies to Carmichael. Moreover, we must note that it has not always been possible to isolate mystical anti-Semitism, as Carmichael understands it, from other forms of anti-Semitism: it cannot be regarded as watertight.

6. See, for example, the clear statement by D. Moody Smith in *Jews and Christians*, ed. James H. Charlesworth (New York: Crossroad, 1990), 76–95; and his essay, "The Representation of Judaism in the Gospel of John," in *Early Christian Thought in Its Jewish Context (Festschrift for Morna Hooker)*, ed. John Barclay and John Sweet (Cambridge: Cambridge University Press, 1996); and C. K. Barrett, *The Gospel of John and Judaism* (London: SPCK, 1975). Caution is necessary; the *'Ioudaioi* of John's Gospel can be variously interpreted. However, this being admitted, they could also very easily be misinterpreted to mean "The Jews" in the sense given by Carmichael. See further, Morton Smith, "Gentiles and Jews," in *The Cambridge History of Judaism*, ed. W. D. Davies and Louis Finkelstein, vol. 3 (forthcoming), for the meaning of *'Ioudaioi*; Alan Culpepper, "The Gospel of John and the Jews," *The Review and Expositor* 89 (1987): 273–88; J. Ashton, *Studying John: Approaches to the Fourth Gospel* (Oxford and New York: Clarendon Press, 1994), 5–36; and Pagels, *Origin of Satan*, 103–5.

7. On this see my essay "Paul and the People of Israel," in *Jewish and Pauline Studies* (Philadelphia: Fortress Press, 1984), 123–52, esp. 130–52.

8. Carmichael does not seem to distinguish between "development" and "evolution." On this see C. F. D. Moule, *The Origin of Christology* (Cambridge: Cambridge University Press, 1977), drawing on Cardinal Newman's famous work. See also Nicholas Lash's *Change in Focus: A Study of Doctrinal Change and Continuity* (London: Sheed and Ward, 1981 edition). He concentrates on Newman's approach to development on pp. 93–97 but is throughout penetrating.

fathers, so Carmichael argues, the supernatural aspect of Paul's thought about Jesus crowded out and superseded his human dimension. What Carmichael calls "the basic Pauline ideas of a Divine being condescending to incarnate himself in a human form, who is then sacrificed for the salvation of others in the struggle against evil, the Being in Christ, the Mystic Body of Christ, the Sacraments of Baptism and the Eucharist" — all these ideas were ultimately to determine the very structure of Christianity.

Certain factors, so Carmichael holds, contributed to this "evolution." First (and in this position he has many predecessors), he underlines the importance of the disappointment experienced by early Christians when Jesus, the Messiah and Son of God, was crucified and did not, as they expected, return from the dead to inaugurate the new order of the kingdom of God. The outcome of this disappointment was to shift the center of gravity of Paul's message away from the kingdom of God, which would embrace the salvation of "all Israel," to the new community, the church, which had come into being largely through Paul's own preaching. The apostle's message came to be separated from the kingdom of God and the hope of the end of the world, and concentrated on the "here and now" in the church, which became, as Carmichael expresses the matter, "a permanent element in the universe: the Church itself became a condition of nature: salvation accordingly could come only through the Church."[9] For Carmichael, the historical Paul had been fundamentally governed by "a passionate conviction that the natural world was about to be transformed": his basic ideas (noted above) described "merely the antechamber to the Kingdom of God at the World's End."[10] Given the deep human yearnings that move all peoples, these basic Pauline convictions naturally had a profound and widespread conceptual and emotional appeal in the first-century Greco-Roman world, as indeed they always have, especially since they were expressed in the extraordinarily powerful prose of the apostle, one of the great writers of the Hellenistic Age.[11] And so Paul's epistles came to serve as the ground of a theology he never dreamed of.[12] For Carmichael, with the evolution of the church and the concomitant understanding of salvation through identification with the flesh of Jesus in the sacraments, there was reintroduced "into the normal workaday world the sacrality that had been eliminated by the Jews a millennium before" (29) — a sentence he does not explain. The ultimate salvation of Jews, which had been assured in the future envisioned by Paul, was no longer an imperative or primary concern of Christians as it had been for the apostle himself.

---

9. Carmichael, *Satanizing of the Jews*, 28.

10. Ibid.

11. See G. Bornkamm, *Paul*, trans. D. M. Stalker (New York: Harper & Row, 1969). This was also the view of my teacher H. J. W. Tillyard in a small volume, *Hellenistic Literature*, which has unfortunately been lost.

12. Carmichael, *Satanizing of the Jews*, 29. Subsequent parenthetical references in text are to Carmichael's volume.

Further, according to Carmichael, a second conceptual factor contributed to the emergence of mystical anti-Semitism at the same time as the first factor indicated. It was a change in the status assigned to Satan in the theology of the church fathers. The Jewish tradition recognized no autonomous Satan, but only a Satan or devil subordinate to the divine being. However, with "the elimination of the contest between God forces and Devil forces underlying Paul's ideas and with the establishment of the Church as a permanent condition of the world, Satan becomes autonomous, that is, the world is governed by both God and the devil — the Church is the only way out" (30).[13] And with the evolution of the church, the incarnation of God in Christ "became the most fundamental fact not merely of religious doctrine but of all life." As the opponents of the incarnation, "The Jews" were assumed to have an ever greater cosmic significance. This assumption grew *pari passu* with the emphasis on the doctrine of the Incarnation in Christendom until "The Jews" became "the symbolical crystallization of the forces of evil on a scale commensurate with the infinite power of Yahweh" (30).[14]

In all this the conversion of the Jews, which Paul had regarded as the prelude to the end of the world, was removed "to the indefinite future, as the immediate World's End was forgotten" (30). Early Christian theologians did not want to eliminate "The Jews" or, to use the modern expression, "to liquidate" them. However, they accepted them solely on the ground that their continued existence in misery and degradation served as a witness to the triumph of Christianity and as "an emblem of the opposition that the Church Triumphant alone stood out against" (30). Augustine's influence ensured that this view of "The Jews" became "the official view of the Church" (36). But, again paradoxically and perversely, even in their misery and degradation, "The Jews" were still regarded as powerful enough to oppose the deity Himself.

According to Carmichael, then, the church theologians changed what, for Paul, had been a temporary blindness on the part of Jews into a characteristic of the very nature of "The Jews." They did this by taking over the Jewish scriptures as their own, making them part of the Christian canon, and interpreting them apart from their original context. By this means they presented "The Jews," not as Jews were historically, but in terms of a timeless cosmic myth or concept which came to constitute the fundamental formulation of mystical anti-Semitism.[15]

All this "evolution" of Christian doctrine coincided with the marked consequences, within Jewish life, of the revolts against Rome in 66–70 C.E. and

---

13. Here Cohn's review of Pagels, "Le Diable au Coeur," is pertinent. See n. 4 above.
14. See also Pagels, *Origin of Satan.*
15. Carmichael, *Satanizing of the Jews,* 31–37.

later.[16] At that time, history conspired with theology against "The Jews." After the failure of the revolts against Rome in 70 and 135 C.E., the dominant form of Judaism became the rabbinic. The rabbis accepted the fall of Jerusalem as a punishment for sin and gradually came to regard the Diaspora, which after 70 C.E. was very greatly enlarged, as part of God's purpose and plan. To seek to "counter" that plan or to "define" it by forcing the end came to be seen as impious. Led by their rabbis, most Jews came to accept their landless condition and, in due course, through the creation of the Talmud — a surrogate for the world's end — to internalize their faith in the "enjoyment of that portable land," the Torah and the Talmud, which had become a substitute for the terrestrial land. Text replaced territory. Furthermore, the study of the Talmud, open to all Jews, so democratized their faith that they required no Temple and no priesthood to interpret it. At the same time the messianic hope, dashed as it had so often been, and its realization, after 135 C.E. generally postponed to the indefinite future in the end time, still continued to give to Jews a tenacious, optimistic resilience and "a sort of psychic independence and an intellectual and emotional prop for sustaining it."[17]

Moreover, all these early rabbinic developments reinforced the self-isolation of Jews: they became more and more "hedged in" by their own institutions and practices; and their increasing isolation made "The Jews" more uncanny than ever to outsiders.[18] It was such a people, turning in upon themselves, suffering from a "siege mentality," whom the church fathers, inconsistently, came to consider threatening, even though they did so in the interest, not of rejecting Judaism (the very Jewish scriptures which they had inherited and cherished forbade this), but "of absorbing Judaism and, indeed, all Jewish history, into the Church" (33).

After defining his term mystical anti-Semitism in chapters 1 and 2, Carmichael proceeds to show how what he interprets as the twist in the interpretation of Paul, to which we have referred, spawned a demonic doctrine of immense power and significance which has worked its way into the very fabric of European culture and vitiated it. Carmichael sets forth the grounds for his position by tracing the history of The Great Hatred through the centuries down to Stalin and Hitler. Carmichael urges that one of the most advanced and sophisticated of all peoples could have succumbed to Hitler's extreme, irrational, chimeric anti-Jewish fantasies only because of the undergrowth of

---

16. The impact of the fall of Jerusalem in 70 C.E. has been much discussed and disputed in recent Jewish scholarship, but the position stated here seems to be still dominant. See L. H. Schiffman, *From Text to Tradition: A History of Second Temple and Rabbinic Judaism* (Hoboken, N.J.: Ktav, 1991), 157–76, esp. 167–71.

17. Carmichael, *Satanizing of the Jews*, 41.

18. Ibid., 42.

hatred which it had inherited from centuries of Christian misrepresentation of Jews.

The thesis Carmichael proposes does not surprise. The role of Christian theology in the perpetuation of hatred toward Jews has long been recognized by Christians no less than Jews. Suffice it to evoke the work of R. T. Herford and James W. Parkes in the United Kingdom, G. F. Moore in the United States, and Jacques Maritain and Jules Isaac in France, all of whom have illuminated the conflict of church and synagogue. The most recent work by a Jewish scholar, Leon Poliakov,[19] points to Christianity as ultimately the root source of anti-Semitism. The Canadian Gavin I. Langmuir, professor of history at Stanford University, has concentrated on the chimeric anti-Jewish developments in late medieval Christendom as supplying a clue to that phenomenon and as the definitive factor in his definition of anti-Semitism.[20]

But Carmichael's work is more unqualified and unequivocal in singling out Christianity as the culprit. He has quite unambiguously reiterated much that is familiar and tacitly accepted, and thus has become so domesticated in Christian — no less than Jewish — circles so as to blunt anti-Semitism's seriousness and tragedy. The accepted can become overlooked and forgotten. Carmichael's concern to underline Christian theology as a determinative component of anti-Semitism is valid: he is not alone in this. For many Gentiles especially his work will be salutary and doubtless sometimes staggeringly informative. How many Christians, for example, will have realized, although the evidence stared them in the face, that the revered Ernest Renan, the author of perhaps the most popular life of Jesus ever to have been written (though emphasizing the humanity of Jesus rather than his divinity), in his *Vie de Jésus* (1863), had played a role in furthering anti-Semitism?[21] Carmichael

---

19. *The History of Anti-Semitism*, trans. Richard Howard, 4 vols. (New York: Vanguard Press, 1965–75).

20. In his important study, *Toward a Definition of Antisemitism* (Berkeley: University of California Press, 1990); see especially his concluding chapter.

21. William Baird, who has so enriched our knowledge of the history of New Testament theology, wrote privately (in a letter dated 5 July 1993) as follows: "That Renan contributed to the advance of anti-semitism in the 19th century is clear." Baird quotes from a paper of his for a "Disciples' Theological Discussion Group":

> The most popular life of Jesus ever published was written by the erudite master of belles-lettres, member of the French Academy, Ernest Renan. First published in 1863, Renan's *Vie de Jésus* went through eleven editions within the first six months, and had been translated into a dozen languages by the end of 1864. On the surface, the book appears to be a wonderful mixture of historical novel and travelogue, but, in any case, it is a literary masterpiece. Jesus, according to Renan, grew up in glorious Galilee, where the wildflowers and the women were beautiful, and where a charming young teacher could inhale the pastoral atmosphere and cultivate spiritual and ethical ideas. In the south, in barren Judea, all was different — harsh and hostile. Jerusalem, the capital, was dominated by a corrupt priesthood and an arid scholasticism. "The science of the Jewish doctor, of the *sopher* or scribe," declared Renan, "was purely barbarous, unmitigatedly absurd, and denuded of all moral element. To crown the evil, it filled with ridiculous pride those who

may be knocking at doors that have long been opened, but since they can, alas, be easily shut again, his knocking must be very seriously heeded. But this being recognized, is his understanding of the origin and development of the tragedy of Jewish-Christian and Jewish-Gentile relations to be endorsed? The following considerations cause pause.

Self-Contradiction and Reductionism

Carmichael's own presentation of the historical development of The Great Hatred might be seen as modifying and invalidating his concentration on one doctrine, that which ascribed demonic status to "The Jews," as exercising such immense influence: is Carmichael not self-contradictory and reductionist?

1. He himself points out, as have others, that for many centuries the status of Jews was "relatively untouched by the stringencies of doctrine." The theological speculations of a small elite, the church fathers, "did not immediately engage the emotions of ordinary Christians."[22] Chrysostom (344–407 C.E.), for example, felt compelled to object virulently to Christians who had friendly relations with Jews: apparently their number was not negligible. This raises the question how far proselytism was practiced by Jews after 70 C.E. The view of Jews as having been driven to total isolation, proselytism thus being eliminated, was contested by Marcel Simon. Recently the

---

wearied themselves in acquiring it" (*Vie,* Modern Library [1927], 214). Things would have gone well for Jesus if he had stayed at home, but traveling to the south, he became contaminated by the apocalyptic and political notions of John the Baptist. Increasingly provoked by the legalism and corruption of Jewish religion, Jesus "appears no more as a Jewish reformer, but as a destroyer of Judaism" (p. 224). "The pride of blood appears to him the great enemy which was to be combated. In other words, Jesus was no longer a Jew. He was in the highest degree a revolutionary; he called all men to worship founded solely on the fact of their being children of God. He proclaimed the rights of man, not the rights of the Jew; the religion of man, not the religion of the Jew; the deliverance of man, not the deliverance of the Jew" (pp. 225–26).

Baird adds two other quotations from Renan's *Life of Jesus:* "But nations, like individuals, have their responsibilities, and if ever crime was the crime of a nation, it was the death of Jesus" (p. 358). "Christianity has been intolerant, but intolerance is not essentially a Christian fact. It is a Jewish fact in the sense that it was Judaism which first introduced the theory of the absolute in religion and laid down the principle that every innovator, even if he brings miracles to support his doctrine, ought to be stoned without trial" (p. 359). For a balanced assessment of Renan's attitude, see also Manuel, *The Broken Staff,* 308–11. What Manuel refers to as Renan's "intoxicating prose" and "dogmatic assurance" helps to account for Renan's immense popularity and influence, but time has not been kind to his linguistic and biblical views. For example, the distinction between Galilean and Judean Judaism cannot be maintained. See Martin Goodman in *The Cambridge History of Judaism,* vol. 3, forthcoming.

22. Carmichael, *Satanizing of the Jews,* 45. That the relationship between the church fathers and Jews and Judaism requires great caution and was far more complex than Carmichael recognizes, for example, appears in a study of some of the early fathers in *Early Christian Thought in Its Jewish Context,* ed. John Barclay and John Sweet (Cambridge: Cambridge University Press, 1996).

much neglected subject has been meticulously examined by L. H. Feldman. He concluded that "even as late as the fifth century" proselytism by Jews was a problem for the church.[23] Only very gradually did the attitude of Christian theologians trickle down to the populace. This took place to any significant degree only after 315, when the Emperor Constantine sponsored Christianity, and when, in 392, Theodosius I made that faith the official state religion. The social and economic consequences of these political developments led to the Christianization of Jerusalem especially, but also of all Palestine, now become "The Holy Land."[24] Jews were squeezed out of that country. The Diaspora became almost complete, and there gradually emerged the "commercial" Jew. In 425, the Jewish patriarchate was abolished. Colonies of Jews, foreign by geographic origin and social custom and not only by theology, spread throughout Europe and elsewhere. These "colonies" were haphazard and uncoordinated: their isolation (although the prelude to their eventual ghettoization) often did not usually cause irritation and friction. For centuries after 70 c.e. some Christians were attracted to Judaism; Jews were not eerie and awesome and threatening.

Before the first Crusade of 1096, there was even an "apparent" relaxation of anti-Jewish sentiment,[25] and in the rules and laws governing the life of Jews in the empire. It was only, then, in the eleventh century, when the first Crusade saw the first giant massacre of European Jews, that there was a marked change.[26] That Crusade, like others that followed, was not motivated solely by theological factors, and certainly not only by the one "demonic" doctrine that Carmichael emphasizes. Political and economic factors were also in play. Economic conditions were particularly hard at that time. "Between 970 and 1040 forty-eight famine years were counted. From 1085 to 1095 conditions were even worse. Misery and unrest prevailed widely."[27] Carmichael does not sufficiently recognize this confluence of causes: to do so would be to incur himself in self-contradiction.

By the eleventh century the understanding of the Diaspora of "The Jews"

---

23. See Marcel Simon, *Verus Israel: A Study of the Relations between Christians and Jews in the Roman Empire (135–425)* (Oxford: Oxford University Press, 1986), esp. 272; L. H. Feldman, "Proselytism by Jews in the Third and Fourth Centuries, *JJS* 24, no. 1 (1993): 1–58, esp. 58; and Robert Wilken, *John Chrysostom and the Jews: Rhetoric and Reality* (London and Berkeley: University of California Press, 1985).

24. See W. D. Davies, *The Gospel and the Land: Early Christianity and Jewish Territorial Doctrine* (Berkeley: University of California Press, 1974), 29f.; and Robert L. Wilken, *The Land Called Holy: Palestine in Christian History and Thought* (New Haven: Yale University Press, 1992).

25. Carmichael, *Satanizing of the Jews*, 50.

26. L. Poliakov writes of "the fateful summer of 1096" in *The History of Anti-Semitism*, 1:v. On the eleventh century, see Langmuir, "Irrational Fantasies," in *Toward a Definition of Antisemitism*, 195–298.

27. Williston Walker, *A History of the Christian Church* (Edinburgh, 1934), 54. See particularly Norman Cohen's *The Pursuit of the Millennium* (London: Secker and Warburg, 1957), esp. 40–52. On the Crusades, see now the pertinent sections in Katz, *The Holocaust in Historical Context*.

as a sign of divine punishment for "the murder of God" had indeed become entrenched in the European mind. At that time also certain strictly theological doctrines which impinged on Jews came to be embraced by Christians — such as that of transubstantiation, bringing with it the prominence of the possibility of the desecration of the Host, and the accusation of ritual murder against "The Jews," implying that they were knowingly evil. Langmuir, whose work Carmichael surprisingly does not refer to, has indicated that these new doctrines generated a climate of doubt and anxiety among Christian laity and clergy and were very unsettling, and this at a time when Oedipal psychological tendencies were also inevitably at work between adherents of ancient Judaism and those of its offspring, Christianity.[28] Any group that rejected or even criticized the Christian faith would be seen as inspiring further doubt and anxiety among believers and would become an object of suspicion. In this climate of increasing religious, monastic, and ascetic zeal, Jews could easily become targets. At the same time, an increase in the power and the reform of the prevailing ecclesiastical system, under a papacy constantly growing and reinforcing its centralized authority, made it more feasible to inculcate and to impose on society the dogmas and the doctrines of the church, including those that dealt with "The Jews." These doctrines became more widespread and influential among the masses. The point here is that the theological "Satanization of the Jews," as Carmichael calls it, by itself — initially and in isolation — up to the eleventh century had not markedly provoked hatred of "The Jews": his own presentation and examination reveal this.

2. There is another self-contradictory element in Carmichael's presentation. In the theology of the church, "The Jews" were witnesses to the triumph of the gospel and were, therefore, to be accepted in Christendom. As a consequence many of the decrees of the church protected Jews from maltreatment. The church provided what Carmichael recognizes as "a sponsorship through dogma" for Jews.[29] The exponents of the theology which created mystical anti-Semitism turn out to be the defenders of "The Jews." Carmichael does seem to recognize the contradiction involved in this, but not sufficiently. He explains it away by referring to the misappropriation of that theology by the masses in the millenarianism which swept Europe at the time of the Crusades and later. Extremists among the populace, unaware of the subtleties of the

---

28. See Langmuir, *Toward a Definition of Antisemitism,* 100–133. It cannot be sufficiently emphasized that the "youth," "the newness" of Christianity as over against Judaism, which was "old," was a disadvantage Christians had to overcome. This needs no documentation, so familiar is it. F. E. Greenspahn, *When Brothers Dwell Together: The Preeminence of Younger Siblings in the Hebrew Bible* (Oxford: Oxford University Press, 1994), holds that the people of Israel, in the Hebrew Bible, often find that the younger sons prevail over the older (e.g., Jacob over Esau), reflecting the ambivalence Jews felt about their "chosenness" from among the family of nations. This thesis deserves further exploration in later sources.

29. Carmichael, *Satanizing of the Jews,* 53.

theologians and mostly incapable of understanding them, could and did embrace only the most easily grasped element of the theology of the church —
the demonic character and role of "The Jews."[30] From the Crusades to the beginning of the sixteenth century, when ghettoes were established, Jews were
often subject to the ruthless violence of "enthusiasts." Carmichael supplies
evidence. This unreasoned and uncontrolled opposition to "The Jews" the ecclesiastical authorities and, by and large, the clergy did not endorse. But they
could not contain it. There was so much in the environment to stimulate it.

On the ecclesiastical side, for a clear reason, the worst excesses of the Inquisition, established in the thirteenth century, were not inflicted on Jews.
Jews could not strictly be branded "heretics" because the church regarded itself as the true heir of Judaism: it would be inconsistent to assert that Jews,
who adhered to that faith, were "heretics," although they were often accused
of being such, and the charge could easily emerge whenever it was convenient. Heresy hunting, however, was in the medieval air. The dilemma of
the church informed the decrees about Jews of the Fourth Lateran Council
of 1215. That council made it clear that, because of their role in the divine
plan, Jews were to be protected and not forcefully converted to Christianity.
They were not to be robbed or killed, their corpses were to be respected, their
cemeteries not to be desecrated. Again, however, one resolution, number 68,
demanded that Jews wear a special mark — the yellow badge — visibly to distinguish them from other people. And "separate" meant not only "unequal";
the visible separation of Jews also reinforced their "otherness." Their role in
the divine plan could easily turn them into depersonalized pawns.

Then, further, this "otherness" fed not only on peculiarly theological and
ecclesiastical factors but on agelong, endemic notions of magic, sorcery, and
witchery, all of which were connected with evil spirits and with heresy. The
thirteenth and fourteenth centuries saw the efflorescence of the understanding of the devil as a real being, not only in the heavens, but in this world:
Poliakov calls the fourteenth century "The Age of the Devil." Heresy was the
devil's work and heretics — not least "The Jews" — his agents, and as such
all sorts of accusations could be made against them. They were claimed to
poison wells, as in the period of the Black Death, which struck Western Europe in 1348. Jewish doctors were suspected of being sorcerers and magicians:
from the thirteenth century on, though kings and princes were conveniently
exempted from this prohibition, Christians were formally forbidden to go to
Jewish doctors. It was in the thirteenth century also that to "The Jews" were
ascribed those physical characteristics of the devil with which the Western

---

30. Ibid. On the enthusiasts or extremists, see especially Cohn, "Le Diable au Coeur." His
work is essential reading on all this section, as is Jacob Katz, *Exclusiveness and Tolerance: Studies
in Jewish-Gentile Relations in Medieval and Modern Times*, Scripta Judaica 3 (London: Oxford
University Press, 1961).

imagination is now familiar — horns, tails, an odious stench, and a peculiar nose. Jews were deemed to have congenital sicknesses, each Jewish tribe having its peculiar form of sickness. At the same time, they had extraordinary sexual virility and habits.

3. Moreover, many economic factors, not only theology, were also to stamp "the damned Jew" and "the wandering Jew" more deeply on the Western imagination. Brute economic and social realities fed into the conceptual theological animus to keep it alive, as we adverted to previously in connection with the Crusades. Although necessary to the developing mercantile economy of Europe and applicable to few of their numbers, the usury practiced by Jews was taken as a further indication of their "demonic" character. Usury was forbidden among Christians by the church, "so that Jews being outside Christian society and its laws, when debarred from other occupations, were often forced into the role of money-lenders and usurers."[31] This "repellent" usage, so necessary and convenient for Christians, further condemned Jews to persecution. At a later date — such is the irony of history — economic changes involved in the development of mercantilism between the thirteenth and fourteenth centuries led to a decline in the need for Jewish usurers, their function having been taken over by members of a new Gentile middle class that emerged and produced its own bankers and financial agents. The Jews ceased to be "necessary and convenient," and could be increasingly dispensed with. Their expulsion from England in 1290 and from most of France in 1366–94, and the destruction of many Jewish communities in Germany — all these occurrences speak for themselves. On top of all this, there were the ravages of the Black Death (1348–49), and in Spain the cruel events of 1492, and later, horrendous massacres in Poland in 1648–49. These events occurred not solely for theological reasons. Non-Jewish financial agents, bankers, and others had come to regard the Jewish usurers and entrepreneurs as their rivals: financial competition exacerbated social and religious suspicion of "The Jews." That this rivalry continued through the Renaissance and the Reformation down to the twentieth century Carmichael unambiguously documents.[32]

But he also emphasizes without letting up that the mystical anti-Semitism which was generated with the advent of Christianity prevailed unbroken down to the present century, and finally fed into the fantasies of Hitler, even though Carmichael recognizes that religious influences were minimal in the

---

31. See "Usury" in the *Encyclopedia of the Jewish Religion*, ed. R. J. Zwi Werblowsky and Geoffrey Wigoder (New York: Holt, Rinehart & Winston, 1965), 394.

32. The various stages of the development of capitalism involved Jews in a sort of seesaw of being economically necessary and used and becoming unnecessary and rejected. See the lucid essay by Salo W. Baron, "Modern Capitalism and Jewish Fate," in *History and Jewish Historians: Essays and Addresses*, compiled with a foreword by Arthur Hertzberg and Leon A. Feldman (Philadelphia: Jewish Publication Society of America, 1964), 43–65.

making of that figure. Carmichael lavishly illustrates his thesis to his own satisfaction. Nor does he overlook, in his concentration on theology, the way in which "The Jews" often conveniently became identified, not only as the economic rivals of the emerging entrepreneurs, but also as the specific political enemies that faced Christendom. In the eighth and ninth centuries "The Jews" were claimed to be on the side of the Moors, in the fifteenth century of the Turks — the Muslim enemies. James Parkes long ago made it impossible to underestimate how easily and constantly down to our own times political interests deliberately have used and fanned "The Great Hatred."[33]

But aware as he is of economic, social, and political factors, does not Carmichael succumb to a kind of myopic self-contradiction in his obsessive emphasis on the theological origins of mystical anti-Semitism? Does he sufficiently consider that the excesses of hatred toward "The Jews" occurred against the will of the church fathers and leaders, and because of influences other than the strictly theological conceptions to which he traces mystical anti-Semitism — factors of a social, economic, and political nature? Theological notions were and are, alas, exploited to fan hatred of "The Jews." Mystical anti-Semitism, however, did not originate only with these theological notions but, as we stated previously, also from endemic, agelong notions of witchery, sorcery, and magic and, in addition, from certain harsh, tangible, inescapable economic realities in a newly emerging mercantile world. Carmichael's presentation of the historical impact of his mystical anti-Semitism, his rigid adherence to this constant, clearly defined concept as the *fons et origo* of The Great Hatred, leads him to elevate it too exclusively above those social, political, and economic forces which, along with the theological, all cohered to give birth to that tragedy.

4. Along with self-contradiction, Carmichael's work demands a degree of reductionism. This reductionism is implicit in what we have written above. We now point to more explicit examples of it.

To begin with, does not Carmichael's almost exclusive concentration on mystical anti-Semitism, which he presents as *sui generis* and unlike all other ethnic hostility, from which it is to be sharply distinguished, lead him to ignore pre-Christian hostility to Jews with which post-Christian anti-Semitism should be compared and connected? In fact, the Greco-Roman world revealed hostility to Jews, which at least to some degree (not, we emphasize, to

---

33. For references to J. W. Parkes's works, see W. D. Davies, "Chosen People: The Approach to Antisemitism," *The Congregational Quarterly* (London) 26, no. 4 (October 1948): 327–41. Baron, in "Modern Capitalism and Jewish Fate" (see previous note), has convincingly shown how Jewish life has always been open to and has unavoidably interacted with the social and political environment: Jews have never been able to escape the larger world, and their responses to it have been immensely rich. Had that world uniformly regarded them as demonic, such rich interaction, despite its frequent animosities and sufferings, would not have been possible.

be exaggerated) foreshadowed what came later in Christendom. The evidence has often been given and need only be summarily noted here.[34]

In the Hellenistic Age, Jews had many privileges.[35] But they were not therefore safe. Privileges usually evoke protests; and attacks upon Jewry then, as so often since, were common. However, it is erroneous to refer to these attacks as anti-Semitic, because that term presupposes the developed racial theories of the nineteenth century. Best is to use the term "anti-Judaism." At first, contacts between Jews and Greeks were of a military nature and highly favorable. To the Greeks, Jews at first appeared as an admirable school of philosophers, and in the persecutions under Antiochus Epiphanes it was to Sparta that many Jews turned. Were not Spartan discipline and Jewish legalism congenial? We do not hear of a specific pogrom until Roman times, when Augustus deprived the Greek inhabitants of Alexandria of their Senate and allowed them only titular magistracies, and at the same time confirmed the Jews in all their rights. There were further outbreaks against Jews in the time of Caligula: the wealthy Jews of Alexandria were driven to the Delta and four hundred of their houses sacked. According to Josephus (BJ XI, xviii, 7–8, iii, I, 3), in the late sixties C.E., fifty thousand Jews were killed in Alexandria. But caution is in order in the acceptance of figures given in the sources. Moreover, while the exact nature of the expulsions of Jews from Rome under Tiberius (19 C.E.) and Claudius (probably 49–50 C.E.) is uncertain, they do point to the insecurity of Jewry even in Rome itself.

And anti-Judaism, although it only broke out into open violence in the Roman period, had old roots. First, the Hellenistic Age was syncretistic. While Aristotle had accepted the near-dogma in Greece that Greeks were essentially superior to other men, Alexander the Great, his pupil, rejected this; for him there was neither Jew nor Greek: he desired their fusion, and that of all men, in a common Hellenic culture. But the universalism of Alexander and of the Hellenistic Age demanded a religious pluralism which religious Jews could not countenance. However far they could go toward assimilation,

---

34. In the following I draw on my essay "The Jewish State in the Hellenistic World," in *Peake's Commentary on the Bible*, ed. Matthew Black and H. H. Rowley (London and New York: Thomas Nelson & Sons, 1962), 686–92. For a balanced presentation, see John C. Meagher, "As the Twig Is Bent: Anti-Semitism in Greco-Roman and Earliest Christian Times," in *Anti-Semitism and the Foundations of Christianity*, ed. Alan T. Davies (New York: Paulist Press, 1979), 1–26.

35. A sharp distinction was drawn in Roman law between Jewish citizens and Jewish resident aliens. The latter could marry according to Jewish law, practice polygamy, follow Jewish laws of succession, be tried by the Roman governor, could be flogged, expelled, imprisoned, and did not have the right to the highest offices in the state. They usually dressed like Romans. Jewish citizens could marry according to Jewish law but only because this was not in conflict with Roman law. They could not practice polygamy, could only follow Roman laws of succession, but could also appeal to the emperor. They were free from flogging, expulsion, and imprisonment, and they had the right to the highest offices (e.g., there were Jewish senators), but had to dress as Roman citizens (Black and Rowley, *Peake's Commentary*, 688).

the commandment under which they lived, "Thou shalt have no other gods before Me," made final assimilation impossible. For the Gentile, freedom and universalism meant in the *sphere of religion* the right to worship any god as one pleased: for the Jew, it could only mean the worship of the one living God before whom there was none other. Thus Jews were accused of being atheists, the point of which was not that they were what we should call speculative atheists, nor that they objected to images (the Jews were not always imageless, and not the only imageless worshipers). They were atheists because they actually opposed gods — the gods of the state and of the Gentile world (see Josephus, *Contra Apion* 1.34).

But this fundamental religious stumbling-block engendered also *social tensions*. The Jew was a creature apart. The fence of the Law which protected him became an offense. Thus the observance of the Sabbath struck Greeks as utterly irrational. For the refusal of the Hasidim to defend themselves rather than violate the Sabbath, the Greeks had only contempt. To them only fanatics could observe the dietary laws, which gave to Jews a reputation not only for blind credulity but for inhospitality; the refusal to participate in Gentile meals, private and public, gained for them the reputation of being unsociable monsters. They were accused of human sacrifice (which they had early condemned). Apion asserted that a captured Greek was found put to death in the Temple by Antiochus Epiphanes. Jews were claimed to have no regard for any man.

Moreover, there were *philosophic attacks* on Jews. The philosophers usually emphasized universalism and rationalism. These were solvents of "nationalism," of ethnic particularism. To recognize distinctions among Jew and Greek and barbarian was objectionable, and the Stoics especially resented Jewish particularism. This comes out in 4 Maccabees 5:5ff. where Antiochus Epiphanes argues philosophically with Eleazar concerning the partaking of swine's flesh: his reasoning was doubtless often followed: "And Antiochus seeing him, said, 'I would counsel thee, old man, before thy tortures begin, to taste the swine's flesh and save your life; ... For wherefore, since nature has conferred upon you the most excellent flesh of this animal, do you loathe it? It seems senseless not to enjoy what is pleasant, yet not disgraceful, and from notions of sinfulness to reject the boons of nature....'"

Again the *political aspect* of anti-Judaism is real. To the Roman government Judaism was merely one among many foreign cults being propagated in the empire and invading Rome itself. And Rome was increasingly being filled with Eastern sects — mystery, magical, astrological, philosophic. Confined to foreigners these were tolerated, but when they began to undermine the ancestral forms of Roman religion measures were taken against them, although on the grounds, not of religion, but of morality. Nor was it difficult to justify these measures. Many of the sects were often immoral; thus

the attacks on the Bacchanalia by Rome in 186 B.C.E. were probably necessary. Not only morally were the sects dangerous but also politically. They
provided cells around which factions could grow. Thus Judaism was included
in a widespread and real suspicion of Eastern groups. Moreover, the intran-
sigence of the Jews in Palestine and especially their openness to Parthian
influences made Jews everywhere more politically suspect: the "central government" had every reason to be wary of them. On the other hand, from
the point of view of the local communities within which they dwelt, the Jews
were especially privileged by the "central government." Many of the privileges were maintained forcibly by Rome so that Jews could easily be regarded
as partisans of Rome against the local population.

Economic reasons for anti-Judaism do not appear to have been especially
operative. But there can be little doubt that Jews would have been unpopular
on account of the export of money for the Temple tax from areas which
could have used it themselves, and measures for the tax's protection had to
be carefully devised: that Vespasian thought it worthwhile to perpetuate the
tax after 70 C.E. indicates how considerable it must have been.

The above factors, and others, combined to produce anti-Judaism. In
Latin authors an item not hitherto mentioned is apparent: Horace, Strabo,
and Ovid found the Jews' *aggressive proselytism* offensive. Conversion to
Judaism, unlike conversion to less demanding religions, usually meant a complete break with nation, family, friends, and the former life: it, therefore,
appeared inhuman. How much Cicero knew about Jews is uncertain. He
does not use the stock terms of abuse to which we shall shortly refer, and
his reference to the Jews as "a nation born to be slaves" is merely rhetorical hyperbole. More important than stray references in Latin authors is the
specific anti-Judaistic literature that developed. This was Alexandrian and expressed the Egyptian point of view. Since the beginning of the sixth century,
Jews in Egypt (at Elephantine) had represented foreign overlords: those who
came with the Ptolemies were likewise "alien." So it came about that with
Egyptians, and also with Greeks, in Alexandria, Jews were unpopular. A long
tradition of anti-Judaism created a convention of anti-Jewish accusations. In
the third century B.C.E. Hecataeus of Abdera, a Greek living in Egypt, gave
the Egyptian version of the exodus. A pestilence caused by the anger of the
gods at the presence of foreign elements in the population led to the expulsion of Jews. Most of these settled in Palestine. There Moses, famous for his
wisdom and valor, ordained for them an inhospitable and inhuman way of
life. Another Egyptian, a priest called Manetho, in the same century wrote a
history of his people, the thesis of which Josephus has preserved for us. The
exodus from Egypt was really the defeat and expulsion of certain rebellious
Egyptians who had been isolated as lepers and criminals. In the second century B.C.E. Mnaseas, a highly rhetorical historian in Alexandria, held Jews to

ridicule because they worshiped God in the form of an ass — the ass being in Egypt a symbol of evil. This charge reappears in the first century B.C.E. in the work of Posidonius, Apollonius Molo, who taught Cicero and Caesar, and in that of Apion, a Greek grammarian of the first century C.E., who wrote a work against the Jews to which Josephus replied in *Against Apion*. Thus while we cannot strictly speak of anti-Semitism in the racial sense in the pre-Christian period (while the Greeks before Alexander had attached a certain theoretical importance to purity of descent and though Romans often made pretensions to this, feelings of racial purity did not play any significant role in the Hellenistic Age), there was a well-marked anti-Judaism.[36] Is Carmichael justified in ignoring this?

The kind of hostility to which we have pointed in the Greco-Roman period is incomparably less horrendous than that of later anti-Semitism, nor had it the racial components and connotations present in the latter. In his penetrating study, "Theological Responses to the Holocaust," Amos Funkenstein rightly finds that "Christian anti-Judaism appears in a much sharper light when compared to its [pagan] antecedents."[37]

Nevertheless, Carmichael's almost total divorce of pre- from post-Christian animosity to Jews is highly questionable. This makes it possible for him to concentrate on the theological cause so as to minimize political, social, and (to a lesser extent in the pre-Christian period) economic factors which must also be considered to have made The Great Hatred possible. The mystical anti-Semitism he postulates doubtless was an ever-present sleeping dog throughout Western European history, but that dog was only stirred to life in its full fury by forces outside itself, particularly as so horrendously in this century. Without the impulsion of those external forces it is reasonable to infer that The Great Hatred might not have continued to express itself so relentlessly. Doubtless the sleeping dog would have persisted, but perhaps slumbering undisturbed. If Christian-generated mystical anti-Semitism formed a backdrop to The Great Hatred, which culminated in Hitler and Stalin, the evidence seems to suggest that there was a customary antipathy to Jews in the Greco-Roman world which (although it has often been overemphasized) also formed a backdrop to any mystical anti-Semitism of the Christian era. Elements found in that earlier classical backdrop, less potent and less pregnant though that anti-Judaism undoubt-

---

36. E. M. Smallwood, in *The Cambridge History of Judaism*, vol. 3, forthcoming; L. H. Feldman and John G. Gager, "Anti-Semitism in the Ancient World," in *History and Hate: The Dimensions of Anti-Semitism*, ed. David Berger (Philadelphia: Jewish Publication Society of America, 1986), 15–42; J. G. Gager, *The Origins of Anti-Semitism: Attitudes toward Judaism in Pagan and Classical Antiquity* (Oxford: Oxford University Press, 1983).

37. In *Perceptions of Jewish History* (Los Angeles: University of California Press, 1993), 306–37; quotation is from p. 313.

edly was, reemerge in odd ways in the later "Mystical Anti-Semitism," as we have already observed.[38] Carmichael's reductionism at this point is clear.

Aspects of Christian theology even in its decline, as Carmichael sees it, could and did provide a *point d'appui* for mystical anti-Semitism, but this was not always, if ever, solely its *point de départ*. Those aspects formed part of the cultural undergrowth of Western European culture, or the mulch of that culture, as Professor E. Cady expresses it,[39] as anti-Judaism had been in the mulch of pre-Christian classical culture. But this theology of the modern world, in decline since the Renaissance and Enlightenment according to Carmichael, was seldom if ever the only source of anti-Semitism.

Hamlet without the Prince of Denmark?

A second question raised by Carmichael's work is inseparable from the first. Has he done justice to the meaning of the encounter between Judaism and the Christian gospel in the first century and later? He concentrates on two phenomena — the demonization of "The Jews" and the delay in the *parousia* — as the root causes of mystical anti-Semitism. These phenomena were real, but how influential were they? The role of demonology in early Christianity was emphasized in recent scholarship by Bishop Gustav Aulen in a significant volume, *Christus Victor,* and by M. Werner in *Die Enstehung des christlichen Dogmas.*[40] Except as it constitutes part of the world of discourse of the New Testament, demonology did not play a dominant part in the interpretation of Christian origins. It is otherwise with the *parousia* — the return of Jesus after his crucifixion. But is it likely that it simply was two concepts —

---

38. I have argued elsewhere (see "Paul and the Gentiles: A Suggestion concerning Romans 11:13-24," in *Jewish and Pauline Studies,* referred to in n. 7) that early Gentile Christians in Rome and elsewhere might have been conditioned by the pre-Christian anti-Judaism of the Greco-Roman world to be prejudiced against Jews. Indeed, the very emphasis on demonology in the confrontation between Christians and Jews to which we refer in the next few pages — it has been suggested — was an inevitable reaction to the emphasis of the rootedness of the Christian faith in a Judaism which had its own demonology (in turn) in its confrontation with paganism. We have been unable to substantiate this claim. We are not quite convinced with J. G. Gager that "we may now put to rest the notion that Gentile converts to Christianity brought with them, *as Gentiles,* the pervasive anti-Semitism of the Greco-Roman world" (*The Origins of Anti-Semitism,* 112). Is the distinction here between *Gentiles* and Gentile converts to Judaism who became Christian later a distinction without a difference? There was no *pervasive* anti-Semitism in the Greco-Roman world but there was a real criticism of Judaism, along with much appreciation of it, among the intelligentsia, and much popular antipathy on grounds summarized here and by Feldman. Carmichael is hardly justified in drawing such an utter distinction as he does between pre- and post-Christian antagonism to Jews, although this former antagonism we prefer to designate "anti-Judaism" rather than "anti-Semitism."

39. In a private communication.

40. G. Aulen, *Christus Victor,* trans. A. G. Herbert (New York: Macmillan, 1951); M. Werner, *Die Enstehung des christlichen Dogmas: Problemgeschichtlich Dargestellt,* 2d ed. (Bern: Verlag Paul Haupt; Tübingen: Katzmann-Verlag, 1954).

"The Jews" as demonic and the delay of the *parousia* — that were the dynamic forces governing Jewish-Christian relations at the beginning and later?

Here it is imperative to recognize that the Christian faith created a crisis in tradition within Jewish messianism in which conceptions of an ideal world, of the restoration of the Davidic kingdom, of the centrality of the land of Israel and of Jerusalem, combined with those of the day of the Lord and the last judgment, were recognized aspects of Jewish revelation and tradition. Belief in a future redemption in the terms indicated had become domesticated within the Hebraic tradition with little discomfort to that tradition. Hopes for a redemption either by the restoration of Israel and the world to a primordial or primeval condition, that is, in a restorative sense, or by the advent of a kind of utopia, which represents "the conception of redemption as a phenomenon in which something emerges which has never before existed, in which something totally new is unmistakably expressed," could coexist, as Gershom Scholem pointed out. He continued:

> Of course, these restorative and Utopian elements in the messianic idea could exist side by side *as long as it was simply a hope that was projected into the distant future, an affirmation of faith that corresponded to no real experience.* As long as the messianic hope remained abstract, not yet concretized in people's experience or demanding a concrete decision, it was possible for it to embody even what was contradictory without the latent contradiction being felt. . . . Messianism could take over even a conservative attitude and in this way become part of the tradition. Messianic *activity*, however, could hardly do this. The moment that messianism moved from the realm of affirmation of faith, abstract doctrine, and synthesizing imagination [that is, from the merely doctrinal or conceptual] into life, and took on acute forms, it had to reach a point where the energies that lay dormant in these two elements would emerge into conflict with each other — the conflict of the tradition of the past versus the presence of redemption.[41]

It was precisely such a conflict that erupted when the Christian gospel confronted Judaism. A familiar realm can illustrate this. In its eschatology Judaism could and did *speculatively* or *theoretically* contemplate changes in the Torah and possibly even a New Torah.[42] But let a movement arise within Judaism actually annulling parts of the Torah and the reaction was swift to reject it, and that with passion.

---

41. Italics added. See Davies, *The Gospel and the Land*, 370–76, for bibliographical details.

42. See W. D. Davies, *Torah in the Messianic Age and/or in the Age to Come*, JBL Monograph Series 7 (Philadelphia: Society of Biblical Literature, 1952). Reprinted in *The Setting of the Sermon on the Mount* (Cambridge: Cambridge University Press, 1964), 109–90.

Early Jewish Christians proclaiming the advent of the Messianic Age and a future coming of Jesus as Lord seem to have found little difficulty in remaining within the ambience of Jewish revelation and tradition, even though they anticipated an imminent incursion of Gentiles to worship in Jerusalem. They could have continued in such a conviction indefinitely, without objection from Judaism. They were free *to speculate* about the restoration of The Land and other matters. What created a crisis both within Judaism and the contiguous Jewish Christianity was no "speculation" or even "conviction": it was a brute historical fact. *Before* Jerusalem had become the center of the New Israel on Mount Zion, a community had emerged in response to Jesus, the Messiah, which dispensed with the oral Law as unnecessary to salvation. Outside the Law and outside The Land, there was a messianic activity, transcending old distinctions, removing the fence of the Torah, a tangible, visible activity, and spreading outside The Land, which could not be masked or made innocuous by "speculation." What were Judaism and Jewish Christianity to make of this fact?

There was no difficulty for traditional Judaism: it rejected the new movement as dangerous. What of Jewish Christianity? It attempted to contain and interpret the new community of the Messiah, Jesus, by insisting that, in accordance with traditional expectations, the gospel was first to be preached to the Jews and in due and proper course to the Gentiles. But facts intervened upon the anticipated procedures. The sheer actuality of Gentile converts, who, it could not be denied, revealed the grace of God, tended to disprove the terms of the messianic redemption expressed by Jewish tradition and accepted by Jewish Christianity. As a matter of history, it had to be recognized, however reluctantly, that the redemption of the Gentiles was not bound up with the prior establishment of the House of David in Jerusalem, to which the Gentiles were later to flow. The pattern imposed on the messianic redemption by Jewish tradition was shattered and had to be abandoned. In fact, the movement inaugurated through Jesus reversed the anticipated course of messianic events; the concourse of Gentiles taking up the collection to Jerusalem was the symbol, the effective symbol, of that reversal.

"There are three ways," Scholem wrote, "in which tradition evolves and develops in history. It can be carried forward with a retention of continuity; it can be transformed through a natural process of metamorphosis and assume a new configuration; and, finally, it can be subjected to a break which is associated with the rejection of the tradition itself."[43] Gentile Christianity, in abandoning the acceptance of the Law as a condition of membership in the People of God and in the messianic redemption, challenged Judaism in its very being, that is, in its interpretation of (1) the Law, the ground and guide

---

43. See Davies, *The Gospel and the Land*, for bibliographical references.

of its life; (2) in its self-identity as a people; (3) and in its promised future in The Land and otherwise. It was not, primarily at least, any impulse derived from Judaism itself that led Paul to accept the removal of the requirements of the Law from his Gentile churches; it was an impulse born of or dictated by the concrete situation, demanding concrete decisions, in those churches. The significance of our statement can be appreciated only if Scholem's discussion, "The Crisis of Tradition in Jewish Messianism,"[44] is taken with full seriousness.

The word "impulse" might suggest a sudden, unreflective reaction. But the writings of the New Testament reveal that such reactions emerged out of an eschatological crisis that demanded intellectual and ethical wrestling with the tradition on several fronts — the suffering of the Messiah, the Law, the People of God, and the remnant and the land of Israel. In coming to grips with Gentile Christianity, early Christians (Jewish and Gentile) had to assess radically all aspects of Judaism, and they either abandoned or transformed them or lent them a new perspective.

It has become a near-dogma in modern New Testament scholarship (another example of overconceptualization applied to Christian origins?) that it was the delay in the *parousia* that initiated early Christian theology. Disappointment with a speculative anticipation, as has been emphasized by Carmichael and by others, spurred on a reinterpretation of the ground and of the content of the Christian faith. But, in the light of Scholem's work, would the delay of the *parousia* in itself have stimulated such activity?[45] There is an essential irrationality in eschatological types such as the early Christians must, in some measure, be taken to have been; they can live with antitheses — the earnest expectation of a near end and extreme activity. It is not unlikely that early Christians were not only moved by the question, "What shall we do now that the end is delayed?" but also by, "How are we to understand our faith in the light of the emergence of these Gentile Christians, who are without the Law and outside The Land, but yet share in the redemption?" The emergence of a community in which there was neither Jew nor Greek, in which Jews and Gentiles were called upon *not only to think together, but actually to eat together, and that consciously and on principle,* compelled the reassessment not only of the place of the Law and The Land, but of the people and of eschatological hopes. The Jewish tradition, within which the earliest Christians arose, had dictated the understanding of the end. Consequently the earliest Christians looked to the *parousia* to confirm their faith. And, at first, Paul himself shared this view. Later, it was the grace of God in the Gen-

---

44. In Gershom Scholem, *The Messianic Idea in Judaism and Other Essays on Jewish Spirituality* (New York: Schocken Books, 1971), 49–77.

45. See now D. C. Allison, Jr., *The End of the Ages Has Come: An Early Interpretation of the Passion and Resurrection of Jesus* (Minneapolis: Fortress Press, 1985), 163–68.

tile churches that amazed him: *there* was the confirmation of his faith. So, too, the Book of Acts has been called "a confirmation of the gospel": Luke saw in the progress of Gentile Christianity the explication and validation of the gospel, and so did Matthew. And in the Fourth Gospel the hope of John (chapter 17) lies in the quality of the life of the redeemed community. Community realized or fulfilled with all the "brute actualities" that this implied in the face of the deepest cleavage probably known to the first century — that between Jew and Gentile — played perhaps as great a part as hope deferred in the reinterpretation of the tradition to which we refer.[46]

The position we have indicated suggests that in his absorption in the demonology of the early church and in the delay of the *parousia,* Carmichael has overlooked the essential nature of the encounter between Judaism and early Christianity. That encounter was not governed simply or mainly by any *concepts* concerning demons and the *parousia,* but by an actual, visible fact — the emergence of the church with the incursion of Gentiles into the "Israel of God." This overriding fact, and not merely theological considerations as such, constituted the unavoidable spearhead of the challenge of the Christian faith to Judaism. That the latter reacted sharply at times, probably violently, to this incursion, is not surprising. Unfortunately Carmichael, by and large, turns a blind eye to this initial but fateful reaction: he never mentions the *Birkath ha-Minim,* for example.[47] Christian scholars have sometimes overemphasized the extent and virulence of the Jewish persecution of early Christians.[48] Nor would the recognition of such persecution, of course, in any way condone that of Jews by Christians, and (need it be said?) it was nothing remotely similar to what the twentieth century has seen. However, Scholem's words, quoted above, deserve pondering and applying to Jewish-Christian relations in the first century. In ignoring the crucial significance of the emergence of a community allowing Gentiles to enter "Israel" on equal terms with Jews,

---

46. In all this discussion a simple fact must not be ignored. It is stated in typically subtle and noteworthy fashion by Bishop Kenneth Cragg in a forthcoming work, a chapter on "Christian Judaica." He writes: "[I]n its very genesis in sequel to Jesus and his Cross, the Christian faith was *by Jewish minds and hands . . .*" (italics added). It was Jews themselves — Jesus, Paul, and others — who issued the challenge to their own Judaism. As Cragg reminds us, Christianity was not (and is not) a Hellenistic excrescence on Judaism (i.e., something which grows out unnaturally), as even some recent scholars such as Haim Maccoby, in his work *Paul and Hellenism* (London and Philadelphia: SCM Press, 1991), have held; but it is a development of and within Judaism itself. For Paul certainly it was the consummation of Judaism. See my essay referred to above in n. 7, and my *Paul and Rabbinic Judaism,* 4th ed. (Philadelphia: Fortress Press, 1980), xxiii–xxv and 1–16, where I urge that, in any case, Judaism itself was already "Hellenized" in certain aspects by the first century, as Martin Hengel has since so convincingly established in his *Judaism and Hellenism: Studies in Their Encounter in Palestine during the Early Hellenistic Period,* trans. John Bowden, 2 vols. (Philadelphia: Fortress Press, 1974).

47. On this, see W. Horbury in *The Cambridge History of Judaism,* vol. 3, forthcoming.

48. See D. R. A. Hare, *The Theme of Jewish Persecution of Christians in the Gospel according to St. Matthew* (Cambridge: Cambridge University Press, 1967).

Carmichael has missed the heart of the matter; he has written Hamlet without the Prince of Denmark. A Jewish scholar, Professor Arthur Hertzberg[49] has recently and powerfully insisted that the doctrine of "Chosenness" is the heart of Judaism — all the rest being merely commentary on it. Even if this might be questioned as too exclusive an affirmation,[50] such a position would inevitably lead us not to be surprised that the heart of the hostility between Judaism and Christianity arose, not from any neat conceptual considerations nor even a merely conceptual denial of the chosenness of the Jewish people, but from the costly actual "denial" of that peculiar chosenness, or rather, more accurately, from the inclusive factual enlargement of it, in early Christianity. This Carmichael has not recognized. It is this same questioning of peculiar chosenness that connects the hostility toward Jews in the Christian world after 70 C.E. with the Greco-Roman world before that date.[51] A quotation concerning the nature of that hostility in the pre-Christian period by Emilio Gabba, referring to a Jewish scholar, makes this clear. Summarizing the situation in the pre-Christian Greco-Roman world, Gabba writes:

> The fundamental reason for the emergence of anti-Semitism has been correctly isolated by V. Tcherikover in the clash between the religious, political, administrative, economic and cultural organism which formed the basis of Greek (and classical) social co-existence, that is to say, the *polis*, and the religious and political organization of the Jewish communities of the Diaspora, founded on total adherence to the traditional laws and special customs of the Jewish people, which were, as a rule, guaranteed by special privileges granted by the Hellenistic kings, and later by the Roman government. So the ethnic Jewish community lives side by side with the Greek community in the same city, and enjoys the advantages of Greek civic life, in which indeed it is anxious to play a part. But it cannot renounce its own traditions and obligations, which means that it does not take its fair share of the city's burdens. Nor, of course, can it recognize the religious foundations of Greek city life. There must have been daily causes for annoyance, arising from the Greeks' inability to understand such an attitude, and the Jews' inability to stop themselves. Thus the phenomenon of anti-Judaism can be read-

---

49. *The Condition of Jewish Belief: A Symposium Compiled by the Editors of "Commentary" Magazine* (New York: Macmillan, 1966), 90. See the discussion of Hertzberg's work in John Murray Cuddihy, *No Offense: Civil Religion and Protestant Task* (New York: Seabury Press, 1978), 101–55.

50. See W. D. Davies, *The Territorial Dimension of Judaism* (Berkeley: University of California Press, 1982; reprint, with a symposium and further reflections, Minneapolis: Fortress Press, 1991), 137–38.

51. Carmichael's insistence on the uniqueness of mystical anti-Semitism, that it is *sui generis*, misleads him in all this. This is not to identify pre-Christian anti-Semitism (Tcherikover's term; we would prefer "anti-Judaism") with The Great Hatred which emerged in the Christian era and introduced a more horrendous dimension to that phenomenon.

ily explained in an urban society where social life is organized on the basis of the *polis.* In Egypt, for example, anti-Jewish manifestations are quite comprehensible in Alexandria (and also those in Memphis, for example, in the first half of the first century B.C.E.). In the country areas, where the Jews were also quite numerous, anti-Jewish outbreaks are much smaller in scale, late to develop, and inspired rather by political reasons of a general nature.[52]

Another implicit element of contradiction and reductionism appears in Carmichael's treatment of "modern times," if we loosely, as do some, take this term to mean what followed the Enlightenment in Western Europe. In two chapters entitled "Secularization" and "Science and Mock Science," he indicates how, since the Enlightenment, other explanations of anti-Semitism, besides the theological, have been offered. Under the former title, he points out how in the Enlightenment in Germany and France, as might be expected, any theological component informing anti-Semitism came to be either discounted or ignored. "Enlightened" rationalism could not seriously husband a theological emphasis. Among the physiocrats and the leaders of the Enlightenment, the hostility toward Jews came to be regarded as a natural and inevitable outcome of the Jews' social, political, and economic circumstances. It was these circumstances that had produced the despicable and despised Jews. It was thought that given an improvement in their circumstances and their consequent acceptance into the mainstream of European life, Jews would in time become "normal" members of society. Tolerance, social and material improvements, and acceptance would be the instruments for the amelioration and eventual disappearance of "The Jewish Problem," although among some of the leaders of the Enlightenment, especially Voltaire, the tolerance espoused did not extend to "The Jews." This sociological approach has been accepted by many in "liberal" and "humanistic" circles ever since — down to the very present. Hertzberg, whose earlier work, *The French Enlightenment and the Jews* (1968), richly illumined this matter, in a recent extended review of some contemporary studies of The Great Hatred, concluded that at the present time the dominant interpretation of the causes of anti-Semitism has become the sociological one.[53]

There are three very clear and telling implications of this sociological approach for an assessment of Carmichael's work. First, the hostility between

---

52. E. Gabba, "The Growth of Anti-Judaism," in *The Cambridge History of Judaism,* vol. 2: *The Hellenistic Age,* ed. W. D. Davies and Louis Finkelstein (Cambridge: Cambridge University Press, 1989), 636–37.

53. A. Hertzberg, "Is Anti-Semitism Dying Out? – Anti-Semitism: The Longest Hatred," *New York Review of Books* (24 June 1993): 51–57. On Voltaire and the Jews, see W. D. Davies, "Reflections on a Pauline Allegory in a French Context," in *The New Testament Age: Essays in Honor of Bo Reicke* (Macon, Ga.: Mercer University Press, 1984), 1:107–26. Essay also appears as chapter 8 in present volume.

Gentiles and Jews is comparable with "the reciprocal paranoia" long recognized as often existing among and between other differing social groups.
Second, it is not necessary to postulate any dominating or exclusive theological grounds to account for anti-Semitism. Third, though this is not often
acknowledged, the sociological approach often involves and even contem-
plates the eventual "normalization" and absorption of Jews in and by the
Western world, and their consequent ultimate disappearance as a people, an
outcome that is often also arrogantly, insensitively, and disastrously implicitly
desired. These three implications run directly counter to Carmichael's thesis.
As we have previously noted, he insufficiently allows for the forces to which
the sociological approach points.

But there are more serious contradictions and weaknesses in Carmichael's
stance. Oddly enough for one who emphasizes the theological grounds for
mystical anti-Semitism, Carmichael takes an inconsistent attitude toward
Christian theology. He writes of the time when "humanists of the nineteenth
and twentieth centuries no longer took theology seriously, the edifice began to crumble, the emotions surfacing in mystical anti-Semitism were left
without a foothold in a larger...sustaining intellectual structure..., when
theology became obsolete through the cooling of faith."[54] Carmichael confidently (far too confidently, we must think) asserts that the Enlightenment
made Christian theology antiquated and irrelevant! If so, one would have
expected him to rejoice in the demise of this prime source of mystical anti-
Semitism. But the brute facts of life after the Enlightenment do not allow
this. The decline of Christian theology, as Carmichael understands it, did
not spell the gradual disappearance of mystical, or of any other form of anti-
Semitism. The period after the Enlightenment saw recurring expressions of
The Great Hatred culminating in the Holocaust. If the Christian theological
grounds for mystical anti-Semitism had declined, yet the phenomenon of The
Great Hatred certainly persisted and intensified.

One inconsistency has led to another. *Before* the Enlightenment, as we
saw, Carmichael points out, paradoxically, that Christian theologians and
ecclesiastics were protective sponsors of Jews against the worst excesses of
the hatred toward them: the very ground of mystical anti-Semitism provided
its own antidote. *After* the Enlightenment, when the Christian theological
ground was eroding, it still operated to create the poison: its effects were actually far more pernicious during its gradual decline than during its heyday!
Carmichael, as we noted, chose simply to ignore animosity toward Jews in
the pre-Christian era. But he cannot ignore the hatred that existed after the
Enlightenment, in a period which apparently, in his mind, is a post-Christian
era, because it has so blatantly culminated in the Holocaust.

---

54. Carmichael, *Satanizing of the Jews*, 133–40.

The decline in Christianity, as Carmichael sees this, coincides, then, with the most horrendous phenomena of hate. He explains this seeming contradiction to which we point by insisting that, despite its demise, Christian theology has left an inescapable residue of hatred toward Jews. That there is such a residue, especially among the least educated, cannot be denied. However, what is not explicable in Carmichael's terms is why this residue — the detritus of Christian theology — has been so much more disastrously productive of hatred of Jews than had been the dominant Christianity that has so surely, albeit so slowly, deposited it across the centuries. If Christian theology were the *fons et origo* of The Great Hatred, why was it only after Christianity's alleged collapse that that hatred became most intense? Is not Carmichael again guilty of self-contradictory reductionism? Were there not other factors than the theological causing this evil?

In fact, Carmichael is fully aware that Christian theology is not the sole culprit accused, and that explanations other than the theological and sociological have been offered for The Great Hatred. In nineteenth-century Europe, theories of race came to be propounded. Literary critics and writers in that century pointed to and dwelled on fundamental cultural differences among peoples. Differences in language were confidently taken to indicate deep racial divisions. For example, the Celtic languages were understood to indicate an unmistakably distinct Celtic people or race. And peoples were to be judged and compared by what they were peculiarly or distinctively in themselves. The work of Matthew Arnold comes to mind in *The Study of Celtic Literature* (1867) and *Culture and Anarchy* (1869). In the same nineteenth century, biologists fed into this ideology of race and lent it "scientific" prestige. On grounds now deemed quite unscientific, there were confident references to Teutonic and Semitic races and peoples. In such a climate it was easy to regard Jews as essentially or radically distinct or different from other peoples and alien to them. This racial approach to Jews was to find its ultimate expression in Hitler's *Mein Kampf* and the Holocaust.

As we saw, Christian theologians always held out the hope that "The Jews" could and would embrace what they considered to be the truth: Jews were always ultimately never beyond hope. This "sponsorship" by Christian theology had provided a bulwark against excesses of hatred. When and where racial theories triumphed, however, they provided no such protective sponsorship: Jews without shelter became exposed to racist hatred. For racial theorists, "The Jews" were what they were by nature, immutably (we would now say genetically) fixed in their characteristics; there was no hope for them and their disappearance and extermination was their assumed, desired and ineluctable, ultimate destiny. This was the logic that led to Auschwitz. Carmichael is fully cognizant of all this and that the theory of race to explain the differences between groups of peoples is now rejected. ("Race" is no longer taken to be a

strictly scientific term.) He is also fully cognizant that the racial theories introduced for Jews a new dimension of despair before The Great Hatred. But
he holds on to the primacy of the Christian origin and influence of that
hatred. For him sociology and the anthropology of race do not oust this
primacy.[55]

A Lachrymose History with a New Twist

In view of what we have written it is not surprising but characteristic of Carmichael that when he deals with the emergence of the theory of race and its
resulting racism, which led to the darkest hours in Jewish history, he finds
one of the influential sources behind racism to have been Christian biblical
criticism. The emphasis on the Bible, as over against tradition, in the Reformation led Protestant reformers to concentrate on the Hebrew scriptures.
At first, this naturally made them more sympathetic toward the Jews, who
had transmitted those scriptures. This was the case with the early Luther.
But, as especially in his case, the comparative honeymoon was brief. Carmichael takes the unambiguous view that, when Luther discovered that Jews
did not accept his interpretation of their scriptures, and did not welcome the
gospel he preached, he vented upon them his unrestrained contempt and
wrath. Some of the most terrible statements ever made about Jews come
from his pen. That Hitler chose to reprint some of Luther's works to further his own anti-Semitism speaks for itself. And although Calvin was more
restrained than Luther, the Protestant Reformation, despite its biblicism, did
not deliver Jews from Christian animosity:[56] the mystical anti-Semitism remained. It must not be overlooked that the Protestant reformers were rooted
in the tradition of animosity toward Judaism which had frequently marked
medieval Catholicism: it was all too "easy" for the new branches to remain
in this tradition.

It was a German pamphleteer, Wilhelm Marr, who in 1873,[57] in the land
of Martin Luther, first coined the term "anti-Semitism" for The Great Hatred. The term is a misnomer, because it has never indicated hatred against
all Semites as such, but only against Jews. The term "Semitic" — derived from
the biblical Shem, one of Noah's three sons — came into currency through
the work of linguists, especially Ernest Renan (1825–92). In his *Histoire*

---

55. The position taken in this essay is now brilliantly and forcefully expressed in the extraordinary work of Steven Katz, *The Holocaust and Mass Death before the Modern Age*, the first of the
three projected volumes in *The Holocaust in Historical Context*.

56. For a very clear statement see Hans J. Hillerbrand, "Martin Luther and the Jews," in
Jews and Christians Exploring the Past, Present, and Future, ed. James H. Charlesworth, assisted by
Frank X. Blisard and Jeffrey S. Siker (New York: Crossroad, 1990), 127–45.

57. Robert S. Wistrich, *Anti-Semitism: The Longest Hatred* (New York: Pantheon, 1992).

Genérale et Système comparé des langues Sémitiques,[58] Renan contrasted Teutonic with Semitic languages and in this way nourished a racial distinction between a "Teutonic race" and a "Semitic race." This terminology came to be generally accepted academically, and the latter "race" was seen as decidedly inferior, as Renan made clear very eloquently in his book on Jesus. Thus the higher criticism of the Bible, which developed in the post-Enlightenment period, because it was concerned with "Semitic" languages and "Semitic" peoples, directly contributed to The Great Hatred. Through biblical criticism the Christian heritage continued its theological animus against Jews to compound it with a racial animus. A Christian component in anti-Semitism thus became inseparable, even when, in and after the Enlightenment (in Carmichael's view) theology was in retreat. Moreover, the use of the term "Semites," rather than the more common term "Jews," lent to anti-Semitism a pseudoscientific academic, and social, respectability: it served as a cultural euphemism to avoid the crudity of referring to "The Jews"!

Christian biblical scholarship, both Roman Catholic and Protestant, has undoubtedly often fed the hatred of Jews. The evidence for this has frequently been documented, and recently was summarized by Charlotte Klein,[59] Carmichael's presentation of his understanding of the impact of biblical criticism has considerable justification. But as baldly or unambiguously stated by him, it is misleading: a blanket indictment of Christian scholarship is unjustifiable. Unfortunately Carmichael's volume has no index; and although I have read it with care more than once, I may have missed pertinent references. If so, I apologize to the author in advance. But it does not seem that he has, at any point, seriously considered whether, and to what extent, at different times and in different countries, there was any intellectual exchange between Jewish and Christian scholars, and whether such exchange was mutually enriching, not merely productive of mutual hostility.

The evidence for the pre-modern period is difficult to come by, having been limited largely to official documents — ecclesiastical, synagogal, and governmental — while the vicissitudes of history and geographical differences make generalizations precarious. But up until the twelfth century, "the open century," when the Western Christian theological tradition was taking shape, despite occasional outbreaks of intolerance (as in seventh-century Spain), Jews and Christians lived as neighbors in varying degrees of mutual respect and tolerance. The situation is described by Aleksander Gieysztor in a survey, "How Jews and Christians Saw Each Other in the West and

---

58. Paris: M. Levey Ferres, 1847. See Heiko A. Oberman, *The Roots of Anti-Semitism in the Age of Renaissance and Reformation* (Philadelphia: Fortress Press, 1984).

59. C. Klein, *Anti-Judaism in Christian Theology*, trans. Edward Quinn (Philadelphia: Fortress Press, 1978).

in East Central Europe in Pre-modern Times."[60] He points out that before the twelfth century it is hardly possible to speak of "a generalized harmful feeling of resentment" between Jews and Christians. There were occasional conversions of Christians to Judaism among the higher clergy and among servants and slaves; sometimes Jews attended Christian services.[61] Theological discussions were held. Although these were mostly hostile "trials" for heresy, the Christians who participated naturally learned about Jews, the only source through whom they could procure the necessary knowledge of Hebrew. Debates between Christians and Jews continued as late as the early eleventh century. Abelard (1079–1142) wrote his *Dialogus inter philosophum, Judaeum et Christianum* at about the same time as Rabbi Yehudah Ha-Levi was writing an apologetic treatise, *Kuzari,* a discussion among a Christian philosopher, a Muslim, a Jew, and the king of the Khazars. Not only hatred but mutual curiosity and respect and enquiry marked such activity. There is convincing evidence that Christian scholars continued to draw on Judaism for illumination down to the Enlightenment.[62]

Moreover, when Carmichael simply points to the pejorative stance of Christian biblical critics in the modern period, he further underestimates two things: first, the way in which Jewish scholars have been influenced by the work of these critics — especially, but not only, in methodology. Modern Jewish biblical scholarship is clearly influenced by the Christian, and that for its enrichment. Second, there is the way in which biblical criticism has helped to revolutionize the understanding of and appreciation for the whole Jewish tradition in our time. Carmichael fails to differentiate the predominant German approach to biblical criticism from that in Britain, France, and other countries. In this connection the unambiguous words of Professor Martin Hengel, in his presidential address for 1993 to the International Society for New Testament Studies, deserve quotation.

[I]n the Anglo-Saxon world the connection between the two Testaments [the Old and the New] was furthered by means of the peculiar discipline of biblical studies, while in the German-speaking world the formulation "biblical theology," which had been in use since [the Pietist] Spener [1635–1705], was more and more pushed to one side. Behind this stands a general distancing from the Old Testament on the part of German idealism . . . as well as a widespread devaluation of Ju-

---

60. In *Jews and Christians in a Pluralistic World,* ed. E.-W. Böckenforde and E. Shils (New York: St. Martin's Press, 1991), 43–56.

61. Ibid. See a convenient statement by Peder Borgen, "Yes, No, How Far: The Participation of Jews and Christians in Pagan Cults," *Explorations* 8, no. 1 (1994): 5–6.

62. We now have the excellent study by Frank E. Manuel already referred to in n. 2. The works of Jacob Katz and Manuel provide the two sides of this question. They both make clear that Carmichael's position has to be made far more nuanced.

daism and of its influence on Christianity, a tendency which then, after 1933, produced fearful results among many German theologians.[63]

Similarly, even Carmichael's reference to Renan, while salutary, indicates that Renan himself distinguished very clearly between the ancient Jews and their descendants in his own time, who were not to be tarred by the same brush. Nor does Carmichael refer to such scholars in France as Jules Isaac, Marcel Simon, Edmund Jacob, Étienne Trocmé, and M. Philonenko, whose sensitive sympathy with Judaism is clear.

In the British world, suffice it to evoke the name of John Lightfoot (1602–75). In the New Testament Seminar at Cambridge University, England, since the time of F. C. Burkitt, its founder, at the beginning of this century, the Reader in Rabbinics was always invited to be a member; Samuel Schechter, Israel Abrahams, Herbert Loewe all attended and contributed, as does the present reader in rabbinics. David Daube, when he was a reader in Roman law at Caius College in the late thirties and forties, regularly contributed: it was his papers at that seminar that led to his immensely influential work, *The New Testament and Rabbinic Judaism* (University of London, 1956), and to a constant stream of illuminating studies in New Testament texts. The atmosphere of that seminar in biblical criticism was governed by mutual respect: criticism was not exclusive of such respect but conducive to it. In my judgment, James Parkes (not a member of that seminar) did more than any other Christian scholar to stimulate respect for Jews in the United Kingdom, although his significance has never been adequately recognized in the history of British scholarship. Carmichael has too narrowly focused his treatment of biblical criticism both geographically and chronologically. To quote Gieysztor, "The answer to the thorny question of whether anti-Semitism has Christian roots needs to be spread over history."[64] We would add: spread over countries and continents and the differing Christian communions, not only over centuries.

As for the United States, the records of its most prestigious group of biblical scholars, the Society of Biblical Literature, bear witness to constant Jewish and Christian scholarly interchange, the effects of which cannot but be immeasurable. Anyone familiar with the programs and conferences of this society can testify to this. There can be few Christian scholars who do not now recognize Judaism as the primary matrix of Christianity and, therefore, as indispensable for its understanding. Nor can there be any who do not acknowledge the immeasurable loss that the Christian world has suffered from

---

63. Translated by Martin Hengel from his presidential address, "Aufgaben der neutestamentlichen Wissenschaft," *NTS* 40, no. 3 (July 1994): 321–57.

64. Gieysztor, "How Jews and Christians Saw Each Other," 51. This is recognized by Manuel, *The Broken Staff,* 318–22.

its past neglect of this truth: it is arguable that through its divorce from the synagogue, the Christian church has suffered profound spiritual and moral impoverishment. In overlooking its Jewish rootage, Christianity has tended to lose the awareness of the Living God at work in history in favor of other-worldliness, mysticism, and "gnosis," to lessen the astringent moral imperative of a call to live out its faith in the world, to lose its sense of itself as, above all, a people rather than as a structured organization, and to forsake the world for the wrong reasons.[65] The separation between the two faiths has "victimized" them both — all too visibly in the case of the one, all too subtly in the case of the other.

Carmichael's focus has another aspect. In recent studies two distinguished historians have independently pointed out the important — though disputed — truth that Christian commitment does not of itself imply or demand rejection, much less hatred, of Jews. Professor Gavin Langmuir, after explaining his reasons for stating this position, writes:

> [T]here is no such thing as *the* Christian faith; there are only faiths of Christian individuals.... whatever we may say about Christian hostility to Jews, we cannot say that it is a result of *the* Christian faith. It can only be an extension of the faiths of individual Christians. And since their faiths have varied, so, too, has their hostility to Jews. Throughout the centuries, individuals who lived at approximately the same time, believed in the divinity of Jesus of Nazareth, and even adhered to the same Christian religion, have varied markedly in faith and in their attitudes toward Jews.[66]

Langmuir takes as examples three prominent contemporaries in the eleventh and twelfth centuries: Peter the Venerable (1092 or 1094–1156), who hated Jews "viciously and libelously,"[67] Bernard of Clairvaux (1091–1153), who protected Jews, and Abelard (1079–1142), for whom "faith, reason and disputation were quite compatible."[68] Langmuir summarizes Abelard's attitude

---

65. See my essay "Reflections on Judaism and Christianity," in *L'Evangile hier et aujourd'hui: Mélanges offerts au Professor Franz J. Leenhardt* (Geneva: Labor et Fides, 1968), 39–54. For the most recent example of the mutual support of Jewish and Christian scholars in the Society of Biblical Literature, see D. Boyarin, *A Radical Jew: Paul and the Politics of Identity* (Berkeley: University of California Press, 1994), ix–xi. Professor Kalman Bland reminds me that the figure of Spinoza deserves a special place in the area with which we are here concerned. See also Manuel, *The Broken Staff.*

66. Langmuir, *Toward a Definition of Antisemitism,* 79. Langmuir insists on meticulous and scrupulous attention to methodological validity and exactitude in his altogether admirable treatment. For an assessment of Parkes's contribution, see K. Cragg, *Troubled by Truth: Life Studies in Inter-faith Concerns,* with which I must concur (reluctantly, because Parkes was a former neighbor and friend). His anxiety to be utterly fair to Judaism sometimes led Parkes to gloss over or muffle crucial affirmations of the Christian tradition.

67. Langmuir, *Toward a Definition of Antisemitism,* 84.

68. Ibid., 87.

toward Jews as follows: "[I]f those who did not know that Christ was God be-lieved in conscience that Christ or his disciples ought to be persecuted, then they would have sinned more gravely had they not persecuted them."[69] The variety of Christian responses to Jews to which Langmuir points in medieval times he finds later also in the modern period. He names Martin Luther and Calvin, Hermann Strack and Adolf Ströcker, and the British scholar James Parkes, to whom we have already referred and whom Langmuir rightly honors for his concern for Jews.

And here we suggest that it would have given Carmichael pause had he compared and contrasted his emphasis on Christianity as the seminal cause of mystical anti-Semitism with the way in which significant Jewish scholars have confronted Christianity. For example, in *Jewish Perspectives on Christianity,*[70] the editor, F. A. Rothschild, summarizes the topics dealt with in the book by five Jewish scholars as follows: (1) The person and significance of Jesus; (2) the polarity of Law and gospel, works and faith, human righteousness and divine grace, first proclaimed by Paul and subsequently elaborated in the theology of the church; (3) the place of the Hebrew Bible in Christianity; and (4) the role of the church as the New Israel (*Verus Israel*) vis-à-vis the Jews as the Old Israel "according to the flesh."[71] It is noteworthy that the five authors included — Leo Baeck, Martin Buber, Franz Rosenzweig, Will Herberg, and especially Abraham Heschel (whom many regard as the greatest Jewish theologian of his day) — do not dwell on the satanizing of the Jews.

Professor Owen Chadwick points to a similar variety of attitudes toward Jews whether the societies in which Jews and Christians found themselves were civil or persecuting. He notes that many anti-Semitic policies have nothing to do with religion (he illustrates this from France and Poland) and that they rise sometimes not from "the difference between Christians and Jews in religion or race ... [but] (in part at least) from something even more basic to humanity ... the difference between a majority inside a state and its minority or minorities." "Any government," Chadwick continues, "from time to time helps itself in governing the majority of the population by being unjust to some minority in the population." In such circumstances dealing with anti-Semitism has nothing to do "with resolving religious differences, but with devising a constitution in which equal rights of minorities are fully protected while not risking the dissolution of the state."[72] Like Langmuir and Chadwick, William McKane, a Scottish biblical scholar, points to a variety of approaches to Jews and their scriptures in *Selected Christian Hebraists*. He

---

69. Ibid., 87–88.
70. New York: Crossroad, 1990.
71. Rothschild, *Jewish Perspectives on Christianity,* 15.
72. "Relations between Jews and Christians in Civil and Persecuting Societies," in ibid., 104–5.

identifies Andrew of St. Victor (d. 1175), William Fulke (1538–89), Gregory Martin (d. 1582), Richard Simon (1638–1712, generally regarded as the founder of Old Testament criticism), and Alexander Geddes (1737–1802), all looking back to Origen and especially to Jerome. So far from fostering anti-Semitism, the study of the Bible by some scholars led to Judaizing tendencies which aroused suspicion.[73]

In more recent times, the record is more tragically sad, but not unrelievedly so. Marshall Johnson, in a preliminary, but typically careful, study of "Power Politics and New Testament Scholarship in the National Socialist Period,"[74] divided New Testament scholars in Germany into four groups: (1) those who were propagandists for the Third Reich as representing a new form of German Christianity; (2) those who were conservative and nationalistic who thought of Nazism as a "return to and revival of traditional Christian values and beliefs"; (3) those who were unaffected by the political developments but carried on with their scholarship undisturbed; and (4) those scholars who protested against the "political prostitution" of scholarship "in the name of either Christianity or simple humanity."[75] All these considerations offered by the scholars mentioned above make clear that generalizations about biblical criticism, as about other matters in this field, can be misleading.[76]

If what we have written is not wide of the mark, Judaism is the beneficiary of Christian biblical criticism, not only its victim. And this evokes a further question. Carmichael has urged that The Great Hatred has persisted because it was a necessity for Christianity. Is it not also true, however, in part at least, that without the constant stimulus of its interaction with the claims of Christianity and Islam, Judaism would not have played so prominent, vigorous, enriching, and significant a role in world history? Jews in the Far East — in China and India — have not been as unmistakably prominent and influential in those non-Christian and non-Islamic countries as in Christian Eastern and Western Europe and the United States. Does not this suggest that Christianity has possibly been even necessary to, or at least has not always totally suppressed, a rich evolution of Judaism, and that Jews are not only victims of the Christian tradition but also even beneficiaries, however indirectly, of it?

Not unrelated to this is Carmichael's failure to refer to the debate among and between Jews and Christians in recent years whether it is legitimate to recognize a joint or common "Judeo-Christian tradition" to which appeal is

---

73. W. McKane, *Selected Christian Hebraists* (Cambridge: Cambridge University Press, 1989), 192.

74. *The Journal of Ecumenical Studies* 23 (Winter 1986): 1–24.

75. Johnson, "Power Politics and New Testament Scholarship," 1.

76. What generalization about anti-Semitism could be justified, for example, to include the wild, peculiar fantasies of Wagner? Must not his irrationality be considered as *sui generis*? See Poliakov, *The History of Anti-Semitism*, 3:429–57.

now almost routinely made in many political, humanistic, and theological circles in the West, and which implies a mutual commonality not only of moral concern but, to a very considerable extent, of religious belief. Such a "hybrid tradition" has been stridently dismissed by some Jews as never having existed.[77] Like oil and water, they assert, Judaism and Christianity have not intermingled or been fused in any fundamental way, and it is disingenuous to pretend that they can and do, the points of divergence between them being so deep as to be nonnegotiable (to use Reinhold Niebuhr's term). The "Satanized Judaism" which Carmichael posits could certainly not have fathered a Jewish-Christian tradition, nor of necessity could it even have allowed for the possibility of such. But "Satanized Judaism" aside, is a mutual or joint tradition or, to adopt Kenneth Cragg's words, an "affiliated" tradition, to be so easily dismissed?

However incredible, and understandably so, this will appear to many Jews in the light of their long experience to the contrary, along with the poisoning "mulch" of anti-Judaism, there is within the Christian tradition an inbuilt reverence, however grudging, for the Jewish people and tradition. Christians took over the Hebrew scriptures as part of their own canon, so that those scriptures have become bone of their bone. Adopted into the Christian canon, those scriptures are never referred to in the New Testament as the Old Testament, and the recognition of them as part of the Christian canon meant that Christians inherited much of their moral and spiritual substance. Even though this did mean their reinterpretation and adaptation, the Christian appropriation of the Jewish tradition did not mean its emasculation. The constant reading of the Hebrew writings and the exegetical and interpretative engagement with them no less than with the writings of the Greek New Testament in the churches of Christendom, could not but, in obvious and in subtle ways, influence Christians. The Jewish names of Christians, male and female, of their towns and villages and of many of the symbols that pepper the Gentile world are not accidental nor insignificant. Certainly theological and intellectual developments, accompanied by economic, social, and political factors, which stimulated, conditioned, and shaped these developments, spawned "The Great Hatred," and ensured a tragic separation between Judaism and Christianity; but all this has often obscured the rich though complex continuity between the two faiths.

Such an assertion of continuity, it is true, must be made with a caveat. It can be too facile and, as R. J. Zwi Werblowsky has again pointed out, may overlook that radical and irreconcilable differences can be glossed over too

---

77. See for example, Arthur A. Cohen, *The Myth of the Judeo-Christian Tradition* (New York: Harper & Row, 1970). Manuel, *The Broken Staff*, 1, points out that though Renan used the term "Judeo-Christian" for a first-century sect in the early church, it became generally used only in this century.

easily in any emphasis on the common use by Jews and Christians of Jewish scriptural and theological terms. Zwi Werblowsky pinpointed, as an example, the term "covenant." Judaism and Christianity understand this term so differently, Werblowsky claims, as to make any continuity in its use ambiguous at best.[78] This hesitation to find a meaningful continuity in the use of a common lexicographical tradition by the two faiths has a very long history. Given the nature of language, from the very beginning, even in Paul himself, with the translation of Hebrew terms into Greek and later into Latin, this ambiguity in the meaning of terms inevitably surfaced. The works of C. H. Dodd (such as *The Bible and the Greeks*, 1935), of George Caird and David Hill, for example, not to mention Kittel's *Wörterbuch* and the reactions to it, indicate the problems raised. It might be argued that Jews and Christians have been separated by a common theological terminology. This came to very clear expression in the medieval "Disputations." Writing in 1991, Werblowsky strangely echoes the Paris Disputation of 1240, when Christians, for example, objected to Talmudic passages "which represent God as grieving over the Jewish exile, or acknowledging a mistake on his own part, or as acknowledging defeat in an argument with a human."[79] For the rabbis this Talmudic conception of a suffering God is in line with the "passable" God of the Hebrew scriptures and opposed what became the dominant Christian conception, born of the influence of Greek philosophy, of the impassibility of God. The materials translated and edited by Hyam Maccoby in *Judaism on Trial: Jewish-Christian Disputations in the Middle Ages*[80] make clear how, historically, a common terminology can bear a very different connotation for those who use it. To borrow Werblowsky's words, "Different trees grow from common roots." While the Hebrew scriptures, when taken over by the church as part of its canon, might, at first, be thought to constitute in themselves a decisive indication of a continuity uniting Judaism and Christianity, so that the notion of a Judeo-Christian tradition becomes natural, caution is in order. Because "*how* a person reads is as important as *what* a person reads,"[81] those Hebrew scriptures in themselves cannot be given such a significance.

Nevertheless, the Hebrew scriptures do point to a decisive common root. Informing Judaism is the confession of the *Shema*: this central affirmation and proclamation of the One God was foundational in Judaism. But this very

---

78. "The Common Roots of Judaism and Christianity," in Rothschild, *Jews and Christians in a Pluralistic World*, 190.

79. Ibid., 120. See also the admirably precise and scrupulous study by Robert Chazan, *Daggers of Faith: Thirteenth-Century Christian Messianizing and Jewish Response* (Berkeley: University of California Press, 1989).

80. London and Toronto: Fairleigh Dickinson University Press, 1982.

81. The work of the literary critic Stanley Fish has become well known especially in his emphasis on the importance of the reader or the community that not only produces writers but that reads and interprets them.

same *Shema* was also the ultimate foundation which sustained Jesus of Nazareth and the Christian faith.[82] Amos Funkenstein, *quem honoris causa nomino*,
has characterized the appeal to origins, as determinative for the understanding of the relations between Judaism and Christianity, as "a fallacious
argument logically as well as historically." But the common commitment to
the One God in both faiths from the beginning (though not to be so sim-
plified as to make it "cheap," and though a too facile insistence upon it can
simply indicate what Carmichael calls "flaccid tolerance") must be given its
full weight. The exploration of the meaning of the One God and of His demands constitutes and has constituted a *point d'appui* and a *point de départ* for
mutual respect and joint endeavor between Jews and Christians. That such
a mutual exploration demands infinite patience goes without saying. Above
all, it calls for a mutual recognition that, in taking over the Hebrew scriptures, Christians have received a terminology which belonged to Jews and
was understood in particular ways by Jews, and also that they themselves have
also, in turn, contributed to that terminology in their own particular Christian ways. Kenneth Cragg has pointed out, with penetrating sensitivity, that
"language is quite literally where religions have to negotiate."[83] The demand
on Jews to negotiate linguistically with Christians in the twentieth century is
a very ancient pre-Christian as well as post-Christian demand on Jews themselves. In fact, as Cragg reminds us, the process of mutual appropriation of
language by Christians and Jews is not without partial antecedent and preparation in the fact that "in each religion words and symbols have themselves
acquired their connotation *through elastic reckoning within their own tradition
and have also coined themselves out of encounter.*"[84] Despite the different connotations that Christians and Jews have ascribed to the Hebrew scriptures, is
it not to be conceded that their common use of them has also inevitably to
a great measure molded both? (Philo, a Jew, for example, could become even
more influential among Christians than among Jews.) Those scriptures provided a scaffolding for the structure of both Judaism and Christianity which
did not preclude an elasticity in the interpretation of the materials with which
that structure was clothed and which helped form the minds of both in common ways. Carmichael should at least have recognized the possibility of such
a development which necessarily involved some degree of "fusion." As C. H.
Dodd, long ago now, taught us: the substructure of the Christian faith is Ju-

---

82. See especially Birger Gerhardsson, *The Shema' in the New Testament* (Lund: Nova Press,
1996); and idem, "The Shema in Early Christianity," in *The Four Gospels, 1992* (*Festschrift* for
Frans Neirynck), ed. F. van Segbroek et al. (Louvain: Bibliotheca Ephemeridum Theologicarum
Lovaniensium C, 1992).

83. Cragg, *Troubled by Truth*, 7.

84. Ibid., 8. Italics added.

daism. This means that it is legitimate to speak of a Judeo-Christian tradition which Carmichael ignores.

With this failure goes another. Maurice Samuel's book *The Great Hatred*, to which we referred earlier, could have alerted Carmichael to a thesis that he does not consider. Samuel urged that Hitler's hatred of "The Jews" coexisted with hatred of Christianity. However, the well-established and powerful status of Christianity in Europe gave Hitler pause. He calculated that it would be impolitic to make a frontal attack on Christians and the Christian churches. But it was otherwise with the marginalized and unpopular Jews. The Christian ethic was as much anathema to Hitler as the Jewish: he detested both, but the status of Christianity in Germany and elsewhere dictated that he could not openly attack that faith. Only the "weaker" faith, Judaism, could he directly seek to destroy. Samuel's thesis has to be carefully assessed. But it is not surprising. The strategy of an indirect attack on Christianity was not new. In the eighteenth century Voltaire used it. Knowing that critics of the establishment in France were not facing "paper tigers," he attacked Christianity and the church only through Judaism. There is in this strategy of Voltaire's an implicit recognition of a commonality between Judaism and Christian which should also give Carmichael pause.

Not unconnected with Carmichael's failure to consider the phenomenon of a Judeo-Christian tradition is an even more surprising failure, that of his neglect of the recent *rapprochement,* like a thaw after a long winter, between the Christian churches, both Roman Catholic and Protestant, and the synagogue. The developments of this *rapprochement* in the Roman Catholic Church have been summarized by Petro Rossano in *Fifteen Years of Catholic-Jewish Dialogue* and need not be repeated here. That it was no "flaccid tolerance" but a profound engagement that informed and governed the deliberations of Roman Catholics appears unmistakably from the history of the changes in the various declarations made on texts proposed, approved, and emended in Vatican II. The changes made in texts proposed between November 1963 and October 1965 and the explanations of these changes are eloquent testimony to the seriousness with which the Roman Catholic Church confronted its past and faced its present and future relationship with Jews.[85] That the official attitude of the Roman Catholic Church toward Jews

---

85. These changes can be conveniently examined in appendices A–F in Arthur Gilbert, *The Vatican Council and the Jews* (Cleveland: World Publishing, 1968). In *Unanswered Questions: Theological Views of Jewish-Christian Relations,* ed. Roger Brooks (Notre Dame, Ind.: University of Notre Dame Press, 1988), the three official documents are also translated into English. They are *Nostra Aetate* ("A Declaration on the Relationship of the Church to Non-Christian Religions," Vatican II, 1965); "Guidelines and Suggestions for Jewish-Christian Relations" (1974); and "Notes on the Correct Way to Present Jews and Judaism in Preaching and Catechesis in the Roman Catholic Church." See also Joseph Neuner on the "Declaration," in *Missions and Religion,* ed. Austin Flannery (Dublin: Scepter Books, 1968); the author's contribution to a symposium

has been in the process of being radically altered cannot be doubted, and need not be documented here, so familiar has it now become. So far from being regarded as satanic, as according to Carmichael they had become in Christianity, Jews are now seen by the papacy as elder brothers.

The process of change seen in Roman Catholic circles has also been evident in Protestantism. Suffice it to refer to the "Colloquium on Judaism and Christianity," held at Harvard University, 17–20 October 1966. There is no need to labor what has now become obvious. Doubtless just as the condemnatory attitude of many of the early church fathers only slowly trickled down to the generality of Christians, as Carmichael recognized, so the reformed attitude of conciliation of the modern papacy and the Protestant leadership will only slowly trickle down effectively to the generality of Christendom. But modern means of communications are more than likely to make that trickle-down much swifter than that of the theology of the church fathers in earlier ages. The sea change in Christian-Jewish relations will, sooner rather than later it is hoped, so dilute the disastrous "mulch" constituting the element of truth in Carmichael's thesis of mystical anti-Semitism as to make it increasingly negligible. It is no accident that a leading Jewish thinker, Arthur Hertzberg, can visualize the end of anti-Semitism.[86]

The emphases and omissions in Carmichael's work noted above explain our choice of title for this subsection, "A Lachrymose History with a New Twist." To judge from *Satanizing of the Jews*, Carmichael seems to share in what Salo Baron, as long ago as 1928, taught us to call "the lachrymose view" of Jewish history, that is, the tendency to regard that history as a "vale of tears," a continuous series of wrongs endured, or as one of unrelieved powerlessness and suffering in which Jews have only been the "objects" of their own history not its "subjects," passive victims rather than active participants. For obvious reasons, given much that makes this view so persuasive in the light of the Jewish past, a Gentile (even one who has been called "an honorary Jew") must hesitate to criticize such an interpretation of Jewish history. Jewish historians can be less inhibited. Over against this lachrymose view, Baron emphasized that that history has always interacted with, has influenced and been influenced by, the various communities and cultures within which Jews have found themselves, that Jewish "separation" has never been only isolation and rejection passively endured.

The rabbis after the fall of Jerusalem in 70 c.e. had perforce to acquiesce

---

on the Vatican-Israel Fundamental Agreement in *Midstream*, January 1995, 22–25 (reprinted in appendix below); and especially Manuel, *The Broken Staff*, 318–33. On p. 320 Manuel cites Pope Paul VI, "The Jewish religion is not 'extrinsic' to us, but in a certain way 'intrinsic' to our own religion.... You are our dearly beloved brethren...our dear brothers" (*New York Times*, 14 April 1986).

86. "Is Anti-Semitism Dying Out?" See n. 53 above.

in their landless existence and to counsel its acceptance. But this must not be equated with passivity. Mere passivity could not have accounted either for the amazing persistence of Jews up to the present nor for the prominent, very significant role they have played in the history of Europe and the West. Doubtless the influence of the rabbinic tradition of the acceptance of landless powerlessness may be the ultimate source of the lachrymose view of Jewish history, but that view, it is very important to recognize, is also to a large degree a corruption of that tradition. Overemphasis among Jews on their wounds in the past to the exclusion of their persistent activism (which has preserved them as a people, paradoxically as it might seem, created nurturing institutions suitable for their needs, produced literature to sustain them, sustained their religious vitality) makes it impossible to understand the amazing creativity of Jews and the striking contribution they have made to the culture of the West and of the world, over many centuries and in many countries, and their extraordinary vigor and dynamism which finally issued in the twentieth century in their creation of the state of Israel. Not surprisingly Baron is not alone among Jewish scholars in protesting the lachrymose approach. Simon Dubnow and Haim Hillel Ben-Sasson have also distanced themselves from it. So also more recently have Amos Funkenstein, Ismar Schorsch, and David Biale.[87] The absence of an index in Carmichael's work makes it precarious to accuse him of having neglected the work of these scholars, but I have detected no awareness of them. Impressive as is the scope of Carmichael's work, it does not attempt to recognize and deal with the way in which Jews have been able not only to survive but to assert their continuing, extraordinarily creative influence in European life as indicated convincingly in Biale's treatment. Such a recognition would have compelled Carmichael to acknowledge that hatred of Jews cannot have been so ubiquitous and powerful as to cause them to be regarded as so unambiguously "satanic" as he claims. Does Carmichael, then, not fall into the category of the lachrymose historians of Judaism? One hesitates to claim this, however, so active has he proven in his advocacy of Israel: he presents us with a paradox, that of a lachrymose and yet forcefully activist historian.[88]

---

87. See A. Funkenstein, "Passivity as the Characteristic of the Diaspora Jews," lecture (in Hebrew), Tel Aviv University School of Historical Studies, 1982; Schorsch, "On the History" (see n. 1 above); and D. Biale, *Power and Powerlessness in Jewish History* (New York: Schocken Books, 1986).

88. I am fully aware that Baron has been criticized at several points by some Jewish historians and rejected outright by others. See the fascinating chapter by Isaac E. Barzilai, "Baer and Shalom (Salo Wittonayer) Baron: Two Contemporary Interpreters of Jewish History," in *Proceedings of the American Academy of Jewish Research*, ed. Nahum M. Sarna, no. 60 (Jerusalem and New York: American Academy of Jewish Research, 1994), 7–69. At the risk of presumption in passing judgment — as I stated in the text — that the lachrymose view cannot account for the amazing, continuing, and vital contributions of Jewry, I simply note that sociologists have long taught us that a crushed people (such as the Jews are in the lachrymose view) is not usually ini-

In the end, Carmichael's sharply and powerfully focused work provokes two reactions. For all Gentiles and especially for Gentile Christians it is a salutary and invaluable reminder of Christian guilt for The Great Hatred. Nothing that we have written above should be allowed to diminish the justifiable accusatory impact of Carmichael's work on Gentile Christians. On the other hand, this volume demands of Jews a degree of caution. Carmichael often writes with a scintillating brilliance. But his brilliance is brittle, because in dazzling the reader with the quick, packed, and concise movement of his thought, he tends to blur the complexities of history.

William Blake, on being asked why he did not want to go to college or university, is reported to have said (I quote from memory), "Because education draws straight lines and life is fuzzy." Carmichael's lines of historical evolution are too straight and too clear. His virtues — a noteworthy synthetic and synoptic gift and a remarkable lucidity — are his strength, but also his weakness. Is he not too simple in his emphasis? There is absent in Carmichael's book the sensitivity of a Cardinal Newman, who, as he pondered the course of human history, found "the progress of things, as if from unreasoning elements *not towards final causes*," and "a vision to dizzy and appall ... which inflicts upon the mind the sense of a profound mystery, *which is absolutely beyond human solution*" (italics added).[89] This calls not for despair, but for eternal vigilance against all the social and political and ecclesiastical forces which are always present to exploit theological differences — differences which, though not to be ignored or dismissed, are now more and more to be embraced in an increasing tolerance. (This is not to be confused with a relativism which overlooks substantial differences with an ultimate indifference.) At long last, *mirabile dictu*, is there not this change in Jewish-Christian relationships?

Here we revert to the illuminating and salutary quotation from the Baeck Lecture by Ismar Schorsch which stands at the head of this essay. Has Carmichael sufficiently freed himself from the "straitjacket of earlier conceptualizations" which has too long governed the approach to Jewish-Christian relationships and to anti-Semitism? Is it not possible to apply to these relationships the same spirit which Schorsch has applied to aspects of Jewish history? To do so would, in our judgment, serve as a salutary and highly enriching corrective.

---

tiative, and certainly not as fecundly so, as Jewry has been. Professor Barzilai is convincing when he points out the difference in the environments which shaped Yishaq (Fritz) Baer and Baron and helped to determine their different approaches to Jewish history. I never knew Yishaq Baer, but Baron was a neighbor for many years in New York. The rejection of the lachrymose view fits in perfectly with the Baron I then knew. Whenever we met him, which was not infrequently, his urbane courtesy and comforting gentleness bespoke a man at home and at peace with his world, although he knew its darkness.

89. Quoted in John Drinkwater, *The Outline of Literature*, vol. 2 (London: George Newnes, n.d.), 551–52.

Appendix:
The Vatican-Israel Agreement

The editor asks whether the Vatican-Israel Fundamental Agreement presages a deeper appreciation for the state of Israel on the part of the Vatican.[90] This question implies a doubt that this may not be so. In our judgment this implied doubt can arise for one reason only. The editor asks for a response to the text of an agreement taken by itself apart, in total isolation. For this reason, I submit, the question itself may be considered malproposed and inviting of a superficial answer.

To examine any phenomenon in isolation is to do two things to it. First, it is to overemphasize or to enlarge its significance, negatively or positively as the case demands, by making it an Everest among other mountains some of which, we know, are almost as high and even more difficult to climb. The signing of the Fundamental Agreement on 30 December 1993 was a truly momentous occasion; but to set it apart and to demand comment on it in isolation is to confer on it a significance which, by itself alone, the agreement cannot sustain. This is because, in the second place, to isolate is not only to magnify, but to distort.

Working on biblical and other texts has long convinced me, as it has most literary critics, that to understand any text demands that it be placed in a continuum or a tradition of circumstances or events and of related texts which preceded it: there are texts behind all texts. Most, if not all, texts are intertextual in the sense that they presuppose other previous texts and reinterpret them, and are conditioned by those previous texts. But all texts are also conditioned by the time and place, when and where, they were themselves composed. The context of a text may not determine but it does define its content. For example, a study of Matthew 5–7, the so-called Sermon on the Mount, one of the most commented-on texts in world history, soon revealed that it can only be rightly understood in terms of its context in first-century Jamnian Judaism, in its setting in the life of the Christian churches of its period, and in the totality of the Gospel of Matthew itself. The isolation of the Sermon on the Mount has often led to grave distortion of its meaning and misinterpretation of its details and of its totality.[91] The same is true of

---

90. This appendix appeared originally in a symposium on the Vatican-Israel Agreement, *Midstream*, January 1995, 22–25.

91. See W. D. Davies, *The Setting of the Sermon on the Mount* (Cambridge: Cambridge University Press, 1964); and a forthcoming study by Betsy Halpern-Amaru, *Rewriting the Bible: Land and Covenant in Post-biblical Jewish Literature* (Valley Forge, Pa.: Trinity Press International, 1994), in which she shows how the earlier Pentateuchal texts are reworked in later documents. After 1944, Nicholas Lash in *Change in Focus: A Study of Doctrinal Change and Continuity* (London: Sheed and Ward, 1981 edition) emphasizes that each document by Vatican II cannot be adequately dealt with in isolation but only in relation to all other Vatican texts. On p. 4 he writes: "It is quite inadequate, therefore, simply to open the text of a conciliar document, and 'see what it

this Fundamental Agreement: its context — textual and historical — lends it significant importance. That context is twofold: it is theological and political.

There is, first, the Christian — and especially the Roman Catholic Christian — context, which is both theological and dialogic. This context is the profound sea change which has taken place since Vatican II in the theology of the Christian approach to Judaism. Joel Carmichael, in his recent book *The Satanizing of the Jews: Origin and Development of Mystical Anti-Semitism*,[92] has reaffirmed and emphasized the major part played by the Christian theological understanding of Jews, whom it turned disastrously into "The Jews," in the origin and evolution of anti-Semitism. Since Vatican II that understanding of "The Jews" and the resulting attitudes toward them have been radically reassessed and their demonic, pejorative aspects rejected. To put the matter succinctly, Jews are to cease to be "The Jews" — satanic or demonic.

Pope John XXIII, who initiated Vatican II, spoke of opening the closed windows of the Roman Catholic Church to introduce fresh air and perspectives. One major, and indeed truly magnificent, result has been the explicit rejection of many traditional Christian theological conceptions of Judaism and of the Jewish people. It is hardly possible to exaggerate the changes in those conceptions and in the actual relations between Christians and Jews since then. The active involvement of Jews themselves in the deliberations of those attending Vatican II contributed profoundly to those changes.

For our present purposes the most important pertinent text is found in paragraphs 4 and 5 of the "Declaration of the Relationship of the Church to Non-Christian Religions." This document, promulgated by Pope Paul VI and the Roman Catholic Bishops in 1965, begins "In our times..." and thus is customarily referred to as *Nostra Aetate*.[93]

> *Paragraph Four.* As this sacred Synod searches into the mystery of the Church, it recalls the spiritual bond linking the people of the new covenant with Abraham's stock.
>
> For the Church of Christ acknowledges that, according to the mystery of God's saving design, the beginnings of her faith and her election are already found among the patriarchs, Moses, and the prophets. She professes that all who believe in Christ, Abraham's sons according to faith (cf. Gal. 3:7), are included in the same patriarch's call, and likewise that the salvation of the Church was mystically foreshadowed by the chosen people's exodus from the land of bondage.

---

says.' We must try to situate it in the historical context of the debates from which it emerged. Only in this way can we hope to discover what is important and what is unimportant."

92. See n. 3 above.

93. I have taken the text of paragraphs 4 and 5 from Brooks, *Unanswered Questions*, 20–22.

The Church, therefore, cannot forget that she received the revelation of the Old Testament through the people with whom God in his inexpressible mercy deigned to establish the ancient covenant. Nor can she forget that she draws sustenance from the root of that good olive tree onto which have been grafted the wild olive branch of the Gentiles (cf. Rom. 11:17–24). Indeed, the Church believes that by His cross Christ, our peace, reconciled Jew and Gentile, making them both one in Himself (cf. Eph. 2:14–16).

Also, the Church ever keeps in mind the words of the apostle about his kinsmen, "who have the adoption as sons, and the glory and the covenant and the legislation and the worship and the promises; who have the fathers, and from whom is Christ according to the flesh" (Rom. 9:4–5), the son of the virgin Mary. The Church recalls too that from the Jewish people sprang the apostles, her foundation stones and pillars, as well as most of the early disciples who proclaimed Christ to the world.

As holy scripture testifies, Jerusalem did not recognize the time of her visitation (cf. Luke 19:44), nor did the Jews in large numbers accept the gospel; indeed, not a few opposed the spreading of it (cf. Rom. 11:28). Nevertheless, according to the apostle, the Jews still remain most dear to God because of their fathers, for He does not repent of the gifts He makes nor of the calls He issues (cf. Rom. 11:28–29). In company with the prophets and the same apostle, the Church awaits that day, known to God alone, on which all peoples will address the Lord in a single voice and "serve him with one accord" (Zeph. 3:9; cf. Isa. 66:23; Ps. 65:4; Rom. 11:11–32).

Since the spiritual patrimony common to Christians and Jews is thus so great, this sacred Synod wishes to foster and recommend that mutual understanding and respect which is the fruit above all of biblical and theological studies, and of brotherly dialogues.

True, authorities of the Jews and those who followed their lead pressed for the death of Christ (cf. John 19:6); still, what happened in His passion cannot be blamed upon all the Jews then living, without distinction, nor upon the Jews of today. Although the Church is the new people of God, the Jews should not be presented as repudiated or cursed by God, as if such views followed from the holy scriptures. All should take pains, then, lest in catechetical instruction and in the preaching of God's Word they teach anything out of harmony with the truth of the gospel and the spirit of Christ.

The Church repudiates all persecutions against any man. Moreover, mindful of her common patrimony with the Jews, and motivated by the gospel's spiritual love and by no political considerations, she deplores the hatred, persecutions, and displays of antisemitism directed against the Jews at any time and from any source.

Besides, as the church has always held and continues to hold, Christ in His boundless love freely underwent His passion and death because of the sins of all men, so that all might attain salvation. It is, therefore, the duty of the Church's preaching to proclaim the cross of Christ as the sign of God's all-embracing love and as the fountain from which every grace flows.

Paragraph Five. We cannot in all truthfulness call upon that God who is the father of all if we refuse to act in a brotherly way toward certain men, created though they be to God's image. A man's relationship with God the Father and his relationship with his brother men are so linked together that scripture says: "He who does not love does not know God" (1 John 4:8).

The ground is therefore removed from every theory or practice which leads to a distinction between men or peoples in the matter of human dignity and the rights which flow from it.

As a consequence, the Church rejects, as foreign to the mind of Christ, any discrimination against men or harassment of them because of their race, color, condition of life, or religion.

Accordingly, following in the footsteps of the holy apostles Peter and Paul, this sacred Synod ardently implores the Christian faithful to "maintain good fellowship among the nations" (1 Pet. 2:12), and, if possible, as far as in them lies, to keep peace with all men (cf. Rom. 12:18), so that they may truly be sons of the father who is in heaven (cf. Matt. 5:45).

To those who have long been occupied with Jewish-Christian relations, in 1994 this statement may appear mild and timid and even innocuous. But in 1965, when it was promulgated, against the background of what Jules Isaac had taught us to call "the teaching of contempt,"[94] it was new and very bold. That "teaching," in Isaac's thought, had three well-defined marks: (1) that the dispersion of the Jews was a divine punishment for the crucifixion of Jesus of Nazareth; (2) that Judaism at the time of Jesus was degenerate and corrupt; and (3) that the Jews were a deicide people. All these elements in *The Teaching of Contempt* were repudiated in *Nostra Aetate* in 1965, and later in "Guidelines and Suggestions for Jewish-Christian Relations,"[95] issued by the Roman Catholic Church in 1974 and published in 1975, and again in "Notes on the Correct Way to Present Jews and Judaism in Preaching and Catechesis

---

94. Jules Isaac, *The Teaching of Contempt: Christian Roots of Anti-Semitism* (New York: Holt, Rinehart & Winston, 1964).

95. Brooks, *Unanswered Questions*, 23–30.

in the Roman Catholic Church,"[96] authorized by Pope John Paul II in 1982 and published in 1985 over the name of Cardinal Johannes Willebrands and others. Although it might very well have been abortive, the painful and even precarious process which gave birth to *Nostra Aetate* did finally culminate in what was "a major accomplishment for Christian Theology and in a decisive and irreversible shift in Roman Catholic teaching about Jews and Judaism."[97]

The documents to which we have referred have "cleared the decks," we can claim, for a mutual respect, a new relationship, and an interaction of mutual enrichment after centuries of contempt. The importance of this "clearing of the decks" can be measured by a reference again to Dr. Joel Carmichael's recent study on mystical anti-Semitism, already referred to, in which he forcefully argues that it was Christian theology that provided the religious and cultural backdrop for the demonizing of "The Jews" in the European (and subsequently the world's) imagination which ultimately made the Holocaust possible. That Carmichael's work is too clear and unambiguous does not detract from the truth in his claim. In *Nostra Aetate* and in the documents it spawned, Roman Catholicism sought to exorcise the demonic in that backdrop.

This very symposium would probably not have been possible without the new climate engendered by Vatican II and this exorcism. The Vatican-Israel Fundamental Agreement of Jerusalem, 30 December 1993, has now led to "full diplomatic relations" between the Vatican and Israel and has paved the way for a new era of interreligious dialogue. Such developments are only conceivable because Christian and Jews have (in principle, if not always in practice) crossed the divide from the "preaching of contempt" to the "preaching of respect." Is it not the failure fully to grasp the significance of the theological crossing of the great divide — from contempt to respect — that helps to create the doubt implied in the question the editor has posed?

But there is another factor fomenting this doubt. It arises from the second context within which the Fundamental Agreement of 1993 is to be understood: what we might call the "political" context. Two aspects of *Nostra Aetate*, and the subsequent documents "expounding" it, aroused criticism among certain Jews as among many Christians concerned with Israel, and their views have reemerged in discussions of the Fundamental Agreement. The two criticisms are the failure to give due consideration to the traumatic significance and impact of the Holocaust and the absorbing importance of the state of Israel for all Jews, in whose minds these two phenomena are inseparable.

---

96. Ibid., 31–46.
97. Wendell S. Dietrich, *"Nostra Aetate:* A Typology of Theological Tendencies," in ibid., 70–71.

To begin first with the latter, the state of Israel is not mentioned in *Nostra Aetate*, which deals solely with the strictly spiritual patrimony which Jews and Christians share; that is, the "Declaration," *Nostra Aetate*, only deals with Jews as a religious people. The same is true of the "Guidelines" and the "Notes." In the "Notes on the Correct Way to Present Jews and Judaism in Preaching and Catechesis in the Roman Catholic Church," on page 45 occur the words: "The existence of the State of Israel and its political options should be envisaged not in a perspective which is in itself religious, but in their reference to the common principles of international law." This reference to the state of Israel many Jews — very naturally — took at best to be gingerly tepid. The political reality of Israel as a state — its actuality — was separated from its religious significance. This meant that, for many Jews, *Nostra Aetate* had separated the inseparable, because it did not grasp the territorial dimension of Judaism in which the deity, the people, and The Land are inextricable.[98] But a comparison of the "Notes" with the Fundamental Agreement reveals immediately how far the Vatican has moved toward the political recognition of the state of Israel and how it implied that there was even more recognition to come, if that were necessary. The Fundamental Agreement is called "the first and *fundamental* agreement... [to] provide a sound and lasting basis for the continued development of their present and future relations" (italics added). The fullest recognition of the state of Israel was clearly anticipated.[99]

If it be urged, again very understandably, that this recognition was very grudging and very slow in coming, certain considerations are pertinent. (1) The Roman Catholic and other Christian churches had to come to terms with and overcome the ingrained and benighted tradition of "contempt." Entrenched attitudes and doctrines die hard. (2) There was opposition to the creation of the state of Israel even within Jewry itself. Certain Orthodox and Conservative Jews regarded that creation as a sinful, rebellious act of impiety in that Zionists had taken upon themselves to do what God had reserved for Himself to accomplish in His own good time. Some Orthodox thinkers went so far as to claim that the Holocaust itself was the direct consequence of Zionist activity, for which it was the divine punishment: arrogant Zionist rebellion had received its due and just reward. On the other hand, Reform Judaism insisted on the purely religious character of the Jewish faith and only very tardily came to espouse concern for The Land and the state of Israel. Since there have been such currents of antagonism against the state of Israel among Jews themselves, the tardiness of its recognition by the Vatican should not be regarded as surprising or unique.

---

98. See Davies, *The Territorial Dimension of Judaism.*
99. See article 14:2.

These considerations do not necessitate or imply that we endorse the tardiness of the Vatican, but they do make it understandable. That that tardiness was governed not by perverse enmity but by good will is now clear. Since these pages were penned, full recognition of the state of Israel, with the full exchange of the customary diplomatic representatives, has been established. The first serious criticism of a political nature has therefore already been invalidated. The recognition of the Palestine Liberation Organization by Israel and the PLO's renunciation of its intent to destroy the state of Israel have removed a political obstacle of great magnitude to ease the way of the Vatican. In recent months theological and political considerations have conjoined in a welcome spirit of compromise. It is not coincidental that the recognition of Israel by the PLO and of the PLO by Israel are taking place at the same time that the Vatican is recognizing Israel. The church had to be concerned with the rights of Arabs and other minorities as well as with Roman Catholics in Israel. It should not be altogether overlooked also that the Vatican had to safeguard the results of the immense energy and devotion, across centuries, which it had "invested," both materially and spiritually, in what it regards as "The Holy Land," which it had vastly enriched by its innumerable places of pilgrimage and worship, hospitals and schools.

But what of the second "political" criticism levied against *Nostra Aetate* — that it ignored the Holocaust? To classify a human tragedy, as staggering as the name "Holocaust" which it bears, as a political datum will strike many as utterly inappropriate. But the Declaration of Independence of the state of Israel, in 1948, made it inevitable that the strictly political significance of the Holocaust became inescapable. The words referring to the horror in that declaration are not many, but they do powerfully and rightly pinpoint the Holocaust, along with other factors, as a most significant reason for justifying the creation of the state of Israel. Moreover, in his book on anti-Semitism already cited, Joel Carmichael also points out how the pursuit of the extermination of the Jews by Adolf Hitler also had strictly political consequences in Germany itself. We are, therefore, justified in this "political" categorization of the Holocaust. And it is not surprising that the papacy also had to consider these "political" dimensions of the Holocaust. The seemingly ambiguous reactions especially of Pope Pius XII, like those of both Roman Catholic and Protestant churches in general, were very widely and furiously condemned. But since those early days of very understandable criticism, the complexities of those reactions have been increasingly recognized. One living in Britain in the days of World War II cannot but recall, for example, such figures as James Parkes and Dr. G. A. K. Bell, the Bishop of Chichester, to name only two, who were outspoken about the Nazi atrocities. It is now difficult to issue a total blanket condemnation of Pius XII, as was once done, nor to paint the Christian reaction as uniformly and unrelievedly one of cruel indifference. One can here only refer to such studies as that of Owen Chadwick on Pius XII, and for a brief statement, to Roger Brooks.[100] Within Israel itself there has also grown the awareness that the unrestrained politicization of the memory of the Holocaust, inescapable and justifiable though that be, is no longer to be indulged in uncritically.[101]

This tragedy was far more than political. Few reflections on it are more rewarding than those of Amos Funkenstein[102] that the Holocaust transcends all simply conceptual theological and political considerations. Before the reality of its horror, silence alone is appropriate,[103] the kind of silence as ascribed to Job before the impenetrability of the mystery of the universe and of the human suffering within it. The Holocaust drives us to recognize anew the sin that at all times and in all places so easily besets all humankind. It reveals the inexpressible and unimaginable depths of human depravity. In short, the Holocaust brings us back to that doctrine of the fall in which we recognize the corruption of the human heart, which as James Fenton, the professor of poetry at Oxford, puts it, makes us "a grave disappointment all around." There is no justifiable explanation for the Holocaust. It is nonrational, and for any nonrational phenomenon, as my mentor J. S. Whale taught me long ago, no "explanation" is possible. This appeal to the fall is not to whitewash the Gentile Christian failure to condemn and oppose the Holocaust, but only to set it in the context of that universal human condition in which Roman Catholic and Protestant churches find themselves. As the record shows, the "silence" of the *Nostra Aetate* declaration points not merely and not mainly to cowardice or insensitivity but to a recognition of the awful reality of the Holocaust and the terrible actuality of the Jewish plight. This awesome silence might appear, to Jews as to Gentiles, pitifully inadequate.

How, then, shall we reply to the editor's question? The Chinese proverb warns that "prediction is precarious, especially about the future." The enormity of the Holocaust, its shame and its guilt, remain in Christendom. But the text of the Vatican-Israel Fundamental Agreement, to which we have

---

100. In the introduction to Brooks, *Unanswered Questions.* See Robert A. Graham, S.J., *Pius XII's Defense of Jews and Others,* with an introduction by Dr. Joseph L. Lichten, sometime director of the Intercultural Affairs Department for the Anti-Defamation League of B'nai B'rith (Milwaukee: Catholic League for Religious and Civil Rights, 1964).

101. See, for example, Amos Elon, "The Politics of Memory," *New York Review of Books,* 7 October 1993, 3–5. See also Kenneth Cragg on Elie Wiesel in *Troubled by Truth: Biographies in the Presence of Mystery* (Cleveland: Pilgrim Press, 1994).

102. *Perceptions of Jewish History,* 306–37. (See n. 37 above.) See also *Twenty Years of Jewish-Catholic Relations,* ed. Eugene J. Fisher, A. James Rudin, and Marc H. Tannenbaum (Mahwah, N.J.: Paulist Press, 1986).

103. See the rich and moving essay by Dale C. Allison, Jr., "The Silence of Angels," *Image,* no. 3 (Spring 1993): 85–97.

responded in its total context, in our judgment justifies a positive response to the editor's question. The very enormity of the Holocaust is itself our condemnation, but we have pointed to signs that out of its jaws of death, *mirabile dictu,* a new life may be emerging, and indeed has emerged already, in Jewish-Christian relations.

Index of Ancient Sources

Index of Classical, Hellenistic, and Extracanonical Christian Names

Index of Mormon Writings

Index of Names

Index of Subjects

adoption, Mormon conception of, 214, 216

allegory, 152
  of two olives, 152–54

analogy, 176

anathemas, 59, 60

anti-Judaism, xvii, xx, 11, 12, 152
  Christian, 156
  Greco-Roman, 260–64, 270–71
  medieval, 156
  traditional, 157

anti-Semitism, xvii, xxi, 7, 10–11, 30, 76, 78, 248–95
  Christian, 76, 156–61, 248–95
  defined, 156, 161
  distinguished from anti-Judaism, 161, 261, 265
  Enlightenment, 163, 166
  eschatological, 161
  "mystical," 248–87
  and racial theories, 274–75
  and the Vatican, 284, 285 288–95
  Voltaire's, 163–68

Apocrypha
  Mormon understanding of, 227–28
  Orthodox understanding of, 228

art, 112–13

asceticism, 11, 67

Atonement, Day of, 66

baptism, 82
  and catechesis, 84

Bible ix, xviii, 1–2, 30, 32
  as canonical book, 1, 2, 10, 44
  corruption of, xx, 243
  geography as barrier to understanding of, 2
  hellenistic approach to, 4–6
  interpretation of, 44
  and megaliths, 1, 2

Mormon, 227–45
  obstacles to understanding of, 2–5
  as sacred book, 1, 2, 54
  as scripture, xvi
  and time, 3
  translations of, 2–3
  world of, 3
  see also canon, Mormonism, scripture, Tanak

biblical criticism, 2, 3, 4–5
  anti-Jewish theological animus of, 275–76, 280

biblical theology movement, 36

Birkath ha-Minim, xviii, 198–200, 208, 269. See also synagogue

book, xvii, xix, 23, 38, 41–42
  Israel as people of, 1, 19, 23, 30, 49, 167
  publication of, 41–42
  see also canon

Book of Mormon, 214, 230–32, 234, 236

canon, xii, xix, 19, 43, 46–47, 48, 50, 51, 86
  authority of, 51
  definition of, 244
  fixing of, 47–49, 51, 53, 54, 197
  Jewish, 8, 42
  Mormon, xix, 227–47
  opposed to "sacred texts," 45, 49
  revelational status of, 244, 245
  Samaritan, 242
  see also book

canon law, 150

canonical criticism, 49

canonization, 44, 48, 77
  and self-definition, 242, 243

casuistry, 85, 149
  "Christian-rabbinic," 139
  see also Christian morality

314